Empty Dreams,
Empty Pockets

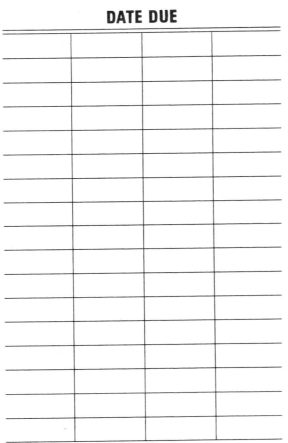

DATE DUE

Empty Dreams, Empty Pockets

Class and Bias in American Politics

John J. Harrigan
Hamline University

Macmillan Publishing Company
New York

Maxwell Macmillan Canada
Toronto

Editor: Bruce Nichols
Production Supervisor: Bert Yaeger
Production Manager: Paul Smolenski
Text Designer: Jane Edelstein
Cover Designer: Cathleen Norz
Cover Illustration: David Tillinghast

This book was set in 10 pt. Century Schoolbook by Americomp,
and was printed and bound by Book Press, Inc.
The cover was printed by New England Book Components, Inc.

Macmillan Publishing Company
866 Third Avenue, New York, New York 10022

Macmillan Publishing Company is part of the Maxwell Communication
Group of Companies.

Maxwell Macmillan Canada, Inc.
1200 Eglinton Avenue East
Suite 200
Don Mills, Ontario M3C 3N1

Library of Congress Cataloging-in-Publication Data

Harrigan, John J.
    Empty dreams, empty pockets : class and bias in American politics
/ John J. Harrigan.
        p.   cm.
    Includes index.
    ISBN 0-02-351420-5 (pbk.)
    1. Political participation—United States. 2. Race
discrimination—United States. 3. Social classes—United States.
I. Title.
JK1764.H37   1993
323'.042'0973—dc20   92-15311
                                                      CIP

Printing: 1 2 3 4 5 6 7   Year: 3 4 5 6 7 8 9

To the reader of this book,
especially if you come from the lower strata.

As you climb up, remember those
who could not.

Preface

What happens to a dream deferred?

Does it dry up
like a raisin in the sun?
Or fester like a sore—
And then run?
Does it stink like rotten meat?
Or crust and sugar over—
like a syrupy sweet?

Maybe it just sags
like a heavy load.

Or *does it explode*?

So wrote Langston Hughes about the desperation of blacks in segregated America at mid-twentieth century. Though no other ethnic group—except the Native Americans—suffered a fate as bad as segregation, the idea of a dream deferred strikes home today among people of many ethnic backgrounds: the unskilled single mother with little hope that her child will move up a rung on the social ladder; the middle-aged man thrown out of work by a corporate "restructuring" and no hope of gaining back a job with comparable pay; the elderly couple whose pension disappeared when the company went bankrupt or was bought out; or even the lower-middle income, two-paycheck family which, despite its two wages, fell behind the cost of living over the past two decades and has little hope that it will catch up over the next decade.

Minority and white, male and female, these people have at least one thing in common. Compared to the richest 40 percent of the population, their pockets are empty. And because their pockets are empty so is the dream of attaining an upper–middle-income American life style. They cannot buy their way into the better neighborhoods, the better schools, the better health insurance programs, or even the better recreational clubs. If they are going to improve their neighborhoods, their schools, their health care, and their living environment, they need the help of government. But the idea of using government for these purposes today does not draw a whole lot of support from the richest 40 percent of the population who dominate the political system.

And that is what politics is about. Deciding who gets to keep most of the income that is generated in the country each year. Deciding for what purposes that income will be used. And deciding what trade-offs to make between private consumption and public investments.

Surely, some will argue, this picture is overdrawn. By most objective measures the average American has better housing, better clothing, better food, better health care, and better schools than the average citizen of just about any sizable country on the face of the globe. Maybe so. Certainly so for the richest 40 percent of the population. For them the past two decades have ranked among the best of times. They enjoyed rising incomes, better health care, abundant consumer products, and the fruits of a complex of political-economic forces that redistributed income upward.

For the bottom 60 percent of the income earners, however, it is hard to argue that these are the best of times. As we will review in coming chapters, average Americans get a smaller share of the national income today than they got twenty years ago. Their comparative advantage in standard of living over the West Europeans and the Japanese has shrunk. And there has been a decline in the ability of government to address effectively their real needs in areas such as public education, health care, and the safety of their living environment. Relative to the top 40 percent of the population, their pockets are emptier than they were twenty years ago. And so are their dreams.

In this book we will examine the relevance of American politics to this bottom 60 percent of the income earners. We will probe especially the biases of the political system as it relates to these people. What aspects of the system are biased to their disadvantage? And what other aspects give them potential for overcoming the system's biases?

Chapter 1 lays out the thesis that the bottom 60 percent of the income earners constitute a lower status population and that the main institutions of politics today have a significant bias against the economic interests of lower status people. If lower status people are to protect their economic interests they need to learn the nature of that bias and ways in which it might be overcome.

Succeeding chapters apply this analysis of bias to the central institutions and processes of American politics. These are the Constitution, federalism, opinion formation, elections, interest groups, Congress, the presidency, and the courts. Finally, the Epilogue reviews the key elements of a strategy for overcoming bias.

The stakes for America in coping with the bias of its political system are high. To function effectively in what promises to be a highly competitive twenty-first century, we need a nation of healthy, skilled, and well-educated people capable of working cooperatively together. If we fail to invest successfully in the health, skills, education, and neighborhoods of our large lower status population, we will become instead a people who are torn by bitter ethnic divisions and who lack the belief that hard work and cooperation can lead to a better life for all. As that happens, the aspirations of the lower status population will, in the words of the poet, dry up, fester, and on occasion explode as they did for blacks in the big city riots of the 1960s. That is not a desirable future for any American. And there is no way to avoid it without coming to grips with the biases built into the political system.

That, at least, is what I have come to believe after two decades teaching about and researching American politics. I wanted to develop this idea in a succinct book that could be used as a companion reading in any college level American Government course. My thanks go to Bruce Nichols of Macmillan Publishing Company for his faith in this idea and for his superb editorial insights. He and his talented colleagues at Macmillan made this book possible. This work also owes a debt of thanks to William R. Thomas, Georgia State University; Herbert Jacob, Northwestern University; Jerome J. Hanus, The American University; David Cingranelli, SUNY Binghamton; Larry Elowitz, Georgia College; James Klonoski, University of Oregon; and Charles Hadley, University of New Orleans, who read various revisions of the manuscript and whose generous criticism forced me to rethink and rewrite much of what appears here. I am especially grateful to my wife, Sandy, who endured many weekends alone while this project took shape and whose own work gave me a glimpse into a slice of life I otherwise would not have seen. Finally, I am indebted to those students whose questions and stories over the years probably taught me much more than I taught them.

John J. Harrigan

Contents

2 The Constitution As Seen from Below   34

3 Federalism: Bias Between State and Nation   63

4 Learning Your Place: Shaping the Minds of Lower-Status Americans   92

5 Staying in Place: How Patterns of Participation and Ideology Foster Lower-Status Subordination   121

7 Congress and the Public Interest

Introduction: Bias and Money in American Democracy

Introduction

American government and politics are not neutral. When governments act, or do not act, some groups of people get most of the benefits, while other groups pay most of the costs. Political processes inherently give more advantages to some people than to others. Some examples will illustrate this idea.

- The 55,000 men who died in the Vietnam War were not a cross section of the American population. They were disproportionately racial minorities and lower-income whites. The sons of upper-and upper-middle-income families found it much easier to get college deferments or find other ways to avoid the war, which contrasts directly with American experience in World War II, when battle deaths cut a swath across all social levels.

- The great conservative movement of the 1980s had the consequence of diluting the political influence of lower-middle- and lower-income people. It also helped, as we will see, to reduce their share of the national income.

- Elections, in democratic theory, give the great mass of lower-middle- and lower-income people a way to influence government to send financial benefits in their direction. But one of the great ironies of American politics is that these same lower- and lower-middle-income people have the lowest voter turnout rates in the American electorate. The people most in need of favorable government policies are those least likely to participate in electing candidates who could respond to their needs.

American government and politics are not neutral. When governments act, or do not act, some groups of people get most of the benefits, while other groups pay most of the costs.

- Higher education funds are not distributed equally to all students of higher education. Elite private colleges and flagship state universities are best able to underwrite the tuition costs of their students. The state colleges, community colleges, and nonprestigious private colleges get less; their scholarships are smaller; their libraries have fewer volumes; and they are less competitive in hiring prestigious faculty.

These examples span four different areas of public life: military action, ideological movements, elections, and public higher education. Despite the breadth of activities they cover, the examples illustrate several common threads in the fabric of American politics. First, in all four cases, some government action was seen to be biased to the disadvantage of lower- and lower-middle-income people. This notion of bias is not an easy concept for many people to admit, because most of us are socialized to think of government as the neutral arbiter of conflicts, much as the football referee arbitrates between two teams. But, as a once-popular song said, "It ain't necessarily so." Doubting the neutrality of American government is the starting point for understanding who gets the most of what there is to get from American politics, and who pays the cost.

Second, these examples raise important questions about the role of wealth and income in our politics. Are these four examples of bias against lower-income groups extraordinary? Or is there a general pattern of bias in favor of the more affluent members of our society and against the less affluent? Third, the examples imply a very broad definition of the term "politics." Politics includes more than simply the competition for elective office. It also involves public policy and social movements, as well as the distribution of wealth and income. Finally, the examples imply that political ideology has important consequences in what government decides to do, who influences government decisions, who benefits from those decisions, and who bears the burden of paying what it will cost to implement them. We shall examine these points in turn.

The Nature of Bias in American Politics _____

To say that politics is biased is not to say that politicians deliberately set out to harm specific groups of people. It *is* to say, however, as political scientist Harold Lasswell wrote, that the political process it-self has a big impact on *who* gets *what* economic advantages in our society, *when* they get those advantages, and *how* they get them.[1] Raising the issue of political bias in American politics thus raises two major questions: Who benefits the most from what government does or does not do? And who pays most of the cost for those benefits?

Bias of Commission and Bias of Omission

Note that the previous questions refer not only to what governments do, but also to what they refrain from doing. For example, the govern-ments of most economically developed industrial democracies see to it that all their citizens have access to health care or medical insurance. The United States government, however, does not. This reflects a bias that works to the disadvantage of thirty million Americans who are not covered by health insurance plans. The burden of this situation, not surprisingly, falls disproportionately on the less affluent members of our society. In 1991, one-third of the families earning less than $26,720 (twice the poverty level) had neither private health insurance nor government-supported medical assistance. By contrast, only 6 per-cent of those with incomes above $53,440 (four times the poverty level) lacked such health coverage.[2] One-fifth of all blacks and more than one-third of all Mexican-Americans lack private or government-assisted health insurance.[3] One of the consequences of this lack of health care coverage among lower income people is that the United States has one of the worst infant mortality rates (infants dying before their first birthday) of the industrialized nations, lagging behind some much poorer nations such as Greece and Spain.[4]

In short, what a government fails to do can reflect a bias just as much as what a government does. We will call these "biases of omission" to distinguish them from the "biases of commission," which refer to the biases of governmental actions. Some of the most serious biases in our political system, such as the lack of health insurance coverage for tens of millions of people, are biases of omission.

Patterns of Bias and Biases of Specific Acts

In analyzing the bias of politics, we are seeking primarily to find out if there are *patterns of bias* that permeate many actions—not isolated instances of bias that are unrelated to a general pattern. In a huge society such as the United States, any significant act of the govern-ment is bound to impose burdens on some people while providing ben-efits for others. To this extent, all government behavior is biased. There is no perfectly fair way to share the costs of some programs.

Raising the issue of political bias in American politics raises two major questions: Who benefits the most from what government does or does not do? And who pays most of the cost for those benefits?

One important example of the inevitability of bias occurred in the late 1980s and early 1990s when Congress passed a catastrophic health insurance plan for the elderly. This plan sought to protect the elderly from being financially wiped out by catastrophic diseases such as some cancers, which may linger for years and require extremely expensive medical treatment. In terms of benefits, a catastrophic health insurance plan would obviously help the elderly more than the young, but there was broad support among most social groups, including the young.

If there was no opposition to the goal, however, there were major conflicts over who should pay for it. Legislation initially passed by Congress in 1988 paid for the program by boosting the income taxes of the elderly. This idea was strenuously resisted by many elderly, however, some of whom brought the point home vividly to the chairperson of the key Congressional tax writing committee (Daniel Rostenkowski, D–IL) when they blocked the passage of his car in Chicago and pounded on the car's fenders, demanding that he repeal the tax. The tax was also resisted by some elderly who already had private health insurance. They would in effect be paying twice, and be penalized for having taken the initiative of providing for their own health care. Another possibility was to pay for the program from the general treasury and thus spread the cost among the whole population. But this idea was resisted by some people in the work force who felt that it took too much of the burden off today's elderly, who would draw huge benefits that far outweighed whatever limited taxes they might pay in support of the plan. Today's working population, by contrast, would pay taxes for 30 or 40 years, and in many cases, they feared that the amount they paid in taxes would exceed whatever benefits they might eventually receive. These conflicts over paying for catastrophic health insurance led Congress to rescind the original plan, and no substitute plan has yet been passed.

In cases such as this one, it might not be possible to find a solution that is fair to everyone. No matter what the solution, somebody is going to pay a larger share of the cost, and somebody else is going to benefit disproportionately.

The realization that you might pay a disproportionate share of the cost for a program that benefits somebody else should be balanced, however, by the knowledge that you benefit disproportionately from other programs. College students might not receive immediate benefits from catastrophic health insurance, but most of them derive enormous benefits from guaranteed student loans, from federal and state tuition grants, and from the billions of dollars of public and private aid to higher education generally. Nowhere does a student's tuition foot the entire bill of his or her education, and the difference is made up from the public treasury or from someone else's generosity. You might ask yourself: Overall, do you receive more benefits from public activities than you pay in taxes? Or vice versa? Do you feel that in the long run the benefits you receive from assistance to higher education more than balance the extra taxes you might end up paying for catastrophic health insurance or other programs that promote the welfare of people other than yourself?

How would you feel if, in the long run, the biases failed to balance out? If you found that some people consistently paid disproportionate costs for government while others consistently received disporportionate benefits, would you still feel that the system was fair and unbiased?

The important question is whether there are *patterns* of bias that underlie government behavior generally. Patterns of bias occur when some groups are systematically excluded from the governmental decision-making processes and their interests are systematically neglected by governmental policy outcomes. Are some people systematically harmed by American political processes? And do some groups of people systematically benefit from those same processes?

Class and Wealth in American Politics _____

In analyzing politics for patterns of bias, one finds many lines of conflict among people. The catastrophic health plan, for example, pitted the young against the old, the working against the retired, and above all, the affluent elderly (who already had health insurance) against the unaffluent elderly (who lacked sufficient coverage). The most persistent lines of conflict in American politics, however, occur around wealth and class. The divisiveness of wealth and class was broadly acknowledged by the original founders of our system of government. America's most important political philosopher, James Madison, wrote more than two centuries ago that "the most common and durable source of factions has been the various and unequal distribution of property."[5] What the founders recognized two centuries ago, however, has become a difficult idea for most Americans to accept today. Most of us are brought up to think that we belong to a broad middle class. To speak in terms of class conflict is somehow viewed as either unrealistic or subversive.

The Myth of a Classless Politics

The Argument that Politics Is Not Class Based. It is certainly true that America does not have a class-based politics comparable to the kind of class-based politics that is common in Europe. In Europe, socialist political parties with a strong working class membership are common. In Britain, for example, there are two major political parties. The Conservative Party draws its strength from the managerial and upper classes. The Labor Party is organized around the labor unions, and draws its voting strength from organized labor and the lower income population generally. In America, socialist parties and labor parties are pushed out to the margins of politics. The two-party system here has a strong bias toward the middle class, and socialist parties have never won much of the national vote.[6] It is true, as we will see in Chapter 6, that the Republican and Democratic parties differ markedly in their constituencies. In the 1988 presidential election, for example, Democratic nominee Michael Dukakis drew almost twice the percentage of votes from low-income voters as he did from upper-income voters. For Republican nominee George Bush, it was the opposite.[7] But in fact, the real battleground in American politics is the middle class. Neither party could hope to win the presidency or control Congress if it appealed only to the very poor or the very rich. And this fact of political life has been a major factor inhibiting the formation of labor parties and leftist parties capable of winning major elections.

Class politics is also discouraged in America by deep underlying cultural values. When sociologist Susan A. Ostrander asked wealthy women to describe their class status, they perceived themselves as different from other people, but reacted vigorously against the word "class" to describe those differences.

> I hate [the term] upper class. It's so non-upper class to use it. I just call it "all of us," those who are well-born.

> I hate to use the word "class." We're responsible, fortunate people, old families, the people who have something.[8]

And a similar plaint was echoed by George Bush who was wealthy from birth. Bush is quoted as saying that class is for "European democracies or something else—it isn't for the United States of America. We are not going to be divided by class."[9]

The reluctance of these upper-class people to acknowledge class as a fact of life in America is shared by the population at large. When researchers ask people to identify their social class, they overwhelm-

The most persistent lines of conflict in American politics occur over wealth and class. This is a difficult idea for most Americans to accept, because most of us are brought up and educated to think that we all belong to a broad middle class.

ingly call themselves middle class, sometimes working class, but rarely lower or upper class.[10]

Self-identification with a social class is also inhibited by the powerful value placed on individualism in our political culture. Because individualism is such a strong value, it is difficult for many people to think of themselves as belonging to such an abstract concept as a social class. To the extent that people do identify as members of social groups, they tend to be ethnic and religious groups. And, of course, ethnic, racial, religious, and geographic divisions have provided some of the most important and violent conflicts in American history: Northerner versus Southerner during the Civil War; Irish, Italians, Poles, and Jews fighting for control of the old political machines in cities in the early twentieth century;[11] blacks versus whites regarding such contemporary issues as affirmative action and busing to integrate public schools. Ira Katznelson invented the term "city trenches" to describe the relations between lower-middle-income Jews, Irish, and blacks sharing the same neighborhoods in New York City. As lower-middle-income residents, they all faced common problems regarding neighborhoods and schools, but the ethnic and religious differences between them were so strong that they found it impossible to work together politically on those common problems. Each was dug into its own city trench and tried to defend it from the encroachments of the others.[12] These ethnic-based city trenches prevented a class-based politics from developing among people who shared a common interest in terms of income, employment, and neighborhood.

Example of a Class-Based Politics. Just because people do not think of themselves as having a class interest, however, does not necessarily mean that class politics are nonexistent. The cartoon presented here about the capital gains tax illustrates this idea. Capital gains are the income derived from selling stocks, bonds, or other assets at a profit. Until 1986, income from capital gains was taxed at a lower rate than income earned from employment. But in that year, in exchange for reducing the maximum income tax from 50 percent to 28 percent, Congress eliminated the preferential treatment of capital gains. No sooner did they receive this sharp reduction in their income tax rates, than financial leaders began pushing to reinstate a lower tax on capital gains. President George Bush, in the late 1980s and early 1990s, became a ma-

A cut in the capital gains tax would benefit mostly people in high income brackets.
(*Source:* Linda Boileau, *Frankfort State Journal.* Copyright © 1989 by Rothco Cartoon Syndicate.)

jor spokesperson for this cause on the grounds that it might stimulate trading in the securities markets and possibly bring in more tax revenue during the first few years. Such a tax cut, however, stood to benefit primarily the rich. A tax committee of Congress calculated that 80 percent of the proceeds of the capital gains tax cut would go to the 5 percent of the people who had annual incomes over $100,000.[13] Such a reduction would, moreover, contribute to the long-term widening of the federal budget deficit, the closing of which would be paid for primarily by middle-income taxpayers and wage earners. Congress did not go along with the president's plan to cut the capital gains tax, but the opponents of the cut were vilified for their efforts. *Newsweek* magazine accused them of waging "class war."[14] And one widely read columnist, George Will, implied that opponents of the capital gains tax cut were communists.[15] In this instance, at least, the American unease with the concept of social class and a class-based politics harmed the credibility of those who opposed a capital gains tax cut.

The conflict over the capital gains tax is instructive, because it reveals so starkly a conflict in which class lines are clearly drawn, and illustrates several features of class and politics today. Most Americans have a class interest, but they fail to recognize it. Those Americans who do recognize it might be accused of engaging in class warfare and being somehow subversive. The more class can be kept from being

The more that class can be kept from being discussed openly, the more such silence benefits the richest members of our society.

discussed openly, the more such silence benefits the richest members of our society.

What Class Do I Belong To?

It is much easier to assert that class-based politics exists than to construct a precise definition of social class. Different people think of class in different terms. Sociologists traditionally define it not only by income, but also by level of education and prestige of occupation. Thus, a physician earning $100,000 per year would think of him- or herself as having higher social status than a high school dropout who won the lottery or struck it rich on Wall Street, even though the dropout might make more money. Lower-class people tend to define class by the amount of money one has, and middle-class people by education level, while upper-class people think of class in terms of life-style and taste.[16]

The problem of trying to decide which social class we belong to is further complicated by the fact that there is a great deal of social mobility between classes, and many of us move through different levels at different points in our lives. A fair percentage of the children of the rich fall out of upper-class status to end up as middle class, and sometimes even in poverty. Conversely, a small share of the poor end up wealthy. Tom Monoghan, the founder of Domino's Pizza and owner of the Detroit Tigers, grew up in an orphanage, hardly a conspicuous place to start out on the road to great wealth. But most of us move up or down only a short distance on the social status ladder.

For our purpose, class is defined in terms of income permanence. A high income today may make you temporarily rich. But you are only permanently as rich as the amount of income you would have if you suffered some disaster, such as the death of your family's chief wage earner, a divorce, a job loss, or an incapacitating illness.[17] Many people with $100,000 incomes, in fact, do not feel rich, precisely because they know that their income does not necessarily translate into permanent wealth. For people in the bottom 60 percent of income earners, financial insecurity is a constant threat. These are the people most susceptible to being laid off from their jobs or to being fired. If they are laid off or fired, they suffer a setback in their quest for financial stability. Your family may be one of those favored with a $100,000 income today, which would place you in the top 5 percent of all income earners in the country and make you temporarily rich. But you cannot think of yourself as permanently rich unless you have enough assets whose investment would replace that $100,000 income in the event your family lost its current sources of income.

Using this concept of social class based on the amount of wealth needed to maintain one's income level, we can identify five social classes as shown in Table 1-1.

1. First are the *well-off* who constitute the top quintile (top fifth) of income earners. To be temporarily well-off in 1989, the most recent year for which data are available, required an income of $54,060; to be permanently well-off required assets of $1.8 million.[18] At the very top of the well-off category are the *rich*, those in the top 5 percent of incomes. To be temporarily rich in 1989 required an income of $98,963; to be permanently rich required a minimum wealth of $3.3 million.

2. Below the well-off is a second category, *the comfortable*, those in the second richest quintile of the population. To be temporarily comfortable in 1989 required a family income of $40,801; to be permanently comfortable required assets of $1.4 million.

3. The third category is that of the *financially precarious*. These are the middle quintile of all income earners. One can live comfortably enough at this level, but there is little margin for error, and any number of misfortunes, ranging from a job layoff to a divorce, could push one down into the near-poverty or poverty level. For this reason, people at this level are in a financially precarious position. A family income between $28,001 and $40,800 would keep one at this level. Nominally it would take assets of $930,000 to keep one permanently at this level, but that figure is less meaningful for the lower 60 percent of the population than it is for the richest 40 percent. Except for farmers with low incomes but large land holdings, few people in this income category could amass $930,000 in assets. Anybody with that much in assets could convert it into at least $28,001 in permanent income, and hence would no longer be in a precarious financial situation.

4. The fourth category is the *near-poor*, the second poorest quintile of the population. These were families with incomes between $16,004 and $28,000 in 1987.

5. The *poor* are the poorest fifth of the population, those in families with incomes below $16,004.

The top two income classes account for 40 percent of the population, but they received 68.3 percent of all the income earned in 1989. We call them the upper strata, or the upper-status population. The poorest 60 percent, are called the lower strata, or the lower-status population. The fundamental economic condition of their lives is insecurity.

When social class is defined in terms of the wealth needed to maintain a given income level, it becomes painfully obvious how unlikely it is that any specific person is going to make it permanently into the ranks of the rich or even the well-off. To become permanently rich, you

TABLE 1-1 Class Structure in America

Social Class	Temporary Income Range Needed in 1989	Permanent Minimum Wealth Needed in 1989
IA Rich Top 5%	$98,963 or more	$3.3 million

Consider yourself temporarily rich if your family earned $98,963 in 1989, and permanently rich if it had a net worth of $3.3 million. The top 5 percent of all families had incomes of $98,963 or more that year. In the absence of Social Security benefits, it would take $3.3 million in assets, including pension funds, to generate this amount of income based on the following two assumptions: First, the figure allows for inflation which has advanced at the rate of about 5 percent per year in recent history. Second, the figure is based on an assumed 8 percent return on investment, which is approximately what U.S. Treasury bills averaged in the 1980s.

IA Well-off Next 15%	$54,060 to $98,962	$1.8 million

Consider yourself temporarily well-off if your family income was $54,060 to $98,962 in 1989, and permanently well-off if it had a net worth of $1.8 million. The top 20 percent of all families earned at least $54,060 that year. This 20 percent received 44.6% of all the income earned in 1989, up from 41.5% in 1980.

II Comfortable 2nd Quintile	$40,801 to $54,059	$1.4 million

Consider yourself comfortable if your family income was $40,801 to $54,059. This would put your family in the top 40 percent of all families. The comfortable received 23.7% of all the income earned in 1989, down from 24.3% in 1980.

III Financially precarious Middle Quintile	$28,001 to $40,800	$930,000

Consider yourself in a financially precarious position if your family income was $28,001 to $40,800. In terms of family income, this puts you in the middle fifth of all families, the heart of the middle class. The financially precarious received 16.5% of all the income earned in 1989, down from 17.5% in 1980.

IV Near-poor 4th Quintile	$16,004 to $28,000	

This is the second poorest fifth of the American population. They received 10.6% of all the income in 1989, down from 11.5% in 1980.

V Poor Bottom Quintile	Less than $16,004	

The poor received 4.6% of all the income in 1989, down from 5.2% in 1980.

Source: United States Bureau of the Census, *Statistical Abstract of the United States: 1991* (Washington, D.C.: United States Government Printing Office, 1991), p. 455. Bureau of the Census, Current Population Survey, *Consumer Income*, Series P-60, No. 172, *Money Income of Households, Families, and Persons in the United States: 1988 and 1989* (Washington, D.C.: United States Bureau of the Census, July 1991), p. 358.

Data Note: Data for families were derived from a Census Bureau survey of 60,000 households in 1989. Income was estimated before taxes and did not include noncash benefits such as food stamps or employer paid fringe benefits.

must be capable of earning $98,963 per year or amassing total assets of $3.3 million. But less than three tenths of 1 percent of all households in the entire nation have net worths in this range; the median net worth of all households is only $36,000.[19] Furthermore, you are aiming at a moving target. At the 5 percent rate of inflation that has prevailed in recent history, the $3.3 million target will grow to $8.8 million in 20 years when today's 20-year-old turns 40, and to $23 million 20 years after that when he or she begins to approach retirement age.

Who Are the Lower-Status People?

At the risk of making another simple idea fiendishly complicated, I ask you to look at Table 1-2. This table compares the lower-status population to the upper-status and shows dramatically that there is nothing random about who ends up in the lower strata. The people in the lower strata are not strange creatures. They are pretty much like people you have known all your life. By birthright characteristics (those you are born with), we note that although a disproportionate number of the lower strata are racial minorities, more than 80 percent are white. They are also disproportionately women, and most of them grew up in families with average incomes.

In contrast to birthright characteristics over which you have no control, you do have some influence over the behavioral characteristics listed in Table 1-2. A pattern of behavior almost certain to keep one in the lower strata would be to drop out from high school, fail to marry and stay married, keep oneself socially isolated by not belonging to any organizations, and live in a place with limited economic opportunities (such as an inner-city neighborhood or a remote rural area). Although people have some influence over whether they will fall into these categories, obviously they do not have complete control. Blacks and native Americans are more likely than whites or Hispanics or Asians to live in places devoid of economic opportunity. They are also more likely to drop out of school. Women are more likely than men to be impoverished by a divorce, because the women usually get custody over the children and face the difficult task of raising them as single parents.

Political Implications of Class Divisions

The great mass of the American population (the lower 60 percent of the income earners) received less than $40,800 in income in 1989, were not among the ranks of the comfortable or the well-off, and had no hope of ever entering those ranks, even temporarily. Politically, the most important aspect of this fact is that no more than a handful of these people identify themselves as belonging to the same social class. There

TABLE 1-2   Characteristics of the Lower- and Upper-Status Populations

Birthright Characteristics

	Percentage of Lower Strata Who Are	Percentage of Upper Strata Who Are
Race		
White	82%	92%
Black	18	8
Sex		
Male	38	51
Female	62	48
Social Status while Growing Up		
Below average	37	25
Average	51	54
Above average	12	21

Behavioral Characteristics

Educational Achievement		
High school not completed	34	8
High school completed	54	35
Post-high school education	32	64
Marital Status		
Married	45	71
Not married	55	29
Organizational Memberships		
None	47	26
One	33	30
Three or more	20	44
Place of Residence		
Central City	23	17
Rural	16	9
Suburb	19	36

Source: James Allan Davis and Tom W. Smith: *General Social Surveys, 1972–1989* [machine-readable data file]. Principal Investigator, Tom W. Smith. NORC ed. Chicago: National Opinion Research Center, producer, 1989; Storrs, CT: The Roper Center for Public Opinion Research, University of Connecticut, distributor.

> . . . there is nothing random about who ends up in the lower strata. The people
> in the lower strata are not strange creatures. They are pretty much like people you
> have known all your life.

are many different kinds of people in this great mass: They come from
many different races and national groups, some of which are in sharp
conflict with each other; they have many different occupations, and
often fight bitterly for the same jobs; they follow different religious
beliefs that often clash sharply on public issues such as abortion or the
saying of prayers in public schools; they live in different regions of the
country that have a long history of competition and sometimes hostil-
ity; they often live in cities where they compete vigorously for the
limited supply of low-income housing and public-assisted housing; and,
of course, some are poorer than others. The financially precarious and
the near-poor can normally live in some comfort, have small luxuries,
and even plan vacations. At the very bottom is a small but desperate
underclass of people living in poor neighborhoods, surrounded by other
poor people, physically removed from the suburban areas of dynamic
job growth, out of personal contact for the most part with middle-class
America, and lacking the skills, knowledge, and behavioral habits that
could possibly improve their situations.[20]

There are, in truth, many forces that keep the great mass of lower-
status people politically divided. Despite the divisions, however, many
in the lower strata share a common situation of economic insecurity. It
is primarily among this group of people that we find those who have no
health insurance, no secure pension, are renters rather than home-
owners, and have relatively little in the way of net worth. Their retirement years will find many of them heavily dependent on Social
Security for their income. In their family-raising years, most find that
they cannot make it economically on one parent's income. Both parents
must work, but the cost of child care absorbs a huge share of their
wages. In single-parent families, this problem is doubled. Many work
at temporary or part-time jobs that provide no health coverage for
their children. It is an irony of American politics that so many people
share a common economic burden but fail to identify themselves as
linked together in any meaningful way. We will explore this irony
further in Chapter 5.

Economic Change and the Class Structure

Furthermore, economic trends at work in the world are likely to
worsen the economic insecurity of these people as we move toward the
twenty-first century. From the end of World War II in 1945 through

Despite the divisions, however, many of them share a common situation of economic insecurity. It is primarily among this group of people that we find those who have no health insurance, no secure pension, are renters rather than home-owners, and have relatively little in the way of net worth.

the 1960s, America dominated world manufacturing, and this dominance provided well-paying jobs and a generally improving standard of living for skilled tradesmen and unskilled factory workers alike. By the 1980s, however, American corporations had begun shifting increasing amounts of their production work to plants in third world countries. From 1980 to 1989 there was a growth of 19 percent in overall employment in America, but employment in manufacturing actually declined.[21]

Harvard economist Robert B. Reich argues that the American labor market is rapidly adapting to these changes by moving to three major types of occupations. Most lucrative are what he calls *symbolic-analytic services*[22] such as computer programming, investment banking, public relations, legal work, accounting, engineering, and music and television production. This work involves the manipulation of data, words, ideas, images, and symbols, hence his term symbolic-analytic services. This is the most lucrative job market in the American economy, and Reich estimates that it accounts for about 40 percent of America's gross national product (GNP) but only 20 percent of all jobs. These are among the most sought-after jobs in the country, are usually salaried positions, and the people classified in Table 1-1 as rich and well-off tend to hold most of them. There are, however, only a limited number of these jobs available; the competition is intense, and getting them usually requires some professional training beyond a college degree.

A second category of labor involves what Reich calls *routine production services* such as typing, data entry, and machine operation. These services account for about 30 percent of the GNP and only 25 percent of jobs. Routine production workers in manufacturing drew good wages and fringe benefits during the 1950s and 1960s when their unions were strong, but unions have had little success expanding among these people in the 1980s and 1990s. Workers in routine production services seldom have a college degree, and have seen their economic situation deteriorate greatly since 1980. Because routine production services can be computerized and automated, there is little economic security in this area, and very little growth potential.

The third category of work Reich calls *routine personal services*. Typical workers here are barbers, sales clerks, cab drivers, child care workers, security guards, and nursing-home attendants. Unlike routine production services, there is considerable job growth in routine personal services, which now account for 20 percent of the GNP but 30 percent of all jobs. Unfortunately for workers in this area, however, the jobs tend to have low pay, poor working conditions, few fringe benefits, and little likelihood of unionization.

According to Reich's estimates, about half of the work force labors in routine production services or routine personal services. During the 1950s and 1960s, poverty was primarily a function of losing one's job; jobholders were seldom impoverished. In the 1990s, however, a great many people working in production services or routine personal services were earning near-poverty incomes. Two-income families and those who hold the cream of the crop of these jobs can climb into the ranks of the comfortable, as illustrated in Table 1-1. But most of the routine production workers and routine personal-service workers find themselves among the lower 60 percent of the population that is economically insecure. Increasing global competition in the 1990s is likely to worsen their economic situation. Their burden of economic insecurity is likely to grow heavier by the year 2000.

This cartoon satirizes the decline of Uncle Sam's economic competitiveness in the modern world.
(*Source*: Danziger in the *Christian Science Monitor*, Copyright © 1988 by TCSPS.)

Political Change and the Class Structure

The great tragedy for most of the lower-strata population is that there are no longer any institutions that effectively represent their economic interests. Historically, from the 1930s through the 1970s there were two institutions that did this to a limited extent. Labor unions, as we will see in Chapter 6, once performed this role for the blue-collar working class. But the political influence of unions has suffered greatly over the past two decades, and most people in the lower 60 percent of the population neither belong to unions nor seem to respond well to union-organizing activities. The second institution was the Democratic Party from 1932 through the 1960s, when it drew strength from the loyalty of the lower-middle-income groups. Since the middle 1970s, however, the Democrats have lost ground in their ability to help their natural constituents in the lower-status population, because they have been unable to win the presidency, which is the central political position for setting the nation's problem-solving agenda. Compounding the decline of organized labor and the immobilization of the Democratic Party, no contemporary political leader has yet emerged to galvanize the lower 60 percent of the population politically around their common burden of economic insecurity.

This decline in the ability of these two institutions to help the lower-status population is in some respects a result of the splintering and fracturing of the lower-status population along racial, religious, ethnic, geographic, and even gender lines that produced the notion of city trenches discussed above. Economically, the people in the lower strata share common economic problems. Perceptionally, however, divisiveness among them impedes their ability to wield as much influence in the electoral and political arenas as their numbers would warrant. We will examine this phenomenon more closely in Chapters 5 and 6.

Why the lower strata has splintered and lost the limited political influence that it had 30 years ago is, of course, open to various interpretations. One provocative interpretation is that of Bennett Harrison and Barry Bluestone, who charge that the nation's top business and political leaders have abrogated an implicit "social contract" that existed in America from 1945 to the early 1970s.[23] Under this social contract, American business was assured of government policies to maintain national economic conditions conducive to corporate profitability. Business in turn agreed to cooperate with labor unions and support general overall improvements in living standards. By the late 1970s, however, inflation was squeezing corporate profits, foreign competition was intensifying, worker productivity was declining, and American industry was losing market share in the automobile markets, steel, consumer electronics, and a growing list of other markets.

According to Harrison and Bluestone, American business responded to this challenge by bailing out of the tacit social contract it had adhered to for a generation. Instead of maintaining the wages and benefits of routine production workers and routine personal services workers, companies forced wage and fringe benefit concessions on them, increased the use of part-time workers, raided pension funds, adopted union-busting strategies, closed older manufacturing plants, and moved manufacturing operations to third world countries where wage costs were a fraction of what they are in America and where environmental and safety regulations are minimal.

Why Should You Care About Income Distribution in American Politics? _____

So what if some people are richer than others? What if political and economic changes can wreak havoc on the lives of the lower 60 percent of the population? Why should you care? It is true that you, along with most readers of this page, are unlikely to become permanently rich, but you are also unlikely to become permanently poor. And most people who persevere through college, work at a steady job with a guaranteed pension, stay sober, don't have too many children, don't get too many divorces, avoid having a family member with an expensive chronic physical ailment, and maintain proper life, health, and disability insurance policies can look forward to living at a reasonable standard throughout their lives. Life is unfair in many ways. Some people are born with horrible handicaps, while others are totally healthy. Some generations send tens of thousands of their men to die in battle, while other generations do not even experience a military draft. In the last analysis, you have to look out for your own self-interest and that of your family. In the face of these responsibilities, why should you worry about seemingly abstract inequities?

There are good reasons why you should care about the income distribution and the contemporary political and economic changes which are pushing this distribution increasingly in the favor of the richest 20 percent of the population.

The Quality of Democracy Is at Stake

There is mounting evidence that the lower strata is being squeezed economically, while the gap between rich and poor is growing. And there is good reason to believe that meaningful democracy cannot exist once this trend gets beyond a certain point.

This squeeze on the lower strata can be seen from a careful look at Figure 1-1, which shows that the poorest 80 percent of American families received a smaller share of the national income in 1989 than they did two decades earlier in 1970, while the richest 20 percent saw its share increase. The middle three categories (the comfortable, the financially precarious, and the near-poor) saw their collective share drop from 53.6 percent of the income in 1970 to 50.8 percent in 1989. While the middle class is being squeezed, the gap between rich and poor grows wider. The top 20 percent earned 9.7 times as much of the national income in 1989 as did the bottom 20 percent. In 1970, the ratio was only 7.4 times as much. In short, recent years have seen a significant redistribution of income upward into the pockets of the already most affluent people in society.

The middle class is not disappearing by any means. But, as Frank Levy has demonstrated in the most persuasive book on income distribution yet written, the middle-income groups are not getting as much of the national income as they used to get. They are falling behind the well-off, and the poor are falling even further behind.[24]

Politically, we must ask how large these gaps can grow before democracy itself is threatened. Jean Jacques Rousseau, whose *Social Contract* laid the philosophical foundation for political democracy, argued centuries ago that the social contract is not possible if the extremes between rich and poor are too large and there is no broad middle class to mediate between the other two.[25] And his warning seems confirmed when we look at the world around us. Democracy is most strongly entrenched in the economically developed societies with substantial middle classes.[26] It is rarely found in nations without a broad middle class or in the poorest nations.

Finally, the worsening economic situation of the lower strata over the past two decades may have contributed to the decline in voter participation during those years. There is evidence to suggest that people experience a drop-off in voting and political participation generally when they are under economic duress. In 1988, for example, people who were unemployed had a significantly lower voting rate than did working people who had comparable levels of education.[27] When times get rough economically and unemployment rates go up, it is an extremely disorienting experience for the people who lose their jobs. They lose self-confidence, question their worth, and feel their status decline within their families and their peer groups.[28] As unemployment increases, social disorientation also gets worse. One study found that a one percentage point rise in the unemployment rate is associated with a 4.1 percent increase in suicide rates, a 5.7 percent increase in homicide rates, and a 3.4 percent increase in the rate of admissions to mental hospitals.[29] If these social disorders are related

The lower 60% received less than a third of the family income in 1989.

Percent of the Family Income by the Five Income Classes

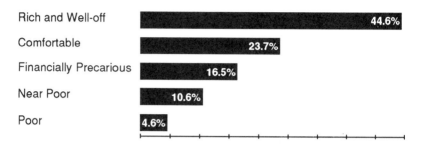

Rich and Well-off	44.6%
Comfortable	23.7%
Financially Precarious	16.5%
Near Poor	10.6%
Poor	4.6%

And their share of the nation's family income declined since 1970.

Percent Change in Share of the Nation's Family Income: 1970-1989

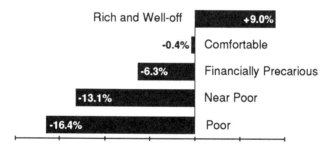

Rich and Well-off	+9.0%
-0.4%	Comfortable
-6.3%	Financially Precarious
-13.1%	Near Poor
-16.4%	Poor

Figure 1-1 Squeezing the Lower Strata the rich and well-off received 44.6% of the national income in 1989. This was an increase of 9.0% over the 40.9% they received in 1970. Conversely, the poor received 4.6% of the national income in 1989. This was down 16.4% from the 5.5% they received in 1970.

Source: United States Bureau of the Census, Current Reports, Consumer Income, Series #P-60, No. 172, "Money Income of Households, families and Persons in the United States: 1988 and 1989" (Washington, D.C.: Bureau of the Census, July 1991), p. 358; Statistical Abstract of the United States: 1971, p. 317.

so strongly to unemployment increases, it is not unreasonable to think that the increasing financial pressures on lower-status people since the early 1970s should also disrupt their participation in political and community life. There are many reasons, of course, why some people do not participate in politics and community life, as we will see in Chapter 5, and poor economic trends is only one of them. But lower participation rates among the lower strata compared to 30 years ago is an indisputable fact. The less the lower strata participate, the more political influence goes by default to those at the top of the economic ladder with no personal incentive to support broad public services for the lower strata. To the extent that growing economic inequalities contribute to nonvoting, they undermine the quality of democracy.

In short, if you care about the quality of democracy in this country, you have a vested interest in caring about growing economic inequities.

There Is a Price to Be Paid for Not Caring

Unless you are among the very rich or the well-off, you have not gotten very much of the upward redistribution of income that took place in the 1980s. Although most of this redistribution resulted from economic rather than political forces, there were ways in which political factors in the 1980s exacerbated the growing economic inequalities and placed significant burdens on average Americans. This was especially the case with deregulation, a major trend during the Reagan-Bush years.

Deregulation was the process of cutting back on the federal government's role of regulating various aspects of the economy. In some areas, deregulation brought positive benefits to American society, but, in three areas in particular, deregulation imposed a significant burden on average Americans. The first involved the dismantling of governmental regulation of the nation's savings and loan (S&L) industry. Many savings and loans banks went under. Over $500 billion in savings and loans losses occurred in the 1980s that must be picked up by the taxpayers. Some of these losses occurred because of bad loans made by the S&Ls once they were freed from the watchful eye of federal regulators. Other losses occurred because of fraud that was easier to perpetrate when federal regulatory staffs were cut back and made incapable of monitoring the S&Ls.[30] The federal government was put in an impossible situation in the 1980s. S&L deposits were insured by the federal government, but the federal regulators were stripped of the capacity to scrutinize how those deposits were invested or handled. As a result, taxpayers will end up paying a substantial portion of the $500 billion in losses that occurred.

A second example of counterproductive deregulation occurred in corporate restructuring in the 1980s. While federal regulators winked,

In short, if you care about the quality of democracy in this country, you have a vested interest in caring about growing economic inequities.

hundreds of companies disappeared in the form of mergers and acquisitions that added enormously to the debt load of corporate America.[31] Finally, because of regulatory cutbacks in occupational health and safety regulation and environmental protection, corporations saved billions of dollars that they otherwise would have had to spend on occupational safety and the prevention of pollution.[32] Safety and the environment are public goods that benefit all equally; profits are specific to stockholders, and thus benefit the most affluent sectors of the population. We will examine the deregulation phenomenon more closely in Chapter 9.

We would not want to deny that positive things came out of the deregulation movement of the 1980s, but it also had its dark side. Insofar as deregulation contributed to the S&L scandal, insofar as it led to laxer regulation of the environment and occupational safety, and insofar as it failed to oversee many pension funds, deregulation imposed enormous costs that will have to be repaid in the coming years. The S&L scandal alone saw hundreds of billions of dollars diverted from governmental programs into profits for somebody. The numbers are so huge and the financial conduits so complex that nobody will ever be able to account for all these sums. But there is no possibility that much of the money found its way into the pockets of average Americans. Environmental decline due to poor government regulation in the 1980s will have to be corrected, at great cost, in the 1990s. The money that disappeared during the S&L crisis will have to be paid back. In both cases, the taxpayer is going to pay a much higher price than he or she otherwise would have paid if Congress and the president had not gutted the regulatory apparatus during the 1980s. And most poignant, the retirees of companies who saw their pension funds raided during the M&A craze will pay a large personal price for the lax regulatory environment that characterized the 1980s.

You or I as individuals could have done very little to prevent these abuses. Had we, however, known how to be effectively vigilant, we could have demanded that our governing officials be better watchdogs over the public treasury and over mergers and acquisitions. Well into the next century the average taxpayer will be paying a price for his or her own ignorance and apathy about political action in the 1980s.

In short, not caring about who gets what from politics can hurt.

You Might Not Reach the Ranks of the Permanently Rich or Well-Off

A 1990 Gallup poll found that a whopping 62 percent of adults under age 30 thought they were somewhat likely to be rich someday.[33] If, however, Robert Reich's estimates are accurate, that only a fifth of all American jobs lie in the lucrative field of *symbolic-analytic services*,

The Personal Side of Politics: Deregulation

For most of us, the merger and acquisitions (called M&A in the financial press) craze of the 1980s was little more than a vague abstraction. But for residents of Kannapolis, North Carolina, S&M would have been a more appropriate set of initials for what happened to them.

For decades, Kannapolis residents worked in the town's Cannon Mills that produced a large share of the nation's towels, wash cloths, and other cotton products. In 1982 the firm was purchased in a leveraged buyout. In typical leveraged buyout fashion, the new owners "restructured" the company by reducing the work force, cutting wages, imposing mandatory early retirement, selling off the mills to new owners while keeping most of the valuable real estate that had come with the original buyout, and getting approval from Reagan administration regulators to cancel the company's pension plan. In a complicated shell game, the owners pretended to protect the pensions of retired workers by insuring them with the Executive Life Insurance Company. But in 1991, the Executive Life Insurance Company went bankrupt.

The net result for 12,900 residents of Kannapolis who had spent their lives in the Cannon Mills was an immediate thirty percent reduction in their monthly pension checks. A huge portion of the money they had spent a lifetime contributing to their pension plans simply disappeared, and the pensioners found it difficult to pin liability on anybody involved. The original owner, the Cannon family, absolved itself of liability by selling the company. The various sets of new owners who participated in the restructuring and apparently made off with various pieces of the pension fund assets bear no legal liability. The Reagan administration regulators who permitted the original pension plan to be terminated bear some moral responsibility, but they are not legally liable.

Ultimately, the State of California took over Executive Life and sold its assets to another insurance group that will assume all or most of the pension obligations. This will keep the Kannapolis pension funds from totally disappearing. If their pension payments are maintained 100 percent, they will be much luckier than a great many retirees in the 1980s who saw similar devastation of their pension funds. Ironically, on the very day that the courts approved California's sale of Executive Life's assets, a bank in Connecticut announced plans to terminate its pension plan for its employees.

Source: Hearings before the Senate Committee on Banking, Housing and Urban Affairs, July 1991. Reported in the *New York Times*, July 30, 1991, p. 1. Also see *New York Times*, August 8, 1991, p. 1 and August 29, 1991, p. 1. *Investor's Business Daily*, December 27, 1991, pp. 1, 28.

most of those young people cannot possibly reach the ranks of the well-off, much less the rich. A fair number of today's college students are going to make their careers in the less lucrative fields of *routine production services* and *routine personal services*. There is nothing wrong with working in those areas; these are, after all, honorable ways to make a living. And depending on one's sense of moral values, the producer of a useful product or an attendant to the elderly in a nursing home might well be doing something more socially useful than the corporate attorney arranging mergers and acquisitions of giant companies.

But if you do decide to seek a career in the less lucrative areas of the job market, it is imperative for the protection of your self-interest that you understand how contemporary economic and political transformations are working to the disadvantage of people in those careers. As you ponder the kind of society you want to inherit and pass on to your children, you are, in the imagery of philosopher John Rawls, behind a veil of ignorance about what your wealth and status will be in that future.[34] You do not know in advance if you will be among the rich, or among the financially precarious. For this reason, you have a self- interest in promoting a political system that treats all of the income classes fairly.

You Can Do Something About It.
Bias Can Be Overcome

As an isolated individual, you can, of course, do nothing effective about the social and economic forces we have been discussing. Denying that you have a class interest, you can do nothing effective; and ignoring the fundamental political realities of life in America, you are doomed to have the biases of the system work against you over and over again.

But the biases of the system are no more than that—biases. People in the lower 60 percent of the population are not predestined to get very little of what can be had through politics. These income strata are not the impenetrable castes of ancient India. The biases can be overcome in some circumstances. And throughout this book we will observe repeated examples of biases having been overcome. There is much to be learned from observing the past.

It Is Healthier to Care

The ancient Greeks in Athens believed that the totally private person is useless. They believed that participating in public life helped develop one's potential as a human being and made one a better person. Of course, the Athenians had a very different democracy from ours. In contrast to our large, representative system where the citizen's major responsibility can be fulfilled by the simple act of voting, Athens was a small society with a direct democracy. When major issues arose, all the citizens were supposed to gather and argue out their differences until a compromise solution was reached.

This Athenian notion that you are a better person if you participate in public life is reinforced by modern psychologists who tell us that it is psychologically healthier to confront our problems and take action

You will be a psychologically healthier person if you care about the kind of society you inhabit, participate in the public activities that seek to make it a better society, and participate with an open mind as well as an open agenda for dealing with the fundamental income, racial, and gender inequities that plague our society.

on them than to ignore them or run away from them. In this sense, you will be a psychologically healthier person if you care about the kind of society you inhabit, if you participate in the public activities that seek to make it a better society, and participate with an open mind as well as an open agenda for dealing with the fundamental income, racial, and gender inequities that plague our society.

Furthermore, it is healthier to care about the effect of politics on income distribution not just because ancient Greeks and modern psychologists say so, but because you develop a sounder moral character by caring about what happens to other people. Psychologists think that the ability to empathize with others is the norm, and they use the term "psychopathic" to describe the extreme character disorder of those who look out exclusively for themselves with no regard for the rights or well-being of others. Even so conservative a public figure as Pope John Paul II wrote an encyclical letter in 1991 urging the capitalistic societies to repair the economic injustices that market capitalism had wreaked on their poor.[35] Government action is needed because private charity is insufficient for coping with the problems of the poor, the near-poor, and the financially precarious. A 1987 poll indicated that barely half the population contributes to charity.[36]

In sum, you have a vested interest in caring about such issues as politics and the distribution of income. First, the quality of American democracy is at stake. Second, growing inequities in income distribution reveal an historic tension in America between who gets what and who pays for it. If political participation and voter turnout continue to shrink, this tension will continue to mean that the lower 60 percent of the population are underrepresented. And finally, individuals become morally and psychologically healthier human beings as they care more about and participate more fully in the public life of their society.

The Meaning of Politics and Power

The Importance of Defining Politics Broadly

It is in the interests of lower status people to think of politics in a much broader sense than the term is usually used. Most television and

Individuals become morally and psychologically healthier human beings as they care more about and participate more fully in the public life of their society.

newspaper news stories portray politics primarily in personal terms as what politicians, political parties, or candidates do during election campaigns. But thinking of politics in such a narrow, individualistic way makes it difficult to conceive of politics as conflict and compromise between social groups over the directions of society. The lower 60 percent of the population particularly must learn to think of politics not only as election campaigns, but as including the decisions of government that allocate the resources of society, and the broader social forces that push government to act in certain ways. If politics mean nothing more than the personal victory of candidate X over candidate Y, then politics is indeed meaningless to the lives of most persons. But if, as we argue here, politics offers the possibility that the lower 60 percent can put in office a slate of candidates who will enact public policies to improve living conditions for the lower 60 percent, then politics becomes very meaningful. Because of this, it is in the interests of lower-status people to think of politics in its broader definition, rather than in its narrow definition.

This broad definition of the term "politics" has long been recognized by political scientists. David Easton defined politics as "the authoritative allocation of values."[37] In this sense, the valuable resources of society are allocated for purposes that society in general considers legitimate and authoritative. Politics is the conflict over the public decisions that results in public policies that allocate benefits, goods, services, and other values in society. Or, as Harold Lasswell stated it, who gets what, when, how.[38]

Political Power

Deeply connected to the term politics is the concept of *political power*. As that term is used here, it refers to the ability of individuals or groups to influence government as it allocates society's resources.[39] To the extent that a group can influence government this way, that group is said to have power.

To learn how to protect their self-interest in politics, lower-status leaders must understand three aspects of political power. First, power is contextual.[40] Most groups have power only in a given political context. Defense contractors, for example, exert considerable influence over the choice of weapons systems that are built and deployed by the Department of Defense, but they have virtually no influence on a whole host of other political contexts, including abortion, desegregaton, affirmative action, or even national tax policy. Lower-status leaders must distinguish between the context in which they can have a great influence on events and those in which their influence is marginal.

A second aspect of political power is that it is structured. Power is not randomly distributed throughout society, and some categories of people are consistently more powerful than others. Least influential of all are unorganized people and people who fail to vote or participate in political action. These people find it virtually impossible to bring their voice to bear on public officials, and since they do not vote, public officials have little reason to listen to them. Somewhat more influential are voters. They exert limited power to the extent that they choose the political leaders and to the extent that they engage in mass demonstrations to influence a public policy. Voters can sometimes be extremely influential when their activities are guided by organized leaders. The affluent elderly, we saw, expressed enough disenchantment with Congress's first attempt to create a catastrophic health insurance plan that they got Congress to revoke the law. Much of this expression came at the urgings of various senior citizens' groups that knew how to organize people to put effective pressure on members of Congress. Without the organized efforts of the senior citizens' groups, it is unlikely that Congress would have paid much heed to a few disparate, uncoordinated complaints of isolated senior citizens.

In contrast to the limited power of the participating electorate and the practically nonexistent power of the unorganized and nonparticipants, some highly organized groups consistently influence public decisions that affect them. Defense contractors, as we noted, are influential on defense policy; bankers and the leaders of financial institutions are generally consulted closely before Congress makes decisions that affect their operations. The political influence of other groups—such as labor unions, political parties, church organizations, and other interest groups—varies widely depending on the issue under consideration. In short, power is distributed in a highly structured way among the major institutions of the economy and society. What is missing for the lower 60 percent of the population is a set of political institutions to represent them effectively in this structure.

Third, political power is inseparable from private power. There is no longer a clear dividing line between actions that are exclusively public and those that are exclusively private. For example, recall the catastrophe that threatened the retirees in Kannapolis. For the purely private motive of maximizing profit, various owners of the cotton mills during the 1980s participated in restructuring the company and raiding its pension fund. The owners took these actions for private reasons, but their actions have far-reaching public ramifications. Government regulators permitted the actions that resulted in the restructurings, the raiding of the pension fund, and the ultimate bankruptcy of the insurance company. Arranging a takeover of the bankrupt insurance company may end up as a cost to the taxpayers of the state that made the arrangement. Kannapolis retirees may not receive 100 percent of their pensions. And if the reduced pensions of the Kannapolis retirees force them onto public welfare, that will be a cost to federal taxpayers as well as those in North Carolina.

Because of the unanticipated consequences of actions taken by large corporations, it often is very difficult to call their actions private rather than public. Even though they may be taken privately, by private business people, for private motives, they often have public ramifications. For these reasons, the distinction between private and public is always blurred.

Money Bias and Radicalism

Finally, if you are to protect your political and economic self-interest, it is important to gain the habit of looking for the ideological origins behind the ideas that people push on you. And you would be forgiven for suspecting that a book emphasizing the role of class and money in politics stems from either a radical or a Marxist perspective. There are many ways of viewing the world, and the Marxist focus on the economic and structural forces behind political power is certainly a useful one. For several reasons, however, this book rejects a radical or Marxist mode of analysis.

First, this book accepts the fact that the people who lived under Marxism, the East Europeans, discarded Marxism as soon as they had the chance. This viewpoint differs from that of Marxists who maintain the fiction that Eastern Europe under communism never experienced true Marxism.[41] But arguing this is a little like proclaiming that people under Catholicism and Protestantism never experienced true Christianity. Whatever their flaws, Catholicism and Protestantism are the only Christianity that most people know, and they draw support from hundreds of millions of people. Likewise, communism is the only Marxism that Eastern Europeans knew, but a third of a billion of them rejected it at their first real opportunity.

Second, radicals and Marxists are revolutionaries; this book is not. They preach that the social ills of America can be addressed only through a revolution that overthrows capitalism, eliminates the greed in human nature,[42] and dismantles the pluralist form of representative democracy that permits greedy interests to have so much influence in the political system.[43] Political scientist Edward Greenberg, for example, writes, "only a radical transformation of the capitalist system will make possible the creation of a society in which justice and democracy are possible. . . . corporate capitalism must be replaced . . ."[44] Another radical political scientist, Michael Parenti, writes, "What is needed then is public ownership of all the major means of production and public ownership of the wealth, the moneyed power itself, in a word, socialism."[45]

In contrast to the radical call for a revolution, this book calls for increasing the influence and affluence of the lower strata within the existing social system. I am certain that a revolution of the radical sort is not going to take place; at least not in my lifetime, and probably not in yours. The inequities in America are too great to put off while waiting for a revolution that is not going to occur. For people trapped in America's bottom strata, the solutions to their problems are not to be found in abstract leftist ideologies preaching a far-off revolution. What they need today is what the great labor leader Samuel Gompers demanded, and to a considerable degree achieved, "More, Now!"

A third reason why this book rejects Marxist and radical analysis of American politics stems from the excessive dogmatism that afflicts Marxists and radicals. In a fair amount of radical writing, ideas are true and facts are recognized only to the extent that they fit into a dogmatic theory. This book, by contrast, is more eclectic and empirical. It does not ask you to accept a political doctrine. It asks instead that you examine the political system for patterns of bias, and then vote and act in ways that might help alleviate those biases. This, indeed, is more difficult than devoting yourself uncritically to a dogma, for I am asking you to accept the premise that nobody has a monopoly on good ideas. Sometimes good ideas come from radicals, sometimes from liberals, and sometimes even from conservatives. And whatever ideas we promote, we have an obligation to make an honest attempt to see if they stand the test of credible empirical evidence.

Conclusion:
Politics as the Art of the Possible _____

In sum, this book is based on Walter Lippman's vision of politics as the art of the possible.[46] The American political system has distinct biases that work against the lower 60 percent of the population. But some of those biases can be overcome. To highlight the possibilities of overcoming them, each chapter that follows will have a section on how the biases of that particular subject can be overcome.

It is in the true interests of all Americans—rich or poor, black, Asian, Hispanic, Native American, or white—to figure out ways to give the lower-status population a greater voice in the political system. In a moral sense, no American becomes a better human being because one more ghetto child grows up illiterate, ignorant, and economically useless. And if the numbers of such children continue to escalate, as they have over the past generation, every American is worse off because of it. The first step in overcoming such biases is to understand how the biases work. And that is the major goal of this book: to examine the biases of our major political institutions and processes, to provide examples of how some of those biases have been overcome in the past, and to point out some ways in which they might be overcome in the future.

Summary

1. Politics are not neutral.

2. There are patterns of bias in American politics. Biases of omission are just as important as biases of commission.

3. Despite the myth of a classless politics, wealth plays a very important role in American life and politics. There are various ways of defining social class, the most straightforward of which is simply to classify people according to their income and wealth. Doing so gives us five income strata: There are two upper strata: (a) the well-off and (b) the comfortable. There are three lower strata: (c) the financially precarious, (d) the near-poor, and (e) the poor.

4. The lower-strata population is not composed randomly. By birthright characteristics, it is overwhelmingly white. But it is nevertheless disproportionately minority, female, and the offspring of families of average income. By behavioral characteristics, it is disproportionately composed of those who have low levels of education, are not married, are socially isolated from membership in organizations, and who live in places such as inner-city ghetto neighborhoods and rural areas that lack extensive economic opportunities.

5. Political and economic changes of the late twentieth century have increased the economic insecurity of the lower-status population.

6. There are several reasons why the average person should care about politics. The quality of democracy, and possibly its survival, are at stake. Most people need government help to alleviate the biases of the marketplace. It is psychologically and morally healthier to care about politics than not to care. And in the proper circumstances, the individual can have an impact.

7. The term politics must be interpreted broadly to have a proper meaning.

8. The term politics must also be conceived of pragmatically as the "art of the possible."

Notes

1. Harold Lasswell, *Politics: Who Gets What, When, How* (New York: McGraw–Hill, 1936).

2. Data from the U.S. Census Bureau, calculated by the Employee Benefit Research Institute. Reported in the *New York Times*, July 29, 1991, p. A8.

3. Data from the American Medical Association. Reported in the *New York Times*, January 9, 1991, p. A10.

4. The official infant mortality rates in 1990 were 10.4 for the United States, 10.3 for Greece, and 6.2 for Spain. United States Bureau of the Census, *Statistical Abstract of the United States: 1991* (Washington, D.C.: United States Government Printing Office, 1991), p. 834.

5. James Madison, *Federalist Paper 10.*

6. The most successful of leftist-leaning presidential candidates were Robert La Follette, who won 13 electoral votes and 17 percent of the popular vote under the banner of the Progressive Party in 1924, and People's (Populist) Party candidate James B. Weaver, who won 22 electoral votes and 8 percent of the popular vote in 1892. See Paul Allen Beck and Frank J. Sorauf, *Party Politics in America*, 6th ed. (Glenview, Ill.: Scott, Foresman and Company, 1988), pp. 50-51.

7. According to the 1988 *Los Angeles Times*/CNN exit poll, voters with incomes under $10,000 voted for Dukakis over Bush by a margin of 64 percent to 33 percent. Voters with incomes over $40,000 favored Bush by a margin of 62 percent to 37 percent. *National Journal*, November 12, 1988, p. 2855.

8. Susan A. Ostrander, "Upper-Class Women: Class Consciousness as Conduct and Meaning," *Power Structure Research*, G. William Domhoff, ed. (Beverley Hills: Sage Publications, 1980), p. 79.

9. Benjamin DeMott, *The Imperial Middle: Why Americans Can't Think Straight About Class* (New York: Morrow, 1991).

10. The National Opinion Research Center has asked over 23,000 people since 1972 to identify themselves in one of four categories. They found that 99 percent of the people were able to put themselves in one of the four, but barely 8 percent were willing to call themselves lower class or upper class. The responses were as follows:

Lower class	5.1%
Working class	46.3
Middle class	44.7
Upper class	3.1

National Opinion Research Center, *General Social Survey: Codebook, 1972–1989* (Chicago: Ill.: National Opinion Research Center, University of Chicago, 1989), p. 237.

11. See John J. Harrigan, *Political Change in the Metropolis*, 4th ed., (Glenview, Ill.: Scott, Foresman, and Company, 1989), chapter 3.

12. Ira Katznelson, *City Trenches: Urban Politics and the Patterning of Class in the United States* (New York: Pantheon Books, 1981), pp. 54-56, 84, 101–102.

13. *New York Times*, October 2, 1989, p. 25. The data were calculated by Congress's Joint Committee on Taxation.

14. A *Newsweek* headline of October 2, 1989, read "Class War Over Taxes: The Demo-

crats Float a Plan to Soak the Rich." p. 24. The following week, October 9, 1989, its headline read, "The Class Warfare Fizzles," p. 37.

15. Will did not directly call the opponents communists. But in the same paragraph, he linked opponents of the tax cut with Lenin and the Communist regime in North Korea. And he accused them of considering wealth as an unspeakable four-letter word. See his column in the *St. Paul Pioneer Press Dispatch*, July 31, 1989, p. 12D.

16. Paul Fussell, *Class: A Guide Through the American Status System* (New York: Summit Books, 1983).

17. This was one finding of the Survey Research Center's nine year study of 5,000 families. James N. Morgan et al., *Five Thousand American Families: Patterns of Economic Progress* (Ann Arbor: University of Michigan, Institute for Social Research, 1974).

18. These calculations were made based on the assumption that inflation will continue at the 5 percent rate it has averaged in recent decades, and that an 8 percent return could realistically be achieved, since that is the approximate average return on Treasury Bills during the 1980s.

19. *Statistical Abstract of the United States: 1991*, p. 469.

20. The concept of underclass is controversial among social scientists. For an excellent set of articles on this topic, see Christopher Jencks and Paul N. Peterson, eds., *The Urban Underclass* (Washington: The Brookings Institution, 1991).

21. *Statistical Abstract of the United States, 1991*, p. 400.

22. Robert B. Reich, "Why the Rich Are Getting Richer and the Poor Poorer," *The New Republic*, 1989. For a fuller treatment of Reich's ideas, see his *The Work of Nations: Preparing Ourselves for 21st Century Capitalism* (New York: Knopf, 1991).

23. Bennett Harrison and Barry Bluestone, *The Great U-Turn: Corporate Restructuring and the Polarizing of America* (New York: Basic Books, 1988).

24. Frank Levy, *Dollars and Dreams: The Changing American Income Distribution* (New York: W. W. Norton and Company, 1988).

25. Jean Jacques Rousseau, *The Social Contract* (New York: Penguin, 1968).

26. Seymour Martin Lipset, *Political Man: The Social Bases of Politics* (Baltimore: Johns Hopkins University Press, 1981).

27. Among college-educated people, voter turnout dropped from 84.3 percent for those who were working to 77.1 percent for the unemployed. Among those with high school education or less, turnout dropped from 71.8 percent to 56 percent. Calculated from James Allan Davis and Tom W. Smith, *General Social Surveys, 1972–1989* [machine-readable data file]. Principal Investigator, James A. Davis; Director and Co-Principal Investigator, Tom W. Smith. NORC ed. (Chicago: National Opinion Research Center, producer, 1989); (Storrs, CT: The Roper Center for Public Opinion Research, University of Connecticut, distributor).

28. Katherine Newman, *Falling From Grace: The Experience of Downward Mobility in the American Middle Class* (New York: Free Press, 1988).

29. M. Harvey Brenner, *Estimating the Social Costs of National Economic Policy: Implications for Mental and Physical Health, and Criminal Aggression* (Washington, D.C.: Government Printing Office, 1976).

30. This was especially true of the Phoenix, Arizona Lincoln Savings and Loan Association. See *New York Times*, November 4, 1989, p. 1; December 5, 1989, p. 1; *Washington Post National Weekly*, November 27–December 3, 1989, p. 10.

31. James B. Steward, *Den of Thieves: The Untold Story of the Men Who Plundered Wall Street and the Chase That Brought Them Down* (New York: Simon and Schuster, 1991).

32. Early in the 1980s, Vice President Bush chaired a Task Force on Regulatory Relief which claimed to have saved industry billions of dollars through the application of cost benefit analysis to the issuing of new regulations.

33. Reported in *Minneapolis Star Tribune*, July 1, 1990, p. 1E.

34. John Rawls, *On Justice* (Cambridge, Mass.: The Belknap Press of Harvard University, 1971).

35. Pope John Paul II, papal encyclical entitled, "Centesimus Annus." Details in *New York Times*, May 3, 1991, p. 1.

36. Roper Poll, Reported in *Minneapolis Star Tribune*, November 15, 1988, p. 2A.

37. David Easton, *The Political System* (New York: Knopf, 1953).

38. Lasswell, *Politics: Who Gets What, When, How* (New York: Meridian Books, 1958).
39. See Robert A. Dahl, *Modern Political Analysis*, 4th ed. (Englewood Cliffs, N.J.: Prentice-Hall, 1984), pp. 23, 41. Dahl describes influence essentially as the ability of actor A to get actor B to do something that B would not normally do. Power is the exercise of influence through the threat of force. "Severe losses for noncompliance can be invoked by the power holder." (p. 41.)
40. This argument is taken from Harrigan, *Political Change in the Metropolis*, 4th ed., pp. 12–13.
41. Edward S. Greenberg, for example, wrote that neither the Soviet Union nor the Eastern European communist countries were truly socialist. See his *The American Political System: A Radical Approach*, 5th ed. (Glenview, Ill.: Scott, Foresman and Company, 1989), p. 356.
42. Charles Reich, *The Greening of America: How the Youth Revolution Is Trying to Make America Livable* (New York: Random House, 1970).
43. See especially, Michael Parenti, *Democracy for the Few*, 5th ed. (New York: St. Martin's Press, Inc., 1988) and Edward S. Greenberg, *The American Political System*.
44. Greenberg, *The American Political System*, pp. 345, 346.
45. Parenti, *Democracy for the Few*, p. 319.
46. Walter Lippman, *Essays in the Public Philosophy* (Boston: Little Brown, 1955).

CHAPTER 2

The Constitution as Seen from Below

Introduction

The Constitution is in many ways the ultimate rule book for American politics, much as Hoyle is for games of cards or other rule books are for various sports. Just as the rules of poker, for example, determine that four aces beat a straight flush, the Constitution provides for such processes as selecting the president, determining how many votes it takes in Congress to override a presidential veto, and setting out vague guidelines for our most fundamental principles, such as freedom of speech, equal protection of the law, and due process of law. Unlike the rule books for cards and sports, however, the Constitution is not neutral. Nor is it enforced by neutral umpires. It was put together in 1787 by the strongest and richest political players of the time, who were keenly aware that the rules of government would deeply affect their economic security. It is enforced in great measure by umpires (Supreme Court justices), most of whom historically have had strong preferences for the property rights of the upper-status population over the human needs of the lower-status population.

To sort out the biases in our Constitution and the body of constitutional law that has grown out of it, however, is no easy task. There are many crosscurrents at work. Different generations interpret the Constitution differently to meet the particular challenges of their day. And at any given moment people with political and economic axes to grind seek to get the umpires (Supreme Court justices) to render constitutional interpretations favorable to their own interests.

This notion that the Constitution and its interpretation are deeply linked to the political conditions of each generation is a difficult one to accept. Many scholars from both the political right[1] and the left[2] argue that the existence of these political linkages proves that the Constitution itself has no inherent meaning; that it is little more than a mechanism to legitimize the privileged position of elites in our society. One critic, for example, argues that the Constitution is meaningless to

> . . . the Constitution is not neutral. Nor is it enforced by neutral umpires. It was put together in 1787 by the strongest and richest political players of the time, who were keenly aware that the rules of government would deeply affect their economic security.

lower-status people because it has no provisions for economic justice, its protections of freedom of speech have been frequently violated, and it took one hundred years to terminate the system of racial segregation that was imposed after the Civil War.[3]

This argument, however, is overdrawn. The laws against murder, burglary, rape, and assault also are violated frequently, but no one would argue that that makes the laws meaningless. It does no disservice to the Constitution to point out that constitutional interpretation is inherently linked to the political conditions of each generation. Indeed, it is the linkage between the Constitution and political reality that makes the Constitution relevant to our lives and difficult to ignore. Many of us could sit down in our studies at night and draft a superior document that would provide economic justice and probably do a better job of spelling out the civil liberties of Americans. But who would pay attention to it? The history of Latin America, for example, is replete with official constitutions modeled on the U.S. document but lacking a real linkage with the cultural and social structures of those societies. And few of these constitutions lasted more than a decade or two.

This chapter argues that the American Constitution, despite the ease with which the upper-status elites can interpret it to legitimate their economic interests, is nevertheless relevant to the interests of lower-status people. To describe this relevance, we must examine: (1) the biases inherent in the drafting of the Constitution, (2) biases in the original content of the Constitution, (3) counterarguments to the notion of a biased Constitution, (4) bias in the interpretation of the Constitution, and (5) how lower-status people can overcome constitutional bias.

Bias at the Beginning _____

The Constitutional Convention that drafted the Constitution in Philadelphia in 1787 is generally held in high esteem by Americans. Two of our most revered historical figures (George Washington and Benjamin Franklin) were among the 55 founding fathers who drafted the document and convinced the nation to adopt it. So many of the other founders were also of such high stature that Thomas Jefferson called the convention an "assembly of demigods." And so stunning were the results of the convention that a more contemporary historian called it the "Miracle at Philadelphia."[4] For the lower-status population of 1787, however, the Constitutional Convention was a far-away event. There were no lower-status people at the convention, and few of the delegates could claim to have been elected by lower-status voters. Historian Charles Beard, in his pathbreaking book *An Economic Interpretation of the Constitution*,[5] calculated that there were five economic groups of people in 1787, and the four poorest groups had no representatives at the convention: women, slaves, indentured servants, and propertyless white men. The delegates all came from the fifth category (white men who owned enough property to give them the right to vote), but even among this group there were at most two or three delegates who were small farmers, and apparently none who were urban tradesmen.

Table 2-1, compiled from Beard's account, tells the story. The 55 delegates to the convention were an economic elite with substantial investments in land, government securities, banking, and commerce. Furthermore, there was substantial overlap among these 5 categories of wealth. Three of the delegates (including George Washington) had holdings in 4 of the 5 categories. Seventeen had holdings in at least 3 of the 5 categories. And 37 had holdings in at least 2 categories. Only 3 delegates were not listed by Beard as having holdings in any of the 5 categories.

It is not surprising that lower-status people were absent from the Constitutional Convention; and documenting their absence would not by itself have made *An Economic Interpretation of the Constitution* the pathbreaking book it became. Lower-status people are seldom present when the initial division of power is being determined in any society in any period. Charles Beard went beyond merely documenting the elite status of the founding fathers, however; he argued that their main motivation was to replace the Articles of Confederation with a new constitution that would freeze into the governing structure their own privileged position in American society.

At first glance, in fact, it was questionable whether the nation even needed a new constitution. For several years America had been governed under a charter called the Articles of Confederation. Under this charter, the United States had scored some important and notable successes.[6] It had inflicted a military defeat on the most powerful nation in the world, negotiated a favorable peace treaty, gained sovereignty over a huge territory stretching from the Appalachian Mountains to the Mississippi River, and passed the Northwest Ordi-

TABLE 2-1 Financial Bases of the Founding Fathers

Financial Security Based on Holdings in:	Number of Delegates in the Category
Speculation in Western Lands	14
Government Securities Issued Under the Articles of Confederation	38 or 40
Banking, Lending or Investing Money	24
Manufacturing, Shipping, or Commerce	11
Plantations and Slaves	15
Number of Delegates with Holdings in All 5 categories	0
Number of Delegates with Holdings in 4 of the 5 Categories (Washington, Mason, Fitzsimmons)	3
Number of Delegates with Holdings in 3 of the 5 categories	14
Number of Delegates with Holdings in 2 of the 5 Categories	20
Number of Delegates with Holdings in 1 of the 5 Categories	15
Unknown or No Holdings	3

nance (1787), which paved the way for settling those territories and bringing them to eventual statehood.

Despite these successes, the founders who met at Philadelphia in 1787 discovered much in the Articles about which to complain. They felt that the Articles provided little more than a feeble confederation, when what was needed was a much stronger national government. They feared that individual states were becoming too democratic and too radical for the good of the nation, and they trembled at the implications of a small and unsuccessful uprising in Massachusetts the previous autumn.

A Feeble Confederation

From the viewpoint of upper-status nationalists such as James Madison and Alexander Hamilton, things appeared to be falling apart for the new nation by the middle 1780s, and the feeble confederation created under the Articles did not cope well with these adverse events. Despite having defeated Great Britain, the new nation had little to show for its efforts. After the end of the Revolutionary War in 1781, the nation fell into an economic slump from which it had not yet fully recovered. Foreign commerce suffered when Great Britain prohibited American ships from trading with the British West Indies, and the new national government under the Articles of Confederation failed to negotiate commercial treaties with France and Spain. In reaction to the economic depression, some states fell into virtual economic warfare with each other. Rhode Island, for example, lowered its import tariffs in an attempt to lure foreign ships to unload their cargoes at its port in Providence, rather than at the one in nearby Boston, which had a high tariff. Massachusetts responded to this challenge by putting a tariff on goods brought into that state from Rhode Island and other low-tariff states.

These problems of foreign trade and interstate rivalry were compounded by a chaotic money system. Indeed, there *was* no single money system; there were 13 money systems, since each state printed its own currency. Some states, such as Rhode Island and Pennsylvania, were controlled by debtors, and issued inflated currencies. Rhode Island's currency became so worthless that merchants refused to accept it as payment for goods. The debtor-controlled legislature then passed the Force Act, requiring merchants to accept the currency, whereupon some merchants closed up shop rather than accept the worthless cash. In creditor-controlled states, on the other hand, the legislatures kept money so tightly controlled that small farmers faced unrelenting foreclosures as they found themselves unable to repay their mortgages and debts. Many of those whose assets could not cover their debts were thrown into debtors' prisons or were forced into servitude to their creditors to work off the debts.[7]

These problems, according to Madison and Hamilton, the most articulate critics of the Articles of Confederation, stemmed from fundamental defects in the charter itself. The national government was simply too weak and disorganized to govern. Congress was especially weak. It lacked the authority to tax, regulate commerce, and control the currency. It was immobilized on controversial issues, because a two-thirds majority was needed to pass laws, and each state had one vote, which meant that any five states could block the passage of bills. Strong leadership in Congress was hindered by the fact that no member could serve more than 3 one-year terms in any six-year period. When Congress succeeded in passing a law, there was no institutionalized executive branch to implement the legislation. Instead of a separate executive branch, laws were executed by a committee of Congress which lacked true enforcement powers. Attempts to remedy these defects failed, because amendments to the Articles required ratification by all 13 state legislatures, and it had never been possible to get all 13 states to agree on giving the national government more powers over the states. In short, the Articles of Confederation created not a true national government but, as its preamble stated, a "firm league of friendship" of 13 sovereign states.

Radicalized States

As Charles Beard and his followers reviewed this history, however, it was not the weaknesses of the national government that upset Madison and Hamilton so much as the radicalization of the states. Following the Declaration of Independence in 1776 and the Revolutionary War (1775–1781), small farmers and people of moderate means increased their representation in the state legislatures. In the three northern states of New York, New Jersey, and New Hampshire, for example, only 23 percent of the legislators were farmers before the Revolutionary War, whereas 55 percent were farmers after the war. In the three southern states of Maryland, Virginia, and South Carolina, the comparable figures were 12 and 26 percent, respectively. As the representation of small farmers increased, the representation of the upper-status population necessarily declined. Before the war, 36 percent of the legislators in New York, New Jersey, and New Hampshire had been classified as wealthy, but only 12 percent were so classified after the war. The story was the same in the South. Before the war, 52 percent of legislators in Maryland, Virginia, and South Carolina had been classified as wealthy, but only 23 percent after the war.[8]

With this improved democratization, the legislatures became more attentive to the concerns of lower-status people. Pennsylvania, in a burst of Revolutionary zeal, adopted a constitution that came about as close to direct democracy as anyone could have hoped for in the 1780s. Not trusting a strong governor, it placed the executive power in a 12-member committee with three-year overlapping terms. It inhibited legislative leadership by providing for annual elections and barring anyone from serving more than four years in any seven-year period. It ensured a citizen voice by requiring that legislative votes and proceedings be made public. No bill could become law until it had been publicized throughout the state and then voted on again at the next legislative session. It was one of the few states to eliminate property qualifications for holding office, and the right to vote was extended to all taxpayers. Even officers of the militia were elected by the people.[9] But even more than Pennsylvania, it was Rhode Island that typified the dangers of democracy in the minds of upper-status elites. Rhode Island, as we saw, issued an inflated currency that favored the interests of small farmers over those of affluent moneylenders or merchants, and then passed the Force Act requiring those upper-status persons to accept payment in the worthless currency.

In the minds of the founding fathers, Rhode Island's Force Act amounted to a repudiation of a contract. How could any upper-status person carry on business, extend credit, and enter into commercial relations with lower-status people if those same lower-status people could elect a majority of the legislature that would repudiate contracts, legitimize bankruptcies, and abrogate their debts by forcing merchants to accept worthless currency as payment for goods and services? These developments in Rhode Island and other states gave upper-status elites little confidence in the common citizen. This, perhaps, is what Alexander Hamilton had in mind when he said, "Sir, your people is a great beast."[10]

Shays's Rebellion

These trends in Rhode Island and Pennsylvania helped predispose growing numbers of upper-status elites to reverse what whey perceived as a democratizing and radicalizing trend in the states. It was as though ideological tinder had been stockpiled, and all that was needed to ignite a bonfire under the upper-status elite was a spark.

That igniting spark came in the fall of 1786 when John Shays, a former Revolutionary War officer and now an indebted farmer, inspired a group of other debt-ridden farmers to invade rural courthouses in Massachusetts. Shays wanted to prevent farm foreclosure proceedings from taking place by preventing the courts from sitting until after the next legislative election, in the hope that a new legislature would provide small farmers with debt relief. He tried to capture a federal arsenal in Massachusetts, and by the time the rebellion was put down, eleven men were killed, and many others injured.[11]

Without Shays's Rebellion, it is doubtful whether Congress would ever have called the Philadelphia Convention. But Shays's Rebellion shocked the upper-status elites into action. George Washington said that the rebellion left him "mortified beyond expression" that the United States should be made to look "ridiculous and contemptible in the eyes of all Europe."[12] But mortified or not, Washington wanted some action taken. He wrote to Henry Lee: "For God's sake . . . if [the rebels] have *real* grievances, redress them; if they have not, employ the force of government against them at once."[13]

Too Much Democracy

With these events in their minds, the 55 delegates who convened at Philadelphia in 1787 were strongly motivated to do something about what they perceived as the democratic excesses of the states. Edmund Randolph, who presented Madison's Virginia Plan to the convention, told his fellow delegates on May 31 that the governmental troubles under the Articles could all be traced to "the turbulence and follies of democracy: that some check therefore was to be sought for agst. this tendency in our Governments." Elbridge Gerry on the same day commented that "the evils we experience flow from the excess of democracy.

It is not surprising that lower-status people were absent from the Constitutional Convention. And documenting their absence would not by itself have made *An Economic Interpretation of the Constitution* the pathbreaking book that it became. Lower-status people are seldom present when the initial division of power is being decided on in any society in any period.

The people do not want virtue; but are the dupes of pretended patriots." And the people in general, argued Roger Sherman, "should have as little to do as may be about the Government."[14] The whole point of calling the convention in the first place was, according to political scientist Michael Parenti, "containing the spread of democracy."[15]

In short, the founding fathers had powerful economic motives for creating a new, strong, national government. The 11 merchants, 24 moneylenders, and 15 plantation owners would benefit from a government that could protect their property rights from the excesses of state legislatures dominated by lower-status people. The 24 moneylenders would benefit from a strong national government that could contain any future Shays's Rebellions threatening the collection of debts. The 14 speculators in western lands would benefit from a strong national government capable of sending an army into the Northwest Territories to pacify the Indians and evict the remaining units of the British army. This would spur population migration westward and enable them to make a tidy profit on their land speculations. Finally, the 40 holders of public securities would benefit by a strong national government capable of maintaining a strong currency and redeeming government notes at full value.

But there was more to this notion of the founders' economic motives than just specific moneymaking opportunities. And despite Beard's extensive research, it is not clear that all, or even most, of the delegates actually voted on their alleged economic motives. What is clear, however, is the founders' concern for the broader issue of the government's role in the political economy. "What was at stake," wrote Staughton Lynd, "was more than speculative windfalls in securities; it was the question, what kind of society would emerge from the revolution when the dust had settled, and on which class the political center of gravity would come to rest."[16]

Bias in the Content

If, as Beard and his followers argue, the founding fathers created the Constitution to protect their economic self-interest, what specific provisions of the Constitution would enable them to do so? Three different types of provisions helped in this regard: (1) Those that protected private property rights, (2) those that insulated the national government from popular rule, and (3) those that minimized the influence of the lower-status population in the ratification process.

The Protection of Property Rights

Several specific provisions of the Constitution were designed to protect the property rights of upper-status elites. States were prohibited from issuing money, and this neutralized the power of debtor-controlled states like Rhode Island to issue inflated currency. States were also prohibited from impairing the enforceability of contracts, and the Constitution's full faith and credit clause made it harder for debtors to escape paying their bills by fleeing to another state. The property rights of slave-owners were secured by the provision that slaves who escape to free states must be returned to their original owners.

Perhaps more important in the long run than these specific provisions was the granting of several new economic powers to the new national government. These included the power to regulate commerce, collect taxes, establish a national currency, borrow money, fix standards of weights and measures, protect the value of government bonds and securities, pay the government's debt, establish uniforms laws of bankruptcies, establish a post office, establish roads, establish copyright and patient protections, suppress insurrections (such as Shays's Rebellion), and finally, legislate for the general welfare of the United States. None of the delegates could have anticipated that these powers would eventually expand as they did over the next two centuries, but the delegates clearly intended to give the government enough economic power to ensure a stable economic environment and promote economic growth.

Insulation from Popular Majorities

In Beard's thesis, the founders not only needed a constitution to protect their particular economic interests, they also needed to do something else. They needed to insulate the national government from lower-status or radical majorities who might take over the government and use its power to redistribute the wealth, as they had sought to do in Rhode Island.

The strategy for achieving this goal lay in what has come to be called the Madisonian model. Madison was very worried about the possibility of tyranny, whether it be the tyranny of the king (as the founders had experienced in colonial days), the tyranny of the masses (which they felt had happened in some of the states), or the tyranny of any faction. And he eloquently argued in the *Federalist Papers* that the best protection against such tyranny lay in an enlarged republic. A republic of the 13 states would be much less susceptible to tyranny than would any individual state, because the larger scope and domain of the national republic would generate so many different economic, regional, religious, and political factions that they would neutralize each other in their quest for influence.

Even though a large republic lessened the chance that one faction could gain control of the government, it did not eliminate that possibility. As a further protection against any one faction gaining control of the government, the Madisonian model called for an extensive system of separation of powers and checks and balances (see Figure 2-1). In *Federalist 51* Madison eloquently described how and why these checks and balances would work.

> ... the great security against a gradual concentration of the several powers in the same department consists in giving to those who administer each department the necessary constitutional means and personal motives to resist encroachment of the others. . . . Ambition must be made to counteract ambition.

And if this device suggested a fairly pessimistic view of human nature, Madison cheerfully admitted that viewpoint.

> It may be a reflection on human nature that such devices should be necessary to control the abuses of government. But what is government itself, but the greatest of all reflections on human nature? If men were angels, no government would be necessary.[17]

Note that Figure 2–1 describes four main institutions of government: the president, the Court, the Senate, and the House of Representatives. Of these, the Beardians point out, only the House of Representatives is elected directly by the people. Thus, even if a huge influx of lower-status voters succeeded in gaining control of the House of Representatives, the elaborate system of checks and balances ensures that they would not be able to impose their will on the whole government. Furthermore, to reduce the chance of lower-status people being elected to Congress, the founders stipulated that congressional districts should contain no fewer than 30,000 people. While this number is small compared to today's congressional district of more than half a million, it was larger than any state legislative district in 1787. Being larger than state legislative districts, the congressional districts

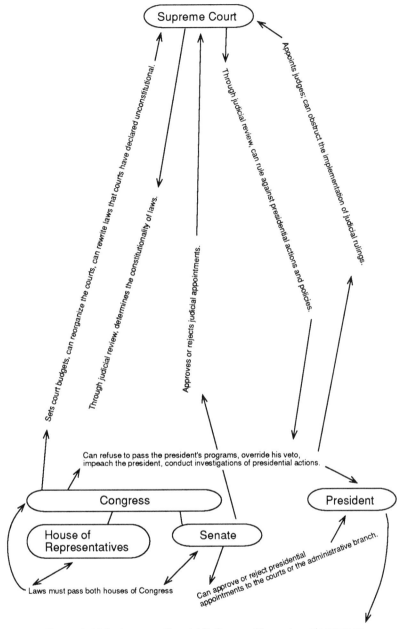

Supreme Court

Sets court budgets, can reorganize the courts, can rewrite laws that courts have declared unconstitutional.

Through judicial review, determines the constitutionality of laws.

Approves or rejects judicial appointments.

Through judicial review, can rule against presidential actions and policies.

Appoints judges; can obstruct the implementation of judicial rulings.

Can refuse to pass the president's programs, override his veto, impeach the president, conduct investigations of presidential actions.

Congress

President

House of Representatives

Senate

Laws must pass both houses of Congress

Can approve or reject presidential appointments to the courts or the administrative branch.

Proposes legislation to congress. Can veto bills. Can use public speeches and appearances to set agenda for Congress.

Figure 2-1 Checks and Balances in the Madisonian Model

would attract "men of intelligence and uprightness" in James Wilson's view, and keep out "men of fractious tempers, of localist prejudices, or of sinister designs," code words by which Wilson and Madison anticipated that few lower-status people would be elected to Congress.[18]

In sum, the main consequence of the Madisonian model, from the perspective of Beard and his followers, was that it minimized the voice of the lower-status population in the national government and insulated that government as much as practically possible from lower-status influence.

Bias in the Ratification Process

In addition to protecting property rights in the content of the Constitution and insulating the national government from lower-status minorities, the Beardians also charged that the founders (who now began calling themselves Federalists) structured the ratification process to minimize the impact of the Anti-Federalists and their supporters among the lower-status voters.

The first thing the Federalists did was to set up a friendlier ratification procedure than the one specified in the Articles of Confederation. Under the Articles, changes had to be ratified by the state legislatures of all 13 states. Since Rhode Island had not even sent a delegation to Philadelphia, it was likely to reject the Constitution and thus send it down to defeat. To get around this unanimous approval requirement, the framers provided that the Constitution would go into effect when ratified by only nine states. A second stumbling block was the state legislatures. Since the new constitution reduced their powers, they were not a friendly forum for ratification. To get around the legislatures, the framers specified that each state must hold a ratifying convention whose sole purpose was to accept or reject the new constitution.

In the elections to choose delegates to these ratifying conventions, the Beardians discovered sharp discrimination against lower-status voters and the Anti-Federalists. Most states had property qualifications for voting, and this alone disenfranchised more than one-third of the adult white men.[19] Turnout was extremely low, with only about 160,000 people voting in all 13 states. Had the turnout been larger, the Beardians imply, the Constitution would probably have been defeated. What might have happened had the turnout been larger, however, is impossible to know. Of the 160,000 people who did turn out, 100,000 (or nearly two-thirds) voted in favor of ratification. This lopsided victory was due, according to one scholar, to the "superior economic position of the Federalists."[20] The Federalists controlled most of the newspapers, which enabled them to play down Anti-Federalist arguments. And Federalist merchants who were regular advertisers in

Anti-Federalist newspapers pressured those newspapers to downpeddle the Anti-Federalist cause. Federalist bankers called in the loans of Anti-Federalist borrowers.[21]

The Beard Thesis in Perspective _____

In sum, Charles Beard and his followers present an overwhelming argument that there was a persistent bias against lower-status people in the drafting and ratification of the American Constitution. In politics, as in life generally, however, it is always a good idea to remember that there are at least two sides to every story. And this is true also of the Beardian thesis about the American Constitution. An impressive number of scholars remain unconvinced that the creation of the Constitution was as biased as the Beardians make it seem.

Historian Robert Brown severely criticized Beard's research methods, claiming that Beard focused only on evidence that supported his thesis, and failed to examine that evidence critically.[22] Forrest McDonald reexamined voting records and discovered enough instances of convention delegates voting against their personal economic interests that he found it "impossible to justify" Beard's thesis.[23] And Garry Wills rejected Beard's contention that the constitutional ratification process was undemocratic.[24]

In addition to these specific complaints about Beard's research methods, three larger issues concern his critics.

Class Divisiveness Overdrawn

First, the Beardians have exaggerated the extent of class divisiveness in 1787. According to the class divisiveness theory, the Constitution betrayed the democratic thrust of the Declaration of Independence and the Revolution. This was a charge leveled by the Anti-Federalists in their attempt to defeat the Constitution, and the charge is not wholly without foundation. As we saw, the Revolution increased the representation of small farmers and middle-class tradesmen in the state legislatures. From this perspective, the founders of the Constitution betrayed the democratic hopes of the Revolution by creating a national government to curb the excesses of the lower-status-dominated legislatures.

However, the class divisions were not that neatly drawn, either at the time of the Revolution in 1776 or at the drafting of the Constitution a decade later. In 1776, many rich men joined the Revolution, especially the wealthy families of Boston and Virginia, the two main centers of the independence movement. And many opponents of the

In politics, as in life generally . . . it is always a good idea to remember that there are at least two sides to every story. And this is true also of the Beardian thesis about the American Constitution.

Revolution were found among the ranks of the non-rich.[25] So even though the Revolution improved the political influence of the lower-status population and reduced the influence of the wealthy, the lines of division over the Revolution were not neatly divided into lower-status supporters and upper-status opponents.

A similar blurring of class lines surrounded the conflict over the Constitutional Convention in 1787. Beard is certainly correct that it was dominated by an upper-status elite that had powerful economic incentives to create a stronger national government, but there were also many lower-status people as well who supported the Constitution. This was especially true of the artisans and skilled laborers in the major cities. In Philadelphia, the Federalist vote was nearly eight times that of the Anti-Federalists. In New York City, it was 18 times as large. The artisans also staged some of the largest parades yet seen in America in favor of ratifying the Constitution. In Boston, 4,000 artisans marched in favor of ratifying the Constitution, in New York City 5,000, Philadelphia 5,000–6,000, and in Charleston, 2,800.[26]

It simply is not clear how much class division existed in 1787. Leftist scholars speak of a sharp bifurcation between rich and poor with a very small middle class.[27] But historian Robert Brown maintains that there was no large propertyless mass. Most men were middle-class farmers who owned or were buying their farms, and thus were qualified voters.[28] Finally, in response to the charge that the founders used the Constitution to protect property rights, Brown further argues "practically everybody was interested in the protection of property. A constitution which did not protect property unquestionably would have been rejected, for the American people had fought the Revolution for the preservation of life, liberty, and property."[29]

What the Convention Rejected

The Constitutional Convention is also significant for what it rejected. A good many delegates wanted a tougher and more centralized national government than they got. The most demanding of them was Hamilton, who proposed a plan that would have provided for a highly centralized national government: a president and a senate elected for life, and a president with an absolute veto over bills passed by Congress, along with the power to appoint state governors.[30] But the convention paid little attention to this plan. Even Madison, who had done so much to create the checks and balance system, felt at the end that the national government should have been given more powers than it had been given. But the delegates were men with practical political experience who understood that they had to temper their own antidemocratic tendencies if they wanted the new government to be ratified.

Madisonian Model Not Undemocratic

Finally, Beard's critics reject the claim that the Madisonian model of checks and balances is inherently a device to "keep the mass of people divided against each other, unable to concert against the opulent class."[31] That may have been one of the intentions of the framers, but some scholars think Madison was worried about the tyranny of religious majorities as well as about lower-status majorities. "Madison's system has thus prevented the formation of conservative religious majorities or majorities behind such figures as Huey Long and George Wallace just as effectively as it has prevented the formation of a unified 'proletariat.' "[32] Today, in fact, we look upon many of the checks and balances as democratic, because they protect minorities from oppression by the majority.[33] Our view of what is democratic has changed over time. Oppressing blacks or Native Americans through a majority vote in a state legislature or Congress would not be viewed as the democratic thing to do these days.

Having admitted these problems with Beard's analysis, however, there are, nonetheless, several persuasive key points in the Beardian thesis. The lower-status population did indeed have nothing to say about drafting the Constitution and (whether by choice or by coercion) had little to say about ratifying it. Important provisions in the Constitution protected economic interests that were more valuable to the upper-status population than to the lower-status population. Class divisions may not have been as exaggerated as the Beardians claim, but they probably existed nonetheless. The founders may not have been as venal as Beard made them seem, but it defies belief to think that they were ignorant of their economic interests and of the role a stronger national government could play in protecting those interests. Because of these factors, it is reasonable to conclude that lower-status people lost influence in the immediate aftermath of 1787.

Bias through Interpretation _____

Whether or not lower-status people lost influence in the aftermath of the 1787 Philadelphia convention, the key question is whether they were better or worse off in the long run because of the Constitution. On the affirmative side, the national government established in 1787 ushered in a long period of political stability that no doubt contributed to the country's rapid economic growth in the next six decades. On the negative side, whether the Constitution facilitated the advancement of lower-status interests ultimately depended a great deal on how the Supreme Court chose to interpret the Constitution.

From the viewpoint of Beard's followers, when faced with a choice between protecting upper-status property rights versus lower-status human rights, most often the Supreme Court gave preference to property rights. One critic wrote that "the U.S. Constitution provides for and secures a capitalist economy."[34] And another wrote that the Constitution continues as a device to protect establishment interests against progressive movements.[35]

In fact there are many crosscurrents at work on the Supreme Court as it interprets the Constitution, and the Court is seldom oblivious to the prevailing political moods of the time. Historically, the most anti-lower-status and pro-property-rights period of Court history occurred during the long period between the end of the Civil War in 1865 and 1937. These were the years of the robber barons, the years of laissez-faire and social Darwinism as philosophies of government. During most of this time the Supreme Court's role was to pave the judicial path for the industrial revolution and the extreme concentration of wealth that resulted from it. In contrast, the most pro-lower-status period of Court history occurred in the 1950s and 1960s. To see how Court interpretation affects the lower-status population, it is useful to compare these two periods.

Laissez-faire as a Constitutional Philosophy

The Court's decisions did not always follow a single, consistent policy direction throughout the long period of 1865–1937, but in general they limited the federal and state governments' ability to regulate the economy. This approach was consistent with the dominant political philosophy of the time, laissez-faire, which held that governments should not intervene in the economy. Closely connected to laissez-faire was the philosophy of social Darwinism, articulated strongly by English philosopher Herbert Spencer.[36] Darwinism, a scientific theory about the struggle for the survival of the fittest in the biological sphere, was easily applied to the socioeconomic sphere. In the biological sphere, the members of each species least adaptable to environmental change die off. Indeed, lest they reproduce their inadaptabilities, it was viewed as essential for the survival of the species that its weakest members die off. In this way the weakest and least adaptable species of life die off so that the strongest and most adaptable survive. Evolution of life thus becomes a struggle for the survival of the fittest.

This precept of social Darwinism became a powerful justification of laissez-faire as an economic policy. Just as the government would not intervene to prevent the weakest members of a biological species from dying, so it should not intervene to prevent the death of the weakest and least adaptable economic units of business in the face of a changing economic environment. To do so would only saddle the economy with a nation of inefficient companies, and prevent the national economy as a whole from growing and adapting to contemporary changes. Once this principle was established, it was only a small intellectual step to apply it to individual human beings as well as economic units such as business corporations.

Reactions to Laissez-faire

Not everybody agreed with these philosophies of laissez-faire and social Darwinism, however. It is one thing to believe in the survival of the fittest social philosophy if you are among the elite of society. Such belief is contrary to your self-interest, however, if you are a member of the lower-status population. Many lower-status people and their interest groups wanted governmental intervention in the economy. Farm groups, for example, demanded that the government help hold down the rates railroads charged for bringing agricultural products to market. Labor leaders demanded that the government help curb exploitative working conditions and wages in the growing industries. Small businesses that were being devoured by giant monopolies, such as Standard Oil, wanted government help to keep from being swallowed up. It was pressure from farmers, workers, and local small business leaders that formed the basis of the Populist movement of the 1880s and 1890s. Under this pressure, several states passed laws that restricted monopolistic practices, regulated the rates banks and railroads charged, and tried in various ways to ease the social costs being wrought by the industrial revolution.

Court Support for Laissez-faire

The courts played a special role in establishing laissez-faire as the prevailing public philosophy of the time. As states, and occasionally Congress, passed legislation to ease the pain caused by the industrial revolution, the corporations that were affected by these laws turned to the federal courts for help in getting them overturned. Two key constitutional clauses provided the basis for many of the Supreme Court decisions that followed: the commerce clause in Article I and the due-process clause of the Fourteenth Amendment.

The commerce clause gives Congress exclusive power to regulate interstate and international commerce. Fourteen times between 1877 and 1886 the Court struck down state regulations of business as infringements on interstate commerce.[37] The Court struck down some important national laws regulating commerce as well. In 1895, the Court ruled that the Sherman Anti-Trust Act could not forbid monopolies in manufacturing because manufacturing was not part of interstate commerce.[38] In 1918, the Court relied on the same principle to strike down a federal law regulating child labor.[39] If exploitative child labor was used only in the manufacture of products but not in their sale across state boundaries, the conservative Court ruled that Congress did not have authority under the commerce clause to put limits on the use of child labor in manufacturing.

In addition to the commerce clause, the conservative Court also used the due-process clause to limit the scope of economic regulation. The due-process clause states simply that no person may be deprived of life, liberty, or property without the due process of law. In the 1880s, the Court defined corporations as persons for the purposes of this clause. Robert McCloskey counted 184 decisions from 1899 to 1937 in which the Supreme Court struck down state laws on due-process or equal-protection grounds.[40] A New York law, for example, regulated bakers' hours, but it was struck down by the Supreme Court on grounds that it violated bakers' due-process rights to engage in a contract with their employers.[41] The Supreme Court did not strike down every attempt to regulate business, but it did so frequently enough to create a "twilight zone in which often neither Congress nor the states could regulate effectively."[42]

The Death of Laissez-faire as Prevailing Judicial Philosophy

This direction of the Supreme Court eventually brought it into a direct clash with other political forces, especially with the New Deal administration of President Franklin Roosevelt in the 1930s. During the depths of the Great Depression in 1932, Roosevelt had campaigned for the presidency on the promise of a new deal for the American people. Under his presidential leadership, the federal government took on broad authority to intervene in the national economy. A system of labor management relations was set up under the National Industrial Recovery Act; a system of railroad pensions was set up under the Railroad Retirement Act; economic subsidies to farmers were set up by the Farm Relief Act and the Agriculture Adjustment Act. All of these acts, however, along with several other New Deal measures, were struck down by the Supreme Court in its 1935–1936 session.

After gaining reelection by an unprecedented majority in 1936, Roosevelt struck back at the elderly justices (their average age was 71) by proposing a plan to pack the Supreme Court with pro-New Deal justices. He asked Congress for a law that would allow him to appoint a new justice for each sitting justice who reached the age of 70 but did not retire. This would have swelled the size of the Court to 15 justices and, of course would ensure majority support for New Deal measures. Despite Roosevelt's overwhelming popularity, this tactic was widely viewed as too blatant a political tampering with the Court. The president was widely criticized for it, and Congress quietly let the plan die a still birth.

Despite losing this battle, however, the president won his war with the Court. Some key justices, perhaps perceiving that they had become dangerously out of touch with majority opinion, began to ease their unrelenting laissez-faire opposition to the New Deal. A key decision came in 1937 when the Court switched its opposition to the New Deal

When President Franklin Roosevelt announced his Court Packing Plan to secure a Supreme Court more favorable to the New Deal, he started a storm of controversy.
Source: Brown Brothers.

and upheld a minimum wage law for women, a decision dubbed by one commentator, "the switch in time that saved nine." Shortly thereafter, two conservative justices retired, and Roosevelt replaced them with New Deal supporters. This signaled the end of the Court's battle to use laissez-faire philosophy to strike down laws that sought to regulate the economy. Since 1937, there has been only one instance of the Court striking down an act of Congress when that act was based on Congress's authority to regulate interstate commerce.[43]

Bias Overcome

Because it inhibited the government from aiding the least-affluent people of our society, the Supreme Court's social Darwinist period was extremely detrimental to most lower-status people; and no group of people was more harmed by the Court's social Darwinist judical philosophy than were the black Americans. With the end of the Civil War in 1865, slavery was terminated and the post-Civil War amendments to the Constitution sought to integrate the former slaves into American society. Especially significant were the Fourteenth Amendment which accorded the full rights of citizenship to the former slaves, and the Fifteenth Amendment which secured for them the right to vote.

For the next 100 years, however, the Supreme Court allowed these amendments to be regularly ignored. An elaborate system of subterfuges such as the literacy test, the poll tax, grandfather clauses (see Chapter 5), and general intimidation were introduced in the late nineteenth century to deprive blacks of their Fifteenth Amendment right to vote. A system of segregation was imposed throughout the South that systematically deprived black Americans of their Fourteenth Amendment rights to equal protection of the laws. Segregation systematically excluded blacks from mainstream American society.

The Legal Origins of Segregation:
The Doctrine of "Separate But Equal"

Despite the Fourteenth Amendment's equal-protection clause that forbade any state to deny any person the equal protection of the laws, the Supreme Court ruled that segregation laws did not violate the Constitution. This strange interpretation of the concept "equal protection" grew out of two specific pathbreaking Supreme Court decisions.

The first decision came in the *Civil Rights Cases* of 1883, a set of five cases that overturned the country's first Civil Rights Act.[44] Following the Fourteenth Amendment's attempt to secure equal protection of the laws for blacks, Congress had passed the Civil Rights Act of 1875, which outlawed racial discrimination in places of public accommodations (theaters, restaurants, public transportation, and so on). A San Francisco theater was found guilty under the Act for having denied entrance to a Chinese man. But when the Supreme Court heard the appeal of the case in the 1883 *Civil Rights Cases*, it overturned the conviction on the grounds that Congress had exceeded its authority by outlawing discrimination by private parties. The equal-protection clause of the Fourteenth Amendment had prohibited only states, not individual citizens, from practicing racial discrimination, according to the Court.

This decision was followed in 1896 by the infamous *Plessy* versus *Ferguson*[45] case which gave a constitutional blessing to state segregation laws. Plessy, who was one-eighth black and seven-eighths white, was expelled from a white railroad car in the state of Louisiana and convicted of violating Louisiana's law requiring segregated railway cars. He appealed his conviction and charged that the law denying him access to the white railway car violated the equal-protection clause of the Fourteenth Amendment, which prohibits a state from denying any person the equal protection of the laws. But the Supreme Court ruled that the segregated public facilities did not violate the equal-protection clause as long as the separate facilities were equal. This rationale became known as the "separate-but-equal doctrine."

These two decisions freed the states to set up whatever segregation systems they wanted without any interference from the federal courts. White individuals were also free to practice racial discrimination, and if a state refused to prevent such racial discrimination, neither the federal courts nor Congress would intervene. The highest court in the nation had sanctioned a segregation system that condemned a tenth of the population to an inferior legal status.

The consequences of this for the black population were disastrous. By the end of the nineteenth century, so-called Jim Crow laws (or segregation laws) made it illegal for blacks and whites to eat in the same restaurants, use the same restrooms, drink from the same water fountains, attend the same schools, sit in the same sections on buses, trains, or theaters, and even be buried in the same cemeteries. Black leaders who objected to this discrimination faced economic sanctions such as dismissal from their jobs, intimidation, mob violence, or even lynching.

Nor was segregation limited to the South. Delaware and Kansas had legally segregated school systems. In many nonsouthern cities, the schools were segregated in practice, since blacks were concentrated in their own neighborhoods, even in the absence of segregation ordinances. Most public accommodations were closed to blacks throughout the nation, and workplace discrimination was the norm.

Overturning Separate But Equal

Once the "separate-but-equal" doctrine was accepted by the Supreme Court, it took 60 years to overturn that principle. During the 1930s and 1940s, the NAACP/Legal Defense Fund began to challenge the doctrine, especially in the area of public education, where repeated documentation showed that the segregated schools were blatantly unequal. The first challenges came to the systems of higher education. On a case-by-case basis, the Supreme Court began forcing state law schools and state universities to stop denying admittance to black students. The first case occurred in Missouri where the law prohibited the admission of blacks to the University of Missouri Law School, but where there was no separate law school for blacks. To get around the requirement of separate but equal, the state offered scholarships to send Missouri blacks out of state for their legal education. In 1938, the Supreme Court struck this action down as a violation of separate-but-equal doctrine.[46] A decade later, the Court forced Oklahoma and Texas to admit black students to their state law schools.[47]

The Texas case was especially interesting, because the state had built a separate law school for blacks, given it a separate building, hired a separate faculty, and stocked its separate library with separate books. The Court pointed out, however, that this law school clearly was not the equal of the prestigious University of Texas Law School at Austin, with its excellent faculty and its extensive library. Based on this Texas decision, it became virtually impossible for any state to maintain that its segregated university system met the demands of the separate-but-equal doctrine.

The doctrine itself, however, was not overthrown until 1954 in *Brown* versus *Board of Education of Topeka Kansas*.[48] In that case the Court reversed the 1896 doctrine and ruled that segregated public school systems are inherently unequal. The next year it ordered public schools to desegregate "with all deliberate speed."

By the end of the nineteenth century, so-called Jim Crow laws (or segregation laws) made it illegal for blacks and whites to eat in the same restaurants, use the same restrooms, drink from the same water fountains, attend the same schools, sit in the same sections on buses, trains, or theaters, and even be buried in the same cemeteries.

The Civil Rights Movement

Because it started the long and difficult process of public school desegregation, *Brown* versus *Board of Education* was a landmark event in the civil rights movement. A second such event came the following year (1955) with the successful Montgomery, Alabama, bus boycott. After a black woman, Rosa Parks, was arrested one day for refusing to give up her seat in the white section of a bus, the Montgomery black community, led by Baptist minister Martin Luther King, Jr., organized a boycott of the city's bus system and sued successfully in the federal courts to have the city's bus segregation ordinance declared unconstitutional.

Just as the *Brown* versus *Board of Education* case had vindicated the legal strategy of attacking the constitutionality of segregation statutes, the Montgomery bus boycott vindicated the effectiveness of a direct-action strategy of protests, boycotts, sit-ins, and demonstrations to overturn local segregation policies. With this signal that direct-action strategies could succeed, the civil-rights movement entered a new, more militant phase based on the application of civil disobedience. Civil disobedience is the tactic of deliberately disobeying a law in the belief that it violates a higher moral law or the Constitution. Proponents of civil disobedience willingly accepted jail sentences for breaking the law in order to challenge the constitutionality of a law they believe is unjust. A favored tactic was staging a sit-in at a local lunch counter. Groups of black and white college students would gather at some counter where racial mixture was illegal, sit peacefully until they were arrested, then appeal their convictions and organize demonstrations against the segregation policies while their cases were being adjudicated.

Civil Rights Legislation

These activities culminated in the passage of the Civil Rights act of 1964 and the Voting Rights Act of 1965. Two of the most important pieces of legislation in American history, these laws continue to be controversial and to have a huge impact on society today. Because we will encounter these two laws in later chapters, it is useful to outline their key provisions here.

The Civil Rights Act of 1964. The Civil Rights Act gave legislative meaning to the equal protection clause of the Fourteenth Amendment. It prohibited discrimination in places of public accommodation such as movie houses, theaters, bars, restaurants, and motels. It also strengthened the role of the Justice Department in overseeing the desegregation of public schools, and prohibited discrimination in any programs receiving federal funds. It established the concept of equal employment opportunity—the prohibition of discrimination in employment on the basis of race, religion, sex, or national origin. When the constitutionality of this act was questioned, the Supreme Court upheld the law on the grounds that Congress had ample authority under its commerce powers to pass such legislation.[49]

The Voting Rights Act of 1965. What the Civil Rights Act did for the equal protection clause, the Voting Rights Act the following year did for the Fifteenth Amendment's guarantee of the right of black Americans to vote. It made a direct assault on the literacy test, which, we will see in Chapter 5, was a major way of keeping blacks from the polling places. By outlawing the literacy test and sending federal voting examiners to conduct voter registration in the South, the 1965 Voting Rights Act brought about a significant increase in black voters and black elected officials. Only 1,469 elected black officials could be identified throughout the entire country in 1970; by the end of the 1980s that number had nearly quintupled to 7,190, including one governor (Virginia) and the mayors of five of the nation's seven largest cities.[50]

TABLE 2-2   The Civil Rights Act of 1964: Main Provisions

Public Accommodations
  Prohibited discrimination in public accommodations.
Desegregation of Government Facilities
  Authorized the Justice Department to initiate suits to desegregate facilities owned or managed by state or local governments.
School Desegregation
  Authorized the Justice Department to initiate suits to desegregate public schools and colleges.
  Authorized the Office of Education (now Department of Education) to give technical and financial aid to school districts in the process of desegregation.
Civil Rights Commission
  Strengthened the Commission's role to investigate civil rights complaints.
Federally Funded Programs
  Prohibited racial discrimination in programs that receive federal funds.
Equal Employment Opportunity
  Prohibited private-sector employers from discrimination in employment on the basis of race, religion, sex, or national origin.
Voting Rights
  Strengthened the role of the federal courts and the Attorney General in dealing with voting rights violations.

TABLE 2-3 The Voting Rights Act of 1965: Main Provisions

Literacy Tests
  Authorized the Justice Department to suspend literacy tests if it was found that they had the effect of discriminating.
Voting Examiners
  Authorized the Justice Department to appoint voting examiners who could register people to vote in counties or municipalities that were identified by a triggering formula.
Triggering Formula
  Any state or local government jurisdiction was determined to have engaged in voting discrimination if it had used a literacy test in determining voter registration eligibility for the 1964 presidential election or if it had a voter turnout of less than 50 percent of the voting-age population in that election.
Prior-Approval Requirement
  No jurisdiction identified by the triggering formula could make any change in voting laws, voter qualification laws, or municipal boundaries without prior approval of either the Justice Department or a three-judge federal court in Washington, D.C.
Enforcement Machinery
  Provided authority to the Attorney General and the Civil Service Commission to enforce the act. Provided fines and imprisonment for convictions for violating the act.

The Meaning of the Constitution to the Civil Rights Movement

In the eyes of some critics, these successes of the civil rights movement had little to do with the Constitution itself. Political scientist Howard Zinn, for example, argues that the Constitution's role in advancing civil rights was marginal. "Black people, in the political context of the 1960s, would have demanded equality whether or not the Constitution called for it, just as the antislavery movement demanded abolition even in the absence of constitutional support."[51]

While this statement is true as far as it goes, it ignores two facets of the Constitution's role in American politics. First, as the highest law in the land, its demand for due process of law, equal protection of the law, and a host of civil liberties, made the Constitution a beacon of hope for fair play for all Americans. Indeed, the most profound book on American race relations prior to the civil rights movement noted the dilemma that this beacon posed for all Americans.[52] For people who truly believed in the rule of law, the denial of legal rights to black citizens made a sham of the American claim to democracy. This belief was a powerful tool in the hands of civil rights leaders like Thurgood Marshall, who successfully argued the landmark *Brown* versus *Board of Education* case before the Supreme Court in 1954. It became very difficult for anyone who truly believed in the rule of law and the primacy of the Constitution to disagree with Marshall that "equal protection of the laws" demanded the dismantling of the segregation system.

Second, the Constitution was critical to the civil rights movement because it provided a means of overturning segregation laws when other avenues of political action were closed to blacks. For almost 30 years beginning with the Missouri University law school case in 1938, direct legislative action by Congress was impossible, and constitutional challenges in the courts were virtually the only tool available to black leaders. Without the power of the courts to strike down segregation laws as unconstitutional, civil disobedience, lunch counter sit-ins, and protests generally would have been much less effective.

Conclusion _____

Although the black population has not achieved parity with the white population in terms of income, job prestige, or most other measures of socioeconomic status, black people clearly are no longer forced into the subordinate legal status they held before the civil rights movement. Although the black middle class still suffers from racial prejudice, middle-class blacks are clearly part of mainstream American society today, a status that they did not enjoy a generation earlier. Between the 1930s and the middle-1960s, black Americans made enormous strides in overcoming the constitutional bias for property rights over human rights.

What made this change possible was a massive, well-organized civil rights movement framed in the context of the Constitution's demand for equal treatment under the law. Both the massive popular movement and the constitutional context were critical to the success of the civil rights movement. Without the protests and the street demonstrations, the judges were under less pressure to overturn the old doctrine of separate but equal. But without the constitutional beacon of equality under the law, the protest demonstrations had little moral force on most of the white population.

Other lower-status Americans have a great lesson to learn from the black experience with the civil rights movement. In the proper circumstances, the Constitution can be a tool for lower-status interests as well as a roadblock to them. Viewing the Constitution from a leftist perspective, Mark Tushnet argued that despite its primary role of protecting established interests against progressive movements, the Constitution

> has enough ambiguous terms in it to allow progressive movements to make credible legal arguments that, were they accepted, would advance the movement's political goals. . . .

When governing elites are divided, progressives can use the Constitution to widen existing divisions and create opportunities for progressive change to occur. Even in the worst of times, progressives can appeal to the aspirations of the Constitution as a means of mobilizing support and strengthening the progressive movement from within.[53]

Summary

1. Charles Beard's *An Economic Interpretation of the Constitution* in 1913 was a ground-breaking analysis that has been a major inspiration for many scholars on the political left. Beard argued that the main motive of the constitutional founders was to protect their personal economic property rights, that lower-status people were absent from the Constitutional Convention that wrote several specific protections of those property rights into the Constitution, and that the Constitution's ratification process was designed to minimize the influence of the Anti-Federalists and the lower-status population generally.

2. Contemporary critics have disputed the validity of Beard's research methods and thrown into doubt a great many of his conclusions. What remains credible from the Beardian analysis, however, is the absence of lower-status people in drafting the Constitution, their minimal role in ratifying it, the existence of several specific provisions in that document that have the effect of protecting the economic interests of affluent people, and the stated antipathy of several key founders to lower-status people and to giving them a meaningful role in government.

3. In terms of the economic interests of the lower-status population, constitutional interpretation is much more important than the original content of the 1787 document.

4. During the 1865–1937 period of social Darwinist judicial philosophy, the Supreme Court's constitutional interpretations were hostile to the lower-status population, especially to the black population.

5. The 1950s and 1960s were a period for overcoming constitutional bias. The key ingredients were: (1) sympathetic Supreme Court justices who were committed to human rights and to dismantling segregation; (2) an active and effectively organized civil rights movement whose civil disobedience tactics forced the courts to rule on the constitutionality of segregation statutes; and (3) constitutional provisions on due process, equal protection, and civil liberties that served as a beacon of hope for fair treatment under the law.

Notes _____

1. Raoul Berger, *Government by Judiciary: The Transformation of the Fourteenth Amendment* (Cambridge: Harvard University Press, 1977).

2. Michael Parenti, "The Constitution as an Elitist Document," Goldwin and Schambra, eds., *How Democratic Is the Constitution?*, pp. 39–58; Edward S. Greenberg, *The American Political System: A Radical Approach*, 5th ed. (Glenview, Ill.: Scott, Foresman and Company, 1989), pp. 55–67. Howard Zinn, "A People's Constitution: Some Truths Are Not Self-Evident," *The Nation* 245 no. 3 (August 1–8, 1987): 87–88.

3. Zinn, "Some Truths Are Not Self-Evident."

4. Catherine Drinker Bowen, *Miracle at Philadelphia: The Story of the Constitutional Convention, May to September 1787* (Boston: Little, Brown, 1966).

5. Charles Beard, *An Economic Interpretation of the Constitution* (New York: Macmillan, 1913).

6. See Jackson T. Main, *The Anti-Federalists* (Chapel Hill, N.C.: University of North Carolina Press, 1961) and Herbert J. Storing, *What the Anti-Federalists Were For* (Chicago: University of Chicago Press, 1981).

7. Herbert Aptheker, *Early Years of the Republic* (New York: International Publishers, 1976), p. 33.

8. Jackson Turner Main, "Government by the People: The American Revolution and the Democratization of the Legislatures," *William and Mary Quarterly* 2nd ser. 23 (July 1966): 405.

9. Alfred F. Young, "Conservatives, the Constitution, and the 'Spirit of Accommodation,'" Robert A. Goldwin and William A. Schambra, eds., *How Democratic Is the constitution?* (Washington, D.C.: American Enterprise Institute, 1980), p. 121.

10. Attributed to Hamilton, in *Bartlett's Familiar Quotations* (Boston: Little, Brown, 1980), p. 108.

11. David Szatmary, *Shays' Rebellion: The Making of an Agrarian Insurrection* (Amherst: University of Massachusetts Press, 1980).

12. Samuel E. Morrison, Henry Steel Commager, and William Leuchtenberg, *The Growth of the American Republic* vol. 1 (New York: Oxford University Press, 1969), p. 244.

13. George Washington letter to Henry Lee, October 31, 1787. In John C. Fitzpatrick, ed. *Writings of George Washington* (Washington, D.C.: U.S. Government Printing Office, 1939), vol. 29, p. 34.

14. Ann Stuart Diamond, "Decent, Even Though Democratic," Goldwin and Schambra, eds., *How Democratic Is the Constitution?*, p. 25.

15. Parenti, "The Constitution as an Elitist Document," p. 41.

16. Ibid., p. 51.

17. James Madison, *Federalist 51*.

18. Gordon S. Wood, "Democracy and the Constitution," Goldwin and Schambra, eds., *How Democratic Is the Constitution?*, p. 13.

19. Parenti, "The Constitution as an Elitist Document," p. 41.

20. Edward Greenberg, *The American Political System*, p. 63.

21. Ibid.

22. Robert Brown, *Charles Beard and the Constitution* (Princeton: Princeton University Press, 1956).

23. Forrest McDonald, *We the People: The Economic Origins of the Constitution* (Chicago: University of Chicago Press, 1958).

24. Garry Wills, *Inventing America* (New York: Doubleday, 1978).

25. Young, "Conservatives, the Constitution, and the 'Spirit of Accommodation,'" Goldwin and Schambra, eds., *How Democratic Is the Constitution?*, p. 124.

26. Ibid., p. 147.

27. Parenti, "The Constitution as an Elitist Document," pp. 40–41.

28. Brown, *Charles Beard and the Constitution*, pp. 195–196.

29. Ibid., p. 197.

30. Young , "Conservatives, the Constitution, and the 'Spirit of Accommodation,' " Goldwin and Schambra, eds., *How Democratic is the Constitution?*, p. 117.

31. Parenti, p. 47.

32. Diamond, "Decent, Even Though Democratic," Goldwin and Schambra, eds., *How Democratic is the Constitution?*, p. 29.

33. Wood, "Democracy and the Constitution," Goldwin and Schambra, eds., *How Democratic is the Constitution?*, p. 3

34. Bernard H. Siegen, "The Constitution and the Protection of Capitalism," *How Democratic is the Constitution?* Goldwin and Schambra, eds., p. 106.

35. Mark Tushnet, "The Constitution from a Progressive Point of View," *A Less than Perfect Union: Alternative Perspectives on the Constitution* (New York: Monthly Review Press, 1988), pp. 40, 49.

36. Herbert Spencer, *Social Statics* (London: J. Chapman, 1851).

37. Robert G. McCloskey, *The American Supreme Court* (Chicago: University of Chicago Press, 1960), pp. 118–127.

38. *United States* v. *E. C. Knight Company* 156 U.S. 251 (1918).

39. *Hammer* v. *Dagenhart* 247 U.S. 251 (1918).

40. McCloskey, *The American Supreme Court*, pp. 127, 141–161.

41. *Lochner* v. *New York*, 198 U.S. 45 (1905).

42. Joel B. Grossman and Richard S. Wells, *Constitutional Law and Judicial Policy Making*, 2nd ed. (New York: Wiley, 1980), p. 324.

43. *National League of Cities* v. *Usery*, 426 U.S. 833 (1976). Nine years later, however, this decision was effectively reversed. See *Garcia* v. *San Antonio Metropolitan Transit Authority*, 105 S.Ct. 1005 (1985).

44. *The Civil Rights Cases of 1883*, 109 U.S. 3 (1883).

45. *Plessy* v. *Ferguson* 163 U.S. 537 (1896).

46. *Missouri* ex rel *Gains* v. *Canada*, 305 U.S. 676 (1937).

47. *Sipuel* v. *Board of Regents of the University of Oklahoma*, 332 U.S. 632 (1948); *McLaurin* v. *Oklahoma State Regents*, 339 U.S. 637 (1950); and *Sweatt* v. *Painter*, 339 U.S. 629 (1950).

48. *Brown* v. *Board of Education of Topeka, Kansas* 347 U.S. 483 (1954).

49. *Heart of Atlanta Motel* v. *United States*, 379 U.S. 241 (1964).

50. *Statistical Abstract of the United States: 1990*, p. 260. These were New York, Los Angeles, Chicago, Philadelphia, and Detroit. Chicago lost its black mayor in 1989. The only cities in the top seven not to have had a black mayor were Houston and Dallas.

51. Zinn, "Some Truths Are Not Self-Evident," pp. 87–88. Quoted by permission of *The Nation*. The Nation Company, Inc., © 1987.

52. Gunnar Myrdal, *An American Dilemma: The Negro Problem and Modern Democracy* (New York: Harper, 1944).

53. Mark Tushnet, "The Constitution from a Progressive Point of View," pp. 40, 49.

Federalism: Bias Between State and Nation

Introduction

In the previous chapter we saw that philosophical arguments about the structure of government at the Constitutional Convention were often a mask for pragmatic considerations about regional and economic interests. For example, there was more than political philosophy behind the process of having the Constitution ratified by special conventions in each state rather than by the state legislatures. The Federalists knew that the Anti-Federalists would have less influence at those conventions than in most of the state legislatures.

In Chapter 3 we will examine a similar relationship between philosophy and self-interest in one of the most important aspects of our Constitution, the federal system of government. This system is not neutral, and the federal division of power between states and the nation is not solely a philosophical issue settled by political theorists like James Madison two hundred years ago. Rather it is an issue that resurfaces every generation or so. And recurring philosophical disagreements about the division of power between Washington and the states almost always mask very practical disputes about how people live, which people will enjoy the greatest benefits of our federal bargain, and which are going to bear the heaviest burdens. These differences have provoked some of the most explosive conflicts in American history.

Example. In 1832, John C. Calhoun persuaded a South Carolina convention to proclaim the Nullification Ordinances. Arguing for extreme decentralization, Calhoun believed that the United States Constitution was no more than a compact (hence his Compact Theory of the Constitution) between the states rather than a charter from the American people. Thus, he insisted, any state, within its own boundaries, could nullify and disregard a law of Congress. This would seem to be based on a philosophical belief, but the philosophical dispute was in fact provoked by the very practical question of whether the power of the federal government would be used to benefit Northern manufacturers or Southern plantation owners.

Northerners wanted a high tariff to protect manufacturing from the competition of foreign imports. Although such a tariff would increase federal government revenues and protect the budding manufacturing industries of the Northeast, it would also invite European retaliatory tariffs that might wipe out the export agriculture of South Carolina and other Southern states.

Example. From 1861 to 1865, the nation fought its bloodiest war to determine whether disenchanted states could secede from the Union. This war claimed more American lives than all the of the nation's other wars combined. But as in the conflict over the Nullification Ordinances, the philosophical issue of secession was little more than a mask for a more practical issue of economics and how people live. In this instance, the issue was slavery. Could slavery be prohibited from the Western territories, and would the abolitionist Republican Party, which had come to power with Abraham Lincoln, try to eradicate slavery from the Southern states too?

Example. From the late nineteenth century to the passage of civil rights legislation in 1964 and 1965, all the Southern states and most non-Southern states maintained a rigid system of racial segregation that kept black citizens out of the voting booth, out of the better public schools, and out of the mainstream of American life. Throughout this period, the quest to end segregation was fought within the confines of a federalism issue called "states' rights." Believers in states' rights argued that the federal government did not have the authority to interfere with the right of any state to legislate domestic issues within its own borders. Opponents argued that the federal government indeed possessed such authority, because segregation was contrary to several provisions of the Constitution, especially its equal protection clause, as we saw in Chapter 2. Underlying this philosophical conflict between states' rights and equal protection, however, were the practical conditions of segregated life for the nation's black population. As long as the states' rights philosophy prevailed, it was impossible to end segregation. When the equal protection philosophy began to prevail, the federal courts became increasingly active in striking down segregation practices.

In this chapter we will examine contemporary federalism to see who makes the best use of the system, and to what end. To do this we will look at the most recent attempt to modify our federal partnership, the "New Federalism" started in the Reagan administration (1981–1989) and carried into the administration of his successor George Bush

(1989–   ). Proponents of New Federalism felt that the federal arrangement that existed on the eve of Mr. Reagan's 1980 election had drifted far away from the original bargain struck at the Philadelphia convention in 1787, and that contemporary federalism had introduced new biases into the system that were counterproductive to an efficient running of the American economy and the governmental machinery. But like the earlier instances of federal conflict cited above, New Federalism had its own biases, and thus presents us with a fascinating example of pragmatic interests that underlie philosophical positions about the balance of power between Washington and the states. The philosophical principles behind New Federalism, we will see, sought to increase the power, influence, and living conditions of some classes of people at the expense of others.

But we are getting ahead of our story. To understand why the New Federalists felt the way they did, it is necessary to understand: (1) the theoretical advantages and disadvantages of federalism as a form of government, (2) how federalism as it exists today differs dramatically from the federal arrangement that came out of the Constitutional Convention in 1787, who pushed for this transformation and who benefits from it, (3) a disenchantment with contemporary federalism that surfaced in the 1970s and paved the way for the New Federalism initiated by the Reagan administration, and (4) the biases of federalism today and their implications for the lower-status population. Accordingly, this chapter will address each of those four topics.

Federalism and Its Attractions as a Form of Government _____

In calling the American system of government a federalism, scholars mean that it has a written constitution that divides power between the national government and the states. Such a system has several advantages and disadvantages when compared to a unitary form of government which concentrates all the governmental authority at the national level. A key issue in examining the advantages and disadvantages of such a form of government is deciding what kinds of roles each level of

. . . recurring philosophical disagreements about the division of power between Washington and the states almost always mask very practical disputes about how people live, which people are going to enjoy the greatest benefits of our federal bargain, and which ones are going to bear the heaviest burdens.

government can best perform, so that the division of powers between the nation and the states will be reasonable and effective.

Advantages of Federalism

Policy Experimentation. The first advantage of federalism is that it allows more experimentation in making and implementing policy than is possible in a unitary system of government. This phenomenon was demonstrated repeatedly during the 1980s when the Reagan administration reduced federal funding for domestic programs. Time and again, in area after area, the most imaginative proposals for dealing with domestic social issues during those years came out of the states, not Washington. California and Massachusetts, among other states, experimented with "workfare" approaches to welfare reform long before Congress picked up on the idea. Connecticut and several other states initiated urban enterprise zones as experiments in central city renewal, which have yet to be authorized nationally by Congress.

Avenues of Access. A second advantage of federalism over unitary government is that it broadens the avenues by which people can influence their government. When MADD (Mothers Against Drunk Drivers) in the early 1980s struck out in many states in the attempt to raise the legal drinking age to 21, they took their case to Washington and got Congress to pass favorable legislation. This legislation provided that states would be deprived of their federal highway grants if they failed to set a 21-year minimum drinking age.

Broadening the avenues of access also works in the other direction. Welfare reformers in the 1970s and early 1980s were unsuccessful in convincing the federal government to write a systematic workfare program into the national welfare laws. After striking out in Washington, they turned to the states, where they scored initial successes in California and Massachusetts with programs that not only put work requirements into the welfare laws but provided day-care assistance, medical assistance, and systematic help in moving welfare recipients into the job market. With workfare initiated in those states, variations of it quickly spread to other states and finally, in 1987, were incorporated into national legislation.

Flexibility. A third advantage of federalism is flexibility in implementing national policies. In transportation planning, for example, densely populated eastern states have the flexibility to use federal transportation funds for mass transit expenses. Less densely populated states in the West have less need of mass transit, but an enormous need for highway construction and maintenance. Federalism gives them the flexibility to direct their transportation dollars to road building and maintenance.

Participation and Human Development. In addition to these advantages, it is also argued that federalism provides more opportunities for citizen participation in public affairs than does a unitary system. In classic Greek theory, a person becomes more fully developed as a human being as he or she participates in public affairs. By requiring important governmental decisions to be made at the state and local levels, federalism fosters a sense of self-reliance and political efficacy among people at those levels that would not be possible if all governmental decisions were made in Washington. In this sense, a tremendous theoretical advantage of federalism is its potential to facilitate an able and politically competent citizenry.

Disadvantages of Federalism

While federalism clearly has some advantages over the unitary forms of government, it also suffers from some important disadvantages. Three of the most important of these have to do with the complexity of the system, the problem of accountability, and the difficulty of securing minority rights in the individual states.

Complexity in the System. The extreme complexity of American federalism makes it difficult to get things done. There are over 80,000 governments in the United States. Many metropolitan areas have several dozen governments, and the New York metropolitan area with over 1,400 governments[1] is the champion in this category. Numerous studies have demonstrated over and over again how the complexity of intergovernmental relations makes it difficult to get the cooperation and coordination needed to bring projects to successful conclusions. A federal program called New Towns in Town sought in the 1960s to rejuvenate neighborhoods in over a dozen cities by constructing economically and racially integrated development projects on land owned by the federal government in those cities. But the program failed without a single such project getting off the ground.[2] And an attempt in Oakland, California in 1965 to put $23 million of federal economic development funds to work in job-creating projects in that city failed to accomplish the goals that had been set for it.[3]

In both of these instances, one of the main reasons the program failed was that so many different agencies and governments had a role in the decision-making process that it was impossible to make timely and effective decisions. Most federal projects do not fail, of

*"We can't come to an agreement about how to fix your car, Mr. Simons.
Sometimes that's the way things happen in a democracy."*

A great asset of American federalism is that it involves more people in the
decision-making process than does unitary government. But in federalism,
as in life generally, the more people involved in decision making, the
more difficult it is to arrive at a decision.
(*Source:* Drawing by Handleman; copyright © 1987 *The New Yorker Magazine,
Inc.*, April 6, 1987, p. 41.)

course. In fact, most succeed.[4] But in many instances they succeed
despite the complexity of the intergovernmental system, not because
of it.

Accountability. The complexity of our federal system has a second
disadvantage—the difficulty of pinning down accountability. Many federal grant programs contribute to the proliferation of government
agencies by requiring that special units of government (called special
districts) be created to administer the grants. Airports, for example,
are almost universally administered by separate airport commissions
that are independent of the cities and counties they serve. Other programs have led to the creation of separate housing agencies, redevelopment authorities, and transit authorities. Welfare programs are
usually run under a complicated set of administrative rules that virtually defy accountability to the elected state and local officials who
are nominally in charge of them. Often the apparently simple task of
getting a traffic signal installed at a dangerous crossing brings many
citizen groups to extreme frustration as they wander back and forth
between city halls, highway departments, and departments of public
safety trying to locate the person with the authority to approve and
install the signal.

The Personal Side of Federalism: Fixing Accountability

In a system of 80,000 local governments, it is often difficult to pinpoint responsibility for simple governmental actions. Some residents of Port Washington, New York, discovered this in the early 1970s, when they tried to do something about a traffic hazard confronting elementary school children.

> So when a group of Port Washington parents decided . . . [that a traffic signal] was needed on Main Street to help shepherd children between the elementary school and the library, they found a jumble of jurisdictions. The school on the south side of the street was located in an unincorporated area of Port Washington, and therefore was controlled by the township. The library on the north side was located in the Village of Baxter Estates. The street itself was a county road, but located in and patrolled by the Port Washington Police District, which is independent of the village, town, and county. Traffic lights on county roads are the responsibility of, naturally, the county. However, parking on the street falls under jurisdiction of the town. As a result, the parents' request for the traffic light, made through the library board of trustees, ended up being passed from one jurisdiction to another. Finally, the county in December turned down the request and recommended that the police district propose to the town the elimination of parking on a section of the street, on the spurious theory that speeding drivers and anxious children would have a better view of each other.[5]

Minority Rights. Finally, because of the autonomy it grants state governments, federalism can create serious problems of equity if a state chooses to discriminate against a minority population. This, of course, was a major drawback of American federalism during the long period of slavery and segregation.

What Role for the Federal Government?

A key premise behind a federal system is that the state and local governments are better at performing some governmental roles and the federal government is better at performing others. It has never been possible in American federalism to make a definitive division of state and federal roles, but there are some things that the federal government does better than others. The 1970s saw an attempt to sort out which governing tasks can be performed best at the federal level and which at state and local levels.[6] But under the Reagan administration the sorting-out exercise quickly degenerated into an excuse to cut programs for the lower-status population. To make a start on an honest sorting-out appraisal, it would help to define what the federal government does well and what it does not do well.

What the Federal Government Does Poorly. The federal government is large, complex, and in many ways quite diffuse. As a result, its general policy failings tend to lie in three categories: those having to do with geography, coordination, and oversight.

Targeting. First, the federal government has a history of ineffectively targeting programs to specific needy geographic areas. Much of this inability to target funds to needy areas is due to the entrenchment of pork barrel politics and log rolling in Congress's decision-making process. A classic case of the difficulty of targeting federal programs occurred in the Model Cities program of the 1960s.

The Model Cities program was first proposed in 1964 by a White House task force that wanted to create a single demonstration of the urban rejuvenation that could be accomplished if all existing federal programs were concentrated on a specific blighted neighborhood of a specific city. The idea of concentrating these resources on a single city was rejected, however, because it would force Democratic President Lyndon Johnson to choose between Chicago, the city of the nation's most prominent Democratic mayor, Richard J. Daley, and Detroit, the city of the nation's preeminent labor leader, Walter Reuther, of the United Auto Workers. To get around this problem the task force originally recommended five cities, but that was rejected because five cities would not attract enough members of Congress to vote for the program. Accordingly, the proposal as sent to Congress was expanded to 66 cities.

To facilitate the program's passage, Congress then expanded the number of Model Cities to 150 and awarded some of them to cities served by members of Congress whose vote was critical. Thus, Smithfield, Tennessee, no great center of metropolitan growth, was awarded a Model Cities program, primarily because it was the hometown of the chairperson of the House Appropriations Subcommittee that would have to approve funds for the Model Cities budget. Montana is not known for its giant metropolises, but was the home state of Senate Majority Leader Mike Mansfield, whose support would be needed; it was awarded two Model Cities programs. Maine, which also is not known as a metropolitan state, was awarded three Model Cities programs. Maine was the home state of Senator Edmund Muskie, who became the floor leader for the bill in the Senate. In all, Congress expanded the number of Model Cities to 150 and appropriated about half as much money as the task force had originally requested. Too little money was spread among too many places for any of them to demonstrate a meaningful impact.[7]

Coordination. A second problem with federal programs usually lies in coordinating the activities of the many federal, state, and local agencies that have something to say about administering the program. The Model Cities program sought to resolve the coordination problem by creating a governing board in each Model Cities neighborhood and giving that government board authority to integrate the activities of all the federal programs that impacted on that neighborhood. But the program never really worked as intended, and when local Model Cities boards crossed swords with other agencies, city halls, and other political forces, the Model Cities boards ultimately lost their ability to coordinate these other political actors. Over the years, a number of other devices were created to improve coordination of federal programs; but most of these eventually withered, as coordination turned out to be much more complicated than anticipated.

Oversight. Third, the federal government does an uneven job of overseeing the hundreds of existing federal programs, seeing that they are carried out as the law prescribes and that the funds are spent as intended. Usually this oversight role means that federal agencies serve as watchdogs over state agencies, which in turn serve as watchdogs over the state and local agencies that actually implement the programs. The oversight role works fairly well in some programs, such as constructing the interstate highway system, for example. In other areas, such as implementing safety, health, environmental, and affirmative action regulations, however, as we shall see in Chapter 9, the system only works well when there is persistent political influence in top echelons of the federal government. One of the most marked features of President Reagan's New Federalism, however, was a disregard for the federal government oversight role in these regulatory areas.

What the Federal Government Does Well. Not all federal activity is unproductive, however. By and large, most intergovernmental federalism programs have been successful and have contributed positively to improving the American quality of life.[8]

Transfer Payments. One area in which the federal government functions fairly well is in transfer-payment-type programs. A transfer payment is a cash payment to an individual, such as Social Security benefits, unemployment compensation benefits, or Aid for Families with Dependent Children. They are called transfer payments, because they literally transfer cash from the federal treasury to individuals. In these types of programs the federal government, either alone or in partnership with the states, determines payment levels, sets eligibility standards, and makes cash available to people who meet the proper eligibility standards. A comparison of Social Security, for example, with the War on Poverty programs of the 1960s suggests that the federal government is much better at mailing out cash payments to people badly in need of money than it is at organizing those same people to develop neighborhood programs for attacking their own poverty.

Transfer-payment programs are not foolproof, needless to say. Some people receive more money than they are entitled to, many others receive less, and most eligible people do not even apply for the benefits for which they qualify; a small number receive benefits fraudulently. But the amount of overpayment and fraud is relatively small compared to the misleading popular image of widespread welfare cheating. Far fewer welfare recipients cheat on their benefits than do college graduates who try to avoid repaying the guaranteed student loans that helped them attend college. The federal government estimates that only about 5.5 percent of welfare recipients fraudulently take benefits to which they are not entitled. This is just a little over half of the 9.2 percent of former college students who have defaulted on their federally guaranteed student loans.[9] In sum, if the purpose of a transfer-payment program makes sense, the federal government, either by itself or working with the states, can usually do a credible job of implementing the program successfully.

Most programs today, however, are not for transfer payments. There are programs to prevent child abuse, to assist senior citizens, to provide nutritious lunches to low-income schools, to protect the environment, to secure occupational health and safety, and even to assist in road maintenance. Some of these programs are implemented much better than others.

Characteristics of Successful Federal Programs. The most successful federal programs seem to share six characteristics: (1) The agency responsible for the program is clearly designated; (2) the program objectives are tangible and measurable; (3) responsibilities are concentrated in a single agency or department; (4) the agencies responsible are given adequate resources to carry out their responsibilities; (5) they do not usually confront strong opposition among interest groups or other government agencies that could divert the program from its primary goals; and finally, (6) a large component of their task depends on technical expertise rather than on mandating significant changes in human behavior.

Example of a Successful Federal Program. To see the importance of these six characteristics at work, it is useful to contrast two extreme examples; the first an extremely successful program and the second an extremely unsuccessful one.

A good example of a successful program that had all these characteristics was the Apollo mission to put a man on the moon in the 1960s. In this program, responsibility for the mission was given exclusively to NASA, the National Aeronautics and Space Administration. The task of building a rocket that could put a team of men on the moon and return with them was essentially a technical, engineering problem that could be organized into tens of thousands of tasks whose completion could be measured and quantified. With the solid support of Congress and three presidents, the Apollo mission was given all the resources it needed to do the job. The agency in charge, NASA, did not have to divert resources or fight a rearguard action to protect itself from interest groups and other government agencies that might try to prevent it from achieving its goal. On the contrary. NASA had so much money to spend and so many contracts to let out that some of the most powerful interest groups supported the program because of the economic boost it would bring to them and to the economy generally. Finally, the task of putting a man on the moon was essentially a technical task as distinguished from a social task to modify human behavior. Although NASA lost its aura of success and was later detoured into the resource-consuming space shuttle program in the 1980s, its early Apollo program was stunningly successful.

To appreciate the importance of these six characteristics in the successful Apollo program, it is useful to contrast that program with an even more difficult program that had none of these six characteristics. This was President Lyndon Johnson's War on Poverty which was initiated during the same time period.[10] First, there was no one single agency in charge; instead responsibilities were scattered throughout several executive departments and bureaus, many of which had overlapping and conflicting missions. Second, the objectives were neither tangible nor measurable. Third, although billions of dollars were spent, the resources were never adequate for a problem of this magnitude. Fourth, instead of the interest group system working to concentrate resources on the central mission as it did in the Apollo program, the interest group system and intergovernmental politics worked to disperse resources throughout the country. As we saw above in the Model Cities program, it was impossible to target resources on a limited number of identifiable places where a substantial impact could be made. As difficult as it was to place a team of men on the moon, that was essentially a technical task, as contrasted with the task of extensive behavioral modification that would be needed to eliminate poverty. That would require not only behavioral changes in the poor themselves but also in the willingness of employers to hire the poor, the willingness of non-poor taxpayers to pay for antipoverty programs, the empathy and attitudes of people running the antipoverty programs, the willingness of hostile interest groups to support the programs, the ongoing support of a majority of the members of Congress, and the willingness of future presidents to continue to support programs that are not identified with them.

Finally, given the magnitude of the task, the War on Poverty would have to have been impeccably designed and executed in order to succeed. Unfortunately, it was neither. In sum, a comparison of the Apollo Mission of the 1960s with the War on Poverty of the same time period shows that NASA was clearly given much better conditions to accomplish its goals than were the multitude of agencies and governments responsible for the War on Poverty.

Federalism Transformed _____

Today's federalism is vastly different from the kind that emerged from the Constitutional Convention in 1787. Even the most vocal advocates of a strong national government, such as Alexander Hamilton, would be amazed at the wide-ranging areas of federal responsibility that we take for granted today: programs for highways, public welfare, public education, public health, child protection, environmental protection, and occupational health and safety protection, among others. This transformation of our federal partnership from 1787 to 1980 is the result of a long evolution from what is commonly called "dual federalism" to a complicated, confusing system today that, for want of a better term, we are going to call intergovernmental federalism.

Dual Federalism

Although the Constitution does not specifically mention the term federalism, that document does directly distinguish between the powers of the national government and the state governments. The national government of the United States was given the delegated or enumerated powers. As shown in Figure 3-1, these were powers such as the power to coin money, raise an army, and declare war. The states, on the other hand, were given a much broader grant of power. States were given the so-called reserved powers, all the other governmental powers not specifically delegated to the national government. Thus, states had exclusive responsibility for most domestic public services such as setting up local governments, maintaining public roads, and conducting elections. Powers exercised by both levels (such as the power to pass laws and establish court systems) are called concurrent powers.

This rigid division of powers between the two levels of government is called dual federalism, or sometimes "layer cake" federalism.[11] The

Figure 3-1 Division of Powers in American Federalism

A. The Dual Federalism Model

Delegated powers of the federal government:
Coin money, conduct foreign relations, regulate interstate commerce, maintain an army and navy, legislate for the general welfare, declare war, establish a post office, establish federal courts.

Concurrent powers of both the federal and state governments:
Levy taxes, borrow money, pass laws, establish courts, exercise eminent domain, charter corporations, spend money.

Reserved powers of the states:
Establish local governments, conduct elections, run public schools and most other public services, regulate intrastate commerce, pass laws in areas not delegated to the federal government.

B. The Cooperative Federalism Model

Federal government, state government, local government:
All three levels cooperate together in providing many of the same services, such as public education, for example. In this service area, the schools are usually run by a local government (the school district), funding comes from all three levels of government, statewide policies such as minimum graduation requirements come from the state, and some other policy mandates (such as desegregation orders) come from the federal government.

federal government's delegated powers were viewed as distinctly separate from the reserved powers of the states, just as the two layers of a cake are separate. And each level of government was considered supreme within its area of authority. For all practical purposes, dual federalism meant that the states were dominant over the federal government in areas such as public education, road construction, public safety, and most domestic issues that directly touched the lives of most people most of the time.

That the states should have enjoyed this dominant position in these areas is not surprising. The founders, as we saw in Chapter 2, were primarily concerned with strengthening the national government to deal with major national issues of economic stability, westward growth and international commerce. There is no evidence that they sought to take traditional domestic responsibilities such as public education, public health, or public safety out of the hands of the states.

Dual federalism came to an end during the Great Depression of the 1930s. What brought it to an end was the states' inability to cope with that economic disaster. By the winter of 1932–1933, the unemployment rate hit 25 percent of the work force. Unprecedented numbers of people lost their life savings due to bank failures. Those with investments in the stock market saw their assets dwindle as the market lost 90 percent of its value in the great crash from 1929 to 1932. With their savings wiped out and their jobs eliminated, millions of working and middle-class people were unable to make their mortgage payments and consequently lost their homes as banks foreclosed on the defaulted mortgages. With the housing market also in a collapse, however, there were no buyers for these foreclosed homes, and the banks suffered huge losses. More banks were forced to close their doors in 1932 than in any year before or since.

The states on their own could not cope with this catastrophe, and over the next several years federal programs were created in areas that had been traditionally viewed as beyond the federal government's scope of responsibility. To provide relief for the millions of needy people, the federal government initiated programs for unemployment compensation, welfare, Aid for Families with Dependent Children, and put in place the Social Security system. To ensure confidence in the banking system, savings deposit insurance was begun and the Federal Reserve Board was given greater authority to regulate banks and the monetary policy. To stimulate home ownership, the FHA (Federal Housing Administration) pioneered the long-term, low-down-payment, federally guaranteed mortgage.

Federalism Today: Intergovernmental Federalism

It was this expansion of federal government powers in the 1930s that ended dual federalism and ushered in the contemporary period of intergovernmental federalism. Figure 3-1 outlines the difference between contemporary intergovernmental federalism and the older dual federalism. The actual division of powers in dual federalism or layer cake federalism was probably never as rigid as shown in Part A of Figure 3-1. But that figure does reflect what was, until the 1930s, the prevailing belief about how power *should* be divided. The states, in this viewpoint, should indeed have primary responsibility for domestic public services, and the federal government should keep its fingers out of the states' areas of responsibility.

Indeed, a great many people today still articulate this viewpoint and argue vociferously that the federal government ought to withdraw from areas in which it has intruded on states' responsibilities since the 1930s. There is something beguilingly attractive about the argument that bureaucrats in Washington should not be allowed to tell local officials how to provide local domestic services. But until you become independently wealthy, you would be wise to be skeptical about this viewpoint, because the overwhelming majority of people who work for a living depend heavily on federal domestic programs. If we adhered to a strict dual federalism division of powers, there would, for example, be no Pell grants or federal loans for college students; no Medicare for our grandparents; no employment compensation when we are laid off from a job; and no worker's compensation when we are injured on a job. There would be no interstate highway system on which most of us drive frequently; no federal food stamps or cash supplements for divorced, single parents with children; and no federal system of environmental protection.

Were the federal government to withdraw from these areas, the states would be left to fend for themselves. And the likely result would be lower levels of public service overall, and even wider discrepancies in service levels than now exist from one state to another. For the person who is very confident that he or she will never need a student loan, never be laid off from a job, never get divorced, never have sick grandparents, never be concerned about national environmental issues such as acid rain, or never be concerned about the living conditions of his or her less fortunate fellow citizens, dual federalism and federal withdrawal might look attractive. But most of us are not immune to those positions.

Indeed, simply listing how some of the federal programs affect our lives shows how far we have moved away from the dual federalism vision. Today the federal government is intimately involved in activities such as school administration, road construction, public health and welfare which the original theory of dual federalism would have left exclusively to the states. In carrying out most domestic public services, the three different levels of government are elaborately interwoven with each other in a cooperative venture, and the analogy of a marble cake is much more appropriate than a layer cake. Hence, in the 1960s scholars began to talk of cooperative federalism[12] or marble cake federalism.[13]

Intergovernmental federalism, the term we use to describe America's contemporary system of federalism encompases an incredibly com-

---

If we adhered to a strict dual federalism division of powers, there would, for example, be no Pell grants or federal loans for college students.

plicated system in which federal, state, and local levels of government all interact with each other to perform most domestic services. For example, consider the child protection program, a program set up many years ago to deal with the widespread problem of child abuse and neglect. The key person in this program is a social worker called the child protection worker.

> Usually employed by and paid by the local county welfare department, the child protection worker is financed partly from county funds, partly from state funds, and partly from federal welfare grants. Although a county employee, the child protection worker functions as an agent of many different governments, acting as a federal officer when getting a client to apply for federally funded food stamps or AFDC and as a state officer when investigating a complaint about a violation of state laws prohibiting abuse of children. When bringing a client to a mental health center in a county hospital, the worker functions as a county officer; but because the center is funded by a federal program, the worker also functions as a federal officer. Investigating a complaint that a city family lets an infant crawl unhealthfully on a floor strewn with the feces of several family pets means acting as a city officer, investigating the ordinance on health and the ordinance on the number of pets permitted in a home. Following up on court orders to ensure that abusing parents continue with court-ordered family counseling means serving as an officer of the court. Visiting a man in jail for having sexually abused his daughter and investigating whether he is taking part in the counseling program there means serving in part as a state corrections officer. The child protection worker may also act as a negotiator with several other local governments and private agencies, such as negotiating with local school districts to get clients into special programs, or with neighboring counties to purchase services for clients that the worker's own county does not provide, or with private agencies, foster homes, halfway houses, or church groups to get their resources applied to clients.
>
> In short, this county-hired street-level bureaucrat acts partly as an agent of the federal government, partly as an agent of the state, and partly as an agent of the county.[14]

Not only is the federal government intimately involved in activities such as child protection and social welfare that were traditionally reserved to the states, but the federal government has in many respects become the dominant actor in this relationship. It controls much of the revenue (through grants-in-aid) for domestic programs, obliges states to do things they might not otherwise do (such as raising the drinking age to 21), and refuses to let states do things they might otherwise want to do (such as prohibiting abortions in the early period of pregnancy). Hence, what started out as dual federalism with the states in the more dominant role has evolved to an immensely complicated intergovernmental system today.

Disenchantment with
the Intergovernmental System _____

The transformation from dual federalism to contemporary intergovernmental federalism brought a dramatic change to the prevailing patterns of governmental relations. In a simplistic sense, these changes can be painted quite starkly. Intergovernmental federalism enabled the national government to attack segregation, which benefited racial minorities; it enabled the federal government to provide financial aid for a broad range of programs ranging from food stamps to medical assistance, which benefited those at the bottom half of the income scale; it enabled the national government to mount a systematic attack on pollution and environmental decline, which benefited the entire population, partly at the cost of the corporate profits of pollution producers, thereby hurting a wealthy group of corporate managers and owners.

Examining the biases of the change in federalism in this simplistic way starkly illustrates some of the interests that benefited and some that were hurt by the change. Of course, tracing the costs and burdens of intergovernmental federalism is much more complicated than this stark portrayal suggests. Compared to dual federalism, intergovernmental federalism indeed is biased in favor of minorities and lower-status people, but the connections are fairly complicated. Each of us benefits disproportionately from some of the programs of intergovernmental federalism, but pays a disproportionately higher share of the costs for other programs. For example, if you or any of your fellow students ever received federally guaranteed student loans or student grants, you and your college clearly benefit from the expansive federal government role. As someone likely to be a middle-income person, however, you are also destined to pay a higher share of the taxes for other programs.

Despite these complications, the truly progressive nature of the 1930s shift to intergovernmental federalism can be seen in that the most vociferous complainers were those high on the socioeconomic ladder. During the early 1980s, a consistent theme of business-oriented publications was that the system's redistributive welfare benefits really entrapped low-income people in poverty rather than helping them to escape from it;[15] that welfare programs and a high federal income tax made the country less productive and less economically competitive;[16] and that the federal regulatory apparatus for environmental protection, occupational safety, and other areas put too heavy a burden on the business community, fueling the inflationary spiral and retarding national economic growth.

In addition to complaints that intergovernmental federalism had put too heavy a financial burden on the nation's upper class, there were also growing complaints from public administration specialists about the incomprehensible complexity of the system, which we noted earlier. Much of this had to do with the complicated system of grants-in-aid that the federal government uses to transfer funds to state and local governments to run domestic programs. In 1930 there were only ten grant-in-aid programs. Even as late as 1960 only 132 such programs were counted. But in the next twenty years the number grew to nearly five hundred programs involving nearly $100 billion. Not infrequently programs worked at cross-purposes. To take maximum advantage of federal funds, enormous amounts of state and local government worker time was spent on grantsmanship, the art of successfully applying for federal grants. State and local flexibility to set their own political priorities was being restricted by requirements to comply with federal guidelines.

The complexity of the system makes a murky playing field for the game of politics. With a system so complex it is very hard for ordinary citizens to determine who is responsible for what. Special watch-dog groups become necessary to watch vigilantly for foul play, which is so hard to detect in the system. The Reagan administration, for example, was able to emasculate the regulatory roles of the Environmental Protection Agency and the Occupational Safety and Health Administration simply by cutting budgets and appointing directors of those agencies who were hostile to the agency missions. (See Chapter 9 for details.)

Ronald Reagan and the New Federalism of the 1980s _____

These controversies over the biases and complexity of intergovernmental federalism festered throughout the 1970s. The Nixon administration had initiated a sweeping proposal called New Federalism to turn much federal authority and budget responsibilities over to the states. But Nixon's attention was absorbed with the Vietnam War and the Watergate scandal, and he soon lost interest in revamping the federal structure. It was not until the election of Ronald Reagan in 1980 that the critics of intergovernmental federalism were able to put federal reform back on the policy-making agenda once more. Promising that he would get government off our backs, Reagan proclaimed in his 1981 inaugural address that "Government is not the answer to our problem. Government *is* the problem."[17] By government, of course, he meant the federal government, and he proposed a broad initiative called New Federalism that would reverse the shift of power from the states to Washington that had taken place over the previous half century.

The key to Reagan's New Federalism in 1981 was devolution, or spinning off, of federal responsibilities. This devolution took place in four areas: the budget, regulation, the role of the private sector, and the role of the federal courts.

Budgetary Devolution

To cut back on federal responsibilities for domestic programs, in 1981 Reagan convinced Congress to consolidate 77 categorical grant programs into nine new block grants. In normal practice, block grants give states and communities much more flexibility and discretion in how they use federal funds than do categorical grants, which can be used only for a very specific purpose. Interstate highway categorical grant funds, for example, can be used only for the construction or maintenance of the interstate highways. But the Community Development Block Grant enabled different cities in different parts of the country to use those funds pretty much as they saw fit. Because of the greater flexibility they gave states and communities, the block grants sharply increased the authority of those governments over the implementation of federal programs in those nine areas. However, the federal dollars going into the programs were cut by 25 percent, and as the cartoon satirizes, this left the states with mixed feelings. On the one hand they were happy for the elimination of so many federal guidelines and the opportunity to set program priorities themselves. On the other hand, however, the sharp cutback in federal funds forced the states to choose between increasing their own state revenues or reducing the programs.

The following year Reagan proposed a "great swap," as it was called, in which the federal government would pick up all the costs of the Medicaid program (medical assistance for the elderly and the poor), while states would assume responsibility for food stamps and Aid for Families with Dependent Children (AFDC). While the costs for food stamps and AFDC were about the same as those of Medicaid, Medicaid expenses were growing much faster. In the end, this idea was rejected by Congress.

In sum, the goal of budgetary devolution was to turn as much responsibility as possible over to the states for funding domestic programs. As Figure 3-2 shows, the Reagan administration made great progress toward that goal. The crosshatched bar shows that federal grants as a percent of state and local expenditures grew steadily from mid-twentieth century to about 1979 when that growth peaked at

"FIXING POTHOLES IS NOT A FEDERAL RESPONSIBILITY"

Cartoonist Herblock lampoons the argument made by critics of Intergovernmental Federalism that the federal government has gotten too deeply into traditional state government functions, such as street repair.
(*Source:* Copyright © 1982 by Herblock in *The Washington Post.*)

"Well I'm tired of this arrangement, too...but...!"

The transfer of federal responsibilities to the states tended to leave state officials with mixed feelings.
(*Source:* Gamble, Copyright © 1986, *The Florida Times-Union.*)

about 23 percent of state and local expenditures. The percent then dropped to about 16 percent in 1985 and has begun edging back up since then. A similar pattern took place for the growth of federal grants as a percent of the gross national product, as the solid bar of Figure 3-2 shows.

Devolution to the Private Sector

In addition to shifting federal burdens onto the states, President Reagan also proposed that private churches and voluntary agencies should take an increased share of the responsibility for funding social services and combatting such problems as hunger and homelessness. Consistent with his conservative philosophy, Reagan believed that the private sector rather than the federal government had prime responsibility in these areas.

Curbing the Federal Courts

Finally, President Reagan threw his support behind efforts that would hamper the judicial activism that he saw as responsible for the growing federal role during the previous two decades. Numerous bills

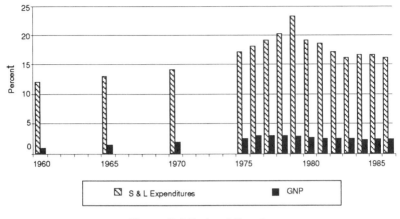

Figure 3-2 Federal Grants

and proposed constitutional amendments were introduced in Congress in the 1980s to restrict federal court authority to hear cases in socially volatile areas such as abortion, school prayer, and busing to desegregate schools, but very little such legislation was actually passed into law. More enduring was the success that Reagan and his successor George Bush enjoyed in appointing political conservatives to the Supreme Court and other federal courts. These judges did not always issue court decisions favorable to Reagan and Bush, but they significantly dampened the ability of federal agencies to impose liberal regulations on the states.

Assessing the New Federalism

Despite Reagan's wide-ranging goal of devolution, in fact it turned out to be a very selective devolution. The administration pushed responsibilities down to the states when such devolution would have the effect of curbing social expenditures for the lower-status population, or when it would serve a conservative social purpose such as weakening occupational safety and health regulations. (See Chapter 9 for details.) But the administration showed no reluctance to impose federal dominance over the states on conservative issues. Thus, the administration supported the move to force states to raise their drinking age to 18. Both Presidents Reagan and Bush supported several measures that impeded doctors or nurses in local public hospitals from participation in abortions, giving abortion counseling to a pregnant woman, or even suggesting where a woman could go for abortion counseling.

As critics examined the New Federalism and the selectivity with which devolution was applied, the philosophical principle of devolution came to be seen as little more than a mask for the administration's true intentions.[18] Those intentions were to curb the welfare system as much as possible and to move the country in the direction of a more conservative social philosophy on issues such as abortion, crime, and race relations. As federal responsibilities were moved to the states, federal funding was cut drastically, and many states were unable to make up the budget shortfall.

How well did New Federalism succeed at these goals? The jury is still out on how this question will ultimately be answered. One school of thought says that very little was really accomplished. Although federal grants-in-aid were cut back from about $95 to about $87 billion in 1981, by the end of the decade they were back above $100 billion. Others, however, think that Reagan has achieved a major permanent shift of financial responsibility for domestic services from the federal government to the state and local[19] governments. And there is little doubt that the brunt of the budget-cutting that accompanied this shift was borne by the least affluent members of our society.

An especially significant consequence of New Federalism has been to give more influence over domestic programs to state legislatures, state governors, and state bureaucracies, while at the same time reducing the influence of federal bureaucracies. What this means in practical terms for the lower-status population is that state political arenas are now a much more important force for determining benefits for the lower-status population than they were a generation ago.

From the increased authority of states over domestic programs comes a second consequence of New Federalism. It exacerbates the already intense competition among states to minimize public services. Paul Peterson and Mark Rom document this phenomenon for welfare expenditures. Each state tries to underspend, or at least appear to underspend, its neighbors on setting welfare levels and this undercuts the heart of welfare programs.[20] But interstate competition to hold down costs goes far beyond welfare programs. States today are under immense pressure to provide a favorable business climate for corporations in the form of low taxes, low levels of public expenditures generally, miserly levels of unemployment compensation and workers compensation (a program of assistance to workers disabled on the job), impediments to organized labor, and lax enforcement provisions for environmental protection and occupational safety and health. Large corporations openly threaten to close their operations and cut jobs in states they view as having hostile business climates, and to expand their job-creating activities in states they view as friendlier. To improve corporate profitability, states are forced into an unhealthy competition to see who can do the least for lower-status people, for occupational safety, and for environmental protection. New Federalism exacerbates this competition because it increases the state burden of financing domestic public services and regulating environmental protection and occupational safety. In this way New Federalist devolution makes the lower-status population hostage to a form of interstate competition for a mythical better business climate.

Another important consequence of the New Federalism has been a persistent decline in public confidence in the federal government since the 1970s. As Figure 3-3 shows, during the 1970s, when asked which level of government gave them the most for their money, most people rated the federal government higher than state and local governments. By the late 1980s, however, the federal government had lost this positive assessment. There are many reasons for its decline. One of them is related, no doubt, to the persistent badmouthing of the federal government bureaucracy that occurred in both the Reagan and Bush administrations. A second reason is also, no doubt, related to expensive scandals that occurred during the Reagan–Bush years in federal agencies dealing with environmental protection, housing, and regulation of the banking and savings and loan industries.

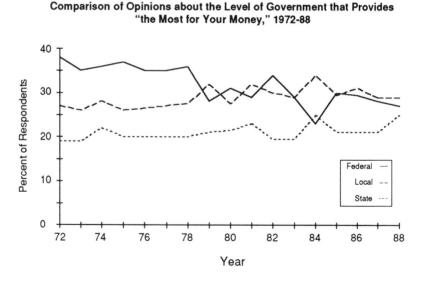

Comparison of Opinions about the Level of Government that Provides "the Most for Your Money," 1972-88

Figure 3–3 Confidence in Federal, State, and Local Governments
Source: International perspective 14, no. 4 (Fall 1988); p.24.

Conclusion: Federalism and the Lower-Status Population _____

In sum, as we move toward the twenty-first century American federalism is an extremely complicated system of government. From the vantage point of the lower-status population, the perennial battle between the federal and state governments for dominance in the system is more often than not a mask for the more important battle of whether there is going to be an expansion or contraction of the social-service state. Liberal administrations seek to centralize authority in Washington and use that authority to expand domestic programs. Conservative administrations seek to devolve authority to states in hopes that the social service system will contract. In times of liberal dominance, Washington tends to become the main arena for fighting over welfare benefits. In conservative times, the states grow in importance.

Because of the many complexities of contemporary intergovernmental federalism, it is no easy matter to sort out the patterns of bias in this system. Nevertheless, there are two areas where the biases seem quite apparent: (1) those affecting racial minorities and (2) those affecting lower-status people generally.

Federalism and the Racial Minorities

While overall political and economic factors affect racial relations more than federalism issues do, dual federalism has generally worked to the disadvantage of racial minorities, especially blacks, while the nationally dominated intergovermental federalism works to their advantage. Most of the civil rights advances for blacks and other racial minorities since mid-century were initiated by the federal government. The Civil Rights Act of 1964, as we saw in Chapter 2, outlawed the practice of racial discrimination in public accommodations such as restaurants and movie theaters. The Voting Rights Act of 1965 outlawed a number of discriminatory practices that had made it impossible for most blacks to register and vote. And a host of Supreme Court rulings struck down state-sanctioned segregation practices ranging from the public schools to interstate bus transportation. From the perspective of racial minorities, the transformation from dual federalism to intergovernmental federalism must be seen as a positive step. The New Federalism of the Reagan and Bush years, however, is another matter. Most civil rights leaders have viewed New Federalism and the retrenchment of the federal government's domestic role as having a negative impact on racial minorities.

Federalism and Lower-Status People Generally

Dual federalism was also biased against the interests of lower and lower-middle income people generally, and this bias has been partially reversed by the contemporary intergovernmental system. This has happened in two ways. First, the growing dominance of the federal government under intergovernmental federalism facilitated the creation of interest groups to represent the lower and the lower-middle classes. Labor organizers, for example, fought an uphill battle to unionize, until the 1930s when federal legislation gave them legal status and provided federal protections for the collective bargaining process. Even today several states have anti-union legislation that inhibits union effectiveness. Without the protective cover of federal law, it is hard to see how unions could have been effective in much of the country. Some of this protective cover of federal law was diluted during the Reagan and Bush years when anti-union people were appointed to head the Department of Labor and labor regulatory bodies such as the National Labor Relations Board.

A second way in which the nationally dominated intergovernmental federalism has benefited the lower and lower-middle classes has been through the creation of numerous programs that brought them tangible financial benefits and helped them gain access to middle-class lifestyles. Federal housing programs, for example, are virtually unthinkable under the older concept of dual federalism, because dual federalism conceives of housing policy as a state responsibility, not a federal government responsibility. But through the assistance of subsidized loans through the Federal Housing Administration and the Veterans Administration, millions of middle-class families since the 1940s have bought homes that they might well have not been able to buy were it not for the federal subsidies.[21]

The same principle is true of other policy areas as well. Consider college education, for example. Millions of people since the 1960s have improved their life-styles with the assistance of federally subsidized grants and loans to help them pursue college educations. These grants and loans would not have been available under the dual federalism approach to government.

Class Bias of New Federalism

Given that the nationally dominated intergovernmental federalism has benefited racial minorities and people of all races in the lower and lower-middle income categories, it is not surprising that the attempts to cut back on the federal government's role under President Reagan's New Federalism were sharply biased against those same categories of people. President Reagan's legacy has been devastating for the lower and lower-middle income residents of the central cities. The policy of New Federalism had relied on economic growth to solve the horrendous social problems of the cities. But judged on its own terms, this policy was a failure.

After a shaky start, the Reagan and Bush administrations saw eight straight years of economic growth until a recession struck in 1990–1991. But the central cities, where lower-status people disproportionately tend to live, did not see their economic condition improve even in the years of economic growth. Despite significant improvements in inflation and unemployment rates, the central cities continue to be rocked by unrelenting poverty, family disorganization, crime, poor schools, and an outmigration of middle-class people to the suburbs. To be fair to Reagan and Bush, all of these problems were well-advanced long before New Federalism was put in place, and New Federalism cannot be blamed for them. What can be said confidently, however, is that the solutions Reagan proposed simply did not work as promised; indeed they made conditions worse. And they exacerbated an interstate competition to minimize public services.

President Reagan's critics judge New Federalism even more harshly. Reagan's administration brought new public housing construction to a halt, cut back social services and welfare services substantially, and instituted a cycle of income tax cuts that put thousands of dollars into the pockets of upper-middle-income people each year while giving a mere pittance to lower-middle-income people and the working poor. These developments contributed to the increasing inequality of the income distribution that we examined in Chapter 1. Compared to two decades ago, a larger share of the national income goes to the richest fifth of Americans, while a smaller share goes to the poorest fifth. The economic and New Federalism policies of Reagan and Bush did not cause the growing income inequalities, but those policies facilitated the inequalities and backed off the half-century thrust of intergovernmental federalism—using federal influence to mitigate the problems of the bottom two-fifths of the income earners.

From this viewpoint, New Federalism was little more than a ruse to reduce federal domestic spending rather than to impose a new political philosophy. Many actions of the Reagan and Bush administrations in fact increased federal dominance at the expense of the states.

For the sake of improving corporate profitability, states are forced into an unhealthy competition to see who can do the least for lower-status people, for occupational safety, and for environmental protection.

Finally, this analysis of federalism's bias carries some important lessons for lower- and lower-middle-income earners. They fared better under the contemporary system of intergovernmental federalism than they did under the old dual federalism. President Reagan's attempts to use New Federalism as a means to undo the the social programs assisting lower-status people, however, illustrate that who runs the federal government is an important factor in determining how the biases of contemporary federalism will be played out.

Summary

1. A federal system of government poses several advantages over a unitary form of government. These include experimentation, broadened avenues of access to government decision makers, flexibility in policy implementation, and increased opportunities for citizen participation.

2. Federalism also has some disadvantages, including greater complexity of government, greater problems of accountability, and greater problems in securing the rights of minorities.

3. As for the proper role for the federal government in domestic affairs, the federal government is better at doing some things than others. It is not very good at targeting programs to specific geographic areas or coordinating programs, and its record in overseeing federal programs is spotty. On the other hand, the federal government usually does a good job of handling transfer payments. Successful federal programs tend to have key characteristics: delegation of adequate responsibility to the proper agency, stipulation of measurable objectives, provision of adequate resources, weak opposition from relevant interest groups, and goals that primarily require technical competence rather than modification of human behavior.

4. In the Constitution, federalism's major provision was the distinction between the delegated powers of the federal government and the reserved powers of the states. This is called dual or layer-cake federalism. In today's intergovernmental federalism, there is no longer a neat division of responsibilities between the national and state levels of government. In a great many areas, the federal government has become the dominant partner in our federal bargain.

5. President Reagan's New Federalism sought to shift responsibility for funding domestic programs from the federal government to the state and local governments.

6. Our system of federalism has several patterns of bias. Lower- and lower-middle-income earners do better under nationally dominated intergovernmental federalism than they did under state dominated dual

federalism. But the advantages of intergovernmental federalism to lower-status people can be mitigated by a presidential administration determined to cut back on the federal domestic role. This was seen in the Reagan administration's New Federalism.

Notes

1. Robert Wood, *1400 Governments: The Political Economy of the New York Metropolitan Region* (Cambridge, Mass.: Harvard University Press, 1961).

2. Martha Derthick, *New Towns in Town: Why a Federal Program Failed* (Washington, D.C.: The Urban Institute, 1972).

3. Jeffrey L. Pressman and Aaron B. Wildavsky, *Implementation* (Berkeley, Calif.: University of California Press, 1973).

4. Paul E. Peterson, Barry Rabe, and Kenneth Wong, *When Federalism Works* (Washington, D.C.: The Brookings Institution, 1984).

5. See, for example, Samuel Kaplan, "The Balkanization of Suburbia," *Harper's* (October 1971): 73.

6. David B. Walker, "The Federal Role in the Federal System: A Troublesome Topic," *National Civic Review* 72, no. 1 (January 1983): 6–23.

7. See Edward C. Banfield, "Making a New Federal Program: Model Cities, 1964–1968," in *Policy and Politics in America: Six Case Studies*, ed. Allan P. Sindler (Boston: Little, Brown and Co., 1973), pp. 124-169.

8. John Schwarz, *America's Hidden Success* (New York: W.W. Norton, 1983).

9. On welfare fraud, see John J. Harrigan, *Politics and Policy in States and Communities*, 3rd ed. (Glenview, Ill.: Scott, Foresman and Company, 1988), p. 362. On student loan defaults the figure is for 1987. See *Statistical Abstract of the United States: 1990*, p. 159.

10. Anthony J. Catanese, *Planners and Local Politics: Impossible Dreams*, vol. 7, Sage Library of Social Research (Beverly Hills, Calif.: Sage Publications, 1974), pp. 55-60.

11. On the term "dual federalism," see, Daniel J. Elazar, *The American Partnership* (Chicago: University of Chicago Press, 1962), p. 20. On the origins of the term "layer cake federalism," see Morton Grodzins, "The Federal System," in *Goals for Americans: The Report of the President's Commission on National Goals* (Englewood Cliffs, N.J.: Prentice-Hall, 1960), pp. 365–366.

12. Elazar, *The American Partnership*, p. 20.

13. Grodzins, "The Federal System," pp. 365-366.

14. John J. Harrigan, *Political Change in the Metropolis*, 4th ed. (Glenview, Ill.: Scott, Foresman and Company, 1989), pp. 227-228.

15. See Charles Murray, *Losing Ground* (New York: Basic Books, 1984), p. 9.

16. See George Gilder, *Wealth and Poverty* (New York: Basic Books, 1981).

17. Ronald Reagan, Inaugural Address, January 20, 1981.

18. Timothy J. Conlan, "Federalism and Competing Values in the Reagan Administration," *Publius* 16, no. 1 (Winter 1986): 29-48.

19. Richard P. Nathan and Fred C. Doolittle, "The Untold Story of Reagan's New Federalism," *The Public Interest* no. 77 (Fall 1984): 96-105.

20. Paul Peterson and Mark Rom, *Welfare Magnets: A New Case for a National Standard* (Washington, D.C.: Brookings Institution, 1990).

21. Harrigan, *Political Change in the Metropolis*, 4th ed., pp. 386-388.

CHAPTER 4

Learning Your Place: Shaping the Minds of Lower-Status Americans

What ordinary people believe and value is very important to the course of a nation's politics. Unless people willingly accept a government's right to govern, the only way the government can stay in power is to impose its rule by brute force. And when the time comes that brute force can no longer be applied, the government will either have to give in to people's demands or get out of the way. Never in our lifetime was this principle dramatized more vividly than in Eastern Europe at the end of the 1980s. Since the end of World War II, Eastern Europe had been run by Communist Parties that were propped up by the military might of the Soviet Union. When demands for greater independence surfaced in Hungary in 1956, in Poland in 1956, and in Czechoslovakia in 1968, the Soviet Army crushed the revolts and in Czechoslovakia in 1968 killed 20,000 people in the process.

A major change took place in June 1989 when Soviet president Mikhail Gorbachev announced that the Soviet Army would no longer put down democratic movements in the Soviet satellite countries in Eastern Europe. By year's end, the communist regimes tumbled in every country except Albania and Bulgaria as mass protesters took to the streets and demanded free elections. The most symbolic event took place in December 1989 when Germans attacked the Berlin Wall with sledgehammers while East German border guards stood by, helpless to stop them. After nearly a half-century of control, the Soviet-led Communist Parties had failed to win the allegiance of the East European peoples. The moment brute force was lifted, the people overthrew the ruling orders.

Ruling orders exist in democratic societies as well as in authoritarian ones, and because brute force is almost impossible to apply consistently for long periods of time in democracies, democratic ruling orders depend even more than authoritarian ones on the allegiance of the people. If they want to be successful, democratic ruling orders, as well as authoritarian ones, are obliged to put great effort into maintaining

If they want to be successful, democratic ruling orders, as well as authoritarian ones, are obliged to put great effort into maintaining belief systems that will support the ruling orders. This is true in the United States as well as in other democracies.

belief systems that will support the ruling orders. This is true in the United States as well as in other democracies.

How the belief system is shaped is of vital concern to lower-status people. To take an extreme example, it will be difficult to move lower-status people to collective action in their self-interest if they can be led to believe, as is commonly preached by some religions, that they will be rewarded or punished in an afterlife, depending on how docile, obedient, and accepting of their lower station they are in this life.

Not only is belief formation critical to the interests of the lower-status population, it is also important to the quality of American democracy itself. Democracy depends on knowledgeable participants in the political process. But the average American, especially the average lower-status American, is woefully deficient in accurate political knowledge. In no small measure this is because of key flaws in the opinion-formation process.

This chapter will argue that the process of forming American political beliefs, while having nowhere near the blatant bias that the process has in authoritarian societies, nevertheless has aspects that are damaging to the self-interest of lower-status people and to the integrity of American democracy itself. We will pursue this argument by examining: (1) how the socialization process through which we acquire our political beliefs impacts differently on the lower-status population from the way it does on the upper-status population and (2) how the role of the media in shaping opinion is harmful to lower-status people.

Learning Political Beliefs: Political Socialization _____

The process by means of which society passes its political culture on to new generations is called political socialization. Political socialization has both a *cognitive* aspect (what we *know*) and an *affective* aspect (what we *feel* about what we know). Thus, our learning about the three branches of government, the two-party system, and other features of American politics is part of the cognitive aspect of our socialization. Our learning to have a positive emotional response to flag ceremonies and the national anthem is part of the affective aspect of our socialization.

The Agents of Political Socialization

By and large we learn about politics through what social scientists call the agents of political socialization. These are principally: *the family*, which has its biggest impact on our pre-teen years and strongly influences whether we view ourselves as Republicans or Democrats;[1] *the schools*, which strive very hard to turn children into knowledgeable citizens who are both patriotic and supportive of the free enterprise economic system;[2] and *peer groups*, which become extremely important politically when we enter adulthood.

Learning Your Place from the Family. At first glance, it seems ridiculous to argue that lower-status families would socialize their children in ways that reinforce their own subordinate situation. After all, few parents would deliberately set out to deprive their children of the knowledge and beliefs needed to gain economic and political influence. Perhaps not. But parenthood does not start as a blank slate. We each come to parenthood with our own experiences and are the product of our own political socialization. And since we vary greatly in our own abilities to participate effectively in politics, we vary greatly in our ability to teach our children how to participate effectively.

One of the starkest realities of political life is that lower-strata people are socialized into the political culture differently than are people in the privileged strata, and these differences persist throughout life. In our early years we acquire our first orientations toward the world outside our family and close friends. Parents who vote regularly, discuss politics frequently, attend political meetings, and become active in community affairs model a participatory role for their children. These activities occur much more frequently among middle- and upper-strata families than they do among lower-strata families.

In contrast to privileged-strata people, those in the lower strata are also much more likely to be raised under authoritarian child-rearing practices. They are more likely to be raised in families that view political participation as a waste of time, and often feel that they have no control over the government and that government does nothing for them. Many are preoccupied with their own day-to-day personal and economic problems. Indeed, engaging in politics can be risky. Since politics is dominated by better-educated, middle- and upper-strata peo-

---

One of the starkest realities of political life is that lower-strata people are socialized into the political culture differently than are people in the privileged strata, and these differences persist throughout life.

ple, the lower-strata person who becomes active often faces considerable psychological risk of being out-argued and out-maneuvered by articulate and skillful middle- and upper-strata activists. For all of these reasons, political activity is much less likely to be an integral part of family life for the lower class than for the middle or upper classes. If one wants to get ahead a little bit in the world, spending time at political meetings and demonstrations is likely to seem less rewarding than moonlighting at a second job in order to buy a new boat, a VCR, or some other consumer product.

The most brutal example of participation as a risky game occurred among African American families during the long period of slavery and segregation in the South. Aggressive black men who sought to advance the interests of their race were in grave danger of harassment, intimidation, or even lynching. Negro mothers knew this and hence sought to raise their sons in ways that inhibited their assertive or aggressive impulses. Two black psychiatrists wrote:

> During slavery the danger was real. A slave boy could not show too much aggression. The feelings of anger and frustration which channeled themselves into aggression had to be thwarted. If they were not, the boy would have little or no use as a slave and would be slain. If any feelings, especially those of assertive manhood, were expressed too strongly, then that slave was a threat, not only to himself and his master but to the entire system as well. For that, he would have to be killed.
>
> The black mother continues this heritage from slavery and simultaneously reflects the world she now knows. Even today, the black man cannot become too aggressive without hazard to himself. To do so is to challenge the delicate balance of a complex social system . . . it is [the mother's] lot in life to suppress masculine assertiveness in her sons.[3]

If the two psychiatrists who wrote that passage are correct and if these conditions prevailed for the 350 years from the arrival of the first slaves in 1619 to the outlawing of segregation in the 1960s, it is little wonder that political cynicism is high and voter participation low among poor blacks, or that repressed rage has led to so much violence among young, poor, black men. The wonder is that anybody who came out of those conditions has even a minimal interest in politics. The amazing thing is that today, barely a quarter-century after the passage of the Voting Rights Act of 1965, the voter turnout rate for blacks is approximately the same as or slightly higher than it is for whites in vir-

---

For all of these reasons, political activity is much less likely to be an integral part of family life for the lower class than for the middle or upper classes.

tually every income category. This achievement is a testimony to black leadership, and we will examine that more closely in future chapters.

The weight of evidence, however, indicates that among blacks, whites, and other races, political socialization within the lower-status family inhibits political participation rather than facilitates it.

Learning Your Place at School. The differences between lower-strata and privileged-strata political socialization at home are reinforced by the schools. Edgar Litt analyzed classroom instruction in three different areas of Boston—a working-class area, a middle-class area, and an upper-class area. In the working-class area, Litt found that "students received some instruction in democratic procedures but were not encouraged in any way to participate in politics." Children in the middle-class area received instruction in democratic procedures, with an additional emphasis on the "responsibility of citizenship," such as the responsibility to vote. The most participatory message came to children in the upper-class area, where "insights into political processes and functions [were] passed on to those who, judging from their socioeconomic and political environment, [would] likely [hold] those positions that [would] involve them in influencing and making political decisions."[4] This observation that nonparticipatory messages are conveyed by the public schools to lower-class children is supported by many other studies of ghetto schools that focus on the debilitating effect that some ghetto school environments have on the self-esteem of the children in those schools.[5]

Fewer Resources in Lower Status Schools. Three factors are at work here. First, the schools in low-income inner-city areas lag far behind most other schools in resources, while at the same time they are overwhelmed by broken families, severe social problems, poverty, and violence. In situations where simply maintaining safety and getting through basic subjects are huge challenges, the teaching of political participation must seem a little esoteric to many teachers.

The Mind of the Public School Teacher. A second factor is also at work, and that stems from the world view of the public school teacher. Most public school teachers come from fairly traditional lower- middle-class backgrounds, are rarely on the cutting edge of social change, and—except for supporting their teachers' unions—are rarely advocates for extending political participation. Psychologically, they tend to identify more with the values of middle-class stability than with values of change. Indeed, in many instances where local neighbors sought to achieve greater input into school policies, the teachers organizations were usually against the change. When New York created neighborhood-based school districts in the 1968, the teachers organization in Brooklyn went on strike and virulently sought to undermine the locally elected school boards.[6] Teachers organizations also opposed decentralization programs in Detroit in the 1970s,[7] open enrollment plans in Minnesota in the 1980s,[8] and educational reform plans in Tennessee in the 1980s.[9] While many dedicated teachers toil for years with little recognition, and most of us have fond memories of those dedicated ones, existing research on the politics of public education does not paint a picture of the typical teacher as prodding his or her lower-status pupils on to greater political participation.

The School System as a Sieve. Even when teachers want to encourage a participatory mentality in their pupils, they are inhibited by a third factor, the role of the public school system as a social sorting mechanism. The system "screens potential workers through a sieve, sorting them according to their capacities to work persistently, to respond to incentives like wages, to conform to work requirements, and to defer gratification."[10] This sifting function can be seen from the highest levels of education to the public schools themselves. People with professional degrees are sorted into prestigious upper-status professions such as medicine and law. A notch below these high-ranking professions are more typical middle-class careers such as public school teacher, social worker, accountant, computer programmer, and registered nurse. These come disproportionately from the state college systems and from the less-prestigious private colleges. Below the bachelor's level, graduates of high schools, technical schools, community colleges, and trade-union apprentice programs get sifted into occupations such as laboratory technician, hairdresser, dental assistant, skilled trades worker, or police officer. Near the bottom of the occupational ladder are the high school dropouts who become the dishwashers, unskilled laborers, and public-relief recipients.

If there is some truth to this vision of the public school system as a social sieve, it would take a teacher of extraordinary perception to regard lower-status children as having the potential to rise above their lower-status level. African American biographies are replete with references to teachers who sought to curb their black pupils who had soaring ambitions and steer them instead toward more modest goals. Malcolm X, for example, tells of the time that he told one of his teachers that he wanted to be a lawyer. Since Malcolm was among the top students in his predominantly white Michigan school, succeeding in law school was not an unreasonable dream. But the teacher replied, "A lawyer—that's no realistic goal for a nigger. You need to think about something you *can* be. . . . Why don't you plan on carpentry?"[11] If a teacher does not perceive his or her lower-status pupils as having the potential to rise on the social ladder, it would take a truly gifted teacher even to think of those pupils as potential participants in, and contributors to, the political system. Not much point in sending them to political caucuses and demanding that they write essays on their experiences. Much better to encourage them to join released time programs so they can spend some of their school hours working at Burger Kings and other occupations that befit their station in life.[12]

Learning Your Place from Your Peers. As children grow into adolescence, the socialization influence of their parents and teachers begins to fade, and the influence of peer groups begins to grow. Most of us seek out peers who reinforce our values. It is not surprising, for instance, that college students majoring in the social sciences tend to be more liberal politically than those majoring in the physical sciences. Since most research shows this to be the case[13] it would take a fairly extraordinary college freshman to major in a field where his or her political values were continuously in conflict with the values of his or her closest friends and associates.

Furthermore, young people usually attend colleges where their values are shared by other students, and to be influenced by the predominant values of those student bodies. This was seen in an examination the *Congressional Quarterly* conducted of 1984 voting results in selected on-campus precincts where all or nearly all the voters were college students. At the colleges with high black-student enrollments and the elite private colleges shown in Table 4-1, the student bodies voted overwhelmingly for Democratic nominee Walter Mondale. By contrast, those in the religious schools and the schools with military traditions voted overwhelmingly for Republican President Ronald Reagan. While the student bodies at most colleges would not be nearly as uniform in their political choices as the ones shown here, the table does illustrate the tendency of people to choose peer settings where they will encounter people with similar values and to be influenced by those people.

Political clustering occurs not only among college students, but also in the occupational world. In the mid-1980s, almost two-thirds of service workers identified themselves as Democrats, while barely 40 percent of people with professional occupations identified themselves as Democrats.[14] It is hard to escape the tendency of like-minded people to cluster together. We should choose our associates carefully, because they tend to influence how we think and how we act.

If a teacher does not perceive his or her lower-status pupils as having the potential to rise on the social ladder, it would take a truly gifted teacher even to think of those pupils as potential participants in and contributors to the political system.

TABLE 4-1 **Vote Clustering by Type of School**

	Percent of Vote for Reagan	Percent of Vote for Mondale
Selected Elite Private Colleges		
Amherst College	25	75
Oberlin College	17	83
Selected Black Universities		
Florida A&M	3	97
Tennessee State	4	96
Private Religious Universities		
Brigham Young	95	5
Oral Roberts	92	8
Baylor University	89	11
Universities with Military Tradition		
Air Force Academy	85	15
Texas A&M	92	8

Source: CQ's Guide to Current American Government: Fall 1986 (Washington, D.C.: Congressional Quarterly, 1986), p. 30.

Summary of Lower-Strata Socialization

In sum, the multiple socialization impacts of family upbringing, school experiences, and peer-group interactions do a great deal to teach us our place in the world. These agents of socialization convey a much less participatory message to lower-strata people than they do to privileged-strata people. Reinforcing this impact, there has been a pronounced trend since the 1960s for younger citizens in their twenties and thirties to vote less frequently and to show less interest in politics than earlier generations of young people. Because young lower-strata people tend to lack the college experiences that encourage participation, among the young, they are the least interested and the least involved in politics.

Learning Your Place from the Media _____

In addition to the agents of socialization (family, school, peer groups), the communications media play a major role in forming our political beliefs. And the media are no more neutral than any other politically important institution. The media do not set out by design to be hostile to the lower-status population. But there are four ways in which they have a hostile effect. Lower-strata people are more dependent for their opinion formation on television news and television commercials than are upper-strata people. Because of a simplistic structural bias in television news, television inhibits the ability of lower-strata people to think critically about the political and economic events that affect their lives. Second, television and the other media convey a negative image of lower-strata life-styles. Third, the media are not as liberal as they seem, and on economic issues central to lower-status interests, they are on balance conservative. Fourth, media concentration reinforces mainstream values that may or may not be advantageous to lower-status persons.

Structural Bias and Lower-Strata Vulnerability

Structural Bias in Television News. Lower-status people, as we shall see shortly, use the media in a less-sophisticated way than do upper-strata people. And this puts them at a disadvantage when trying to determine how media coverage affects their economic self-interest. These disadvantages are most pronounced in the case of television, because that is the medium relied on most heavily by lower-status people for their political news. The very nature of television news has a structural bias[15] that favors some kinds of news events over others. Producers want to telecast visually dramatic or sensational events that will attract a wide viewing audience. This bias was expressed clearly by CBS president Van Sauter who displayed in his office a plaque that read:

> Television is not the truth! Television is a goddamned amusement park, that's what television is. Television is a circus, a carnival, a traveling troupe of acrobats and storytellers, singers and dancers, jugglers, sideshow freaks, lion tamers and football players![16]

Emphasizing the Visual. With this structural guide-post of television news as entertainment, the television networks are highly selective in what they broadcast. They favor visually dramatic events that make an emotional impact on the viewing audience. Television reports violence, scandal, conflict, or disaster more often than stories of the mundane or the ordinary. It prefers reporting familiar people and familiar settings to reporting the unfamiliar. But, of course, it seeks out familiar people doing novel things that are timely.

Perhaps the worst impact of TV on public life in America is its tendency to dull the critical-thinking ability of the American public in observing the political arena. PBS correspondent Bill Moyers reached this conclusion at the end of a four-part series on the role of images in public discourse. The power of the TV image outweighs the words spoken by the commentators. One of the most graphic examples of this occurred in an anecdote told by CBS correspondent Leslie Stahl. She expected the Reagan White House to be angry about a report she did that juxtaposed pictures of Reagan in front of a senior citizen housing project with a verbal commentary that Reagan had cut the budget for such housing projects. Instead, she received a thank you call from Reagan's chief media strategist Michael Deaver who told her that the viewing public would forget her verbal commentary but would be left with the very favorable visual image of Reagan empathizing with senior citizens.[17]

Emphasizing the Sound Bite Because of its structural bias in favor of the visual over the oral, the amount of time that television news programs will give to a political candidate or public official has shrunk dramatically over the years to what is currently referred to as a "sound bite," a 10- or 15-second statement. One analysis found that the average length of a candidate's uninterrupted talking in 1968 television election coverage was 42.3 seconds. In 1988, that had shrunk to 9.8 seconds.[18] Political candidates might make thoughtful speeches on complicated topics, but the TV news coverage will show at most the dozen or so most inflammatory words in the speech, regardless of whether they reflect the intentions of the candidate or are merely taken out of context. Sound-bite journalism has had a debilitating impact on public discourse, because political candidates quickly learn to play the game that will get them the television coverage they need in order to win. They engage in sound bites and visual imagery instead of rational analysis of the nation's problems.

Contrast this situation today with the famous Lincoln–Douglas debates of the 1858 senatorial campaign in Illinois. Abraham Lincoln and Steven Douglas presented Illinois voters with a clear and eloquently articulated choice between their approaches to the divisive issue of slavery that soon would engulf the nation in its bloodiest war. Lincoln argued against extending slavery into the new territories that would come into the union as states over the next few years. Douglas, in the name of popular sovereignty, argued that each state should decide for itself about slavery. In the current era of sound-bite journalism, it is difficult to imagine television spending much time covering such debates. It is also difficult imagining that candidates today, knowing the importance of having their sound bites aired, would think it worthwhile engaging in such an intellectual exercise as developing reasoned arguments about their vital and divisive political issues.

Trivializing Politics. Instead of campaigns educating voters on complicated issues, television news coverage dwells on sound bites and action shots of candidates working their way through crowds, and focuses on who is ahead of whom—what is often called the horse-race

This cartoon speculates on what the Gettysburg Address might have sounded like if President Lincoln had had to worry about today's emphasis on 15-second sound bites for the television evening news.
(*Source:* Ohman for the *Oregonian.* Found in *Washington Post National Weekly*, October 31–November 6, 1988, p. 30.)

aspects of campaigns. This type of television news coverage trivializes the campaign.[19]

The response of candidates to the visual nature of campaign coverage compounds the trivialization. Candidates hire advisers to organize media events that will produce powerful images but will say little about how the candidate may handle real issues. In the 1984 election, for example, Ronald Reagan strategists Michael Deaver and David Gergen wanted to defuse a potential campaign charge that the 74-year-old president might be too old to withstand four more grueling years in the White House. To defuse this potential attack on the president's age, they

> arranged for Reagan to arm-wrestle weight lifter Dan Lurie, publisher of *Muscle Training Illustrated.* A White House photographer snapped a setup shot of Reagan pinning Lurie's biceps to his desk, and Deaver put it out to the press, getting front page play. David Gergen arranged a similar photo layout of Reagan pumping barbells for *Parade* magazine. Antidotes to fears about a seventy-four year-old president.[20]

Election campaigns today have become exercises in media manipulation, photo opportunities, and visual demagoguery in which the issues the candidates address are subordinated to the visual imagery in which the candidate appears on the TV screen. If the mass of the American population had a variety of information sources to double-check the images they acquire from television, the visual demagoguery of television would not have as pernicious an effect on the ability of the American public to think critically about politics. Unfortunately, television has become the dominant source of information on news for most of the population.

Lower-Status Dependence on Television News

There is reason to think that lower-strata people are the ones most dependent on television news. They spend much more time each day watching television than do upper-strata people, and are much less likely to read a newspaper every day.[21] The print media is becoming highly segmented, with different magazines targeted to different audiences. Magazines targeted to lower-income readers, except for *Readers Digest*, seldom cover political issues. Most of the politically oriented magazines, by contrast, are targeted to a more upscale reading audience. These include opinion magazines and journals such as *The Public Interest*, *National Review*, *The New Republic*, *The American Prospect*, *Harper's*, and *The Atlantic Monthly*. Although the number of readers of these publications is very small compared with the number of viewers of television news broadcasts, the readers are often influential persons such as government and business leaders, educators, politicians, professional people, and organizational leaders.

Not only do upper-strata and lower-strata people use the media differently, they also differ in their ability to perceive bias in the media or to view it critically. A 1985 survey for the American Society of Newspaper Editors found that bias in the media was perceived by 52 percent of college-educated persons, but only 41 percent of the high school-educated, and only 36 percent of those who lacked a high school education. Lower-strata people were also less likely to view the media critically. When asked to rate the accuracy of the newspapers they read, 49 percent of those who lacked a high school education gave a very good rating for accuracy to their newspapers, compared to only 39 percent of those with a high school education, and only 31 percent of the college educated.[22]

What we see, in sum, is a pattern in media usage and understanding that works to the disadvantage of the lowest-income strata of the population. The lower strata are much more dependent on television for their information. Given the simplistic nature of television news coverage, with its emphasis on sound bites and visual demagoguery, the dependence of the lower strata on television for their coverage makes

What we see, in sum, is a pattern in media usage and understanding that works to the disadvantage of the lowest-income strata of the population.

it much more difficult for them to think critically about events or issues than for the upper-strata people. Those who rely on TV news programs simply will lack the breadth of information to make critical judgments. The less able they are to think critically about political reality, the more susceptible they are to manipulation and the less likely they are to determine their own economic self-interest from the sound-bite messages they see on television.

An Unflattering Media Portrait of Lower-Status Life

In addition to the structural bias of television news that dulls the critical faculties of lower-status people, television and the print media also paint an unflattering picture of the lower-status population. Media executives do not set out to do this, of course, but nevertheless it occurs in two different ways. The first has to do with the treatment of lower-status political or labor movements, and the second with the treatment of lower-status people generally.

Capitalism and Labor Strife in the News. Because the media is intimately connected with the corporate world, the media necessarily is defensive of the free-enterprise system and unreceptive to lower-status movements that criticize any aspects of that system. In the 1960s, the owners of the Wilmington, Delaware, *Morning News* and *Evening Journal* objected to an editorial that praised President Kennedy's appointment of Byron White to the Supreme Court, so they wrote their editors not to "devote space to one who is an enemy of private enterprise and the capitalistic system."[23] (White, in fact, sides with the conservative and moderate blocs of the Supreme Court justices, not the liberal bloc.) In 1973–1974, when automobile companies were seeking the repeal of safety laws requiring them to install air bags in automobiles, the nation's most prestigious newspaper, the *New York Times*, virtually gave its pages over to the automobile advertisers. Michael Parenti writes:

> The *Times* ran stories that were, as one *Times* staff person admitted, "more or less put together by the advertisers." *Times* publisher Arthur Ochs Sulzberger openly admitted that he urged his editors to present the industry position in coverage of safety and auto pollution because, he said, it "would affect the advertising."[24]

The most persistent class-based news distortion of the media probably occurs in the treatment of conflicts between big business and organized labor. A good example of media treatment of labor issues could be seen in a detailed analysis political scientist Michael Parenti conducted of a strike by coal miners in 1977–1978.[25] This case study is worth examining because many of the aspects of media treatment of labor strife that were reflected in this particular strike are commonplace in the media's treatment of labor strife generally.

The workers' demands in this particular strike are not difficult to understand. High on their agenda of demands were safety and job security issues. There had been instances of foremen disconnecting the alarm system that warns miners of dangerous gas buildup in the shafts. In fact, well into the 1990s companies followed a regular pattern of tampering with detection devices that warned workers of coaldust buildup, a prime cause of black lung disease, a debilitative and fatal disease common among coal miners.[26] To protect themselves from these company practices, the miners in 1977 refused to enter the mines when the safety devices were disconnected, thus conducting an unauthorized "wildcat strike." The company planned to phase out the United Mine Workers (UMW) health plan and health clinics, and shift the workers to insurance plans the company selected. It wanted to initiate work speed-ups that would force the workers to dig out the coal at a faster, and perhaps more dangerous, pace, and keep them in the mines during periods of hazardous buildup of gases or coal dust. In addition to these safety, health, and working condition issues, there were, of course, traditional issues of wage increases and other working conditions. In short, the mine workers demands were fairly straightforward. They wanted the companies to stop tampering with safety devices; did not want to be forced to go into the mines when these devices were disconnected; did not want work speed-ups that would keep them in the mines during unsafe periods or for unsafe lengths of time; did not want reductions in the quality of their health insurance and health coverage. And, of course, during a period of high inflation, they wanted wage increases that would keep them ahead of the increased cost of living.

These concerns of the workers, according to Parenti, were downplayed by the media, but management's side of the dispute was portrayed sympathetically. Management's wage offer was described as "hefty" by the *Wall Street Journal*[27] and "whopping" by *Time* magazine.[28] And management's only demand was for "labor stability."[29] Undiscussed in the media were the implications of the term "labor stability." By labor stability, the companies were demanding the right to discipline or even fire any employee for encouraging or participating in strike activity. In practice this meant that workers had no choice but to go into the mines when foremen disconnected the safety-warning devices. If they refused to go into the mines during unsafe periods, that action would be termed a "wildcat strike" and they would be subject to discipline by the company. If the companies were given this right, the only recourse of the workers would be to go into the mines and then later initiate a labor grievance leading to arbitration in which the arbitrator could force the company to reconnect the devices and perhaps level a small fine on the company. But labor grievance procedures can drag out for months, during which time the miners would be exposed to unsafe levels of gas and coal dust. Thus, from the miners' viewpoint, the "right to strike can be a matter of life and death. None of this was made clear in the news coverage. Instead, wildcat strikes were characterized as wanton and self-defeating."[30]

In preparation for the contract negotiations, the mining companies stockpiled large amounts of coal so that they would be able to keep selling it even if a strike occurred. With these large stockpiles on hand, the companies rejected the UMW proposal in December 1977 and closed the mines, hoping to force the union to give in. Closing the mines this way is called a "lock-out," but the press continued to call the closure a strike. When the mine owners and the UMW finally agreed upon a contract, it was submitted to the workers for a vote, and they rejected it by a two-to-one margin. Media coverage of the vote did not focus on the reasons why the miners rejected the contract (mainly inadequate safety and health provisions). Instead the union was charged with being in a "state of virtual anarchy"[31] and with being unable to keep the workers in line.[32] Before the issue was finally resolved, the mines stayed closed for 112 days, during which time the national media continued to protray the miners negatively. The miners were "hell-raising and violent, promiscuous and enduring" according to *Newsweek*;[33] "traditionally quick to resort to violence" and "not addicted to regular work" according to *Time*;[34] and "a breed apart" and "clannish" by the *New York Times*.[35] Michael Parenti wrote sarcastically:

> No such conjectures were offered regarding the mine owners, nothing about their "clannish" country clubs, and "inbred" and "promiscuous" social lives; their irregular, leisurely, and often nonexistent work hours; and the tradition of violence expressed in their reliance on goon squads, Pinkertons, gun thugs, state troopers, and National Guardsmen. No reporter wrote about management's "strange ways," nor would any editor or publisher have allowed a story to pass.[36]

Despite the general media assessment of the unreasonableness of the miners' position in this particular labor conflict, we will see in

Chapter 9 that this strike was a critical event in getting the federal government to strengthen OSHA (the Occupational Safety and Health Administration) to come to grips with mine safety issues. The miners had been conducting their unauthorized wildcat strikes because neither OSHA nor the UMW itself had been standing up for the safety and health of the men who went into the mines. In historical retrospect, the worker demands in fact became critical steps in improving mine safety. At the time, however, the national media portrayed those demands as wanton and irresponsible.

The negative media treatment of coal miners did not end in 1978. The years since have been dotted with conflict between the coal companies and the miners. In 1989, the Pittston Coal Company sought to terminate its contributions to health plans for its miners, and the miners staged a sit-down strike that lasted for nine months. Over the entire nine months, the three television networks allotted only 22 minutes to covering the strike. By contrast, when Russian coal miners went on strike in the Soviet Union that summer, our networks covered that strike for eight consecutive days. The *New York Times* coverage of the two strikes described the Russian strikers in glowing terms but focused its coverage of the Pittston strike on a fine levied on the UMW for violent behavior. While portraying the Russian strikers as heroes, the media portrayed American strikers as violent. No mention was made of the nine months of nonviolence that had characterized the strike.[37]

What lesson should the lower-status person draw from this anecdote of the media treatment of the mine workers? A very simple one. The way the media treated the workers in this strike is typical of the way in which the media treat workers in most situations of labor conflict. When you read stories or see television sound bites about the irresponsibility of strikers, do not accept those accusations at face value until you have taken the trouble to examine the same issue from the striker's viewpoint. Especially, guard against the "fishing" explanation of the strike; that is, the charge that the strikers simply want a little more vacation time to go fishing. When the coal miners again went on strike in 1981, the *Wall Street Journal* claimed that an anonymous union official had told them that "it's fishing season in Appalachia, and a lot of miners are off in Fort Lauderdale on vacations they booked months ago."[38] *Newsweek* picked up this story and gave it wider publicity.[39] Before accepting the absurd notion that the majority of economically marginal workers would vote to give up two or three months of paychecks and health insurance coverage just to have some more fishing time, it would be useful to demand that the newspaper making such reports back them up with concrete evidence and data. As we have said often in this book, there are always at least two sides to every story. Media treatment of labor conflict, however, usually lines up on the side of management.

Lower-Status Life-Styles on TV. Given the persistently negative treatment the media give workers in situations of labor conflict, it is not surprising that most Americans have negative views of lower-status workers generally. These views are reinforced by the entertainment media. The International Association of Machinists and Aerospace Workers (IAM) in 1980 published a study of the treatment of working-class people on prime time television. The study showed a persistent distortion of the kinds of people who do ordinary work in America. Machinists, for example, were outnumbered by prostitutes by a ratio of twelve to one; welfare workers were outnumbered by witch doctors by a ratio of two to one; miners were outnumbered by butlers by a ratio of eight to one; and production-line workers were outnumbered by private detectives by a ratio of twelve to one.[40] A labor force that is disproportionately prostitutes, witch doctors, butlers, and private detectives is obviously not a cross-section of the average lower-strata population. But this is the image that prime-time television projects of that population.

In the late 1960s and early 1970s, an eminently popular television sitcom, *All in the Family*, used the character of Archie Bunker to portray lower-status whites as beer-swizzling, ignorant, opinionated, racist, sexist bigots. By the 1990s, lower-status white life-styles were epitomized by the popular *Roseanne* show. Roseanne and her family are clearly not the bigots that Archie Bunker was, but they are still portrayed as beer-swizzling, ignorant, opinionated ne'er-do-wells who are too incompetent to gain control over their own lives.

If the portrait of lower-status whites on television is negative, racial minority commentators complain that it is even worse for them. When a lower-status black male appears on television, he is more likely than not portrayed as in trouble with the law or up to no good in general. For example, a study by Black Entertainment News showed that when drug usage was discussed on television news, it was associated with blacks 50 percent of the time but with whites only 32 percent of the time. In reality, blacks constitute only a minority of drug users in the country.[41] Most lower-status men and women—white, black, or of whatever race—lead lives that are far removed from the images of their lives shown on television. They go to work regularly, pay most of their taxes, do not have trouble with the law for anything other than traffic tickets, try to raise their children as best they can, are sexually faithful to their spouses for years on end, do not steal from their employers, have no connection with drug traffickers or organized crime, and live from paycheck to paycheck without much margin for economic setbacks. But those people would not make for a very interesting television drama or a very funny sitcom. And this is why the television view of lower-strata America includes more prostitutes than social workers and more private detectives than production-line workers.

The Damage of Media's Unflattering Portrait of the Lower-Strata. Although there is no conclusive way to link television images with specific lower-strata behavior, there is good reason to think that television's unflattering portrait of lower-strata life contributes to both a higher sense of alienation among lower-strata people and a lower level of political participation.

Lower-Strata Alienation. As Table 4-2 shows, people in the lower strata are more alienated from society than upper-status people. This alienation is not caused by television, but the unflattering portrait television paints of lower-status people feeds into and facilitates their greater sense of alienation. They are more inclined to be pessimistic about the fate of the average person, much more likely to think that public officials do not care about them, and much less trusting of their fellow human beings.

Some scholars think that these higher levels of alienation among the poorest strata are not a reflection of their self-image but an accurate reflection of their powerlessness in the system. Bernard Barber writes that the "50 percent of the population that seems to express distrust and alienation is understandably less powerful than the other half of the population and . . . withdrawal from politics to the comforts of trustworthy family, friends, and job is sensible, not irrational."[42]

Barber may be right in believing that it is rational for poor people to withdraw from the political arena and devote their efforts to improving their own economic status. Engaging in politics puts little money in the pocket, and as every political participant can attest, it takes an enormous investment of time to achieve just the smallest political victories. If one took the time spent in political agitation and spent it working at a second job, one might earn enough extra income to move up a notch from near-poverty to financial precariousness.

Lower-Strata Participation. From an individual viewpoint, alienation and withdrawal might make sense, as Barber argues. From a collective standpoint, however, it is disastrous. The greater the number of lower-strata people who withdraw from politics, the more the political process is left in the hands of the upper-strata. It is not ratio-

TABLE 4-2 Alienation Among the American Population

	Percent Making an Alienated Statement		
	Lower-Strata People		**Upper Strata**
	Bottom of the stratum (i.e., the poorest 40%)	**Top of the stratum (i.e., the middle 20%**	**(i.e. the richest 40%)**
Query			
The lot of the average man is getting worse, not better.	69.1	*57.9*	*52.4*
Most public officials are not really interested in the problems of the average man.	*62.1*	*60.0*	49.3
Most people would take advantage of me if they got the chance.	46.3	*34.6*	*27.4*
Most people get ahead by their own hard work rather than by lucky breaks.	14.9	*13.2*	*13.2*
I am not satisfied at all with my present financial situation.	40.4	*23.7*	*13.1*

Note: Italic numbers are used to show whether the top of the lower strata population stands closer to the poorest of the lower-strata or to the upper-strata population.

Source: James Allan Davis and Tom W. Smith,: *General Social Surveys, 1972–1989* [machine-readable data file]. Principal Investigator, James A. Davis; Director and Co-Principal Investigator, Tom W. Smith. NORC ed. Chicago: National Opinion Research Center, producer, 1989; Storrs, CT: The Roper Center for Public Opinion Research, University of Connecticut, distributor.

nal to assume that political leaders electorally beholden to upper-status groups will subordinate the interests of their upper-status supporters to advance the interests of lower-status people.

Because of the unflattering picture that television paints of lower-status activists, other lower-status people are inhibited from becoming active. Recall that when the striking miners in 1978 refused to enter coal mines during unsafe periods, those miners were branded by the nation's most prestigious newspapers and magazines as promiscuous, lazy, wanton, violent, irresponsible, and the dupes of selfish, greedy leaders. No reasonable person wants to be thought of in those terms by respectable members of society. And to join in a labor strike, a protest demonstration, or in fact in any demonstration not sanctioned by media elites is to risk being painted as such a person. It is difficult to believe that this does not inhibit the political activity of most members of lower-strata America.

More Conservative Than They Look

A final impact of the media on lower-status Americans is that the media in general are much more conservative than they appear. The general perception of the media is that they are not conservative at all, and that they have a liberal bias. This perception is the result of a long-term effort by conservatives to show that the media, especially television, reflect an "Eastern-liberal media-establishment" bias. This effort stems from the years of the Nixon presidency (1969–1974) which, in fact, was treated very negatively by the media, especially by television. The charge of media bias was put most colorfully by Nixon's vice president, Spiro Agnew, who railed against the television network commentators as "nattering nabobs of negativism" and "supersensitive, self-anointed, supercilious electronic barons of opinion."[43] And in 1988, when reporters and television interviewers bored in on embarrassing events in the background of vice-presidential candidate Dan Quayle, Republicans accused the media of engaging in a "feeding frenzy." Conservatives were so convinced of a liberal bias in the press and on the air that Accuracy in Media was founded in 1984 to monitor media reports.

The radical left, on the other hand, accuses the media of censoring out news that is critical of the capitalistic system and ignoring leftist candidates in the electoral process.[44] By ignoring such criticisms and such candidates, goes the charge, the media deny them legitimacy in the public mind. Liberals accused the conservative watchdog Accuracy in Media of simply trying to pressure the media into adopting a more conservative tone, and soon a liberal group, Fairness and Accuracy in Reporting (FAIR) was formed to monitor conservative bias in the media and create pressure for better treatment of liberal views.

Ideological Leanings of Journalists. How can we judge the merits of these charges that emanate from opposite ends of the political spectrum? It is no easy task to figure out which way journalists lean. But a number of studies have attempted to do so.

Newspaper and television reporters are generally perceived as more liberal than conservative. Stephen Hess asked a sample group of Wash-

---

... a long-term effort by conservatives to show that the media, especially television, reflect an "Eastern-liberal media-establishment" bias.

The radical left, on the other hand, accuses the media of censoring out news that is critical of the capitalistic system and ignoring leftist candidates in the electoral process.

ington reporters whether the Washington press corps was politically biased. Half the sample agreed that the press corps had a liberal bias. However, when asked their own ideological leanings, 58 percent identified themselves as conservative or middle-of-the-road, versus only 42 percent who were liberal.[45] This suggests that reporters are not as liberal as is generally believed. Other studies, however, have reached the opposite conclusion.[46] A survey by the *Los Angeles Times* of 2,703 reporters, editors, and staffers on 621 newspapers found that 55 percent described themselves as liberal, compared to about 23 percent of the public generally.[47]

What reporters mean when they call themselves liberal or conservative, however, is not necessarily clear. The *Los Angeles Times* survey of 2703 journalists found them to be most liberal on social issues such as abortion, but there is reason to doubt that they are very liberal on economic issues of importance to lower-status people. They were no more likely than the general public to sympathize with labor unions, and they were less liberal than the general public on the question of using government to reduce income inequalities.[48] A 1981 survey of the political leanings of media elites on 20 separate questions found them to be split. Conservative biases predominated in responses to 11 of the 20 questions, while liberal biases predominated on only nine.[49]

However liberal the media might seem to be, the fact is that conservative viewpoints are strongly articulated every day. Television programs such as the *McLaughlin Group, Firing Line,* and *Crossfire,* and conservative personalities such as TV preacher Jerry Falwell reach millions of viewers on a regular basis. The liberal group Fairness and Accuracy in Reporting (FAIR) analyzed the guest list on the popular TV news analysis program *Nightline* and found a pervasive conservative bias. Only 7 percent of the guests represented public interest groups, while 80 percent represented government, business, or professional organizations. The guests who appeared most frequently were overwhelmingly conservative, with some of the most frequent guests being the conservative stalwarts Jerry Falwell, Henry Kissinger, and Alexander Haig. American critics of President Reagan's foreign policy were seldom invited to be guests. Not only were liberals rare among the guest lists, but few programs dealt with liberal issues. Of the 865 programs studied, only one program dealt with class conflict, only two with gender issues, and only 11 with racial conflict. *Nightline* host Ted Koppel admitted the conservative bias in his guest list but attributed it to the fact that conservatives were in power throughout the 1980s when the program aired, and his job was to interview those in power.[50]

Bias in Media Output. Even if reporters were as liberal as they are generally perceived to be, this does not necessarily mean that such views would stand out very prominently in their publications and broadcasts. What is printed and broadcast is ultimately not up to reporters but to teams of editors, producers, and executives who rewrite the copy that is filed by the reporter, or who may simply kill stories on certain topics. As a consequence, reporters who prize their jobs learn which kinds of stories to pursue and which to avoid. Columbia Broadcasting System news correspondent Leslie Stahl on a Bill Moyers PBS documentary frankly admitted that CBS news censored what she could cover and the terms under which she could report critically on the Reagan White House.[51]

Why do media executives censor the work of reporters in this way? There are many reasons, and they range from the honest exercise of professional judgment, to the desire not to offend a sensitive advertiser, to making the end-product conform to the political ideology of the company executives.

The concerns of advertisers are given much more weight by communications organizations than the average newspaper reader or television viewer would believe. Advertisers are the central revenue source for both newspapers and television stations, and if they have alternative outlets, advertisers are understandably reluctant to place large dollar amounts of advertising with newspapers or television stations that run news stories that might be costly to the advertisers. We saw earlier (p. 104) that even the nation's most prestigious newspaper, the *New York Times*, let its 1970s news stories on automobile safety be colored by the concerns of the automobile companies. In cities where a dominant industry reigns, it is very difficult for newspapers or television stations to run stories critical of that industry. Thus, the oil industry is treated very carefully by media in Texas, the auto industry by media in Michigan, and real estate development by the media in Phoenix. What the reporter reports may not necessarily wind up in the end-product you read in the newspaper or view on television.

We would not want to conclude that the *New York Times* or other reputable media giants consistently follow a path of distorting news coverage, but it is important to recognize that newspapers and television stations are businesses with economic interests to defend, and that that fact can influence how they present the news. Especially if lower-status collective action such as a strike might threaten the economic interests of a newspaper, it is unreasonable to expect the paper to present the news in a manner sympathetic to the lower-status people involved. Realizing this, the sophisticated citizen cannot rely exclusively on television and the daily newspapers for his or her information on important political issues. It is very important to branch out one's sources of information to include opinion magazines such as *The Nation* or the *Utne Reader* on the left, *National Review* on the right or from public television productions such as McNeill-Lehrer and Bill Moyers.

Media Concentration and Lower-Status Interests

One last way in which the media affect lower-status interests stems from the concentration of news gathering efforts. If thousands of information outlets competed with each other for peoples' attention, there would be a high possibility of overall media neutrality as the viewpoints of one organization conflicted with those of others. In fact, however, television news is dominated by the three giant broadcast networks (ABC, NBC, CBS) and the Cable News Network (CNN) which decide what national news will be sent to two-thirds of the homes in the country.[52] Most news stories are generated by what Stephen Hess calls an inner ring of twelve news organization. These include the three major television networks (ABC, NBC, CBS), the Cable News Network (CNN), the three major national news magazines (*Time, Newsweek*, and *U.S. News and World Reports*), three newspapers of national stature (*Washington Post, New York Times*, and *Wall Street Journal*), and the national wire services (The Associated Press and United Press International).[53]

The inner ring media not only decide what the news is, they also influence the thinking of other journalists. A survey of 1,933 newspaper and magazine journalists found that six of the seven newspapers and magazines they read most frequently were those of the inner-ring media (*Time, Newsweek, U.S. News, New York Times, Wall Street Journal*, and *Washington Post.*). The only non-inner-ring publication to make the top seven was the nonpolitical *Sports Illustrated.*[54]

This concentration of the media does not directly threaten lower status people, but it does indirectly affect them. The news you receive is generated by a very limited number of news organizations. As can be seen in the "Personal Side of Politics" illustration, most of the news presented to *Minneapolis Star Tribune* readers on a typical day was generated by inner-ring media giants such as the *Washington Post* and assorted news wire services. Only two of the eighteen articles were written by *Star Tribune* reporters. Almost 40 percent of the 16 pages allotted to the national and international news section was taken up by advertising. Not a single news story was picked up from labor newspapers, from alternative press publications such as *In These Times*, or

The Personal Side of Politics: Getting the News

A useful exercise that can help you discover the origins of the news you receive is simply to examine your daily newspaper. The two columns below on the left show how often various news sources were the origins for national or international stories or opinion pieces that appeared in my local newspaper on a typical summer day in 1991. If this newspaper were a person's only source of information about the world, he or she would learn little of the viewpoints expressed in the labor press or the alternative press. And most of this person's information would have been generated by inner or middle-ring media organizations. Your local newspaper may, perhaps, give a broader view of the world than mine does. To see if that is the case, the third column gives you a chance to apply this same analysis to your own daily newspaper.

Source of News Story	Number of Occurrences in:	
	Minneapolis Star Tribune	Your Newspaper
Associated Press	5	
Los Angeles Times	2	
Washington Post	1	
Other news wire services (e.g., Cox, Scripps-Howard)	8	
Star Tribune staff	2	
Total number of stories	18	
Locally written editorials	3	
Syndicated columns	3	
Op-ed. pieces picked up from *New York Times* and *Washington Post*	2	
Total pages of advertising	6	
Total pages in the national and international news section	16	

Source: *Minneapolis Star Tribune*, July 22, 1991.

from ideological news outlets of either the political left or the political right. Furthermore, about half of the stories originated either from press releases by government or private organizations, or from statements by governmental or established political leaders.

In short, the news that Minnesota readers scanned at breakfast that day essentially reflected the concerns of mainstream institutions oriented to the values and cares of upper-status Americans. There is nothing devious or conspiratorial about this. In fact, the *Minneapolis Star Tribune*, like most metropolitan dailies, goes out of its way to produce and print complimentary stories about racial minorities in the Twin Cities, about the gay community, about women's groups, about neighborhood organizations, about some labor leaders, and about virtually any conceivable group that does anything commendable or out of the ordinary. But on broader national issues of eco-

Most of the news you consume is generated by upper-status institutions oriented to upper-status concerns. For this reason it is absolutely imperative to broaden your news sources if you want to be a sophisticated citizen.

nomics and politics, the vast majority of stories are generated by mainstream news-gathering organizations of a fairly narrow ideological spectrum.

This analysis of one day in the *Minneapolis Star Tribune* is consistent with an analysis of the sources of news stories that appeared in the *New York Times* and the *Washington Post* in the early 1970s. Fully three-fourths of those stories originated from official government agencies, either American or foreign. Less than one percent of stories originated from a reporter's own analysis.[55]

What this means to you as a consumer of news is that you must be alert to the fact that a lot of developments important to lower-status people do not appear as news. Most of the news you consume is generated by upper-status institutions oriented to upper-status concerns. For this reason it is absolutely imperative to broaden your news sources if you want to be a sophisticated citizen.

Overcoming Bias

It is very difficult for individuals to overcome the impact political socialization and media bias have on them. There are, nevertheless, several habits you can develop which will give you a more sophisticated appreciation for contemporary events and how they are presented by the media.

1. Broaden your sources of information.
2. Be skeptical of news stories based on anonymous sources.
3. Become aware of code words such as "going fishing" or "military leader vs. military strongman" that can easily be used to create a negative impression of events or people.
4. Ask how a news organization's treatment of a story relates to its economic interest.
5. Look for the sources behind news stories.
6. Check your peers carefully to see how they interpret the news.
7. Discuss the news with people who disagree with you as well as those who agree.
8. Be a watchdog at your school to see how the sieve works.

Conclusion _____

This chapter explored how the lower-status population is affected more than the upper-status population by political socialization and the media. It is important to note that there is nothing conspiratorial about this process. It is simply that the socialization process and the media reflect the dominant values of society, and in American society—as in most societies—the concerns of upper-status people carry more weight than do those of lower-status people. There are several ways in which socialization and the media work to the disadvantage of lower-status people.

First, the major agents of political socialization—the family, schools, and peer groups—tend to downplay the value of political participation among lower-status people. This message is reinforced by the media, which give a fairly negative treatment of lower-status political movements and of lower-status life in general.

Second, the greater difficulty that lower-strata people have in sorting out their economic self-interest is compounded by the differences between the way they and the upper-strata use the media. Lower-strata people depend more on television for information about the world than upper-strata people do, and they are much less likely to read newspapers daily, or to read political opinion magazines. It was argued earlier that the pervasiveness of sound-bite television and visual demagoguery serve to dull the critical-thinking habits of the public. If this argument is accurate, the critical-thinking habits of the lower strata are dulled more than are those of the upper strata. There is very little on network television news that would stimulate lower-strata viewers to examine political events from the standpoint of their economic self-interest.

Third, the high levels of political alienation and political withdrawal among the lower-strata people work to their disadvantage. The more they withdraw, the more politics are left in the hands of people with entirely different economic self-interest.

Finally, there is a systemic bias in the process of producing television news. The excessive reliance on visual demagoguery and sound-bite journalism, it was argued, dulls the viewing public's ability to think critically. The net impact of this is that it lowers the quality and level of public discourse about major issues of foreign relations, international economic competition, and the national welfare as we move toward the twenty-first century. Lowering the level of public discourse as we enter a critical turning point in the nation's history probably is to no one's advantage, rich or poor. But it is especially hard on lower-status people because they depend on the electronic media for their information and for helping to form their opinions.

Summary _____

1. Political beliefs are acquired through the process of political socialization, especially through the family, the schools, and peer groups, the primary agents of political socialization. Upper-strata people are socialized into a much more participatory role than are lower-strata people.

2. The electronic news media have a structural bias in favor of drama and visual demagoguery. To the extent that this structural bias inhibits television from focusing on public issues in a meaningful way, it imposes a burden on the lower-strata population, because those people are more dependent on television than are upper-strata people.

3. The news media generally give a negative portrayal of lower-status political movements, especially organized labor.

4. Entertainment television also portrays lower-status life-styles very negatively. Entertainment television and news television combine to reinforce political alienation among the lower strata and to inhibit participation in strikes, demonstrations, or protest activities.

5. The high level of concentration of media ownership means that most news originates from a very narrow section of the American political spectrum.

Notes _____

1. Fred Greenstein, *Children and Politics* (New Haven: Yale University Press, 1965), especially pp. 71–73. Greenstein found that almost two-thirds of children identified with a political party as early as the fourth grade.

2. An examination of high school social studies texts, for example, found that they stressed the strengths of the American political system, downplayed its weaknesses, generally portrayed communism unfavorably, and seldom examined the pitfalls of capitalism. See C. Benjamin Cox and Byron G. Massialas, *Social Studies in the United States* (New York: Harcourt, Brace and World, 1967).

3. William H. Grier and Price M. Cobbs, *Black Rage* (New York: Basic Books, Inc., Publishers, 1968), pp. 62–63.

4. Edgar Litt, "Civic Education, Community Norms, and Political Indoctrination," *American Sociological Review*, 28, no. 1 (February 1963): 69–75.

5. See Jonathan Kozol, *Death at an Early Age: The Destruction of the Hearts and Minds of Negro Children in the Boston Public Schools* (Boston: Houghton Mifflin, 1967); Bel Kaufman, *Up the Down Staircase* (Englewood Cliffs, N.J.: Prentice-Hall, 1964); Robert Coles, *Teachers and the Children of Poverty* (Washington, D.C.: Potomac Institute, 1970); Herbert Kohl, *36 Children* (New York: New American Library, 1967).

6. Mario Fantini and Marilyn Gittell, *Decentralization: Achieving Reform* (New York: Praeger, 1973), pp. 48, 53–55.

7. Ibid.

8. John J. Harrigan, *Politics and Policy in States and Communities*, 4th ed. (New York: Harper, Collins Publishers, 1991), p. 409.

9. See a series of articles by Steve D. Williams in the *Comparative State Politics Newsletter*: "Alexander's Master Teacher Program Fails in Tennessee," 4, no. 3 (May 1983): 11–12; "Master Teacher Program Update," 4, no. 6 (December 1983): 21; "The First Year of Merit Pay for Tennessee Teachers," 6, no. 5 (October 1985): 33; and "The Politics of Merit Pay for Tennessee Teachers," 10, no. 5 (October 1989): 52–63.

10. David M. Gordon, *Problems in Political Economy: An Urban Perspective*, 2nd ed. (Lexington, Mass.: D. C. Heath, 1977), p. 213.

11. *The Autobiography of Malcolm X* (New York: Grove Press, Inc., 1965), p. 36.

12. In 1983 Boston started a program called the Boston Compact which made it a graduation requirement for students to have held a part-time job between the end of their sophomore year and graduation. Joel Spring, "From Study Hall to Hiring Hall," *The Progressive* 48, no. 4 (April 1984): 31.

13. See Alexander M. Astin, *Four Critical Years: Effects of College on Beliefs, Attitudes, and Knowledge* (San Francisco: Jossey-Bass, 1978), p. 38.

14. Frank J. Sorauf and Paul Allen Beck, *Party Politics in America*, 6th ed. (Glenview, Ill.: Scott, Foresman and Co., 1988), p. 175.

15. Austin Ranney, *Channels of Power: The Impact of Television on American Politics* (New York: Basic Books, 1983).

16. Richard M. Cohen, "Good Morning Journalism," *Mother Jones* 13, no. 6 (July/August 1988): 12.

17. Leslie Stahl interviewed by Bill Moyers on the Bill Moyers special *Images*, part 4; broadcast, Fall 1989.

18. Kiku Adatto, "Shrinking Sound Bites Put Voters on a Starvation Diet," *Minneapolis Star Tribune*, December 17, 1989, p. 30A. Originally a *New York Times* op. ed. piece.

19. Ranney, *Channels of Power*, p. 116.

20. Hedrick Smith, *The Power Game: How Washington Works* (New York: Ballantine Books, 1989), p. 41.

21. See *General Social Surveys, 1972–1989: Machine Readable Data File* (Chicago, Ill.: The National Opinion Research Center, University of Chicago,1989). In the 1989 survey, 61.9 percent of lowest-strata people watched three or more hours of television per day as contrasted to only 34.4 percent of those in the upper strata.

22. Schneider and Lewis, "Views on the News," p. 7.

23. Michael Parenti, *Inventing Reality: The Politics of the Mass Media* (New York: St. Martin's Press, 1986), p. 15.

24. Ibid., p. 48.

25. Ibid., pp. 81–83.

26. *New York Times*, April 5, 1991, p. A8. The U.S. Labor Department indicated in 1991 that 40 percent of all coal mines under surveillance had devices that had been tampered with in ways that would make it seem that coal-dust levels were safe when they were unsafe. The Department levied $5 million in fines on 500 companies, an average of $10,000 per company. This amounted to little more than a slap on the wrist, according to labor advocates.

27. *Wall Street Journal*, March 16, 1978.

28. *Time*, March 20, 1978.

29. Curtis Selzer, "The Pits: Press Coverage of a Coal Strike," *Columbia Journalism Review* (July/August 1981).

30. Parenti, *Inventing Reality* p. 82.

31. *Washington Post*, March 6, 1978.

32. *New York Times*, March 28, 1978.

33. *Newsweek*, March 20, 1978.

34. *Time*, March 6, 1978.

35. *New York Times*, December 4, 1977 and March 5, 1978.

36. Parenti, *Inventing Reality,* pp. 82–83.

37. Jonathan Tasini, *Lost in the Margins: Labor and the Media*, A Special FAIR Report (Washington, D.C.: Fairness and Accuracy in Reporting, September 1990), pp. 7–9.

38. *Wall Street Journal*, April 2, 1981.

39. *Newsweek*, April 13, 1981.

40. Parenti, *Inventing Reality*, pp. 76–77.

41. Ishmael Reed, "Tuning Out Network Bias," *New York Times*, April 9, 1991, p. A11.

42. See Bernard Barber, *The Logic and Limits of Trust* (New Brunswick: Rutgers University Press, 1983), pp. 92–93.

43. *Newsweek*, November 9, 1970, p. 22.

44. For a coherent articulation of these charges see Edward S. Herman and Noam Chomsky, *Manufacturing Consent: The Political Economy of the Mass Media* (New York: Pantheon Books, 1989). Herman and Chomsky argue that there are five institutional mechanisms in the media that serve as filters to impose considerable censorship on what the media reports. These five filters are: the concentration of ownership, the important influence of advertisers, the narrow reliance on a few government and corporate officials as news sources, flak created by right-wing media watchers, and an ideology of anti-communism shared by most of the high executives in the newspaper and television business.

45. Hess, *The Washington Reporters*.

46. S. Robert Lichter and Stanley Rothman, "Media and Business Elites," *Public Opinion* (October/November 1981): 42–46, 59–60. This article has been heavily criticized for methodological shortcomings. See Herbert J. Gans, "Are U.S. Journalists Dangerously Liberal?" *Columbia Journalism Review* 24, no. 1 (November/December 1984): 29–33.

47. William Schneider and I. A. Lewis, "Views on the News," *Public Opinion* 8 (August/September 1985): 7.

48. Ibid.

49. *Public Opinion* (October/November 1981): 44.

50. "Are You on the Nightline Guest List?" *Extra! A Publication of FAIR (Fairness & Accuracy in Reporting)* 2, no. 4 (January/February 1989): 1–15.

51. Leslie Stahl interviewed by Bill Moyers on the Bill Moyers special *Images*, part 4; Broadcast, Fall 1989.

52. Doris Graber, *Mass Media and American Politics*, 2nd ed. (Washington, D.C.: Congressional Quarterly, 1989), p. 52. Data was for 1987, down from 91 percent market share a decade earlier.

53. Steven Hess, *The Washington Reporters* (Washington, D.C.: Brookings Institution, 1981). Hess did not include CNN, but its growth in recent years would certainly give it a place among the inner ring today. Also, the UPI has been struggling with bankruptcy for much of the 1980s and may soon drop out of the inner ring. The most likely candidate to replace UPI would be the *Los Angeles Times*.

54. G. Cleveland Wilhoit and David H. Weaver, *The American Journalist: A Portrait of the U.S. News People and Their Work* (Bloomington: Indiana University Press, 1986), pp. 34, 37.

55. W. Lance Bennett, *News: The Politics of Illusion* (New York: Longman, 1983), pp. 53–54.

CHAPTER 5

Staying in Place: How Patterns of Participation and Ideology Foster Lower-Status Subordination

A very useful demonstration of political participation occurred in 1989. Congress passed a plan to provide catastrophic health insurance for the elderly, but at the cost of an increase in their Medicare premiums to pay for the plan. People do not like their costs going up, however, and senior citizens groups around the country staged noisy protests against the increase. To express their displeasure, one group of seniors surrounded the automobile of the House tax-writing chairman, Daniel Rostenkowski, pounded on the car's hood, and belligerently impeded his route. The angry seniors also pointed out quite boldly that they have high voter turnout rates and are capable of punishing politicians they dislike. Faced with this rebellion, Congress backed down and reversed its action.

Political participation seldom brings such an immediate reaction from government. If seniors had failed to participate in those demonstrations, however, and if they had had a history of non-voting rather than voting, it is doubtful that Congress would have been so quick to respond to their demands.

And this leads us to a general principle of politics: Although political participation will not bring a category of people everything they want, *the lack of participation* will almost certainly ensure that they get very little of what they want. To give two historical examples, it is inconceivable that Congress would have passed the civil rights and voting rights legislation of the 1960s, had it not been for the active participation of millions of blacks in the civil rights movement over the previous decade. It is also highly unlikely that political leaders around the country would pay as much attention as they do to women's issues if women were still denied the right to vote.

> Although political participation will not bring a category of people everything they want, *the lack of participation* will almost certainly ensure that they will get very little of what they want.

A major political problem facing lower-status people is that they have the lowest participation rates of any income category. Clearly, increased participation would not solve the economic problems of lower-status people, for many of their problems lie beyond the political arena. But the federal and state governments would be much more attentive to their problems if lower-status citizens were as consistently astute about their political interests as the senior citizens were about paying for catastrophic health insurance.

What this chapter will argue is that lower-status people suffer in the political arena because they lack sufficient political participation and a coherent vision of how to further their economic self-interest. We will do this by examining the following: (1) how different types of political activity form a hierarchy of participation, (2) how participation rates of the lower strata compare to the upper strata, (3) how lower-strata and upper-strata people view political ideology, (4) how lower-strata people differ from upper-strata people on key political issues, and (5) how the lack of a coherent political philosophy undermines the lower strata's political participation and reinforces their subordinate political role.

Participation and Subordination _____

Political participation refers to a wide variety of individual or group activities that seek to influence the selection or actions of government officials.[1] These activities form a hierarchy that ranges from the simple act of voting to the complex and demanding activities of campaigning for office and lobbying public officials. As Table 5–1 shows, the more demanding the participation is in terms of time and energy, the fewer the number of people who want to participate.

The Lower-Status Participation Gap _____

Not only is there a drop-off in participation rates as the type of participation gets more difficult, there is a huge gap between the participation of lower-status people and upper-status people. This is shown

TABLE 5-1 Types of Political and Community Participation

Activities Requiring Little Initiative	**Percent Saying They Did That Activity**
Voted in 1988	66.6
Ever contributed money to a group	63.2
Read a newspaper every day	32.6
Ever contributed to a political candidate or a political cause	21.4
Activities Requiring Greater Initiative	
Ever worked with others to solve some local community problem	33.4
Ever contacted a local government official about a problem	32.7
Ever worked for a political party or candidate in an election	27.7
Attended a political meeting in the last 3 or 4 years	19.5
Ever contacted government officials on behalf of a group	18.1
Ever picketed in a labor strike	10.5
Ever took part in a civil rights demonstration	4.5

Source: James Allan Davis and Tom W. Smith: *General Social Surveys, 1972–1989* [machine-readable data file]. Principal Investigator, James A. Davis; Director and Co-Principal Investigator, Tom W. Smith. NORC ed. Chicago: National Opinion Research Center, Producer, 1989; Storrs, CT: The Roper Center for Public Opinion Research, University of Connecticut, Distributor.

in Figure 5-1, which graphs participation rates in the least demanding type of activity, voting in the presidential election. The poorest and least-educated people vote far less frequently than the more affluent and better-educated citizens. Of these two variables of income and education, most research concludes that education is the more powerful. Lower-status people vote less frequently than upper-status people not because they have less money but because they have less education.[2] They are less likely to have been socialized at home and at school to participate, and less likely to have the confidence and communications skills needed to engage in community organizing, campaign work, and lobbying.

But there is more involved than low education levels. Education levels have risen since the 1960s, but voting turnout rates have gone down. If education alone could explain voting turnout, turnout should have risen as education levels rose.[3] Furthermore, the biggest drop-off in voter turnout has been among the young, the people who have had the largest increase in education levels. From 1972 to 1984, voting turnout rates were virtually unchanged for middle-aged people (ages 45–64) and actually increased for the least-educated age group, those over 65. By contrast, turnout rates dropped from 59 percent to 54 percent among the highly educated 25- to 34-year-olds.[4] Because of these patterns of education and turnout, we must examine some other barriers to lower-status participation: psychological, historical, legal–political, and organizational.

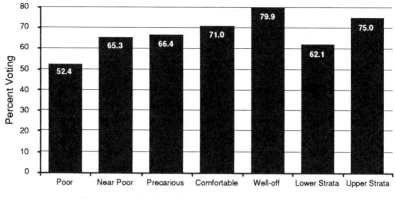

Figure 5-1 Voting Turnout by Income Status

Psychological Barriers to Lower-Status Participation

As noted, lower-status people are less likely than upper-status people to have been socialized in their early upbringing to participate. They are also less likely than upper-strata people to have internalized a sense of civic duty to participate.[5] They are less apt to work in professions (such as the law, teaching, management), which would give them extensive experience in verbal, analytical, or human management skills. For this reason, persuasion tactics, organizing activities, and promoting cooperative solutions to common problems do not come as second nature to the lower status as they do to many in the upper strata. And the lower strata are likely to lack a highly developed sense of political efficacy. This is a term that political scientists use for a person's belief that participating in politics can have an impact. The lower the sense of one's political efficacy the less likely one is to participate.[6]

Historical Barriers to Lower-Status Participation

If we refer to the last three decades of the nineteenth century, we find that voter turnout rates among the lower-status population were high. Overall turnout of the eligible adult population in presidential elections never dropped below 70 percent from 1868 to 1910. After 1910 it began to drop sharply and never again reached its late-nineteenth-century levels.

It is no accident, say Frances Fox Piven and Richard Cloward,[7] that voter turnout began dropping about that time. Two interrelated developments started in the 1880s that would drive voter turnout rates down. These were progressive reforms in the North and anti-black laws in the South.

Targeting Lower-Status Northern Whites. In the North, progressive reformers sought strenuously to curb the political influence that lower-status immigrants and white ethnics had achieved through the big-city political machines.[8] It is easy to see why progressive reformers wanted to do this. Progressive reformers were refined, upper-status professionals and businessmen who resented their cities being dominated by the unrefined lower-status people who ran the political machines. What the reformers were up against could be seen in an analysis of the backgrounds of the delegates to the 1896 Cook County (Chicago) Democratic convention.

A Cook County convention of 1896—held, it may be well to remember, before the Illinois legislature had undertaken mandatory reform—indicates the appalling degradation that might be observed occasionally in the politics of the period. Among 732 delegates, 17 had been tried for homicide, 46 had served terms in the penitentiary for homicide or other felonies, 84 were identified by detectives as having criminal records. Considerably over a third of the delegates were saloon-keepers; two kept houses of ill fame; several kept gambling resorts. There were eleven former pugilists and fifteen former policemen.*[9]

It is also not hard to understand why reformers' calls for change had such a seductive appeal to the broader population. Most of the political machines stuffed the ballot boxes as a matter of course. In one Chicago ward in that same 1896 election, for example:

The bars were open all night and the brothels were jammed. By ten o'clock the next morning, though, the saloons were shut down, not in concession to the reformers, but because many of the bartenders and owners were needed to staff the First Ward field organization. The Bath, Hinky Dink and their aides ran busily from polling place to polling place, silver bulging in their pockets into which they dug frequently and deeply.[10]

Party workers often made the rounds of different polling places to vote in each. So common was this practice that even anthropologist William Foote Whyte used it while conducting research as a participant observer in Boston for his classic book, *Street Corner Society*.[11] As long as machine bosses controlled the immigrant vote through such devices as these, upper-status reformers could not hope to defeat the machines. Hence the introduction of secret ballots, election judges, campaign fair-practice laws, and voter registration, all in the hope of severing the political bonds between the lower-status immigrants and

---

*The author commented, "The policemen of Chicago at that period were not highly regarded."

the machine bosses. By making registration difficult, establishing long residency requirements for registration, requiring registration to be done several weeks or months in advance of the election, and by requiring frequent reregistration, voter registration laws inhibited voter turnout. These laws necessarily impacted the upper-status population less than the lower-status population, with its high concentration of renters who were more likely to move frequently than were home owners.

Targeting Southern Blacks. In looking at the South, the motives of voter registration reformers were even more obviously aimed at reducing voter turnout, especially among blacks. In the 1880s, a populist movement was gaining strength among small farmers, and in 1892 the Populist candidate for president even won 8 percent of the vote. If white Populists had coalesced with black Republicans, they would have posed a considerable threat to the dominant economic and political elites in the South. Voting turnout among black Southerners was actually quite high until the 1890s. One historian estimated that 60 percent of black adult men voted in presidential contests in the South from 1876 through 1892. By 1920 that had dropped to zero. Not only did the new registration requirements bring an end to black voting in the South, they severely crimped voting among poor whites as well, thus putting an end to the Populist threat. An estimated 69 percent of Southern whites had voted in the presidential elections between 1876 and 1892, and that dropped to 32 percent by 1920.[12] One witness to the attempts of poor illiterate whites to pass the literacy barriers gave a poignant account of its impact on the people involved.

> It was painful and pitiful to see the horror and dread visible on the faces of the illiterate poor white men who were waiting to take their turn before the inquisition. . . . This was horrible to behold, but it was still more horrible to see the marks of humiliation and despair that were stamped on the faces of honest but poor white men who had been refused registration and who had been robbed of their citizenship without cause. We saw them as they came from the presence of the registrars with bowed heads and agonized faces; and when they spoke, in many instances, there was a tear in the voice of the humiliated citizen.[13]

What happened between 1892 and 1920 was the widespread implementation of a voter registration system combined with literacy tests, poll taxes, white primaries, and other devices that sought to disenfranchise the blacks but also disenfranchised many poor whites. The poll tax reduced turnout among minorities and the poor, because it had to be paid each election year and it accumulated for each year it was not paid. In a short time, one could owe a considerable amount of money just for the right to vote. The poll tax was finally outlawed by the Twenty-fourth Amendment, in 1964.

There was also a widespread requirement that citizens pass literacy tests before being allowed to register to vote. These were usually conducted in a blatantly discriminatory fashion. In some instances, blacks with graduate degrees were failed on the test. In other instances, black applicants would be given abstruse passages of the state constitution to interpret. Some states passed a grandfather clause which exempted people from the literacy test if they had a grandfather who had voted in 1866. This obviously was designed to exempt whites but not blacks from the literacy tests, and it was struck down by the Supreme Court in 1915. Other states, such as Texas, had a white primary. Blacks were allowed to vote in the general election but not in the primary election of the Democratic Party. Because Texas was a one-party Democratic state, the Democratic primary really determined who was elected to office. White primaries were declared unconstitutional in 1944.[14] When the number of black voters became large enough to determine local elections, communities sometimes changed their boundaries or gerrymandered election districts to dilute the impact of black voters. The most flagrant example took place in Tuskegee, Alabama, which in the 1950s changed its boundaries from the shape of a square to a twenty-eight-sided polygon in order to dilute the impact of black voting in city elections. This was struck down by the Supreme Court in 1960.[15]

The key to ending these blatant forms of voter discrimination was the Voting Rights Act of 1965 which we examined in Chapter 2. This law and its later amendments effectively eliminated the literacy test, allowed federal registrars to register voters in counties with evidence of racial discrimination, and prohibited changes in election laws or municipal boundaries without prior federal approval in places where previous discrimination had been shown to exist.

Legal and Political Barriers Today

It is fair to ask if these voter registration measures still reduce voter turnout. There are many reasons why some people fail to vote, and difficulty in registering is only one of them. The voter registration reforms took place a century ago, and the most flagrant ones, such as literacy tests, poll taxes, and long residency requirements, have been

---

One historian estimated that 60 percent of black adult men voted in presidential contests in the South from 1876 through 1892. By 1920 that had dropped to zero.

eliminated. In some states you can now register on election day itself, with only a thirty-day residency requirement and no more proof of identification than a driver's license or a friend to vouch for you.

There is still reason to believe, however, that registration laws themselves restrict voter turnout. Each state sets its own registration requirements, and consistently in election after election the highest turnout rates occur in the states with the least-rigid requirements. Raymond E. Wolfinger and Steven J. Rosenstone examined voting turnouts in all 50 states and estimated that voting turnout would be increased by nine percentage points if all states relaxed their voter registration laws to the level of the laws of the most lenient states.[16] The real trick is to get people registered. Once they are registered they tend to vote. Eighty-five percent of people who are registered, in fact, do vote in presidential elections, but voter turnout is brought down because so few people register. In 1988, only 69 percent of eligible voters were registered.[17] One of the categories of people most vulnerable to losing their registration is that of the people who move in the summer or fall prior to an election. To increase registration among people who move, Congress in 1990 deliberated on a National Voter Registration Act that would have permitted their voter registration to be transferred automatically to their new address through the use of driver's license records and U.S. Post Office change of address records, and cancelled their registration at their previous address. This bill passed the House of Representatives but did not make it through the Senate.

Organizational Barriers to Lower-Status Participation

Another important factor in political participation is the existence of organizations that mobilize people to participate. The senior citizens who rebelled against paying for catastrophic health insurance coverage, for example, did not simply show up spontaneously at demonstrations around the country. There is a network of senior citizen organizations around the nation that actively recruit participants. There is also a strong relationship between belonging to organizations and voting.[18] People who belong to churches, labor unions, social service clubs, or civic groups are deluged with messages not only urging them to vote but often also suggesting for whom they should vote. The more politically oriented the organization, obviously, the more forceful will be its impact on voter turnout.[19] Since membership in organizations is much more typical among upper-strata people than among the lower strata, lower-strata people receive fewer messages urging them to vote and participate.

The dynamics of organizations in mobilizing voter turnout was illustrated in a study comparing West Virginia counties with neighboring Virginia counties of a similar socioeconomic character. The West Virginians voted much more regularly than the Virginians because for many decades labor unions had organized the West Virginia coal miners and instilled in them the habit of voting. In contrast, in Virginia, politics were dominated by a political organization called the Byrd Machine, named after U.S. Senator Harry F. Byrd, which discouraged participation because it thrived on low voter turnouts.[20] Another study found that black voting in Mississippi increased when federal voting examiners moved in to register blacks and outside organizers showed up to mobilize them to go to the polls.[21]

Voters can also be mobilized by voter registration drives, especially minorities such as blacks and Hispanics.[22] A study of such drives in Houston in1976 found not only that voter registration drives increased turnout that year but that the drive had long-term impacts as well: Most of the people who registered during the 1976 voter registration drive also turned out to vote in the elections four years alter.[23]

Summary of the Participation Gap

Several factors combine to reduce voter turnout rates and other forms of political participation among lower-status people. Their early-life socialization experiences do not foster participation to the degree that such socialization does among the upper strata. Their lower levels of education probably combine with other psychological factors to inhibit their sense of civic duty and the sense of political efficacy that would encourage participation. There probably is still a residue of nonparticipatory attitudes remaining from the decades-long discriminatory barriers that prohibited black voting. Voter registration laws reduce turnout as much as 9 percent from what it would otherwise be, and most of this reduction occurs among lower-status people. And finally, because they belong to fewer organizations, lower-status people experience less organizational pressure to vote than upper-status people.

The reduced levels of political participation work to keep lower-status people in their place. While full participation would not transform the political system, there is no doubt that lack of participation makes the system less responsive. It is unlikely, for example, that Congress would have passed civil rights legislation and affirmative action legislation had blacks not participated in the civil rights movement. It is unlikely that political leaders would support abortion rights if women did not vote. And it is unlikely that Congress would have reversed the catastrophic health insurance fee had it not been for their political participation of senior citizens.

The reduced levels of political participation work to keep lower-status people in their place. While full participation would not transform the political system, there is no doubt that lack of participation makes the system less responsive.

Political Ideology and Lower-Status Subordination

Not only do low participation rates help keep lower-status people politically subordinate, but the context of their thinking about politics does so also. A major conclusion of Chapter 4 was that upper-status elites go to extraordinary lengths to influence the thinking of lower-status people. Therefore it is not unreasonable to question whether the political ideas of lower-status people are consistent with their economic self-interest.

A Tendency Toward the Middle

Aristotle, who preached moderation in all things, would have been proud of the average American's political views. Most Americans reject ideological extremes. Figure 5–2 shows the results of a 1989 interview that asked a representative sample of Americans to define themselves in one of seven categories, ranging from extremely liberal on the left to extremely conservative on the right. Of the people who did so, 39

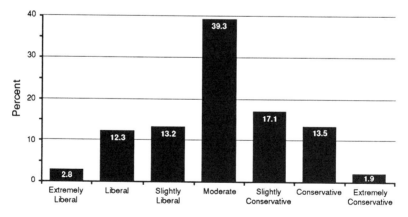

Figure 5-2 Ideological Spectrum

Source: James Allen Davis: *General Social Surveys, 1972–89* [Machine-readable data file]. Principal Investigator, James A. Davis; Senior Study Director, Tom W. Smith, NORC, ed, Chicago: National Opinion Research Center Producer, 1989; Storrs, CT: Roper Center for Public Opinion Research, University of Connecticut, Distributor.

percent called themselves moderates or middle-of-the-roaders. If the people leaning slightly to the left or right can be counted in the middle-of-the-road category, then a whopping 69 percent of Americans think of themselves as moderate or leaning slightly to the left or the right, and only 30 percent of the population defines itself sharply as either liberal or conservative. Not only did this 1989 interview find that most Americans cluster around the middle of the ideological spectrum, but the same tendency has existed for years. During some periods, such as the early 1970s, there were a few more people on the left side of the spectrum than there are today, and during the early 1980s there were a few more people on the right side of the spectrum than there are today.[24] But whenever pollsters ask the question, the general results are the same: the vast majority of Americans place themselves in the middle of the ideological spectrum.

Lower Strata Less Ideological and Less Conservative

Table 5-2 breaks down these results for the lower and upper-strata populations as well as for each of the five income categories we discussed in Chapter 1. Four patterns are evident in Table 5-2. First, this table clearly shows that lower-strata people are less ideologically inclined than upper-strata people. While 40.2 percent of lower-strata

TABLE 5-2   Ideology by Income Strata

	The Lower-Status Population			The Upper-Status Population	
	Poor	**Near-Poor**	**Financially Precarious**	**Comfortable**	**Well-Off**
Liberal	31.9% Total for entire lower strata 28.9	28.8%	26.7%	26.0% Total for entire upper strata 27.8	29.9%
Moderate	37.2 Total for entire lower strata 40.2	43.0	39.1	41.0 Total for entire upper strata 35.9	29.9
Conservative	30.9 Total for entire lower strata 30.8	28.1	34.2	33.0 Total for entire upper strata 36.4	40.3
N =	188	302	243	312	268

$X^2 = 16.145$ p$<$.05

Source: James Allen Davis: *General Social Surveys, 1972–89* [Machine-readable data file]. Principal Investigator, James A. Davis; Senior Study Director, Tom W. Smith, NORC, ed, Chicago: National Opinion Research Center Producer, 1989; Storrs, CT: Roper Center for Public Opinion Research, University of Connecticut, Distributor.

people considered themselves moderates, only 35.9 percent of upper-strata people did so. Lower-status people are also less conservative. Only 30.8 percent of them considered themselves conservatives, but a much larger 36.4 percent considering themselves conservatives, and 29.9 percent liberals.

A second pattern evident in Table 5-2 is that few people in the poor and near-poor categories are attracted to conservatism. A third pattern is that the ideology of the most prosperous of the lower strata (the financially precarious) resembles the upper-status comfortables more than it does the ideology of the rest of the lower strata. The financially precarious are the least likely of the lower strata to call themselves liberals and the most likely to call themselves conservatives. Finally, liberals show up most frequently among the very poor and the very well-off. These last two patterns, we will see shortly, cause sharp political problems among liberal Democrats.

In general, however, Table 5-2 shows that the ideological differences between lower and upper-strata people are not great. The mass of the American population is not divided sharply along ideological lines.

More Liberal on Close-to-Home Economic Issues

Just what Table 5-2 means in concrete terms is confused, however, because the terms liberal and conservative are not clear: They are heavily value-laden terms, and mean many different things to many different people. Hence, when people are asked to identify their political ideology in general terms, the easiest response is to take refuge in saying that they are middle-of-the-road or lean only slightly to conservatism or liberalism. When asked, however, about their views on specific issues that strike close to home, most people have a very definite opinion, and many feel strongly about those opinions. To examine differences in political thinking between lower and upper-strata people, we have to examine their opinions on specific political issues. And if you will be patient enough to bear with two more complicated illustrations, we can do this by looking at Tables 5-3 and 5-4.

Table 5-3 shows that lower-status people generally are liberal when it comes to having the federal government spend more money on Social Security, reducing the income gap between the rich and the poor, and a number of domestic problems ranging from the nation's health system to the environment. The only issues in the table that do not command majority support for greater spending are mass transportation and welfare. This does not mean that the American public is opposed to programs that help poor people; it just means that they do not like programs called "welfare." This was evident in a *New York Times*/CBS poll in 1978, which showed that 58 percent of the people surveyed were opposed to government welfare programs. Yet when the question was

TABLE 5-3 Differences on Domestic Spending Preferences by Income Strata

We're spending too little on:	The Lower-Status Population		Financially	The Upper-Status Population	
	Poor	Near-Poor	Precarious	Comfortable	Well-Off
Social Security	60.7%	63.0%	60.0%	52.4%	45.6%
	Total for entire lower strata 61.4			Total for entire upper strata 49.3	
Reducing income gap between rich and poor	55.4	68.1	54.7	56.4	30.4
	Total for entire lower strata 59.8			Total for entire upper strata 48.7	
Welfare	40.0	21.3	26.3	18.6	16.7
	Total for entire lower strata 28.2			Total for entire upper strata 17.7	
Improving the nation's health	Total for entire lower strata 73.6			Total for entire upper strata 68.9	
Dealing with drug addiction	74.8	73.9	75.4	72.2	69.2
	Total for entire lower strata 74.6			Total for entire upper strata 70.8	
Problems of big cities	56.5	57.1	55.8	52.6	51.2
	Total for entire lower strata 56.5			Total for entire upper strata 52.0	
Mass Transportation	33.7	33.2	31.5	31.1	36.5
	Total for entire lower strata 32.8			Total for entire upper strata 33.6	
Improving the nation's education	64.1	67.3	73.8	74.5	72.4
	Total for entire lower strata 68.6			Total for entire upper strata 73.5	
Improving the environment	68.3	70.6	78.0	79.3	81.6
	Total for entire lower strata 72.2			Total for entire upper strata 80.4	

Source: James Allen Davis, *General Social Surveys, 1972–89.*

reworded so that it described welfare programs without using the word "welfare," overwhelming numbers of people expressed support. Eighty-one percent supported a program to help poor people buy food at reduced prices (the Food Stamp Program), 81 percent supported giving financial aid for children in low-income, one-parent homes (the AFDC program), and 82 percent supported paying the health costs of the poor (the Medicaid program).[25]

Not only is the American public liberal on most questions of economic policy, but there are sharp differences between the views of the lower strata and the upper strata on Social Security, reducing the income gap, and welfare. On these issues, the lower-status population is significantly more liberal than the upper-status population, and es-

TABLE 5-4   Differences on Social Policy by Income Strata

| Important Issues in Recent Presidential Elections | | | Percent Giving a Liberal Response: | | | | |
| | | | Lower Strata | | | Upper Strata | |
Issue	Lower Strata	Upper Strata	Poor	Near-Poor	Financially Precarious	Comfortable	Well-Off
Capital punishment	Conservative	Conservative	29.6	23.6	20.8	19.4	17.9
Require prayer in public school	Liberal	Liberal	74.3	62.2	56.2	50.0	50.6
Permit abortion for any reason	Conservative	Liberal	25.4	33.8	38.7	50.5	51.1

| Issues of Tolerance and Civil Liberties | | | Percent Giving a Liberal Response: | | | | |
| | | | Lower Strata | | | Upper Strata | |
Issue	Lower Strata	Upper Strata	Poor	Near-Poor	Financially Precarious	Comfortable	Well-Off
Would permit an advocate of each of the following to teach in college:							
Homosexuality	Liberal	Liberal	55.0	60.5	64.3	75.6	78.7
Communism	Conservative	Liberal	43.1	52.1	51.0	61.3	65.5
Atheism	Conservative	Liberal	40.9	46.7	58.7	55.7	68.2
Letting the military run the country	Conservative	Liberal	31.3	35.2	43.1	47.8	56.6

| Issues of Race (Responses Only of Whites) | | | Percent Giving a Liberal Response: | | | | |
| | | | | | Financially | Com- | |
Issue	Lower Strata	Upper Strata	Poor	Near-Poor	Precarious	fortable	Well-Off
Busing to desegregate public schools	Conservative	Conservative	33.3	27.5	23.0	26.0	21.5
Assert we are spending too little to improve condition of blacks	Conservative	Conservative	23.5	25.2	36.5	32.3	28.6
Would send their child to a school where more than half the pupils were black	Conservative	Liberal	32.9	49.6	44.0	57.7	43.4
Would prohibit homeowners from refusing to sell their house to someone because of race	Liberal	Liberal	55.8	56.1	57.2	58.2	64.7

Source: James Allen Davis: *General Social Surveys, 1972–89* [machine-readable data file]. Principal Investigator, James A. Davis; Senior Study Director, Tom W. Smith, NORC, ed. Chicago: National Opinion Research Center, Producer, 1989; Storrs, Conn.: Roper Center for Public Opinion Research, University of Connecticut, Distributor.

pecially more so than the richest category, the well-off. Furthermore, this finding that the lower strata is more liberal than the upper strata on social welfare programs to raise living standards is a finding of long standing. As early as 1947, the Gallup Poll found that 58 percent of manual workers favored government action to guarantee everyone a job, but only 28 percent of the prosperous favored such action.[26]

What Table 5-3 suggests is that the closer to home an economic issue is, the more likely it is that people are to take a liberal position on it. Spending for Social Security, for welfare, and for reducing the income gap would translate into significantly more spendable cash for large numbers of lower-strata people. But such spending would put very little into the pockets of upper-strata people. The benefits of increased federal spending for most of the other issues areas in Table 5-3, however, would be more universally spread about and not concentrated in the lower-status population. For this reason, the self-interest of upper-strata people leads them to support more spending in those areas.

It is worth noting the position of the financially precarious people on these economic issues. Because they have the highest voter turnout rates among the lower strata, they play a critical political role. If they side with the rest of the lower strata on a political issue, then their voting power might be enough to push public policy in that direction. But if they side with the dominant upper-status groups, there is little chance that the views of the poor and near-poor could prevail. On only three of the nine issues in Table 5-3 were there significant differences between the positions of the upper-strata and lower-strata people. On two of these (spending for Social Security and welfare), the financially precarious stand solidly with the rest of the lower strata.

More Conservative on Social Policy Issues

In addition to economic issues, a wide range of social policy issues divide liberals and conservatives. Table 5-4 divides these social issues into three sets: (1) those that played important roles in recent presidential elections (capital punishment, school prayers, and abortion), (2) those that concern tolerance and civil liberties, and (3) those that touch on the nation's racial problem.

In contrast to their generally liberal position on economic issues, lower-status people on balance tend to be conservative on social issues. On the recent election issues highlighted in Table 5-4, for example, lower-status people generally took the conservative position on abortion and capital punishment, although they took the liberal side on whether or not prayers should be said in public schools. Interestingly, however, only on the abortion question did their opinions differ sharply from those of the upper strata.

On the question of whether people with deviant views should be allowed to hold college teaching positions, lower-status people were consistently intolerant of all that category except for homosexuals. Lower-status people were much less tolerant generally than upper-status people.

The data in Table 5-4 that deal with race refer only to whites, and it is apparent that lower-status whites generally have a slightly more conservative view of how to deal with racial problems than do upper-status whites. Only on the question of busing were the upper-status respondents more conservative than the lower-status respondents. However, one must question upper-status liberalism on the two questions dealing with open housing and school segregation. If people say they will send their child to a school where a majority of pupils are black but then choose to live in a suburb or neighborhood where this is unlikely to occur, one is inclined to suspect that their actions speak louder than their words.

Selective Commitment to Constitutional Freedoms

Finally, one other set of issues important to lower-status people are constitutional freedoms. Americans have a "selective commitment" to their constitutional freedoms. It is selective in the sense that people strongly hold those freedoms in principle for people in the mainstream of American society. But they are much less likely to uphold them for people whom they conceive to be dangerous to society, such as revolutionaries or criminals.

The selective commitment to constitutional freedoms is illustrated in Table 5-5. Approximately three-fourths of the people interviewed in 1985 upheld the right to organize public meetings to protest against the government, but only 52 percent of the same people would allow "revolutionaries" to hold public meetings to express their views. Nearly two-thirds approved of publishing a pamphlet to protest against the government, but only 52 percent would allow "revolutionaries" to publish a book expressing their views. And if someone tagged a "revolutionary" should aspire to be a high school teacher, he or she had best change career goals; barely 18 percent of the people would allow that person to hold such a job.

The same sense of selective commitment to constitutional freedoms is seen in the questions relating to privacy and fair treatment by criminal justice officials. There is an overwhelming commitment to privacy and fair treatment in general, as Table 5-5 shows. Given the hypothet-

---

In contrast to their generally liberal position on economic issues, lower-status people on balance tend to be conservative on social issues.

TABLE 5-5 Selective Commitment to Constitutional Freedoms

	Percent giving the civil libertarian response
Questions about revolutionaries	
Would allow people to organize meetings to protest against the government	72.7%
Would allow revolutionaries to hold public meetings to express their views	51.8
Would allow people to publish pamphlets to protest against the government	62.5
Would allow revolutionaries to publish books expressing their views	52.0
Would allow revolutionaries to teach in public high schools	17.6
Questions about criminals	
"Suppose the police get an anonymous tip that a man (with no criminal record/with a long criminal record) is planning to break into a warehouse."	
Would *not allow* police to tap the telephone of the	
man	73.0
criminal	50.0
Would *not allow* police to open the mail of the	
man	84.2
criminal	71.9
Would *not allow* police to detain overnight for questioning the	
man	60.4
criminal	35.6
Perceives the ability of the federal government to use computers to bring together pieces of information on individual citizens a serious or fairly serious threat to privacy	57.3

Source: James Allan Davis and Tom W. Smith: *General Social Surveys, 1972–1989* [machine-readable data file]. Principal Investigator, James A. Davis; Director and Co-Principal Investigator, Tom W. Smith. NORC ed. Chicago: National Opinion Research Center, producer, 1989; Storrs, CT: The Roper Center for Public Opinion Research, University of Connecticut, distributor.

ical situation of an anonymous tip to the police that a particular man was going to burglarize a warehouse, 73 percent of the people would deny police the authority to tap the man's telephone without a judicial warrant, 84 percent would not permit authorities to read his mail, and 60 percent would refuse police the authority to detain him overnight for questioning. If the man had a prior criminal record, however, this overwhelming support for civil liberties drops off markedly to 50 percent in the case of tapping his phone and to 36 percent in the case of detaining him overnight.

Historical Background. This selective commitment to constitutional freedoms has deep historical origins. A classic study by Samuel

Stouffer at the height of the Cold War in the 1950s found the American public highly intolerant of communists and atheists;[27] but college-educated people were more tolerant of those groups than were people with lower levels of education. Because more and more people were going to college, Stouffer optimistically predicted that future years would see a greater level of tolerance among the American population and a higher degree of commitment to constitutional freedoms.

Indeed, as time passed, public opinion surveys found that the public did become more tolerant of communists and atheists.[28] Rather than signaling an increase in overall tolerance, however, this simply signaled that communists and atheists were not perceived to be as dangerous as they had been decades earlier. And there was very little tolerance toward groups that came to replace communists and atheists as dangerous groups in the public mind. One imaginative team of researchers asked a sampling of people to indicate the groups of people they most disliked. When each person's tolerance toward his or her least-liked group was compared to the Stouffer data from the 1950s, there was very little increase in tolerance. Three-fourths of the people would prevent members of their disliked groups from teaching in public schools, and two-thirds of them wanted to outlaw their most disliked group.[29] Who were these newly disliked groups in the 1970s? Not surprisingly, the groups disliked by liberals differed markedly from those disliked by conservatives. Liberals disliked the John Birch Society, fascists, the Ku Klux Klan and the anti-abortionists the most, while conservatives disliked Black Panthers, atheists, communists, the Symbionese Liberation Army, socialists, and pro-abortionists the most.

Constitutional Freedoms and the Poorest Strata. There is a substantial body of research showing that commitments to constitutional freedoms are weakest among the poorest and least educated members of society. As far back as the 1950s, sociologist Seymour Martin Lipset studied the prevalence of tolerance and antidemocratic feelings among manual laborers and professionals (lawyers, doctors, etc.). He used the concept of working-class authoritarianism to explain the higher levels of intolerance among the poorer strata of people. Authoritarianism is the belief that people must be compelled to submit to a strong central authority in order for society to remain stable. Lipset found a stronger belief in authoritarian values among manual workers than among professionals.[30]

What Lipset found in the 1950s for the most part has been confirmed by more recent studies. In the 1980s, Herbert McClosky and Alida Brill found not only that political elites are more committed to civil liberties than the mass public is, but within each group the people who put a high value on authoritarianism were less committed to civil liberties than those who didn't.[31] There is also a correlation between authoritarianism and intolerance and the level of education; the more years of formal schooling people have, the more inclined they are to hold tolerant views. Since there are fewer college-educated people among the poorest strata than among the richest, it is not surprising that lower- and lower-middle-income people are the most likely to express selective commitment to constitutional freedoms. We saw this in Table 5-5, which showed lower-status people to be intolerant of deviant viewpoints.

The Bias of Selective Commitment to Freedom. It is ironic that selective commitment to constitutional freedoms is most prevalent among lower-strata persons, because they, more often than the upper strata, have been the victims of selective freedom. Historically, most political movements among the lower strata have been opposed by the upper strata. The union movement, for example, was rooted in the lower-strata population, and it always had to struggle against the notion that it was somehow subversive, communist, and undeserving of constitutional protections. During the 1930s, when unions finally won the right to collective bargaining and began to organize factory workers around the nation, the major union for factory workers, the Congress of Industrial Organizations (CIO), was roundly denounced by the mainstream media as part of a communist conspiracy to overthrow America. In Chapter 4 we saw that media treatment of unions and labor causes continued to be negative in the 1970s and 1980s.

In actuality, selective commitment to constitutional freedoms is especially threatening to lower-status people, whose representatives usually lack access to the mainstream media and so have to rely on non-mainstream kinds of tactics (such as demonstrations and protest marches) to publicize their political messages. These are also the types of groups and tactics most likely to be denied constitutional protections under most forms of selective commitment to constitutional liberties.

Prospects for a Lower-Status Movement to the Left

We have seen that most lower-status people lack a coherent political ideology. When asked to place themselves along the ideological spectrum, they are more inclined than upper-status people to reject liberalism or conservatism and place themselves in the middle. Notwithstanding this lack of a sharply defined ideology, on most domestic issues lower-status people have a distinctly liberal bias concerning government spending, and on redistributive issues such as social security and legislation to reduce the income gap they are significantly more liberal than upper-status people. On issues of social policy and political tolerance, however, lower-status people tend to be conservative on balance. In short, most lower-status people tend not to think of themselves as liberals or conservatives, but tend to lean toward the liberal side of the spectrum on economic issues and the conservative side on social issues.

Would lower-strata people be better off if they had a more coherent political philosophy? And, since it is the left of the political spectrum that claims to support the lower-status cause, what are the chances that lower-status people might adopt a more coherent political philosophy of the left? Three big impediments stand in the way.

Low Levels of Issue Conceptualization

First, the lower strata lack of ideological consistency exemplifies what the Survey Research Center (SRC) called low issue conceptualization.[32] At the highest level of conceptualization are the *ideologues* and *near ideologues* who have a coherent enough understanding of the terms "liberal" and "conservative" to apply these terms to specific political issues and voting decisions.

The *group-benefits* voters have a slightly lower level of issue conceptualization; they take a position on an issue or a candidate depending on whether they will benefit directly from it. Upper-status people who support domestic spending on the environment because they think they might benefit from it but oppose spending on welfare because they will not directly benefit are essentially group-benefits voters.

A third and still lower level of issue conceptualization is held by the *nature of the times voters*. When times are good, they support incumbents, and when times are bad, they vote for the challengers, without regard to the specific issues of the campaign or even to whether the incumbents are responsible for the good times or the bad times.

Finally, at the lowest level are the *no issue content* voters. These are people who fail to articulate any issue content whatsoever in expressing their likes or dislikes about politics. A highly quoted example was the North Carolina man in 1956 who just could not think of anything that he liked or disliked about either Republicans or Democrats:[33]

(Anything you like about the Democrats?)	"No Ma'am, not that I know of."
(Anything you dislike?)	"No Ma'am but I've always been a Democrat, just like my daddy."
(Anything you like about the Republicans?)	"No."
(Anything you dislike?)	"No."

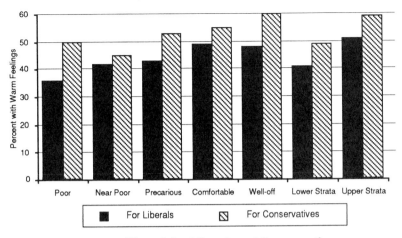

Figure 5-3 Warmth for Liberals and Conservatives

The percentage of "no issue content" and "ideologue" voters varies greatly from one election year to another. The presidential election of 1956, for example, stands as the least ideological election, with only 12 percent of people being identified as ideologues. But in the highly issue-oriented elections of 1964 and 1968, the percentage of ideologues rose to 27 percent and 26 percent, respectively.[34]

Although the SRC did not break down his analysis of issue conceptualization by social status, the lower levels of political ideology among lower-status voters make it reasonable to conclude that there are fewer ideologues and near-ideologues among the lower-strata population than there are among the upper-strata population.

Little Warmth for Liberalism

In addition to a low level of issue conceptualization as an impediment to a liberal resurgence among the lower strata, a liberal resurgence would also be impeded by the data shown in Figure 5–3, which indicate that most lower-status people do not feel very positive about liberals generally. This graph depicts the results of a "feeling thermometer" question about liberals and conservatives. Each respondent was shown a thermometer ranging from zero degrees (coldest) to 100 degrees (warmest) and asked to indicate the degree of warmth he or she felt toward liberals and conservatives. Figure 5-3 shows the percentage of respondents who expressed warm feelings (60° or higher). Three things are immediately apparent from Figure 5-3 that make it seem unlikely that a resurgence of liberalism will occur soon among the lower-status population. First, most lower-status people do not express warm feelings about liberals. Second, lower-status people feel even less warmth toward liberals than they do toward conservatives. Third, lower-status people feel even less warmth toward liberals than upper-status people do.

Abandoned by the New Political Left

A third factor that inhibits lower-status people from lining up consistently on the left side of the political spectrum stems from the splintering of the left that has become pronounced in recent years.

When the terms liberal and conservative first came into use about the time of the American Revolution, a conservative stood for a strong central government and the preservation of the society's social structure; a liberal, on the other hand, stood for social change, for individualism, and for a weaker central government. By the Great Depression of the 1930s, a major reversal of positions occurred as liberalism came to mean strengthening the central government's ability to regulate the economy and to impose economic controls on individual companies or people. Conservatism by this time had come to stand for individualism and a weak governmental ability to regulate the economy.

This is how liberalism and conservatism compared for the next thirty years. The defining difference between liberals and conservatives was essentially economic: whether one approved or did not approve the use of government power to improve the economic conditions of lower-status people. But in the great political upheavals of the 1960s and 1970s, two new dimensions emerged in the definitions of political ideology—a social dimension and a foreign policy dimension. On the social dimension, the new key issues were prayer in public schools, freedom of choice on abortion, busing to desegregate public schools, and the use of affirmative action and racial and sexual preferences to eliminate disparities in employment and admission to professional schools. Liberals tended to support these measures, and conservatives to oppose them. On the foreign-policy dimension, liberals tended to oppose the Vietnam War, protest against nuclear weapons, and object to American intervention in the affairs of other nations. Conservatives tended to support such initiatives as necessary to the pursuit of American security.

As the idea of liberalism expanded to include social as well as foreign-policy issues, the term itself became confusing in a way that

---

A liberal resurgence would also be impeded by the data in Figure 5-3 shown, that most lower-status people do not feel very positive about liberals generally.

Today, however, liberalism means one thing regarding economic policy, another regarding social policy, and something entirely different regarding defense policy. There is no longer a single label that is generally recognized by the poorest 60 percent of the population favoring them economically.

was disadvantageous to lower-status people. When political ideology was essentially a one-dimensional phenomenon of economic ideology, it was much easier for people in the poorest 60 percent of the population to see which candidates and parties advanced their economic interests. To identify a candidate as liberal in that context was to identify one who was willing to use the power of government to improve the economic position of the mass of the population. Today, however, liberalism means one thing regarding economic policy, another regarding social policy, and something entirely different regarding defense policy. There is no longer a single label that is generally recognized by the poorest 60 percent of the population favoring them economically.

As these new social and foreign policy issues came to predominate in American politics, the leaders of the various organizations on the political left became divided. Among Democrats, for example, great bitterness exists between those who are liberal on economic issues but conservative on social and foreign policy issues. Many of these people began to call themselves neoconservatives; typical of them was President Reagan's first United Nations ambassador, Jeane Kirkpatrick, who switched from the Democratic Party to the Republican Party and at one point entertained hopes of a vice-presidential nomination.[35] In contrast to the neoconservatives, another new group called themselves neoliberals. They believed in liberal approaches to social policy but were much more conservative on economic issues. They were especially frustrated by the Democratic Party's traditional reliance on strong centralized governmental regulation of the economy, and wanted the government to scale back much of its welfare legislation.[36]

The most prominent neoliberals today are probably Richard Gephardt, the Majority Leader of the House of Representatives, and Senator William Bradley of New Jersey.

Further to the left are several concentrations of radicals who generally refer to themselves as belonging to the New Left.[37] They are consistently liberal on all three ideological dimensions, most of them harbor a deep antipathy toward the capitalistic economic system, and they generally oppose any foreign policy initiative the American government undertakes.

Finally, the New Left has also splintered further into numerous single-constituency groups. Prominent are militant movements among

There is very little indication in the rhetoric of many prominent leftists that they *even want to appeal* to this audience.

the black leadership, the feminist leadership, and the gay and lesbian coalition leadership. All three of these groups come from the liberal side of the liberal political spectrum, all are extremely vocal and command considerable attention from the media, and all have a strong voice in the liberal political institutions, especially the Democratic Party. And all three tend to pursue the issues of their constituency with single-minded intensity, to the exclusion of pursuing issues that might unite various potential constituencies of the left.

There are two fundamental problems facing the left if it wants to capture the minds and hearts of lower-status Americans. First, the left is so splintered that the average lower-status voter has no idea which groups or leaders to look to for political cues. And this is a fundamental change from periods of leftist progress in the past. During the union-organizing battles of the 1930s, the union itself was the defining issue of liberalism. During the desegregation attempts of the 1950s and 1960s, there was an identifiable civil-rights movement, which had a few highly visible leaders to advise people on how to think and act on racial issues. Today the left is so splintered that there is no single movement, no institution, no individual, overarching cause to command the attention of the lower-status population.

The second fundamental problem of attracting the loyalty of lower-status people to the left is that the rhetoric of many prominent leftists does not suggest that they *even want to appeal* to this audience. It is doubtful that many lower-status people pay much attention to the writings of leftist leaders, but if they did they would find much there to turn them off. For example, feminist columnist Ellen Goodman, in discussing a movie in 1991, included the phrase "the only good man is a dead man."[38] Civil rights leader Julian Bond ridiculed whites who opposed the 1991 Civil Rights Bill as having an inferiority complex on the grounds that the only way they could get ahead was to discriminate against women and blacks. "Without having to compete with minorities or women, any white man, no matter what his qualifications, had a head start. All he needed was a membership in the favored race and gender."[39] And a Syracuse University philosopher asserted that "white males have committed more evil cumulatively than any other class of people in the world . . . [but] white males regard themselves as morally superior to all others."[40] Liberal-leaning upper-status white male intellectuals might be willing to overlook this sort of language as hyperbole and put it in the larger context of sexual and racial relations in the nation. But lower-status white males, who con-

> But lower-status white males, who constitute a sizable proportion of the lower-status population, are likely to jump to the conclusion that Goodman, Bond, and the philosopher are contemptuous of them and are really out to do them in; that there will be little room for their own upward mobility if the likes of these social liberals come to power.

stitute a sizable proportion of the lower-status population, are likely to jump to the conclusion that Goodman, Bond, and the philosopher are contemptuous of them and are really out to do them in; that there will be little room for their own upward mobility if the likes of these social liberals come to power.

This sort of reaction of lower-status white men was seen in interviews the *Washington Post* conducted with Chicago fire fighters who were upset with the "race-norming" of the fire department tests for employment and promotion. They wanted the 1991 Civil Rights Bill to ban those tests. Race-norming is a practice, common in the 1980s, of adjusting overall scores on employment tests to compensate for the fact that blacks and Hispanics do not do as well as whites on those tests. By race-norming, blacks were to be compared only with blacks, and Hispanics only with Hispanics. This meant that when the overall rankings of test scores were compiled, whites would have to have scored 20 or 30 percent higher than blacks or Hispanics to achieve the same ranking.

As someone who has already experienced the Scholastic Aptitude Test and a variety of achievement tests, probably you have your own questions about what these kinds of tests really measure. And, in fact, there are many legitimate concerns about the validity of aptitude-type tests and whether they actually measure anybody's potential for future performance. But you can also appreciate that the white fire fighters in Chicago were not concerned with these subtleties when they pondered the effects of race-norming on their prospects for advancement, and they blamed their reduced prospects on liberal Democrats. The *Washington Post* quoted one angry fire fighter as saying, "The guys they are stepping on are middle-class white Americans, and we are leaving in droves for the Republican Party."[41] A *Washington Post*/ABC News Poll in 1991 echoed these feelings when they showed 88 percent of whites opposing racial preferences even in the absence of rigid quotas.[42]

Political Implications of Lower-Strata Political Views

We have gone into great detail on these views of lower-status people, because they have important ramifications for the political influence of the lower-status population and the future of liberalism. Two generalizations: First, lower-status people are cross-pressured between the left and the right. Second, many of them resolve their conflicts by avoiding participation.

Ideological Cross-Pressure

Out in the Cold on the Left. For most of the past 30 years, the ascending issues of the political left have not been the economic issues of vital concern to the lower-status population. This is not because the left has failed to support federal spending for domestic issues, but because the defining issues of the political left have been opposition to virtually every foreign-policy venture of the United States government, as well as issues of immediate concern to single-constituency groups such as black militants, feminist militants, and gay and lesbian militants. Each of these groups has its own litmus test of support, and since the lower-status population usually are social conservatives, it tends to fail the litmus tests.

In a sense, the political left has downplayed a significant component of its lower-status audience in favor of issues of more concern to upper-status black militants, feminists, and gays.

At Risk from the Right. If the lower strata has a natural allegiance to the political left on economic issues but is alienated from it on social issues, it has just the opposite relationship with conservatives. However, the dominant thrust of conservatism opposes increased spending on domestic issues that would assist the lower-status population. Indeed, conservative politicians, such as former President Reagan, in fact seek to cut funding for such programs and offer specious arguments that such programs only harden lower-status dependency on government programs.[43]

Nonparticipation as a Response to Cross-Pressure

In sum, the thinking lower-status person has a dilemma. On economic issues, his or her natural allies are found on the political left. However, since the early 1970s the political left has shown a remarkable inability to win the presidency and to shift the federal budget in the direction of domestic spending. Furthermore, from the perspective of lower-status white males, who constitute a sizable part of the lower-status population, the political left looks even more bleak. It is beset by vicious disagreements over ideology and issues and tactics that leave leftist organizations splintered. Lower-status white males believe that a leftist political victory would result in preferential treatment for blacks, women, and gays and would leave the typical lower-status male out in the cold. Lower-status white men might be wrong in that assessment, but substantial numbers do believe and distrust the political left, accordingly.

On the other hand, the conservative message does not appeal to them either. No single conservative of stature today supports increased federal expenditures for domestic programs.

The typical thinking lower-status person, then, is ideologically cross-pressured between the left and the right. The left supports lower-status interests on economic issues, but differs markedly on a host of social issues. The right is more closely aligned with lower-status preferences on social and foreign policy issues, but does not empathize with the economic conditions of lower-status people.

Given this ideological configuration it is easy to understand why so many lower-status people sit out presidential contests. In every presidential election since the 1930s the Democratic candidate has been to the political left of the Republican candidate. But if you believe the political right is opposed to your economic interests, the political left is out of touch with your social-policy preferences, and you do not believe leftist leaders could do much about your economic problems even if they came to power, *why vote?*

Overcoming Bias _______________________________

Is there any way to overcome the participatory and ideological disadvantages of the lower-status population? There may not be, but there are ways to reduce the biases.

Voter Reform

Two immediate steps would significantly increase voter turnout among the lower-status population. These are voter-registration reforms that would make it easier to register, and persistent voter-registration drives targeted to the lower-status population. As we saw earlier, considerable research supports the belief that these steps would increase lower-status voter turnout.

Rhetoric of the Left

The way to make the political left more relevant to the lives of lower-status people is not to ask leftists to give up ideological viewpoints. Feminists, for example, *should* continue to be concerned about the role of women in our society; blacks *should* care about the fate of the black population; and gay leaders *should* be concerned about the civil rights of gays and lesbians. If they want to draw political support from the great bulk of the lower-status population, however, then at some point these leaders' rhetoric must stop portraying politics as a zero-sum game between the various components of the lower strata.

Organizational Leadership

Finally, and perhaps most importantly, there is very poor leadership in the lower sectors of the lower-status population. Many organizations do address sub-elements of the lower-status population. Civil rights groups, for example, want the black population's economic situation improved; Hispanic groups want greater upward mobility for Hispanics; labor unions bargain for improved benefits for their members; but there is no broad organizational leadership seeking to mobilize large segments of the lower-status population to political action. As we shall see in Chapter 6, the institutions most likely to do this have suffered declining influence over the past generation.

Summary _____

1. There is a hierarchy of political participation. The more demanding the activity is, the fewer the people who engage in it.

2. There is a significant participation gap between the lower- and upper-status populations. While closing this gap would not eliminate the economic problems of lower-status people, it would give them better government representation and make the government more attentive to their concerns.

3. Americans are not ideologically inclined, and lower-status Americans are less ideologically inclined than the upper status.

4. Although not ideologically inclined, lower-status people do tend to take a more liberal stance than upper-status people on a wide range of economic issues, but a more conservative stance on social issues.

5. A resurgence of liberalism among the lower strata is unlikely because of three factors: lower levels of issue conceptualization among the lower strata, very little warmth felt by lower-strata people for liberals, and a splintering of the political left combined with a rhetoric among many on the New Left that is essentially hostile to lower-status people.

6. If the political position of the lower strata is to be improved, three

developments would help: voter registration reform combined with persistent voter registration campaigns; a toning down of New Left rhetoric hostile to segments of the lower-status population; and the emergence of organizational leadership devoted to the political mobilization of the lower-status population.

Notes

1. Sidney Verba and Norman Nie, *Participation in America* (New York: Harper and Row, 1972), p. 2.
2. Raymond E. Wolfinger and Steven J. Rosenstone, *Who Votes?* (New Haven: Yale University Press, 1980), pp. 23–30.
3. Roy A. Teixeira, *Why Americans Don't Vote: Turnout Decline in the United States* (New York: Greenwood Press, 1987).
4. Harold W. Stanley and Richard G. Niemi, *Vital Statistics on American Politics* (Washington, D.C.: CQ Press, 1988), pp. 66–67.
5. The importance of a sense of civic duty voting is discussed in the work of William Riker and Peter Ordeshook, "A Theory of the Calculus of Voting," *The American Political Science Review* 62, no. 1 (March 1968): 25–42.
6. Angus Campbell et al., *The American Voter* (New York: Wiley, 1960), ch. 4.
7. Frances Fox Pivens and Richard Cloward, *Why Americans Don't Vote* (New York: Pantheon Books, 1988).
8. On the class-based motives behind the progressive reformers, see especially Richard Hofstadter, *The Age of Reform: From Bryan to F.D.R.* (New York: Knopf, 1955), p. 181. Also see Samuel P. Hayes, "The Politics of Reform in Municipal Government in the Progressive Era," *Pacific Northwest Quarterly* 55 (October 1964): 157–166.
9. Howard Penniman, *Sait's American Parties and Elections,* 5th ed. (New York: Appleton–Century–Crofts, 1952), p. 283.
10. Lloyd Wendt and Herman Kogan, *Bosses in Lusty Chicago* (Bloomington, Ind.: Indiana University Press, 1967), p. 269.
11. William F. Whyte, *Street Corner Society* (Chicago: University of Chicago Press, 1970) pp. 313–315.
12. Data cited in Pivens and Cloward, *Why Americans Don't Vote,* p. 84. Original source is Paul Kleppner, *Who Voted? The Dynamics of Electoral Turnout* (New York: Praeger, 1982), pp. 53, 55.
13. Quoted in Pivens and Cloward, *Why Americans Don't Vote,* pp. 83–84. Original source, William C. Pendleton, *Political History of Appalachian Virginia* (Dayton, Va.: Shenandoah Press, 1927).
14. *Smith* v. *Alwright* 321 U.S. 649 (1944).
15. *Gomillion* v. *Lightfoot* 364 U.S. 339 (1960).
16. Wolfinger and Rosenstone, *Who Votes?* p. 73.
17. Raymond E. Wolfinger, "How To Raise Voter Turnout," *New York Times,* June 6, 1990, p. 14A.
18. In 1988 the voter turnout rate among people claiming three or more organizational memberships was 80 percent. Among those with no memberships it was 44 percent. The turnout rate was 73 percent among people who attended church at least twice a month, but it dropped off to 55 percent among those who only attended a few times a year. Data calculated from: James Allen Davis: *General Social Surveys, 1972–1989.* [machine-readable data file]. Principal Investigator: James A. Davis; Director and Co-Principal Investigator, Tom W. Smith. NORC ed. Chicago: National Opinion Research Center, producer, 1989; Storrs, Conn.: Roper Public Opinion Research Center, University of Connecticut, distributor.
19. One study found that participation in campaigning and political contacting was

higher among those who belonged to purposed groups (such as political clubs) than those who belonged to material benefit groups (such as labor unions or professional associations). See Philip H. Pollack III, "Organizations as Agents of Mobilization: How Does Group Activity Affect Political Participation?" *American Journal of Political Science* 26, no. 3 (August 1982): 485–503.

20. Gerald W. Johnson, "Research Note on Political Correlates of Voter Participation: A Deviant Case Analysis," *American Political Science Review* 65, no. 3 (September 1971): 768–776.

21. Lester M. Salamon and Stephen Van Evera, "Fear, Apathy, and Discrimination: A Test of Three Explanations of Political Participation," *American Political Science Review* 67, no. 4 (December 1973): 1288–1307.

22. Bruce E. Cain and Ken McCue documented this finding for Hispanics in their analysis of Los Angeles County voter registrations from 1980 to 1982. See their "The Efficacy of Registration Drives," *Journal of Politics* 47, no. 4 (November 1985): 1221–1230.

23. Arnold Vedlitz, "Voter Registration Drives and Black Voting in the South," *Journal of Politics* 47, no. 2 (May 1985): 643–651.

24. Since the *General Social Survey* first began asking this question in 1974, the most liberal year was 1974 and the most conservative was 1984.

	1974	*1984*	*1989*
Percent liberal	30.4%	24.0%	28.4%
Percent moderate	40.1	40.3	39.3
Percent conservative	29.5	35.7	32.4

25. *New York Times,* August 3, 1977, p.1.

26. *The Gallup Poll: Public Opinion 1935–1971, vol. 1, 1935–1948* (New York: Random House, 1972), p. 645.

27. Samuel Stouffer, *Communism, Conformity, and Civil Liberties* (New York: Doubleday, 1955).

28. The National Opinion Research Center since 1972 has asked a sample of the national population whether communists and atheists should be allowed to hold teaching positions in college. In 1972, 60.7 percent of the people interviewed felt that communists should not be allowed to teach in college, and 55.4 percent felt that atheists should not be allowed to teach. By 1989, these percentages dropped to 43.2 percent opposed to communists teaching and 44.3 percent opposed to atheists teaching. See *General Social Surveys, 1972–1989: Cumulative Codebook* (Chicago, Ill.: The National Opinion Research Center, University of Chicago, 1989), questions 79 and 80. Also see the *General Social Survey, 1972–1982: Cumulative Codebook,* questions 72 and 75.

29. John L. Sullivan, James E. Piereson, and George E. Marcus, "An Alternative Conceptualization of Political Tolerance: Illusory Increases, 1950s–1970s," *American Political Science Review* 73, no. 3 (September 1979): 781–794. This viewpoint has been contested by John Mueller, however, who argues that no other groups have yet emerged who appear as dangerous as communists and atheists appeared in the 1950s. Mueller, "Trends in Political Tolerance from 1984 to 1984," a paper presented at the annual convention of the American Political Science Association, Washington, D.C., August 30–September 4, 1984.

30. Seymour Martin Lipset, *Political Man* (Garden City, N.Y.: Doubleday, 1963), p. 87.

31. Herbert McClosky and Alida Brill, *Dimensions of Tolerance: What Americans Believe about Civil Liberties* (Sage Publications, 1983), p. 339.

32. Angus Campbell et al., *The American Voter* (New York: Wiley, 1960), ch. 9.

33. Ibid.

34. See Paul R. Hagner and John C. Pierce, "Correlative Characteristics of Conceptualized Voting in the American Public: 1956–1976," *Journal of Politics* 44, no. 3 (August 1982): 779–809.

35. See Peter Steinfels, *The Neoconservatives: The Men Who Are Changing America's Politics* (New York: Simon & Schuster, 1979).

36. Randall Rothenberg, *The Neoliberals* (New York: Simon & Schuster, 1984). Also see Victor Ferkiss, "Neoliberalism: How New? How Liberal? How Significant?" *Western Political Quarterly* 39, no. 1 (March 1986): 165–179.

37. There are too many movements on the radical left to give a representative list. Some

of the more prominent publications are *Dissent, Monthly Review,* and *In These Times.*

38. Ellen Goodman column, *Minneapolis Star Tribune,* July 16, 1991, p. 8A

39. Julian Bond, "Civil Rights Act: White Man's Hope," *New York Times,* August 13, 1990.

40. Laurence Thomas, "Next Life, I'll Be White," *New York Times,* August 13, 1990, p. A15.

41. Tom Kenworthy and Thomas B. Edsell, "The Voices of Those Who Think Civil Rights Have Gone Too Far," *Washington Post National Weekly,* June 10–June 16, 1991, p. 14.

42. Ibid.

43. Few people articulate these ideas more forcefully than Charles Murray. See his *Losing Ground* (New York: Basic Books, 1984).

CHAPTER 6

The Political Process: Leadership to Overcome Bias

Ordinary people in a political system must have leadership if they are to have influence. That leadership can come only through political processes and institutions that enable lower-status people to make their voices heard in the government. In America, those institutions are political parties, elections, interest groups, and political movements. Parties and elections are especially critical, for they enable average citizens to vote their leaders into office. Once in office, those leaders can support policies that help average citizens. Interest groups and political movements are also important, because they enable people to put pressure on governing officials. In fact, American history is replete with examples of disadvantaged groups using the political process to overcome biases in the American political system that affected them.

- Organized labor, for example, struggled with very little success until the decade of the 1930s when pro-union forces passed National Labor Relations legislation that created a legal framework for collective bargaining between labor and management. Through difficult unionizing drives in the 1930s, organized labor succeeded in unionizing much of American industry and vastly improving the wages and working conditions of unionized workers.

- African Americans and most other racial minorities were virtually shut out of the mainstream of American society by a rigid system of segregation and widespread discrimination. Through the civil rights movement of the 1950s and 1960s, blacks got most segregation legislation stripped from the law books. The movement culminated in the 1964 Civil Rights Act which outlawed discrimination in virtually all areas of public accommodations, and the 1965 Voting Rights Act which for the first time since the 1890s made it possible for blacks to vote. The most dramatic illustration of the success of this legislation can be seen in the number of black elected officials in the United States, which increased fivefold from 1,479 in 1970 to 7,335 twenty years later.

- Women were for the most part denied the vote until 1919, and even after achieving the vote they remained on the sidelines of American politics and institutional life for the next half-century. The suffragette movement of the early twentieth century was critical to women's achieving the right to vote. And the women's movement of the 1970s and 1980s was critical to effecting affirmative action programs for women, appointing more women to high political office, and passing laws sought by women's groups.

Despite these successful uses of the political process to overcome bias against workers, racial minorities, and women, the most dramatic benefits of these movements have gone to upper-middle-class minorities and women, and it is clear that effective political influence is still beyond the grasp of the lower-status population generally (including both men and women, whites and minorities). In some respects events since the mid-1970s have kept many lower-status Americans from fully enjoying the fruits of these earlier victories of labor, the civil rights movement, and the women's movement. Middle-income and lower-middle-income Americans were unable to prevent the tax system from becoming more regressive in the 1980s, a development that increased their tax burden while reducing the taxes of the wealthy. The 30 million Americans without health insurance have been unable to use the political system to gain medical coverage. And the millions of lower-status families and single parents needing day-care facilities for their children have been unable to get much government help to pay for this expensive service.

Today it is very difficult for average and lower-status people to use the political process to achieve these simple goals. Most of the time the political process in America has a strong practical bias against lower-status citizens. As we saw in the last chapter, lower-status people vote less often than do upper-status people, and political reforms have weakened their political leaders. In this chapter we will examine further the impact of political processes on lower-status people by looking at: (1) the differences between the political parties, (2) the biases inherent in the contemporary electoral cycle of "dealignment," (3) the biases inherent in the contemporary style of "high-tech media" political campaigning, and (4) upper-status biases inherent in interest group politics. Then we will explore the possibility that a rainbow coalition of lower-status people might emerge in the 1990s. Finally, we will review what would-be lower-status leaders must do to make the political process work better for the lower-status population.

Why Parties Are Important to Democracy and to Lower-Status Citizens

Political parties are vital to the proper functioning of a democracy. In the words of E. E. Schattschneider, political parties "created democracy and democracy is unthinkable save in terms of parties."[1] This is because, as another political scientist V. O. Key expressed it, "Political parties are the basic institutions for the translation of mass preferences into public policy."[2] Each party seeks to translate mass preferences into public policy by nominating a slate of candidates and endorsing a platform of policy proposals in the hope of attracting the most voters. Elections allow voters to choose which set of candidates and policies they prefer. The winning candidates then enact the policies that get them the winning votes.

There is a great concern today that parties and elections do not perform these functions very well anymore. *Washington Post* columnist David Broder wrote two decades ago that "the governmental system is not working [today] because the parties are not working."[3] Parties have strengthened their organizational structures since then, but they nevertheless continue to lose influence over the voters. This in no small measure is because their historical role of nominating candidates and running their campaigns is being taken over by television, computers, direct-mail techniques, political action committees, and independent media consulting firms. As party influence declines, the typical voter is left facing an election choice without a good idea of how his or her self-interest is best served by one candidate or the other.

No group of citizens has been left more at sea in this regard than lower-status citizens. Lacking other channels of political and economic influence, the lower-status citizen needs a strong, disciplined, and well-led political party to represent his or her economic interests. Strong parties based on a lower-status constituency can provide effective leadership by endorsing candidates favorable to lower-status interests and advising voters about the candidates favored by the party. Without strong party leadership, the lower-status voter has no systematic method of getting this information. It was this fact of political life that led the great scholar of parties, Maurice Duverger, to write that a regime without parties "is of necessity a conservative regime. To sup-

> Lacking other channels of political and economic influence, the lower-status citizen needs a strong, disciplined, and well-led political party to represent his or her economic interests.

press parties would be an admirable way for the right to paralyze the left."[4] If one were to substitute the word "disempower" for suppress, this is precisely what has happened to the historic tie-in between the American party system and America's lower-status population since about 1970.

Historically, there were days when the political parties were not weak, when they vigorously courted the support of the lower classes and rewarded their lower-status constituents with favorable policies. Republicans after the Civil War sought the vote of poor farmers with the slogan "Vote yourself a farm!" And Democrats during the Great Depression sought the vote of poor and middle-income people alike with their promise of a "New Deal." To a much greater degree than they are given credit for, the New Deal Democrats fulfilled that promise.[5]

But the days of political party relevance to the lower-status population appear to be gone. At issue today is whether party relevance can be brought back. And this is an important issue to people of all income levels. For it is unlikely that a meaningful democracy can survive in the United States if 40 to 60 percent of the potential voters are permanently isolated from the election process through which the nation selects its leaders.

Democrats and Republicans Differ—Significantly _____

As the parties' ability to influence the vote weakened, more and more people came to believe that there are no longer any important differences between the Democratic and Republican Parties. This feeling was put most tersely by George C. Wallace when he campaigned for president in 1968 on a third-party ticket: "There isn't a dime's worth of difference between the parties."[6] This sentiment is reflected in public opinion surveys. When asked which party was better able to handle the most important problems facing the country, nearly half the people interviewed failed to see any difference between the two parties in 1976; this was up from one-third of the people just eight years earlier in 1968.[7]

Differences between Democrats and Republicans in Congress

Despite the growing sentiment that the political parties are alike, there are three ways in which the Republican Party differs significantly from the Democratic Party. First, when Democrats get into office, they enact more liberal economic policies than do Republicans. This can be seen in Table 6-1, which shows that even the most conservative bloc of Democratic members of Congress (the Southern Democrats) vote more liberally than the most liberal bloc of Republicans (the non-Southern Republicans). Remembering from Chapter 5 that lower-status and middle-status people were more liberal economically than the rich or the near rich, this means that the Democrats are more inclined to the economic policy views of the middle- and lower-status population than the Republicans are.

On foreign policy and social-policy issues, however, the results are not quite so clear-cut. In Chapter 5, we saw that lower-status people had relatively conservative views on foreign policy, but that their views were split on social policy. Lower-status people were more liberal than upper-status people on race issues but were more conservative on questions of abortion and school prayers. For these reasons, it is not possible to say whether Table 6-1 indicates that either congressional Democrats or Republicans are in fact closer to the views of lower-status Americans on social and foreign policy issues; but it clearly shows that Democratic members of Congress are more liberal on average than Republican members on social and foreign policy issues as well as on domestic economic issues.

Differences between Democratic and Republican Voter Base

A second difference between the parties, as Figure 6-1 shows, is that Democrats draw more of their voting strength from lower-status people than do Republicans. This supports the common notion of the Republicans as an upper-status party and the Democrats as a lower-status party. The people who disproportionately identify as Democrats are low income non-Southern whites, blacks, Hispanics, and people of all races whose formal education stopped at the grade school or high school levels. Democratic supporters also tend to be big city dwellers, Jews, and Catholics. The core of strong Republican support is found among farmers, white Protestants, small-town and rural residents, Westerners, and most whites with college educations, high incomes, and high-status occupations. A dramatic partisan change in recent years involves gender. Until the 1960s, men's and women's party iden-

TABLE 6-1 Policy Differences Between Democratic and Republican Members of Congress, 1991

Percentile rankings on:*	Economic Liberalism	Foreign Policy Liberalism	Social Policy Liberalism
Senate			
Southern Republicans	15	9	10
All Republicans	22	21	25
Non-Southern Republicans	24	23	28
Southern Democrats	57	55	49
All Democrats	69	68	65
Non-Southern Democrats	73	72	70
House of Representatives			
Southern Republicans	14	11	11
All Republicans	19	18	19
Non-Southern Republicans	20	20	21
Southern Democrats	52	51	50
All Democrats	66	66	64
Non-Southern Democrats	72	73	76

*Each score represents the group's average percentile ranking on a range from least liberal (0) to most liberal (100). The median percentile is 50. For example, on economic liberalism, the average Southern Republican senator is more liberal than 15 percent of all senators. (This means, of course, that the average Southern Republican senator is also more conservative than 85 percent of all senators.)

Source: Richard E. Cohen and William Schneider, "Partisan Polarization," *National Journal,* January 18, 1992, pp. 132–155. Copyright 1992 by the National Journal, Inc. All rights reserved. Reprinted by permission. The *National Journal* has calculated these rankings annually since 1981 for each individual senator and representative. The scores shown here are averages for the members in the specific subgroups indicated.

tifications were approximately the same. But by the 1980s, more women have come to be Democrats than men.

Differences between Democratic and Republican Activists

A third important difference between the two parties is in the party activists who serve as delegates to the national convention or are national committee members. Whereas the rank-and-file Republican and Democratic voters tend to cluster around the middle of the ideological spectrum, Democratic activists tend to be very liberal and Republican activists very conservative. Figure 6-2 shows this relationship for 1988, but surveys dating back to 1956 have consistently revealed the same phenomenon.[8]

Not only are Republican activists much more conservative than Democratic activists, but they also produce more conservative party platforms. In 1984, for example, the Republican Party platform op-

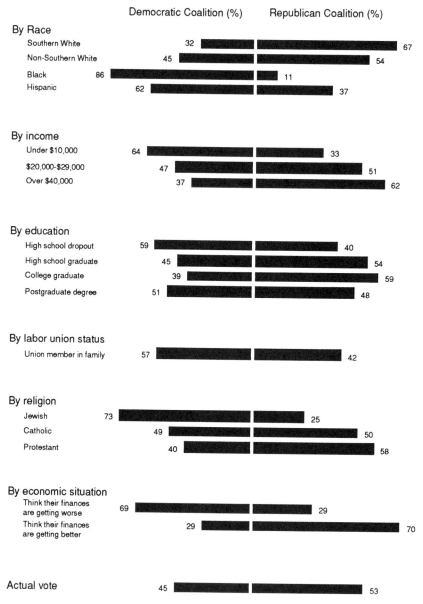

Figure 6-1 Democratic and Republican Voter Bases: 1988

Source: CNN-*Los Angeles Times* exit poll, November 8, 1988. Copyright 1988 *Los Angeles Times* reprinted with permission.

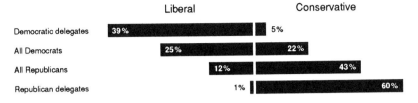

Figure 6-2 Party Activists and the Ideological Spectrum
Democratic activists tend to be more liberal than typical Democratic
voters, while Republican activists tend to be more conservative than
typical Republican voters.
Source: Copyright © 1988 by the New York Times. Reprinted with permission.

posed the Equal Rights Amendment, which the Democratic platform
endorsed. And the two parties' platforms also differed sharply on their
handling of many other issues that related to the economy, taxes, civil
rights, the environment, and national defense.[9]

In sum, important differences separate Democrats from Republicans.
The Democratic Party draws more of its voting strength from the
lower-status population than does the Republican Party. Democrats in
office usually are more attuned to the economic policy preferences of
the lower-status population; and Democratic activists tend to be much
more liberal than the average voter, while Republican activists tend to
be much more conservative. One of the most important aspects of these
differences is that most (but not all) upper-status people recognize
these differences between the parties and identify their own interests
with the Republican Party. Lower-status people, however, are less able
to see the differences between the parties and to calculate where their
economic interests lie.

Party Dealignment Has Hurt Lower-Status Americans _____

A Cyclical History of Party Alignments

Despite the clear differences between the Democratic and Republican parties, lower-status voters have difficulty perceiving that those
differences are relevant to their lives. Part of the reason for that difficulty stems from the process of party dealignment that has persisted
since the late 1960s. This period of dealignment is the most recent
period in a long cyclical history of six periods in American politics
since the founding of the party system in the early 1800s.[10] During

each of these six periods, the parties were organized around coalitions of voters who were divided over the central issues of the times.

The first two periods in American political history (1800–1828; 1828–1860) were dominated by the early Democrats, first under the guidance of Thomas Jefferson and then reborn under the leadership of Andrew Jackson starting in 1828. During both of these periods, Democratic dominance was based on coalitions of rural voters and later Western voters reacting against the mercantile and banking interests of the Northeast. These early party systems splintered in the 1850s over the question of slavery and whether it would be permitted to extend into the Western territories. The Republican Party was founded in 1856 as the party of abolition and came to dominate the next two historical periods which stretched from 1860 to 1896 and from 1896 to 1932. The fourth period, from 1896 to 1932, is especially relevant to modern times, for it was in this period that the Republican Party organized its voter coalition around the interests of the big business. This period ended with the economic disaster of the Great Depression in the 1930s, which brought the Democrats back as the majority party.

The fifth period in the historical cycle was one of Democratic dominance from 1932 until 1968, and politics during this period were characterized by a division between Republicans and Democrats on economic issues. Democrats blamed Republicans for the Great Depression, but Democrats took the credit for the economic expansion that took place throughout most of this period. Democratic dominance during the fifth period rested on the so-called *New Deal coalition* which consisted of lower-status workers and middle-class voters, many of whom had been thrown into poverty by the Depression. They responded enthusiastically to President Franklin Roosevelt's attempts to reinvigorate the nation. With the exception of the Eisenhower presidency (1953–1961), Democrats dominated the White House throughout this period and regularly controlled Congress except for two short periods from 1947 to 1948 and 1953 to 1954.

Realignments Follow Disasters. It has always taken massive historical tragedies to create a new electoral cycle. To bring the Republican Party to dominance in 1860 required the nation's inability to resolve the slavery question as well as a Civil War that destroyed the Southern economy and cost half a million lives. It also took a disaster to bring the New Deal coalition to power in the 1930s, the worst economic breakdown in the nation's history. One-fourth of the work force was unemployed by the time of Franklin Roosevelt's inauguration in 1933, with no national system of unemployment compensation, no Social Security, and no welfare programs to soften the shock. Banks were failing left and right, and there was no federal deposit insurance as there is today; when a bank failed, the depositors simply lost most of their savings. Faced with these tragedies, it is not surprising that voters threw the Republicans out of the White House in 1932. And when economic matters improved under Roosevelt, it is not surprising that voters reelected him.

Realignments Bring Profound Change. Not only does it take a national tragedy to create new party realignments, but those realignments bring drastic policy changes that resolve issues that had been unresolvable before. A new political majority is created, and that new majority runs the country according to its own vision of what the country needs. The Republican majority following the Civil War, for example, resolved the issue of slavery by eliminating it. And it ended the thorny issue of whether a state was obliged to obey national laws. Republican political dominance after the Civil War coincided with a period of Northern dominance that kept the South in an underdeveloped state for most of the next century. In short, the political realignment that took place in the 1860s had profound consequences for the next half-century.

The results of the New Deal realignment of the 1930s were nearly as dramatic. In the face of the economic catastrophe of the Depression, popular support disappeared for the political philosophy of "laissez-faire," the philosophy that the government should take a hands-off approach to the economy. In its place came a liberal economic philosophy demanding that the federal government regulate the economy and sponsor social welfare policies to help people the Depression had driven into poverty. President Roosevelt reacted to these demands by promising a "New Deal" for the American people, hence the term "New Deal" for his administration and for the new majority political coalition that formed around him.

The Politics of Dealignment

By the end of the 1960s, the New Deal period in America's six-cycle political history was getting old. In the past, realigning elections had surfaced like clockwork every 28 to 36 years (1800, 1828, 1860, 1896, 1932). On the 36th anniversary of the New Deal's ascension to power, 1968, a conservative Republican, Richard Nixon, was elected president, and a young analyst, Kevin Phillips, argued brilliantly that Nixon's election signalled the end of Democratic dominance and the emergence of a new Republican majority.[11]

Phillips was correct in foreseeing that Democratic dominance was over, since the Republicans held onto the White House for 20 of the next 24 years. He was wrong, however, in thinking that 1968 had brought in a new Republican majority. Despite their hammerlock on the White House, Republicans have yet to outnumber the Democrats in terms of people's party identification (see Figure 6–3); they have been unable to dislodge Democrats from control of Congress (except for a short period of Republican control of the Senate, 1981–1985); and they have had little success in dismantling Democratic dominance of the 50 state legislatures and governorships.

Because these key ingredients of a realignment are still missing, most political scientists argue that the period since 1968 has been one of a *partisan dealignment* rather than a realignment. In this dealignment, as Figure 6-3 shows, the Democratic majority has shrunk visibly, but a new Republican majority has not yet emerged. Thus, the sixth and most recent period of election cycles from 1968 to the present has not been one in which one party dominates the political landscape. Rather it has been a period of weakening party ties, split control over the government, and declining voter turnout.

Why Dealignment? Much of the deteriorating party fortunes since 1968 can be traced to the change of generations. The generation that formed the New Deal coalition was shaped politically by the Great Depression of the 1930s and World War II in the 1940s. New Deal voters came mainly from the lower-status portion of society: lower- and middle- income people, blue collar workers, union members, Catholics,

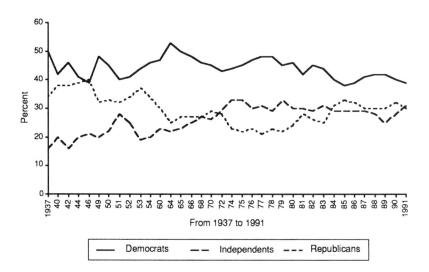

Figure 6–3 Trends in Party Identification
Source: The Gallup Poll: Public Opinion 1981 (Wilmington, Del. Resources, Inc., 1982), p. 128. *The Gallup Report,* no. 286 (July 19), p. 2; *The Gallup Poll Monthly,* no. 311 (August, 1991), p. 48. Used by permission of The Gallup Organization.

Jews, Southern whites, and blacks as they gained the right to vote. The dominant political institutions of the New Deal were the big city political machines of the North, the labor unions, and the rural political machines of the South. With the memory of the Great Depression vividly in their minds, the members of the New Deal coalition resoundingly supported liberal economic measures to regulate the economy and create a system of social welfare ranging from Social Security to unemployment compensation to general welfare programs such as AFDC. Also in the memory of this generation was World War II, the 290,000 lives that it cost, and the realization that this war had in no small measure resulted from policies of appeasement toward an expansionist Nazi Germany in the late 1930s. As a consequence, the New Deal coalition members became strong supporters of a strong military and virtually any foreign policy initiative taken to counter perceived communist expansion during the 1950s and early 1960s.

The issues that shine in the memory of one generation, however, glow more dimly in the minds of their children, and more dimly yet in their grandchildren, who face an entirely different sort of world. And this is what happened to the New Deal coalition. The dominant issues for the generation that came to adulthood in the 1930s were usually economic. Starting in the 1960s, however, a wide range of new issues began to surface in the minds of the children and grandchildren of the Great Depression generation. These issues were civil rights for African Americans, desegregation of schools through the use of court-ordered busing, the environment, gay rights, women's issues, abortion, and above all, the war in Vietnam.

The emergence of these issues profoundly disrupted both political parties, but especially the Democratic Party, because these issues bitterly pitted some parts of the New Deal coalition against other parts. As the Democratic party became the champion of civil rights in the 1960s, for example, it lost the loyalty of a great many Southern whites. As abortion became an important issue, it created a dilemma for many Catholics who now faced an issue that pitted the historical teaching of their church against a highly vocal wing of their party. As Democratic activists pushed for affirmative action policies for women and racial minorities, they did not give much incentive to lower-status white men to continue to vote Democratic. And as other Democratic activists pushed for busing to desegregate schools, they gave middle-income whites no incentive to remain in central cities or continue to vote Democratic.

A Two-tiered System of Politics. The practical outcome of this splintering of the New Deal coalition was a two-tiered system of party control.[12] Democrats dominate the lower political tier that includes

The issues that shine in the memory of one generation, however, glow more dimly in the minds of their children, and more dimly yet for their grandchildren who face an entirely different sort of world. And this is what happened to the New Deal coalition.

Congress and most of the states, but the upper tier, the big prize, the presidency, has gone Republican in every election but one (1976) since 1968.

Everett Carl Ladd contends that it was the rising importance of symbolic social issues (such as abortion, race relations, crime) in the 1970s that split the Democratic Party and led to the two-tier system of divided government. Older, blue collar, New Deal-oriented Democrats (called Old Class Democrats by Ladd) supported liberal economic policies but often were conservative on social issues. This social conservatism put them at odds with younger, better-educated Democrats with managerial and professional backgrounds (called New Class Democrats by Ladd). This division was exacerbated in the 1980s by foreign and defensive policy issues. Many traditional Democrats responded positively to President Reagan's hawkish approach to international relations.[13]

These divisions were directly related to the political beliefs of the lower-status and middle-status people that we examined in Chapter 4. In that chapter we saw that lower- and middle-status people were distinctly more liberal on economic issues than were upper-status people, but they were much more conservative on some social issues (especially prayer in public schools and abortion) than were upper-status people. When these lower-status people looked at the political parties, they saw, as Table 6–1 shows, that Democratic officeholders and activists tend to be more liberal and Republicans more conservative, not only on economic issues but on social issues as well. This same principle is true of presidential candidates. Every Democratic nominee for president since 1968 has been more liberal on social and foreign policy issues than has his opponent. So the average lower-status voters found themselves in a dilemma, especially if the lower-status voter was white and male. To vote his economic interests he had to vote Democratic, but if he were a social and foreign policy conservative, which was very likely, he may have found it more appealing to vote Republican.

There were two ways for individual voters to resolve this dilemma between party loyalty and social issue sentiment. One was not to vote at all, which apparently is what a great many people did, since voter participation rates dropped off precipitously in the 1970s. The more imaginative resolution, however, was to vote their economic interests at the congressional level and their social policy interests at the presidential level; and evidence indicates that large numbers of people did precisely this, especially Southern white men.[14]

Weakened Party Identification. A second characteristic of dealignment has been a progressive weakening of peoples' attachment to political parties. This can be seen in Figure 6-3 which shows a growing disenchantment with political parties[15] from the 1960s though the early 1980s. The weakening of parties is also seen in the rising incidence of split-ticket voting, as discussed above. At the height of New Deal dominance in the early 1960s, split-ticket voting was rare. By the 1980s, however, more than two-thirds of the Democrats or Independents and half of the Republicans split their ballots in some elections.[16] Neither party can claim the loyalty of its voters it had a generation ago, but the problem is worse for the Democrats than it is for the Republicans.

What makes this weakening of party ties most threatening to the future viability of political parties is that the youngest voters are the ones with the weakest partisan attachment.[17] A panel study compared the attitudes of 1965 high school graduates with their parents in 1965, 1973, and 1982 and found partisanship much weaker among the younger generation.[18]

Dealignment and the Lower-Status Population

Given the above analysis, the contemporary period of dealignment has been difficult for the average lower-status and middle-status voters. Lower-status Americans made out well during the New Deal period precisely because there was an institution, the Democratic Party, which depended on their vote and for 30 years rewarded that vote with a broad array of distributive programs such as unemployment compensation, GI bills for veterans, subsidized mortgage insurance, and Social Security that promoted upward mobility or at least provided some assistance when times were bad. For reasons that we will discuss below, most Democratic congressional members do not depend on the lower-status vote any more. And the party itself has become so weakened that it has very little ability to initiate new programs that might resurrect the enthusiasm of the lower-status non-voter.

In sum, since about 1968, the political events called dealignment have led to a two-tiered system of politics, declining voter participation, split control over government, and the absence of a clear choice that was obviously in the best interests of lower-status voters. From an economic point of view, the Democrats serve lower-status interests better than do Republicans. But evidence from public opinion polls and voting returns suggest that a great many lower-status people think the Republicans do a better job of serving their symbolic interests on social issues and foreign policy issues. And the high rate of non-voting among the lower-status population suggests that neither party is perceived as very important to its interests.

The End of Dealignment?

As long as this situation persists, dealignment will persist.[19] But not everybody thinks the situation will persist forever. To a great extent there is rolling realignment as older people die off and newer voters enter the electorate. That is what accounted for the growth in Republican voters in the 1980s. More young voters tend to become Republicans than Democrats.[20] Eventually the issue dilemmas will be resolved, of course. The post-New Deal generation has been immobilized by the trauma of Vietnam, foreign policy issues generally, and social policy issues such as abortion, prayer in schools, and race relations. But for the children of the post-New Deal generation, the split over Vietnam will be less traumatic, and the collapse of the Soviet Union will make anti-communism less important an issue. New issues will arise, and eventually some new crisis will emerge that will bring the dealignment period to a close, just as the Vietnam War signified the end of the New Deal dominance.

Which party will benefit from this new alignment? It is impossible to know, because we do not yet know what issues or what crisis will provoke it. But several guesses are appropriate. If the realignment is brought about by a crisis, whichever party is in the White House when the crisis reaches its climax will suffer greatly unless it is able to resolve the crisis in a reasonable time. The Democrats will most likely benefit if economic issues are the dominant ones and if they are able to convince lower-status voters that a strong federal government can cope with the economic problems of the lower-status population. The Republicans will most likely benefit if social issues are dominant and if they are able to convince lower-status voters that government is irrelevant to the economic problems of the lower-status population.

High-Tech Campaigning and Its Impact on Lower-Status Voters _____

If partisan dealignment has worked to the disadvantage of the lower-status voter, the same can also be said of the high-technology-media

> If partisan dealignment has worked to the disadvantage of the lower-status voter, the same can also be said of the high-technology-media campaign style characteristic of national and statewide races today.

campaign style characteristic of national and statewide races today. The high-tech campaign relies upon a careful orchestration of public-opinion polling, highly sophisticated voter analysis techniques such as focus groups, the design of television and radio advertising to use persuasively the results of this elaborate voter research, and the use of computers to develop highly specialized direct-mailing campaign strategies both to solicit contributions and votes. During the 1980 and 1984 campaigns, Ronald Reagan's personal pollster, Richard Wirthlin, used a sophisticated computerized polling system he called PINS (for political information system) which helped Reagan's handlers make strategic campaign decisions. Each night Wirthlin polled 100 to 200 people to track how various social groups responded to the campaign. The results of these polls were given to campaign decision makers the next morning.[21] On the basis of PINS, Reagan's strategists made key decisions on how to maximize the labor vote[22] and how to choose campaign themes. For example, prior to the Republican convention in 1984, Wirthlin's tracking polls showed that in voters' minds Reagan was weak on whether he could deal effectively and boldly with the problems of the future. Based on that information, the strategists decided to hit hard on the future theme during the convention and the campaign.[23]

George Bush took hi-tech campaigning to new heights in 1988. In late spring 1988, he was trailing Michael Dukakis in public opinion polls by about 10 percent, and he was persistently criticized for lacking the forcefulness and independence of a presidential leader.[24] Bush's chief media adviser, Lee Atwater, decided to conduct a strong negative campaign that would both smear Bush's opponent, Dukakis, and picture Bush as tough and daring. To develop his campaign themes, Atwater borrowed a research technique called the "focus group" from the commercial advertising industry. Advertisers commonly employ psychological researchers to probe deeply into the intellectual and emotional responses that marketing themes provoke in small groups of people. Atwater tested out various political themes on two focus groups of 30 Democrats who had voted for Reagan in 1984 but were leaning toward Dukakis in 1988. The researchers hit pay dirt when they discovered powerful emotional responses to two items of information. First was the news that Dukakis as governor of Massachusetts had vetoed a bill requiring the obligatory saying of the pledge of allegiance to the flag each day at school. Second was the Massachusetts prisoner furlough program under which a convicted murderer, Willie Horton, had raped a woman and killer her husband while he, Horton, was out of prison on a weekend furlough. Faced with such carefully selected information, half of the focus group members changed their minds about supporting Dukakis.[25]

The next step in Atwater's strategy was to develop a media campaign that would link these findings to symbolic and emotional themes such as patriotism, fear of violence, and desire to punish wrongdoers. The net impact was an extremely negative mud-slinging campaign that portrayed Dukakis (and liberals generally) as aloof, uncaring, unpatriotic, and out of touch with the concerns of middle-class America. On the Willie Horton theme, for example, Bush in October exclaimed "Clint Eastwood's answer to crime is, 'Go ahead, make my day.' My opponent's answer is slightly different. His answer is, 'Go ahead, have a nice weekend.'"[26] The Republican Party of Illinois took these charges a step further in a campaign flier charging that "all murderers and rapists and drug pushers and child molesters in Massachusetts vote for Michael Dukakis."[27] Perhaps most effective was Bush's support for the death penalty for drug dealers. When contrasted to Dukakis's opposition to the death penalty, this went a long way towards dispelling the image of Bush as a wimp, and established him as the more forceful of the two candidates. In fact, Bush was soon sounding so tough that his speechwriters found it necessary to tone down his rhetoric. Accordingly, in his acceptance speech at the Republican National Convention in August, he proclaimed his desire for a "kinder, gentler America."

Having established an extremely effective media strategy based on symbolic themes rather than substantive issues, Atwater tied that strategy to the daily campaign schedule. Each morning Bush's advisers agreed upon a "line of the day" which coordinated Bush's campaign appearances that day with the broad campaign themes. They fed the "line of the day" to television and newspaper reporters, who dutifully transmitted it to the American public. Bush's campaign appearances were used to reinforce the "line of the day" and the broader themes. Bush never appeared in an unstructured environment where media reporters could question him at will. Instead, his appearances were carefully orchestrated to reinforce his advertising campaign. To reinforce his advertising attack on Dukakis's veto of the pledge of allegiance bill, for example, he made the evening television news one day by visiting a flag factory and proclaiming that increased flag sales were good for America.[28]

In sum, Bush conducted a high-tech-media campaign in 1988 that was based on highly emotional political symbols such as patriotism and crime, but was devoid of any substantive discussion of how a Bush administration might tackle the social deterioration in America that underlay public concerns over patriotism and crime. Highly sophisticated research was used to establish the themes for the campaign. High-tech-media advertising was used to sell those themes to the public. Personal contact between the candidate and the press was minimized. Instead, his personal appearances were used to provide "sound bites," "photo opportunities," and "visual scenes" that would play well on the evening television news.

This is the way national campaigns and large statewide campaigns are conducted today. The candidate who fails to do these things does so at his or her peril, as Dukakis found out in 1988, and Mondale before him in 1984.

From the standpoint of the lower-status population, however, these contemporary styles of campaigning are detrimental in three respects.

The Illegitimacy of Targeted Voter Groups

For lower-status voters to be brought to the polling booth, they must first be targeted, and many of the targeting appeals are made to specific groups such as blacks, or other racial minorities, labor-union members, and central-city dwellers. In old-fashioned personalized politics, candidates and party leaders met with representatives of such groups and worked out agreements on policies, on positions in the campaign, and on positions in the administration, should the candidate win. In a media-oriented campaign, however, this is harder to do. A pro-union television message is heard not only by union members but also by anti-union people who are likely to be offended by it.

How a campaign targeted to specific subpopulations can backfire on a Democratic candidate can be seen in Walter Mondale's presidential campaign in 1984. Endorsed in his presidential bid by the AFL–CIO and by feminist groups, Mondale quickly was tagged the candidate of special interests. His opponent, President Ronald Reagan, rode a wave of patriotism coinciding with the 1984 Olympic games, the 40th anniversary of the D-Day invasion of Europe, and Reagan's emotional, televised visit to the Normandy landing sites of the invasion. In a contest of images, candidate Mondale and the Democrats "were seen as captives of special interest: organized labor, blacks, feminists, gays. The flip side of this explanation was that the Democrats had turned their backs on the middle-class, on 'mainstream' white America."[29] In such a contest, special interest candidate Mondale was no match for the all-American Reagan, candidate of traditional values and all the people.

Displacement of Intermediary Groups

In traditional politics, there were large numbers of groups (churches, clubs, unions, professional associations, parties, and work groups) that were important intermediaries in helping people decide how to vote. The citizen's role within such groups was interactive; you could argue and discuss issues or candidates with your minister, your union steward, or your fellow group members. Now, most political information comes from television, which has displaced intermediary groups as the major source of political news and interpretation. And you cannot carry on a dialogue with a political advertisement on the television screen.

This decline of intermediary groups' ability to influence the vote especially hurts lower-status people because it deprives them of personal contact with groups that can brief them on which candidates represent their interests. Lower-status people are much less likely to belong to groups than are upper-status people, and people who fail to belong to groups vote much less often than do group members.[30] In short, a situation exists in which lower-status Americans are much less able to cross-check their political information with intermediary groups than are upper-status Americans, are much less likely to vote, and are much less likely to belong to groups that would give them cues on when and for whom to vote.

The Issueless Nature of High-Tech Campaigns

Historically, American campaigns have been nonideological. But until the 1970s, the structure of political organization made it relatively simple for people to understand where their self-interest lay. As intermediary groups and political parties decline, however, lower-status voters find it more difficult to sort out their self-interest, because there are few firm issues that distinguish clearly between the candidates. Television coverage of campaigns has a strong bias toward covering visual events and playing up what analysts call the "horse race" aspect of campaigns. That is, television news focuses more on the question, "Who's winning?" than it does on the question, "How do the candidates differ on their ability to deal with the major problems our society faces?" The second question is about eight times longer than the first, and is a much more complicated idea. Television news dislikes complicated ideas; it loves conflicts. Especially simple conflicts. And even more so, simple conflicts that are dramatic. "Who's winning?" has a brevity, simplicity, and drama that are much more conducive to television news than the longer question is. In a satiric account of television coverage of the 1976 campaign, one commentator wrote:

> I saw President Ford bump his head leaving an airplane . . . I saw Carter playing softball in Plains, George. I saw Carter kissing Amy, I saw Carter hugging Lillian. I saw Carter, in dungarees, walking hand in hand through the peanut farm with Rosalynn. I saw Carter going into church, coming out of church . . . I saw Ford misstate the problems of Eastern Europe—and a week of people commenting about his misstatement. I saw Ford bump his head again. I saw Ford in Ohio say how glad he was to be back in Iowa. I saw marching bands and hecklers, and I learned about the size of crowds and the significance of the size of the crowds.
>
> But in all the hours of high anxiety that I spent watching the network news, never did I hear what the candidates had to say about the campaign issues. That was not news.[31]

One would only need to change a few words to adapt that description to the 1988 campaign. Dukakis rode a tank. Bush welcomed back the space shuttle. Dukakis said the pledge of allegiance; so did Bush. Bush visited a flag factory; Dukakis draped his campaign appearances in flags. Bush pitched horse shoes; Dukakis played catch with a baseball. Both men got off airplanes and shook hands with crowds. The 1988 campaign became a classic instance of an issueless campaign in which substantive issues were subordinated to visual demagoguery.[32]

These anecdotal impressions of the issueless nature of television coverage of campaigns are substantiated by systematic research. As television coverage focuses increasingly on the drama of campaigns, the amount of news time given to candidates' issue positions drops. In 1978 the average TV time allotted to a candidate's speeches was 45 seconds. By 1984 this dropped to 14 seconds and by 1988 to nine seconds.[33] This meant that candidates were forced to compress their issue positions into 9-second pithy sound bites if they wanted them shown on the evening television news. A study of 1976 campaign coverage by the three networks and five print media sources did not find a single instance in which news about "substantive" issues of politics received most of the time or space devoted to the election.[34] This focus on the horse-race aspect of elections tends to trivialize campaigns.[35] Just how much impact television coverage has on people's actual vote is unclear. Some observers argue that television news is watched most intently by people who have already made up their minds; the undecided voters pay much more attention to the issues that are important to them than to the daily campaign coverage.[36]

"Let's run through this once more—and, remember, you choke up at Paragraph Three and brush away the tear at Paragraph Five."

What counts in television campaigning is not the substance of one's speeches so much as the emotional appeal that can be aroused over political symbols.
Source: Drawing by D. Reilly; © 1988 *The New Yorker Magazine*, Inc.

Interest Groups as Channels of Influence _____

Interest groups are another area of the political process that gives average people a chance to influence public policy. In the pluralist school of political theory, interest groups are considered the core of democracy, because they represent channels through which people can band together to counteract the advantages that the economic elite have in the political system. The essence of democracy, to interest-group theorists (also called pluralist theorists), thus is a democratic competition between groups in society.[37] Groups mediate between the individual and the government. In the huge American society of 250 million people, it is not possible for government policy-makers to respond directly to individuals, but they can respond to groups that represent individuals.

As long as people are free to band together in this way, the political system will necessarily be forced to confront any major grievances that exist in the society. And if any significant numbers of people have grievances that the government fails to address, those people constitute a *potential interest* group that will eventually form when the grievances get serious enough and leadership emerges. Women, for example, constituted a potential interest group that during the 1970s transformed itself into an actual political movement. Finally, the great democratic advantage of a group-based politics is that the proliferation of groups prevents any one specific group from dominating the government.[38] Interest group politics is thus a bulwark against tyranny.

The Class Basis of Interest Group Membership

That groups form the basis for American politics is hard to dispute. But from the perspective of lower-status Americans, the group system has two biases that work to their disadvantage. First, as Table 6–2 shows, lower-status people are the Americans least likely to belong to political groups. Almost twice as many persons in the highest income and educational categories belonged to interest groups as did people in the middle category. And the proportion of people in the poorest category who belong to interest groups dropped off precipitously. This limited participation of the lower strata in groups is probably related to the socialization process we examined in Chapter 4. Lower-status people are not as likely as upper-status people to experience a socialization that encourages political or group participation. If groups are the primary vehicles for making demands on the political system, the lack of membership in such groups among lower-status Americans puts them at a special disadvantage. Theoretically, these lower-status people could form their own interest groups. But on a national level this is very difficult to do.

The Bias of Policy Planning Organizations

The upper and upper-middle-class bias of interest-group membership is compounded by the increasingly important role that policy planning organizations play in forming public policy. Some policy-planning organizations such as the Brookings Institution, the Council on Foreign Relations, or the American Enterprise Institute; these organizations stimulate research and publish reports on major public problems and propose policy solutions to them.

The use of policy-planning organizations is a major way for business

TABLE 6-2 The Class Basis of Interest Group Membership

Category of People	Percentage of People Belonging to Interest Groups
All Americans	13
By income level	
$25,000 and over	22
$15,000–24,999	12
Under $15,000	7
By education level	
College education	21
High school education	11
Grade school education	2

This table refers to groups that took positions on issues such as abortion, environmental protection, birth control, the rights of Vietnam veterans, the rights of blacks, women's rights, tax reductions, nuclear power generation, antiwar attitudes, homosexuals' rights, the promotion of the free enterprise system, and the protection of endangered animal species.

Source: The Gallup Poll. *Public Opinion 1981* (Wilmington, Del.: Scholarly Resources, Inc., 1982), pp. 177–178.

interests to put their goals on the political agenda. The Council on Foreign Relations, for example, serves as a forum through which major corporations, top government officials in the foreign and defense agencies, and a few elite university intellectuals generate ideas that may later be translated into U.S. foreign-policy proposals. The directors of the Council on Foreign Relations all serve on boards of directors of large American corporations, forming "interlocking directorates." This is a term used by sociologists for persons serving on the boards of directors of more than one corporation, thus providing an interlinking between corporations. Many directors of the Council on Foreign Relations are graduates of elite universities and have held high appointive positions in the Department of Defense and the Department of State. The Council publishes the journal *Foreign Affairs,* which has historically played a significant role in developing major foreign policy initiatives for the United States. Thomas R. Dye maintains that the Council on Foreign Relations was behind most of the important foreign policy initiatives of the United States during the twentieth century, from the Kellogg Peace Pact of the 1920s, to the toughening of relations with the Soviet Union in the early Reagan years, to the warming up to Soviet glasnost policies in the late Reagan years.[39]

The success of the conservative movement in the 1980s in no small measure grew out of a rise in funding for conservative policy-planning organizations during the 1970s. Organizations such as the American Enterprise Institute and the Heritage Foundation laid much of the intellectual groundwork for President Reagan's New Federalism that we examined in Chapter 3.[40]

Not all policy-planning organizations are on the right of the ideological spectrum. Liberal think-tanks include the Urban Institute, the Institute for Policy Analysis, and the Citizens for Tax Justice. There are also specialized policy-planning institutes that focus on the environment and on energy policy. But there are few influential policy-planning organizations that focus on the problems confronting the lower half of the population. Those who do, such as the Urban Institute, are outweighed in number, in budget, and in prestige by the mainstream policy-planning organizations such as Brookings, or the conservative ones such as the Heritage Foundation. Policy-planning organizations derive most of their funding from interest groups, corporations, foundations, and contracts to do research for government agencies. Given these sources of funding, it is not surprising that most of them focus on national problems from the viewpoint of the upper-status rather than that of the lower-status population.

Decline of Organized Labor

Finally, the lower-status population's ability to use the interest-group process to its advantage has suffered from a progressive weakening of organized labor over the past quarter-century. It might not seem at first glance that the lower-status population has much to lose in the decline of organized labor, since only a minority of lower-status people belong to labor unions, and unions are generally viewed as selfishly seeking economic improvements only for their own members. In fact, however, lower-status people tend to do better when unions are strong. This can be seen most easily by comparing key measures of equity in nations with strong unions (such as Sweden and Denmark) and nations with weak unions (such as the United States). The countries with strong unions have lower unemployment rates, spend a greater share of their economy on social welfare programs, and have a smaller income gap between the rich and the poor.[41]

Even in the United States, with its comparatively weak unions, it is obvious that unions have done a great deal over the years to benefit the bottom half of the income earners. Historically, organized labor has played a critical role in passing most of the country's social welfare legislation. From the Social Security Act of 1935 to the Civil Rights Act of 1964, the Voting Rights Act of 1965, the Medicaid and Medicare programs in 1965, and much of the expansion of social welfare programs in the 1960s and 1970s, the political influence of organized labor was critical. Much of this legislation would have failed had it not been for organized labor.

From the Social Security Act of 1935 to the Civil Rights Act of 1964, the Voting Rights Act of 1965, the Medicaid and Medicare programs in 1965, and much of the expansion of social welfare programs in the 1960s and 1970s, the political influence of organized labor was critical. Much of this legislation would have failed had it not been for organized labor.

Today, however, organized labor is a pale imitation of what it was in its heyday in the 1950s and 1960s. Membership dropped drastically from one-third of the work force in 1955 to about one-sixth of the work force—16 million workers—in 1989,[42] and it is still falling. Along with the dropping membership has come a decline in political influence.

This was especially pronounced during the Reagan years of the 1980s. In 1981, President Reagan fired 12,000 air traffic controllers who conducted an illegal strike. He also appointed anti-union members to the National Labor Relations Board so that it could use its influence to reject union grievances, delay collective bargaining elections, and support businesses that illegally fired workers for engaging in union activities.[43] With the federal government in an anti-union mode, corporations in the 1980s felt free to step up their own anti-union drives, hire consultants to advise them on union-busting tactics, demand give-backs from workers with union contracts, and fire union organizers. According to one account, recent years have seen a dramatic increase in employees fired for participating in union activities. In 1957, about 100 such cases were identified; in 1983, there were 10,000 such cases.[44]

In addition to the anti-union frontal attack launched by government and business, the union movement suffered some self-inflicted injuries as well. Most important of these has been a generally negative image of unions as being somehow a little shady. This negative image is bolstered by occasional incidents of union corruption. The International Brotherhood of Teamsters has seen four of its last seven presidents sent to prison for illegal activities, and the International Longshoremen's Association saw more than two dozen union officials convicted of illegal activities in the early 1980s.[45] Compounding the problems of a shady image, union leaders generally resisted many of the social changes taking place over the last quarter-century. The AFL–CIO PAC political director in 1972 described the Democratic National Committee as composed of "kooks, crazies, queers, and feminists,"[46] hardly a description to endear him to the DNC.

By 1990, there was some indication that organized labor was regaining influence. The Bush administration did not seem as reflexively anti-union as the Reagan administration had been. And organized labor won a number of symbolically important strikes, including a strike of the Northeastern Telephone Company workers in 1989 and a bitter coal miners' strike in 1990.[47]

The Prospects for a Cross-Ethnic Political Coalition _____

If the lower-status population is to gain greater political influence, its main hope lies in developing effective leadership in the central institutions of America's political process: political parties, elections, and interest groups. Union leaders, for example, must create a way to convert their own support for lower-status causes into political support from the lower-status population. Democratic Party leaders must do the same thing among lower-status voting groups. The voting turnout rates of the lower-status population must be increased so that more legislators find themselves as dependent upon the votes of their lower-status constituents as they are on their upper-middle-class campaign contributors.

Above all, would-be leaders of the lower-status population must find ways to build voting coalitions among the various ethnic, religious, and ideological groups that currently pit the members of the lower-status population against each other. For example, if low-income Hispanics, whites, American Indians, and Asians could form an electoral coalition capable of swinging key races for governorships, the United States Senate, and the United States House of Representatives, that coalition alone would vastly increase the political influence of lower-status people. The outspoken advocate of this approach was presidential candidate Jesse Jackson who called for a "rainbow coalition" in his 1984 and 1988 campaigns. Just as the rainbow's natural beauty lies in its spread of colors, the political rainbow coalition would draw its strength from the unity of peoples of different colors: whites, browns, reds, yellows, and blacks.

Seeing the need for a rainbow coalition is easier than constructing one, however. Jackson had modest success in his 1988 primary campaign for the Democratic presidential nomination and emerged the top vote-getter in some states. But he had little success among one of the crucial constituencies for a successful rainbow coalition, the lower-middle-income white vote. Jackson gained as much as 30 percent of the white vote in some primaries, but almost all of that came from upper-middle-income white liberals; very little came from white blue-collar workers and lower-middle-income whites generally.[48]

Cross-ethnic coalitions are growing more common, but they still face several obstacles, as can be seen by looking at state and local government elections. In most cities where blacks have won the mayor's office, they did so in the face of massive opposition from the white wards which was usually overcome by huge majorities in the black wards. Chicago black mayor Harold Washington (1983–1987), for example, won nearly all the black vote and a large majority of the Hispanic vote, but still depended on a small upper-middle-class, white, liberal vote for his margin of victory.[49] Of all the big-city black mayors, only Los Angeles' Thomas Bradley has consistently won a large cross-section of the white vote.

Black–Hispanic voter coalitions are more common than are black coalitions with lower-status white voters. But even here the obstacles are numerous. Chicago's black mayor, Harold Washington, received 57 percent of the Hispanic vote in his 1987 election.[50] But Houston Mayor Kathy Whitmire tended to divide that city's black and Hispanic voters. She won a majority of blacks in her first mayoral election, but lost a majority of the Hispanics. New York City Mayor Edward Koch did the reverse; he drew strong support in the Hispanic neighborhoods but tended to lose in the black neighborhoods. In Miami, relations between blacks and Cubans are openly hostile.[51] And a widely praised study of minority-group politics in northern California found alliances between blacks and Hispanics difficult to achieve.[52]

The missing ingredient for a consistently successful rainbow coalition is the lower-status white voter. Most of the white vote for minority candidates comes from upper-status white liberals who have an *ideological* motivation for joining multi-ethnic coalitions. But there are not enough upper-status white liberals to make the rainbow coalition viable. What is missing is the mass of lower-status white voters who might support a rainbow coalition if they could be convinced that such support was in their economic *interest*.[53] Upper-status white liberals might vote for ideological motives, but lower-status white voters are less likely to do so.[54] A substantial portion of lower-status white voters constitute what the Center for Political Studies terms "group benefits voters" and "nature of the times" voters.[55] To bring them into the rainbow coalition it would be necessary to convince them that they have an economic *interest* in doing so rather than to appeal to their ideological motivation.

In sum, there are large but not insurmountable obstacles to the formation of a lower-status cross-ethnic voting coalition. The unspoken but critical obstacle is probably economic opportunity and affirmative-action policies. A prominent candidate with a viable scheme for promoting the economic opportunities of all these lower-status peoples would stand a chance of gaining broad voter support. A campaign theme that pitted one element of the potential coalition against the other elements would be doomed to failure. One that promised to abandon affirmative-action programs would most certainly alienate blacks and Hispanics, who would accurately perceive it as an attack on themselves. One that promised to expand affirmative action would probably alienate lower-status whites, especially lower-status white males, and most especially Southern lower-status white males, who would accurately view it as an attack on them. What is needed is a scheme that would expand opportunities for all categories of lower-status workers without obviously singling out any subcategory for preferential treatment. There probably is no white politician capable of doing this today without alienating black and Hispanic voters. But the victory of moderate Democratic black gubernatorial candidate Douglas Wilder in Virginia suggests that it might be possible for a minority candidate to pick up white voters by campaigning on such a schema.

Conclusion: To Overcome Bias _____

In reviewing the political process, we have pinpointed several obstacles that lie in the path of any movement to improve the political influence of the American lower-status population.

1. Many lower-status people, especially whites, do not see the Democratic Party as more sensitive than the Republican Party to their economic interests.
2. Many lower-status people, especially whites, *do* see the Republican Party as more sensitive to them than the Democratic Party on important symbolic social issues.
3. As the old New Deal coalition has lost its dominance, people are less inclined to vote along party identification lines and class lines than they were a generation earlier. This makes it difficult for lower-status voters to perceive that elections make a difference to their self-interest.
4. The two-tiered system of politics has given the Republicans an edge over the Democrats in defining the issues of national politics. Because they have controlled the highly visible White House, Republicans have been better able than the Democrats to get elections fought on the basis of social issues that would be to their advantage.
5. The decline of party identification as a voting turnout determinant has been hastened by the rise of high-technology campaigning. Because high-technology campaigning lends itself to

campaigns based on highly symbolic social and foreign policy issues, it compounds the problem that lower-status voters have in perceiving their economic self-interest in the election process.

6. In the era of high-technology campaigning, appeals to lower-status voters suffer an image problem. Such appeals usually have to be made by targeting specific subcategories of the lower-status population such as blacks, Hispanics, union members, central-city dwellers, or poor women. But such appeals, made via television, are seen by non-members of the subcategories as well as members, and such appeals can alienate the non-members. The broad-middle-class voters especially tend to get alienated, and the candidate who overtly makes such targeted campaigns risks being tabbed as the candidate of special interests.

7. The displacement of intermediary groups in the electoral process by television has robbed the lower-status voters of a mechanism that might have helped them sort out their economic self-interests.

8. The issueless nature of contemporary high-technology campaigns compounds the problems that lower-status voters face in sorting out their self-interest among the campaign appeals.

9. Interest groups offer a potentially powerful avenue for lower-status influence in the political process. But lower-status people are less likely to belong to political interest groups than are upper-status people, and the interest groups based on the lower-status population (especially labor unions) have seen their influence decline in recent years.

10. A powerful multi-ethnic coalition of lower-status voters is not out of the question, but enormous obstacles stand in its way.

Outlined so starkly, these obstacles to lower-status influence appear formidable. But ignoring the obstacles will not make them disappear. As we have said repeatedly, bias understood is bias overcome. To understand the biases inherent in today's political process is to outline the steps needed to overcome the biases. In this instance, the steps are fourfold.

A Massive Educational Effort

First, would-be leaders of the lower-status population need to promote a massive educational campaign among that population. Lower-status people need to learn that turning out to vote makes a difference in terms of their economic interests. Unless a third party can be created for them (which does not seem very likely), lower-status voters need to perceive that their economic interests are better met by the

Democratic Party today than the Republican Party, which caters more to some of their symbolic interests. They need to develop a more sympathetic outlook toward unions and toward collective action generally.

Stimulate Group Participation

Second, would-be leaders of the lower-status population must do everything possible to stimulate lower-status participation in the group life of American neighborhoods, churches, schools, and workplaces.[56] Because lower-status people are less likely to be group participants than are upper-status people, they are less likely to get the interpersonal cues and signals that help people calculate where their best interests lie. It is important for all Americans, but especially for the less well-educated and less-sophisticated lower-status Americans, that there be a revival of the political role intermediary groups play in mediating the political messages that come from the television screen.

Strengthen Lower-Status Institutions

Third, would-be leaders of the lower-status population should lend whatever support they can to strengthening the political party system and organized labor. Strong parties and strong unions are the main institutional mechanisms in contemporary democracies for promoting the political leadership of lower-status populations. Where parties and unions are strong, lower-status populations tend to do better economically. Where they are weak, those populations tend to do worse.

Build Cross-Ethnic Lower-Status Coalitions

Fourth, would-be leaders of the lower-status population must cooperate in creating cross-ethnic political coalitions. Included in this cooperation would be supporting candidates capable of appealing to voters across the rainbow coalition. Because of the limited number of ideological upper-status white liberals in the voting population, this coalition cannot be built solely on the basis of ideological motivation. It must also offer economic incentives to lower-status whites to join the coalition.

Notes _____

1. E. E. Schattschneider, *Party Government* (New York: Rinehart, 1942), p. 7.
2. V. O. Key, *Public Opinion and American Democracy* (New York: Knopf, 1961), p. 432.
3. David S. Broder, *The Party's Over: The Failure of Politics in America* (New York: Harper & Row, 1972), pp. xxi, xxiii.

4. Cited in Walter Dean Burnham, "Elections and Democratic Institutions," *Society* 24, no. 4 (May/June 1987): 39.

5. John E. Schwarz, *America's Hidden Success: A Reassessment of Twenty Years of Public Policy* (New York: W. W. Norton and Co., 1983), especially pp. 57–59.

6. Quoted in Samuel Lubell, *The Hidden Crisis in American Politics* (New York: Norton, 1971), p. 76.

7. Martin P. Wattenberg, "The Decline of Political Partisanship in the United States: Negativity or Neutrality?" *American Political Science Review* 75, no. 4 (December 1981): 941–950. The surveys were the quadrennial National Election Studies conducted by the Center for Political Research at the University of Michigan.

8. This was first discovered in 1956 by Herbert McClosky, Paul J. Hoffman, and Rosemary O'Hara, "Issue Conflict and Consensus among Party Leaders and Followers," *American Political Science Review* 54, no. 2. (June 1960): 406–427.

9. The *Congressional Quarterly Weekly Report,* October 22, 1988, pp. 3042–3043.

10. Walter Dean Burnham, *Critical Elections and the Mainsprings of American Politics* (New York: Oxford University Press, 1975).

11. Kevin Phillips, *The Emerging Republican Majority* (New York: Arlington House, 1969).

12. Everett Carll Ladd, Jr., *Where Have All the Voters Gone? The Fracturing of America's Political Parties* (New York: Norton, 1978), pp. 23, 42–43.

13. David Gopoian, Derek Hacket, Daniel Parelman, and Leo J. Perrotta, "The Democratic Party Coalition in the Eighties: A Reassessment of Ladd's Old Class/New Class Explanation of Intra-Party Conflict," *Western Political Quarterly* 40, no. 2 (June 1987): 247. This article dismisses Ladd's "New Class/Old Class" distinction as significant to the Democratic decline and argues that foreign issues rather than social issues were the ones that did in the Democrats.

14. Charles D. Hadley has found a dual partisanship among Democrats. This occurs among people, mostly Southerners, who consider themselves Democrats at the state level but Republicans at the national level. See his "Dual Partisan Identification in the South," *Journal of Politics* 47, no. 1 (February 1985): 255–268.

15. Martin P. Wattenberg, "The Hollow Realignment: Partisan Change in a Candidate Centered Era," *Public Opinion Quarterly* 51, no. 1 (Summer 1987): 58–74; "Do Voters Really Care About Political Parties Anymore? A Response to Craig," *Political Behavior* 9, no. 2 (1987): 114–125. Another study found a growth in positive feelings toward both parties since 1968. See Thomas M. Konda and Lee Sigelman, "Public Evaluation of the American Parties, 1952–1984," *Journal of Politics* 49, no. 3 (August 1987): 814–829.

16. William Crotty, *American Parties in Decline,* 2nd ed. (Boston: Little, Brown and Co., 1984), pp. 35–36.

17. One study found that lower partisanship among new voters was the most common reason for the decline in party identification between 1965 and 1976. Helmut Norpath and Jerrold Rusk, "Partisan Dealignment in the American Electorate: Intermixing the Deductions Since 1964," *American Political Science Review* 76, no. 3 (September 1982): 552–538.

18. M. Kent Jennings and Gregory B. Markus, "Partisan Orientation over the Long Haul: Results from the Three Wave Political Socialization Panel Study," *American Political Science Review* 78, no. 4 (December 1984): 1000–1018.

19. One political scientist, W. Phillips Shively, has expressed doubt whether contemporary conditions permit a new majority party to be formed. See his "The Electoral Impact of Party Loyalists and the 'Floating Voter': A New Measure and a New Perspective," *Journal of Politics* 44, no. 3 (August 1982): 679–695.

20. Helmut Norpoth, "Under Way and Here to Stay: Party Realignment in the 1980s?" *Public Opinion Quarterly* 51, no. 3 (Fall 1987): 376–391.

21. *New York Times,* April 23, 1984.

22. See David S. Broder, "'How They Rehearsed the Election," *Washington Post,* November 16, 1980.

23. See Wirthlin interview in *Public Opinion* 8, no. 1 (February 1985).

24. *Newsweek* ran a cover picture of Bush that boldly proclaimed there was a "Wimp factor" in the election. George Will caricatured Bush as a lap dog for Reagan.

25. See Paul Taylor and David S. Broder "Early Volley of Bush Ads Exceeded Expectations," *Washington Post,* October 28, 1988, p. A1.

26. Michael Rezendes, "Bushwacked on Law and Order, Dukakis Points to His Record," *Washington Post National Weekly Edition,* October 24–30, 1988, p. 7.

27. Quoted in Marjorie Randon Hershey, "The Campaign and the Media," in *The Election of 1988: Reports and Interpretations,* Gerald M. Pomper, ed. (Chatham, N.J.: Chatham House Publishers, Inc., 1989), p. 95.

28. Shown on Bill Moyers, *The Public Mind,* a PBS television series broadcast in the Fall, 1989.

29. Hershey, "The Campaign and the Media," p. 79.

30. The National Opinion Research Center's General Social Survey annually asks people how many groups they belong to. Among the bottom 40 percent, those who belong to three or more groups reported a 77 percent voter turnout in the 1988 presidential election, while those belonging to less than three groups reported only a 60 percent turnout.

31. Malcolm MacDougall, "The Barkers of Snake Oil Politics," *Politics Today* (January/ February 1980): 35.

32. Hershey, "The Campaign and the Media," pp. 96–100.

33. *Newsweek,* November 21, 1988, p. 24.

34. Thomas E. Patterson, *The Mass Media Election* (New York: Praeger Publishers, 1980), p. 29. The three networks devoted 58 percent of their time to the "game" aspects of the elections and only 29 percent to the "substance." Print media were only slightly more inclined than television to cover the substance. The *Los Angeles Times* devoted 52 percent of its space to the game and 33 percent to the substance, while *Time* and *Newsweek* magazines combined devoted 54 percent to the game and only 31 percent to the substance.

35. Austin Ranney, *Channels of Power: The Impact of Television on American Politics* (New York: Basic Books, 1983), p. 116.

36. Michael J. Robinson, "The Media in 1980: Was the Message the Message?" in Austin Ranney, ed., *The Elections of 1980* (Washington, D.C.: American Enterprise Institute, 1981), p. 178.

37. See especially Robert A. Dahl, *Polyarchy, Participation and Opposition* (New Haven: Yale University Press, 1971) and David B. Truman: *The Governmental Process* (New York: Knopf, 1951).

38. This was Madison's great insight in his *Federalist 10.*

39. Thomas R. Dye, *Who's Running America: The Bush Era,* 5th ed. (Englewood Cliffs, NJ: Prentice Hall, 1990), 248–257.

40. Joseph G. Peschek, *Policy-Planning Organizations: Elite Agenda and America's Rightward Turn* (Philadelphia: Temple University Press, 1987).

41. These were the findings of a study done by economist David R. Cameron and reported in Edsall, *The New Politics of Inequality,* pp. 146, 255. The weak-union countries had an average unemployment rate of 4.6 percent from 1965 to 1981, compared to 2.8 percent in the strong-union countries. They spent 13.7 percent of their GNP on social welfare programs compared to 21.3 percent in the strong union countries, and the richest two-fifths of the population received 38.8 percent more of the national income than did the poorest two-fifths, compared to only 28.3 percent more in the strong-union countries.

42. Union members comprised 33.2 percent of the non-agricultural work force in 1955, compared to 16.4 percent in 1989. *Statistical Abstract of the United States: 1975,* p. 371 and *Statistical Abstract of the United States: 1991,* p. 425.

43. See David Moberg, "Obstacles to Union Organizing," *In These Times,* July 11–24, 1984, p. 5 and Dennis Schall, "How Bad Can the NLRB Get?" *Guardian,* January 16, 1985, p. 7.

44. *Washington Post,* July 20, 1986.

45. Edsall, *The New Politics of Inequality,* pp. 172–174.

46. Quoted in Ibid., p. 161. The official was Alexander E. Barkan of the AFL–CIO Committee on Political Education.

47. See David Moberg, "Innovative Pittson Strike Nears End," *In These Times,* January 17–23, 1990, p. 7. *New York Times,* February 21, 1990, p. A10.

48. Jackson was the top vote-getter in seven states, the District of Columbia, and Puerto

Rico. In California and New York, he drew much stronger support from white liberals and from college-educated whites than he did from other whites. Gerald M. Pomper, "The Presidential Nominations," in *The Elections of 1988,* Pomper, ed., pp. 40, 45.

49. See Michael B. Preston, "The Election of Harold Washington: Black Voting Patterns in the 1983 Chicago Mayoral Race," *PS* 16, no. 3 (Summer 1983): 486–488; *The New York Times,* April 9, 1987, p. 11; Paul Green, "The Message from the 26th Ward," *Comparative State Politics Newsletter* 7, no. 4 (August 1986): 16.

50. *New York Times,* April 7, 1987, p. 11.

51. See Joan Didion, "Miami: La Lucha," *New York Review of Books* 34, no. 10 (June 11, 1987): 15.

52. Rufus P. Browning, Dale Rogers Marshall, and David H. Tabb, *Protest Is Not Enough: The Struggle of Blacks and Hispanics for Equality in Urban Politics* (Berkeley, Calif.: University of California Press, 1984), pp. 121–124.

53. The distinction between ideology and self-interest as a motivation for whites to join multiracial coalitions is formulated by Raphael J. Sonenshein, "Biracial Coalitions in Big Cities: Why They Succeed, Why They Fail," *Racial Politics in American Cities,* eds. Rufus P. Browning, Dale Rogers Marshall, and David H. Tabb (New York: Longman, 1990), pp. 193–211.

54. A substantial body of research supports this contention. See especially the categorization of voters into ideologues, near ideologues, group-benefits voters, nature-of-the-times voters, and no-issue-content voters by the Center for Political Studies. Philip E. Converse, "Public Opinion and Voting Behavior," in Fred I. Greenstein and Nelson W. Polsby, eds., *Handbook of Political Science,* vol. 4 (Reading, Mass.: Addison–Wesley, 1975), p. 102.

55. Ibid.

56. See Paul Starr, "Civil Reconstruction: What to Do Without Affirmative Action," *The American Prospect* No. 8 (Winter 1992): 7.

CHAPTER 7

Congress and the Public Interest

As the nation turned the calendar to the last decade of the twentieth century, an AFL–CIO-supported research group, the Citizens for Tax Justice (CTJ), reported the results of a study it had just completed on the consequences of tax reform over the previous dozen years.[1] Tax reform is not usually a barn-burning issue, but the CTJ findings were eye-catching to say the least. During the dozen years studied (1978–1989), Congress made three major revisions in tax law (1981, 1984, and 1986) along with countless minor fine tunings. As a result of all this tinkering, when citizens sat down at their kitchen tables to fill out their 1990 income tax returns, 90 percent of them owed more taxes than they would have owed had tax laws been left as they were in 1977. Despite this increase in taxes for 90 percent of the people, the federal government collected $70 billion *less* in tax revenues than it would have collected had Congress left the tax codes alone. Since the bottom 90 percent of the people paid more in taxes as a result of the changes, the richest 10 percent received virtually *all* of the tax savings. And the richest 1 percent paid $84 billion less in taxes than they would have if taxes had been left alone.

Not only did the richest 1 percent of the people save $84 billion in taxes in 1990, they saved another $84 billion in 1991. Another $84 billion in 1992. And so on until the tax laws are changed again.

We know by now, of course, that nobody in politics is neutral, so you will be forgiven if you suspect that an AFL–CIO-supported research group might have exaggerated the inequities resulting from these tax changes. The poorest citizens were virtually taken off the tax rolls in 1986, and upper-income people complain that they shoulder an even larger share of the tax bill now than they did in 1980. But there can be little doubt that the general conclusion of the CTJ study was correct: the rich got most of the benefits from government taxing and spending policies in the 1980s. There simply have been too many other studies reaching that same conclusion to doubt that the Citizens for Tax Justice report was essentially correct on that point.[2] But perhaps the CTJ exaggerated the extent of the inequities. Let us assume, arbitrarily,

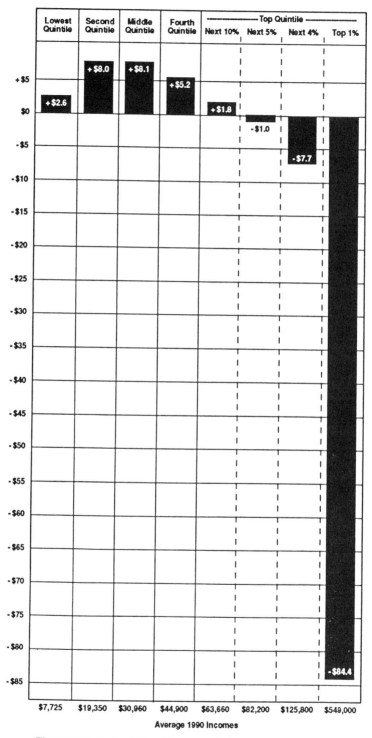

Figure 7-1 Federal Tax Changes, 1977 to 1990, in Billions of Dollars (1990 Taxes Versus 1977 Taxes Adjusted for Inflation)

Source: Inequality and the Federal Budget Deficit (Washington, D.C.: Citizens for Tax Justice, 1990), p. 8.

that the results were exaggerated by as much as 25 percent. If so, then the richest 1 percent of the people received only $63 billion in tax savings each year, not $84 billion. And only two-thirds of the people were paying higher taxes, instead of 90 percent of the people as calculated by the CTJ. If that were the case, would you feel any better about the way Congress treated your pocketbook during those years? Probably not.

The change in federal tax policy from 1978 to 1986 stands as one of the starkest examples in American history of the redistribution of wealth from the middle and lower-middle classes to the rich. Congress bears a heavy responsibility for this redistribution, because Congress is the predominant branch of government in writing tax legislation. While this redistribution was taking place, one house of Congress was controlled all the time by the Democrats, the party that draws its votes disproportionately from the lower-strata population. And the other house of Congress was controlled most of the time by the Democrats. Not only did the Democrats predominate in Congress during this period, but Republican control of the presidency rested in no small measure on the ability of Presidents Reagan and Bush to convince millions of lower-status voters that Republicans would look out for them better than the Democrats would.

How could a government-sponsored upward redistribution of wealth of this magnitude take place during a period when the political party beholden to lower-status voters (the Democrats) dominated Congress and the Republicans, who dominated the presidency, were deeply indebted to the large numbers of middle and lower-middle-income voters who had deserted the Democrats?

This is a question that screams out for analysis. Are politicians so cynical that they blatantly plunder the lower-status population immediately after winning their votes? Many people would say yes to this question, but the correct answer to this question is more complex. The answer lies in four great changes that have occurred in the past 20 years in the way Congress goes about its business. These four changes have to do with (1) the relationship of congressional Democrats to their voting constituencies, (2) the Republican relationship to their constituencies, (3) the resurgence of the traditional conservative coalition at critical moments in the tax-reform process, and (4) some structural features of Congress that impeded its ability to set its own decision-making agenda most of the time.

Analyzing these four changes and their consequences will shed some light on how Congress operates and what patterns of bias are involved in those operations. In this chapter we will first review the tax changes that occurred between 1978 and 1990 and, second, examine the way in which each of the above political changes helped bias the treatment of tax reform to the disadvantage of the lower-status population. Third, we will explore what will be needed for Congress to overcome the biases that put the lower-status population at such a disadvantage in the tax-reform process of the 1980s. Finally, we must keep in mind that in conducting this analysis we are observing here only a small, albeit important, slice of Congress. Were we to analyze Congress working in a different area of public affairs—constituent casework, for example, or environmental-protection legislation—we might conceivably find totally different patterns of bias. But the issue of tax reform is central to anyone who is concerned with how Congress treats the lower-status population, for it touches on a fundamental question of democratic theory. Whose voice will be heard when it comes to parceling out the burden of paying for government? The great rallying cry of the American revolution, after all, was "No taxation without representation!"

Tax Reform

The federal income tax is a relatively new phenomenon. When started in 1913 it touched only the highest incomes in the land and imposed a top tax-bracket of only 7 percent.[3] Over the next 60 years, however, the income tax became increasingly widespread as the federal government was called upon to fight major wars, finance the Cold War, pick up the pieces from the economic collapse of the 1930s, and meet persistent demands that the federal government promote social-welfare policies at home that were commonplace in the other industrialized nations. By the mid-1970s, virtually everyone with an identifiable source of income was subject to the tax, and the marginal tax rate[4] reached as high as 70 percent.

Complaints About the Federal Tax Structure

Historically, the federal income tax was highly regarded as an admirable way to raise money to meet the federal government's responsibilities, but as time went on it became less popular. By 1979, public-opinion surveys began to show that people now looked on it as the worst tax, the least fair among the major taxes they paid.[5] Why this transformation occurred can be seen in the complaints of scholarly economists and political conservatives.

The Complaint of Scholarly Economists. Looking back on the criticisms of mainstream economists about the income tax in the late 1970s, it seems clear that they never intended for tax reform to become the huge giveaway to the very rich that it eventually became. On the contrary, much of their criticism sought to broaden the tax base and make it fairer. Three main features of the income tax came in for the greatest criticism.[6]

First was the growing use of "tax preferences." Commonly called loopholes, tax preferences are tax deductions, credits, or exclusions that are granted to people or corporations in order to promote some public goal. To encourage employers to form pension plans for their workers, for example, the amount of your pay that is contributed to your pension plan is deducted from your taxable income before your taxes are calculated. This gives a substantial tax savings to you, and it was the single biggest tax preference in 1980, costing the federal treasury nearly $20 billion.[7] Economists disliked tax preferences mainly because there were so many of them ($145 billion in 1980) that they drove up the budget deficit, narrowed the tax base, and put an unfair burden on people who were not eligible for tax preferences. Well over one-third of all tax preferences in 1980, for example, were for employer-paid pension contributions, employer-paid health insurance benefits, and tax-deductible home-ownership taxes and interest. Obviously, you did not qualify for these tax savings if you were a renter who worked for a company that did not provide a pension or health-insurance plan. This was, and still is, the situation of most lower-status workers. They pay higher taxes to compensate for the tax savings being given to the higher-status home owners working in higher-status jobs that are covered by pension plans and health insurance.

A second criticism was that the growing list of tax preferences was distorting the investment decisions of corporations and individuals. Instead of investing their profits primarily in expansion and greater productivity, companies were increasingly pressed to make investments for garnering the biggest tax breaks. This consequence of the income tax drew more and more attention as the economy of the 1970s and early 1980s lapsed into a condition called "stagflation"—the simultaneous occurrence of economic stagnation and inflation.

Economists' third criticism focused on the "bracket creep" that resulted from inflation. There were 15 different income-tax brackets by the late 1970s, each with its own tax rate, and the higher income-tax brackets paid higher tax rates. (The $22,500–24,999 bracket, for example, had a higher rate than the $20,000–22,499 bracket.) If inflation rose 5 percent and you received a 5 percent salary increase, you only broke even in real dollars, but because of your salary increase you probably crept into a higher tax bracket. As a consequence of inflation and bracket creep, millions of families were driven into progressively higher income-tax brackets during the 1970s and early 1980s, even though their real, spendable income was barely increasing.

The Complaint of Political Conservatives. Added to the criticisms of the mainstream economists was the complaint of political conservatives that the high marginal income-tax rates were acting as a drag on the economy. This was especially the complaint of "supply side" economists. In their view, the rich simply paid too much of the tax burden. The richest 10 percent of the people paid half of all federal income taxes, and the richest half paid over 90 percent of all the income taxes. [8] From the supply-side perspective, high marginal rates of up to 70 percent discouraged people from working hard and seeking financial independence. By soaking the rich and redistributing wealth through social-welfare programs to the lower-status population, the federal government was taking money away from the people most likely to invest in job-creating enterprises and giving the money to those most likely to squander it. If we would just cut income taxes generally and eliminate the high marginal rates that prevailed in the 1970s, the private sector would generate so much economic activity that unemployment would be reduced, inflation cured, and the federal budget deficit would disappear.[9] Rather than a progressive income tax based on ability to pay, supply-siders wanted a "flat tax" rate for all, regardless of their income level.

Reforming the Tax System

In sum, by the late 1970s there was growing dissatisfaction with the federal income tax. Public opinion had become hostile, and a sharp intellectual challenge was being mounted by mainstream economists and supply-side conservatives alike. President Carter summed up much of this criticism with his simple comment that the tax system was "a disgrace."[10]

Economic Recovery Tax Act of 1981. The Economic Recovery Tax Act of 1981 (ERTA) reflected the influence of supply-side conservatives on the early Reagan administration, and it was the single most important cause of the huge tax savings granted to the rich in the 1980s. It reduced individual income taxes by 23 percent, cut the top marginal tax bracket from 70 percent to 50 percent, and provided a host of generous tax preferences for corporations and upper-income persons. Among the most generous of these were the short time periods allowed for depreciating investments in real estate property and capital equipment. No small number of doctors, for example, discovered that the new law enabled them to buy a Porsche in November or December, drive it once to a professional conference before year's end, and make a substantial reduction in their income tax liability by writing off the automobile's purchase as a business expense. Partially as a result of the dramatic increase in tax preferences, the supply-side promise that the tax cuts would stimulate so much economic growth that the federal deficit would disappear did not materialize. On the contrary, the federal debt more than tripled from approximately $1 trillion in 1981 to more than $3 trillion by decade's end.

Tax Reform in 1982 and 1984. To slow the growing flow of red ink, Congress passed the Tax Equity and Fiscal Responsibility Act of 1982 (TEFRA) and the Deficit Reduction Act of 1984 (DEFRA). These acts sought to recoup some of the government's lost tax revenues without undoing the income-tax-rate cuts that Reagan had urged on Congress in 1981. They did this by increasing user fees for federal services, increasing non-income-tax revenue sources such as liquor taxes or cigarette taxes, and closing some of the more flagrant tax loopholes that had been opened in 1981, such as the one cited above for writing off all the cost of luxury automobiles.

Tax Reform Act of 1986. If the 1981 tax act was a great gift to the wealthy, the Tax Reform Act of 1986 (TRA) is notable for making the most revolutionary changes in the structure of the tax codes in nearly a half-century. It was essentially revenue neutral in that it did not dramatically increase or decrease the amount of tax revenues collected by the federal government. But it made a dramatic reduction in the tax preferences available to many middle-class citizens (deductions, for example, for state sales taxes, for consumer loan interest, and for money saved in an IRA). In exchange it moved in the direction of a flat-rate tax by consolidating the previous fifteen brackets into just two brackets, 15 percent and 25 percent, although a marginal rate of 33 percent was tacked onto upper-middle incomes.[11]

Getting this act through Congress took remarkable legislative leadership by its chief adherents, Daniel Rostenkowski, Democrat from Illinois, who chaired the Ways and Means Committee of the House of Representatives, and Robert Packwood, Republican from Oregon, who chaired the Senate Finance Committee. These are the two tax-writing committees of Congress. The act offered something for virtually everyone. Liberals were attracted because the act completely removed most poor people from any income liability, increased the tax on capital gains, and reduced a large number of business deductions. Conservatives were attracted by the overall reductions in tax rates and the "flat tax" feature of having just two tax brackets. And the votes of key individual congressional members were secured by the traditional logrolling practice of giving tax breaks that would affect their districts. The *New York Times* published a list of 655 such breaks that were included in the legislation.[12] For example, to push the bill through the

House, Rostenkowski needed the help of Rules Committee Chair Claude Pepper, so Rostenkowski put into the act special tax breaks for a football stadium in Pepper's home town (Miami, Florida) for the Miami Dolphins, a convention center, and a redevelopment project. In return, Pepper pushed through the Rules Committee a rule that made it impossible to amend the bill when it came to the House Floor for debate. When criticized for the concessions that he wrote into the bill for Pepper and others, Rostenkowski simply replied that he did what was needed to get the bill passed. "Politics," he said, "is an imperfect process."[13]

Why Tax Reform Produced Its Unintended Break for the Rich

Aside from supply-siders who influenced the early Reagan administration, it does not appear from this cursory review that most of the economists and members of Congress who played leading roles in the tax reform of the 1980s deliberately sought to give $84 billion per year in tax savings to the richest 1 percent of the population, while increasing the tax burden on most everybody else. Yet this massive redistribution—or at least something approaching it—is indeed what resulted. To understand why this unintended consequence happened we have to explore the internal politics of Congress itself. Although it is not possible to trace the thousands of congressional decisions that produced the tax policies of the 1980s, we can identify four features of the congressional process that support an anti-lower-status bias in Congress and that facilitated the upper-class tax breaks that resulted from tax reform.

Democrats and Their Lower-Status Constituents

We saw in Chapter 5 that the Democrats in Congress are much more inclined than Republicans are to support economic policies that aid lower-status voters. But evidence reviewed here suggests that the Democrats did not do a good job of looking out for their lower-status constituents when it came to tax policy in the 1980s. Part of the reason for this lies in changes that occurred in the 1970s and the 1980s in the relationship between Democratic Congress members and their constituents. This is the thesis of *Washington Post* reporter Thomas B. Edsall, who in 1984 wrote *The New Politics of Inequality*[14] to sort out the political connections between government policy in the 1980s and the state of the Democratic Party.

The Personal Side of the Tax Code:
The Super Bowl High Roller

If you run a business, many of your expenses count as legitimate income tax deductions. For example, no one could reasonably expect you to pay income taxes on the cost of travel to recruit a staff member or even on the costs of entertainment that could help you run your business better. It is not hard to abuse these tax privileges, however, as shown in the case of the Super Bowl High Roller, Dr. Dale Helman of Monterey, California. The *Minneapolis Star Tribune* reported:

> The 32-year-old neurologist was tooling around the Twin Cities Saturday afternoon in a blue-and-gold chauffeur-driven 1962 Rolls that rents for $1,200 a day.

> He says he made the trip to the Super Bowl because he needed a $10,000 tax writeoff: "On Dec. 30, my tax accountant said I have 36 hours to get an entertainment deduction." In a New Year's Eve rush, Helman bought four tickets over the phone from Ticket Exchange, a ticket broker in Phoenix, Ariz. . . . The price: $1,550 a ticket.

> Helman wanted only the best seats. He said he'll write the trip off because he's taking three neurologist friends to the game and plans to discuss neurology with them "in the limo. . . . Maybe at halftime we'll talk about the neurology of football injuries." He also went to Minneapolis Veterans Medical Center yesterday afternoon in his limo to interview a neurologist for a position on his staff.

> "It is rare that I get a weekend off, but when I get a weekend off I play hard," said Helman, who flew first class from San Francisco on Friday night. He and his buddies went to a Champps sports bar, where they met some Buffalo Bills cheerleaders.

> He calls his visit "clean fun."

Source: Minneapolis Star Tribune (Minneapolis–St. Paul) January 26, 1992, p. 15–A. Reprinted by permission.

The Thesis of Democratic Desertion

Edsall's thesis that the Democratic Party deserted its traditional lower-status constituency is built on the demographic fact that the traditional Democratic bastions in the central city are losing political influence while the suburbs are gaining influence. Because of population shifts, the central cities lose representation in Congress and the suburbs gain representation when congressional districts are reapportioned after each census. Since suburbanites tend to be slightly more affluent and much more inclined to be political independents than are average central-city residents, suburban Democratic congressmen have to make accommodations in their political behavior if they wish to be reelected, or even elected in the first place.

Procedural Reform and the Shift of Power in the Democratic Party. According to Edsall, many of these representatives made their accommodations in the 1970s and 1980s by pushing for *procedural* reforms within Congress and the Democratic Party, rather than substantive *redistributive* reforms designed to improve the economic position of the lower-status Democrats voter. The critical class of congressmen were those Democratic elected during the post-Watergate reform era of 1974 and 1976. "Many of these . . . won election in previously Republican districts, and their first priority was to prevent largely middle and upper-class voters from returning to the GOP fold."[15] Such Democrats feared that substantive, redistributive reforms would disaffect their suburban constituents who were less liberal and less Democratic than were central-city residents. These Congressional members hoped that these same suburban constituents would respond positively to procedural reforms aimed at curbing the influence of organized labor and big-city machines on the Democratic Party while opening up the party to feminists and minorities.

In Chapter 5 we examined how these reforms took place within the Democratic Party. The net effect of these reforms, argues Edsall, was to shift influence away from an older elite of union leaders, Democratic officeholders, and urban bosses who drew their own political influence from the support of lower-status voters and thus had a vested interest in advocating the economic concerns of those lower-status voters. The winners in this shift of influence consisted of a newer elite whose interests lay in paying attention to the concerns of upper-middle-class people rather than lower-status people. This was reflected in the kind of voters that dominate the primary elections that choose delegates to the Democratic national convention. For example, a study of 13 states in 1976 found that primary voters earned higher incomes than general-election voters in 9 of the 13 states, had higher education in all 13 states, and had a lower level of black participation in all but one of the states.[16] Upper-middle-class activists seeking to become delegates to the national convention through primary elections dominated by other upper-middle-class voters do not have to care as much about the economic concerns of lower-status Democrats as they do about the symbolic social and foreign-policy concerns of liberal, upper-status Democrats.

Procedural Reform and the Shift of Power in Congress. What goes on at conventions also influences what happens in Congress, especially the Senate. Many senators see a potential president or vice president staring back at them when they look in the mirror each morning, and know that their hopes for a presidential or vice-presidential nomination rest on the favor of the people who vote in the Democratic primaries. Given the fact that these voters are more affluent than the average Democratic voter, Edsall argues, ambitious senators are more attentive to the concerns of upper-status Democrats than to their lower-status Democratic constituents, who do not turn out in the primaries in great numbers. In the words of one caustic observer, the reformers succeeded in Republicanizing the Democratic Party.[17]

The procedural reform ethos had an even bigger impact on the House of Representatives. Reforms in the House reduced the power of committee chairs, gave unprecedented influence to subcommittees, opened congressional procedures to public observation, revamped the system of campaign finance regulation, imposed more rigid ethics rules than Congress had ever had in the past, weakened seniority rule, weakened the positions of central leadership, and greatly decentralized influence in the House.[18]

Such reforms may have played well in suburbia, but, says Edsall, they had the unintended consequences of making the Democrats less responsive to the needs of their lower-status constituents. Especially, they weakened the influence of organized labor in Congress in its attempts to limit the tax giveaway to the rich in the early 1980s.

A highly revealing illustration of this inability of Congressional Democrats to respond to lower-status interests on this score occurred in the testimony of AFL–CIO president Lane Kirkland during the House Budget Committee hearings on the 1981 Economic Recovery Tax Act. Kirkland accused the administration's tax plan of "gambling with the well-being of those who can ill afford to gamble in order to provide a sure winner for the wealthy who are not asked to take any of the risk." Addressing the supply-side rationale for the tax cuts, Kirkland argued that "Tax cuts loaded on the side of the rich ignore the evidence of history that such cuts do not produce the type of investment society needs most and do not trickle surely down to enhance the general welfare." Despite the fact that what happened in the rest of the 1980s confirmed the accuracy of Kirkland's prediction, he was not well-received by the Democrats on the committee. Committee member Leon F. Panetta (Democrat from California) chided the labor leader:

> Mr. Kirkland, I think your testimony has obviously some weaknesses. . . . We came through a November election in which the issue of growth in government, tax burden, and deficits were major issues. I think it is generally accepted that President Reagan won the victory he

did largely based on the frustrations of the people with a lot of what government has been doing over the years. Your proposals generally endorse more of the same.[19]

Interestingly, Panetta fit Edsall's definition of the new Congressional Democrat to a tee. He was elected to Congress by defeating an incumbent Republican in the post-Watergate year of 1976. He represents a sprawling, heavily suburban district that voted decisively for Reagan in 1984 and then reversed itself and voted with equal decisiveness for Dukakis in 1988. In terms of ideology, he has consistently been more liberal on social issues than on the economic issues of concern to labor leaders like Kirkland.[20]

Not only did organized labor lose influence among Democrats in Congress, but, Edsall argues, so did the more liberal older members of Congress. This was because the congressional reforms of the 1970s "led not to the transferring of power from a recalcitrant, conservative old guard to the party's liberal wing; rather, much of the transfer of power was away from the party's liberal elders who, through seniority, became eligible for chairmanships, to an ideologically mixed, if not confused, collection of junior members."[21]

Evaluating the Thesis of Democratic Desertion

To sum up, Edsall's thesis lays much of the responsibility for the increasing inequities of the 1980s on younger Democrats like Leon Panetta, cited earlier. Coming from suburban districts with large numbers of upper-middle-income constituents, they did not empathize with lower-status voters as strongly as did older Democrats such as former Speaker of the House Thomas P. (Tip) O'Neill (Democrat from Massachusetts), who more often than not represented less-affluent central-city districts. By throwing their support behind procedural reforms, the younger Democrats impeded the leadership ability of the older, more liberal Democrats to protect the economic interests of lower-status people when those interests came under attack by Reaganomics.

Is this thesis supported by systematic empirical evidence?

Before accepting the thesis of Democratic desertion, we must note that there are some other plausible explanations for the success of Reaganomics in 1981 that have little to do with Edsall's thesis. Much of the success of Reaganomics was due to Reagan's legislative strategists. They used a poorly understood feature of the budgeting process (called reconciliation) to make sure that the 1981 tax bill and the 1981 budget cuts in domestic programs were not allowed to be amended on the floor or even submitted to the traditional committee revision process.[22] Much of the success is also due to the White House's decision to focus on a limited number of issues, thereby putting Reaganomics (the budget and tax cuts) at the top of Congress's agenda and keeping it there.[23] And a substantial share of the success of Reaganomics was due to Reagan's stunning electoral victory that brought Republican control of the Senate as well as the White House. This led Reagan supporters in Congress and in the media to claim that the voters had given a mandate for Reaganomics.

Later analyses of public-opinion data showed clearly that the public not only had *not* given a mandate, but most of the public did not even support the President's domestic budget cuts. By 1983, the NBC News poll found that 52 percent of the people surveyed agreed that Reagan had gone too far in cutting back federal programs, and a 1986 *New York Times*/CBS poll found 66 percent wanting more money spent to help the poor.[24] But what scholars discovered later did not provide any solace to lawmakers who at the time had to deal with the repeated claims in the media of a mandate for the president.

These alternative explanations do not disprove Edsall's thesis. However, they do provide a context within which Reagan's legislative victories took place. To assess Edsall's thesis of Democratic desertion directly, we need to examine studies that sought to correlate the vote of congressional members on the 1981 tax cuts and budget cuts with the districts that the members represented. If there is empirical evidence for Edsall's thesis, then we would expect to find a pattern in the differences between congressional districts and how their representatives voted. The most systematic attempt to make such a study was conducted by political scientist Darrell West.[25]

While not all of West's data support Edsall's thesis, the bulk of the data do support it. Most contrary to Edsall's thesis was West's finding that there was very little relationship between representatives' votes and the socioeconomic status of their constituents. Edsall's thesis suggests that the representatives from the more affluent districts should have supported the tax and budget cuts, while those from the poorer districts should have opposed them. But neither the per-capita income of a district nor the percent of constituents working in blue-collar jobs had a significant relationship to how the representatives voted. Not even public opinion in the districts had much impact on the votes. Representatives from districts where public opinion was hostile to Reaganomics were no more likely to vote against the tax cuts and budget cuts than were representatives from districts where public opinion was favorable.

The factors that did make a difference in members' votes, however, strongly supported Edsall's thesis. First, although public opinion in general did not influence the representatives' votes, the *activists'* opinions very strongly influenced them. It is often difficult for representatives to accurately assess district opinion in general. They cannot afford to take public opinion polls on all major issues. But they can get a sense of the opinion of activists by looking at newspaper editorials, listening to local leaders, and attending to the mail, telephone calls, and telegrams that come into their offices each day. What often happens is that representatives interpret the opinion of activists as the general opinion of their constituents. And the activists were overwhelmingly for Reaganomics, while general public opinion was lukewarm at best. Among representatives who supported the tax cuts, 81 percent of their mail on the issue favored Reaganomics. Among representatives who opposed the tax cuts, only 55 percent of the mail favored Reaganomics. The key voting group consisted of Southern Democrats who called themselves Boll Weevils and who deserted the party position to support the tax cut. In the Boll Weevil districts, 91 percent of the mail favored Reaganomics.[26]

This discrepancy between public opinion in general and activist opinion was a classic illustration of what political scientists call the "intensity problem."[27] The silent majority tended to oppose Reaganomics but did not feel intensely enough about their opposition to let their legislators know about it. Among the supporters of Reaganomics, however, were many who did indeed feel intensely enough about it to communicate their opinions to their legislators. And this communication appears to have been one of the decisive factors in gaining enough votes to push the tax and budget cuts through Congress in 1981.

A second set of correlations that were powerfully related to voting on the tax cut were political party and ideology. Ninety-nine percent of Republicans voted for the final bill, and 80 percent of Democrats opposed it. The 20 percent of Democrats who supported it were overwhelmingly the Boll Weevils who, as we saw, were subjected to considerable pressure from their districts. On a scale of ideology, supporters of the tax bill rated themselves almost twice as conservative as those who voted against it.[28]

Democratic Desertion and the Future of Lower-Status Influence

We have paid so much attention to Edsall's thesis of Democratic desertion for a very important reason. If Edsall is correct that the new breed of congressional Democrats have less reason to care about the interest of lower-status Americans than do the older Democrats in Congress, then lower-status Americans face a continued threat to their influence. The congressional reapportionment following the 1990 census will increase suburban representation and decrease that of the central cities. And if the Democrats want to remain the majority party in Congress, they will have no choice but to continue to accommodate themselves to their upper-middle-class constituencies.

It is also conceivable that this will not happen. The political differences between central-city and suburban voters might not be as important in the future as they were in the 1980s. After all, much of the lower-status population now lives in suburbia. It is also possible that a populist backlash against the growing inequalities of recent years could bring millions of lower-middle- and middle-income suburbanites back to the Democratic fold. And if this were to happen, congressional Democratics presumably would become more sympathetic to their concerns. But up to this point, the central city–suburban split among voters has worked to the disadvantage of the lower-status population.

Republicans and Their Constituents _____

If congressional Democrats deserted their core constituency in the 1980s, Republican strategist Kevin Phillips uses even stronger language to describe the relation of congressional Republicans to the large numbers of lower-middle- and middle-class voters who fled the Democrats and voted Republican during the 1980s. Phillips essentially accuses the Republicans of betraying their new converts.[29] Having won over much of the traditional Democratic constituency, the Republicans could have followed policies that would have given economic help to their new voters; instead they followed policies that Phillips says created "a new plutocracy" and left America with "too many stretch limousines, too many enormous incomes and too much high fashion. . . . Accelerating economic inequality under the Republicans was more often a policy objective than a coincidence. A disproportionate number of women, young people, blacks, and Hispanics were among the decade's casualties."[30]

Insofar as Phillips's accusations concern congressional Republicans, the accusations are too harsh. There are basic problems facing a possible alliance between congressional Republicans and lower-status voters. Most Republican members of Congress come from suburban or rural districts where it is very difficult if not impossible to attract a majority of the votes by following policies that give preferences to the lower-status population, especially when the lower-status population is perceived, erroneously, to be nonwhite. Furthermore, if they wanted to stay in the good graces of party leaders, most Republicans in Congress really had no choice but to support President Reagan's economic and tax policies.

The basic problem is that it was Reagan, not congressional Republicans, who won the substantial share of lower-status votes in the

1980s. Republicans in Congress had no political reason to give those converts many of the benefits that were enacted into tax policy in the 1980s. This could change in the future, as more and more lower-status voters reside in suburbia, where Republicans have a stronghold. This could make suburban Republican members of Congress more attentive to concerns of the lower-status population. But more real to Republican Congress members is the possibility of a populist backlash against the growing economic inequalities and the economic scandals that pervaded the Reagan administration.

In sum, Republican as well as Democratic members of Congress bear responsibility for the $84 billion per year in tax savings given to the top 1 percent of the population in the 1980s. If the prospects seem slim for strengthening the traditional marriage between lower-status voters and Democrats in Congress in the 1990s, the prospects for turning their flirtation with the Republicans into a marriage seem even slimmer.

Resurgence of the Conservative Coalition _____

A third trend in Congress that worked to the disadvantage of lower-status voters was the resurgence of the conservative coalition in the 1980s. This is a loose voting alliance of Southern Democrats and conservative Republicans who vote together to oppose initiatives of Northern Democrats in areas such as social policy, foreign affairs, and economic policy. The coalition emerges on about 20 percent of the roll-call votes in Congress. While its ability to affect policy outcomes has fluctuated through the years, the coalition enjoyed a resurgence of influence in the late 1970s,[31] and it never really disappeared. Some scholars go so far as to argue that it, rather than the Democratic or Republican Party, is the true permanent majority in Congress.[32]

The conservative coalition played an especially influential role in the early Reagan years. In the 1980 elections, Republicans gained control of the Senate and cut the Democrats' House margin to 51 votes. Because of the presence of several conservative Southerners in the Democratic delegation, President Reagan could often count on 30 to 40 Democratic votes when the chips were down in the House. In 1981, the conservative coalition emerged on 20 percent of the roll-call votes taken, and it prevailed in more than 90 percent of those votes.[33] By the end of the eighties, the coalition's influence had diminished greatly. But Reagan did not need the conservative coalition all of the time— only when his priority items were on the line. And during the early years, when the domestic policy agenda for the rest of the decade was being set, the conservative coalition was there much of the time when Reagan needed it most.

As we noted, conservative Democrats who voted for Reagan's Economic Recovery and Tax Act of 1981 called themselves "Boll Weevils," and the Democratic Party leaders in the House were powerless to bring them into line. This was especially illustrated by the case of Texas Democrat Phil Gramm. As one of the leaders of the Boll Weevils, Gramm was a major force in the passage of the Economic Recovery and Tax Act of 1981, and he openly collaborated with the Reagan administration in using the reconciliation process to push the president's domestic budget cuts through the House of Representatives. In 1983, House Speaker Thomas P. (Tip) O'Neill sought to punish Gramm for his lack of party loyalty, and refused to reappoint Gramm to the House Budget Committee. When House Republicans heard about this, they promised to give Gramm one of their seats on the Budget Committee if he would defect from the Democrats and become a Republican. Gramm accepted the offer, resigned from Congress, and ran as a Republican in the special election that was called to replace him in Congress. Gramm easily won reelection, took the Republican position on the Budget Committee, and the following year was elected to the Senate.

In short, the resurgence of the conservative coalition in the early 1980s provided the votes needed for passage of President Reagan's tax-cut plans. Without the conservative coalition, it is unlikely that the great tax benefits given the top 1 percent of the population could have occurred.

Other Structural Impediments to Lower-Status Influence _____

In addition to the conservative coalition and the relation of congressional members to their constituents, the controversy over tax reform reveals some other structural impediments to lower-status influence in Congress. The most important of these are congressional relations with the president, the dispersion of influence in Congress, and the weakness of the political parties in Congress.

Relations with the President

It is very difficult for Congress to resist a legislative program when it is pushed strenuously by a popular president, fresh from a stunning electoral victory, bolstered by a solid contingent of votes in both houses of Congress, highly adept at using the media to his advantage, and highly successful at conveying the notion that his program would address a national crisis. This set of conditions does not happen very often, but it did prevail in 1981 and 1982 when so much of the redistributive tax action took place. It previously happened in 1964–1966 under Lyndon Johnson's Great Society and 1933–1935 under Franklin Roosevelt's New Deal. In those two earlier periods, presidential programs sought to link the concerns of middle-income people and the poor.

But in 1981–1982, the president's legislative program of tax and budget cuts sought to link the concerns of middle-income people with those of upper-income people. Given the ever-present conservative coalition and the transformation in the relationship of congressional Democrats with their lower-status constituents that Edsall described, it is not surprising that lower-status people lost out in the tax reforms of the early 1980s. The real surprise was the legislative and political effectiveness of the Reagan White House in pressing its economic agenda in those early years. Despite his impressive election victory, Reagan generally had been underrated when he assumed the presidency. But his first administration saw a very adept team of legislative and political strategists. This combination of favorable political circumstances and effective presidential leadership were vital to the success of Reaganomics.

Once the 1981–1982 tax and budget cuts were in place, it was back to business as usual for Congress until the 1986 Tax Reform Act. Under business-as-usual conditions, power is widely dispersed in Congress, and the widely dispersed power centers function better at protecting existing interests than they do at setting a new agenda for Congress as a whole. Even if congressional Democrats had wanted to set a new agenda furthering the causes of the lower-status population, the original success of Reaganomics made that unlikely. The huge budget deficits that resulted from Reaganomics have made budget-deficit reduction the main driving force behind Congressional initiatives ever since. It is impossible to reduce the deficit and dramatically increase funding for domestic programs at the same time. It is objectively true that the lower-status population has urgent needs in critical areas such as health insurance, day care, public education, and neighborhood safety; but it is hard to see, under the circumstances that have prevailed since 1981, how Congress by itself can set an agenda for dealing with these issues.

Dispersion of Influence in Congress

Although Congress seldom has been highly centralized, much of the vast dispersion of influence in Congress today is due to the congressional reforms of the 1970s. To a certain extent this dispersion of influence helps the lower-status population. The most critical points of influence today are the subcommittee chairpersons. Subcommittee chairs are able to predominate in the narrow policy areas that are within the jurisdiction of their subcommittees. Thus, subcommittee chairs responsible for programs such as those for food stamps, highway maintenance, or old age assistance would see their own influence diminished if these programs were gutted. Consequently, the subcommittees worked fairly successfully during the remainder of the 1980s to protect such programs from the Reagan domestic budget cuts.

But the same dispersion of influence that facilitates the protection of a multitude of unrelated narrow interests also makes it difficult to centralize the influence needed for Congress as a whole to set a new agenda to tackle some of today's pressing problems. Health insurance coverage, for example, is a pressing need for most of the lower-status population. But there are no subcommittees in Congress jealously protecting nationally mandated health insurance, simply because there *is* no system of nationally mandated health insurance. To create such a system would require putting together a new majority of subcommittee leaders who would fight as much among themselves for jurisdiction over the new program as they would fight to get it passed. In this instance, the absence of centralized leadership facilitates the status quo and works against setting an initiative-taking agenda for Congress as a whole.

Weak Parties in Congress

In a legislature, the agency for strong centralized leadership is the political party, but in Congress the parties are weak. Sometimes, as in the case of the 1986 Tax Reform Act, it is possible for party leaders to overcome the decentralization of influence in Congress. The congressional reforms of the 1970s did much, it is true, to strengthen the role of the Speaker of the House. But by and large, most of the time the forces for decentralization win out over party leadership. One of the most dramatic examples of that, as we saw earlier, was the inability of Speaker of the House Tip O'Neill to punish Texas Democrat Phil Gramm for working directly against the Democratic leadership on the budget and tax cuts in 1981. When O'Neill tried to punish him, Gramm simply bolted the Democratic Party and came back to Congress as a Republican.

Overcoming Bias: The Lower-Status Agenda _____

The normal state of affairs in Congress today is characterized by two features: (1) dispersion of influence that inhibits the formation of a policy-making agenda for Congress as a whole, and (2) a deficit-shrouded policy-making environment that leaves little budgetary room for expanding domestic programs. Given this environment, there is little chance that Congress could undertake any massive new initiatives on behalf of the lower-status population.

It has not always been this way in Congress. From 1933 through the mid-1970s, Congress may well have done a better job of protecting its lower-status constituents than it has done since. It was during those four decades that most of the social-welfare legislation that exists today was set up. If lower-status people are to benefit greatly from new domestic initiatives, they probably need a strong block of representatives and senators to champion their economic concerns more effectively than the Democrats champion them now. For such a bloc to emerge and gain influence, it seems that four steps would have to be taken.

A Receptive President

There really has not been a president with a strong electoral vested interest in lower-status economic concerns since Lyndon Johnson (1963–1969). It is hard to see how a lower-status agenda could be established in Congress without a receptive president to take the lead. Congress relies heavily on the president to set its policy-making agenda. He often fails to get what he wants, but he usually determines much of what Congress deliberates over. Although the Democratic presidents have usually been more receptive to lower-status economic concerns than have Republicans, this does not need to be the case in the future. But whether he or she be Republican or Democrat, without a president to take the lead, lower-status economic concerns will probably continue to be dealt with piecemeal.

Stronger Political Parties in Congress

Better representation of lower-status economic interests in Congress also seems to depend upon strengthening the centralized leadership of the parties. This is particularly the case for the Democrats. Until the Democratic leaders develop the ability to discipline their Boll Weevil members of the conservative coalition or until those Boll Weevils themselves come to depend on their lower-status constituents for more votes, there is not much hope for a successful Democratic initiative addressing lower-status issues.

Strong Lower-Status Interest Groups

The decline of lower-status influence in Congress has paralleled the decline of organized labor. For a lower-status agenda to be put before

Congress, either organized labor has to be rejuvenated, or some other conglomerate of interest groups has to be created to do for the lower-status population what organized labor did for workers in the 1930s and what the civil rights movement did for blacks in the 1960s.

More Effective Activism

Given the impact that local pro-Reaganomics activists had on the vote of key representatives in the 1981 budget and tax-cut votes, it is reasonable to conclude that the lower-status population is hurt significantly by lower-status citizens being much less active politically than the rest of the population. To the extent that they fail to vote, their congressional representatives have good reason to respond to the concerns of their upper-middle-class voting constituents; to the extent that they fail to send letters on key issues or make telephone calls, they make it easier for the activist constituents to influence their representatives. To the extent that they fail to make even small campaign contributions, they throw away an easy chance to be listened to a little more carefully when they do communicate to their representatives. One senator went so far as to give his campaign contributors blue stickers to put on letters they sent him so that his staff would know a letter came from a contributor and thus merited higher consideration than mail received from his other constituents.[34]

Summary _____

1. Tax reform from 1978 to 1986 promoted a significant tax savings for the richest taxpayers and a tax increase for the rest of the population. It does not seem to have been the intent of tax reformers to produce such a massive shift of the tax burden, but the shift occurred nevertheless, and it can be attributed to politics in Congress and the relations between Congress and the president.

2. The Economic Recovery Tax Act of 1981 was the most important step in shifting the tax burden off of the rich. It did so by huge tax cuts and by expanding tax preferences that benefit high-income people the most.

3. The Tax Reform Act of 1986 reduced some of the inequities of the 1981 Economic Recovery Tax Act by removing most poor people from the income-tax rolls. But its most notable feature was to move away from the progressive income tax to a flat tax with two brackets, and to make a big reduction in tax preferences for middle-income earners.

4. Thomas Edsall's thesis of Democratic desertion holds that this shift of wealth could not have occurred without the connivance of the

congressional Democrats. They deserted the interests of the lower-status constituents in hopes of attracting the votes of their upper-middle-class constituents. The evidence on the Edsall thesis is mixed. Some evidence does not support it, but other evidence does, especially the evidence that activists in congressional districts played an important role in convincing key representatives to support Reaganomics.

5. A second explanation for the shift of the tax burden is Kevin Phillips' thesis that the Republicans betrayed the middle-class and lower-class voters. While evidence shows that congressional Republicans indeed supported Reaganomics by overwhelming margins, the accusation of betrayal does not apply very well. This is because most congressional Republicans do not represent districts with large lower-status voting blocs to begin with.

6. A final explanation was seen in some structural characteristics of Congress itself. Congress relies on the president to set an agenda for congressional deliberation. Congressional political parties are weak, and the interest group most directly attached to the lower-status population, organized labor, has suffered declining influence in Congress. The result is a dispersion of influence in Congress. Although this dispersion does not always work to the disadvantage of the lower-status population, it does hinder the ability of Congress to set its own decision-making agenda, and to that extent hinders the ability of Congress to propose a set of programs directed at lower-status economic concerns.

7. If Congressional bias against the lower-status population is to be overcome, a strong bloc in Congress must emerge to champion lower-status interests as so-called "Great Society" Democrats did in the 1960s and "New Deal" Democrats did in the 1930s. Such a bloc is not likely to emerge and achieve decisive influence unless (1) a president is elected who is responsive to lower-status economic interests, (2) political-party leadership in Congress is strengthened while subcommittee chairs and diverse caucuses are weakened, (3) powerful interest groups in the private sector find it in their interest to push for lower-status concerns, (4) the conservative coalition is reined in, (5) the lower-status population itself becomes more active politically.

Notes _____

1. *Inequality and the Federal Budget Deficit* (Washington, D.C.: Citizens for Tax Justice, March 1990), p. 8.

2. For a conservative Republican's assessment of these charges, see Kevin Phillips, *The Politics of Rich and Poor: Wealth and the American Electorate in the Reagan Aftermath* (New York: Random House, 1990). On the conservative argument that the rich actually pay more taxes now, see Tax Foundation, *Tax Features* 33, no. 4 (May/June 1989): 1–2; Michael Novak, "A Hanging Judge," *Forbes,* August 6, 1990, p. 73.

3. For a history of federal tax policy, see Timothy J. Conlan, Margaret T. Wrightson, and David R. Beam, *Taxing Choices: The Politics of Tax Reform* (Washington, D.C.: CQ Press, 1990), chap. 2.

4. The marginal rate is the rate you pay on any increase in income that you earn. Nobody paid 70 percent on all income. To use 1989 as an example, a married couple with a taxable income of less than $30,950 had an "effective tax rate" of 15 percent, which means that their taxes amounted to 15 percent of their taxable income. Any income over $30,950 was taxed at the "marginal rate" of 28 percent.

5. Advisory Commission on Intergovernmental Relations (ACIR), *Changing Public Attitudes on Government and Taxes: 1989* (Washington, D.C.: U.S. Government Printing Office, 1989). This is an annual survey in which the ACIR asks people to compare the fairness of the federal income tax, the local property tax, the state sales tax, and the state income tax. Prior to 1979, the local property tax was viewed as the least fair tax, but starting in 1979, the federal income tax consistently held the top spot as the most unpopular tax.

6. See Conlan, Wrightson, and Beam, *Taxing Choices,* pp. 25–30. The leading critical economist was probably Joseph A. Pechman, who sought to broaden the tax base by reducing the federal reliance on tax preferences. See his *Federal Tax Policy,* 5th ed. (Washington, D.C.: Brookings Institution, 1987) and "Tax Policies for the 1980s," *Economics in the Public Service,* eds. Joseph A. Pechman and N. J. Simler (New York: W. W. Norton, 1982).

7. *Statistical Abstract of the United States: 1989,* p. 308.

8. *Tax Features* 33, no. 4 (May/June 1989), p. 1. *Tax Features* is a newsletter of the Tax Foundation, a business-oriented think-tank. In 1979 the top10 percent of tax filers paid 49.5 percent of all federal income taxes, and the top 50 percent of filers paid 93.2 percent of all income taxes. Ironically, the massive shifts of wealth in the 1980s increased the share of taxes paid by the rich. For 1987, the comparable figures were that the top 55.4 percent of filers paid 94.1 percent of taxes. Even though they paid lower rates and received generous tax breaks, they also received such a huge increase in their share of the national income that their share of taxes went up accordingly.

9. To verify that this is not a caricature of the supply-side argument, see Conlan, Wrightson, and Beam, *Taxing Choices,* pp. 30–35. Supply-sider Paul Craig Roberts, who became undersecretary of the treasury under Reagan, wrote: "The progressive income tax was implemented to 'soak the rich' and redistribute income. In practice it works as a barrier toward mobility and discourages people from making their best effort. In pandering to envy, the tax system has made it almost impossible for the average taxpayer to obtain financial independence." See his "Supply-Side Economics, Growth, and Liberty," *To Promote Prosperity: U.S. Domestic Policy in the Mid-1980s,* ed. John H. Moore (Stanford, Calif.: Hoover Institution Press, 1984), p. 75.

10. Quoted in Conlan, Wrightson, and Beam, *Taxing Choices,* p. 25.

11. For a concise outline of the chief features of the Tax Reform Act of 1986, see Conlan, Wrightson, and Beam, *Taxing Choices,* pp. 4–5. The 33 percent marginal rate for upper-middle-income taxpayers was called the "tax bubble." In 1988, for example, a married couple paid the 33 percent rate on income between $71,901 and $171, 090. On incomes above $171,090, the rate reverted to 28 percent. See *1989 Tax Guide for College Teachers and Other College Personnel* (Washington, D.C.: Academic Information Service, Inc., 1988), p. 11.

12. *New York Times,* September 27, 1986, p. 33.

13. Rostenkowski's quip was widely reported. See *New York Times,* November 27, 1985, pp. 1, 14; Neal R. Peirce's syndicated column, *Minneapolis Star and Tribune,* December 8, 1985, p. 35A; David Broder's syndicated column, *Minneapolis Star and Tribune,* December 8, 1985, p. 34A.

14. Edsall, *The New Politics of Inequality,* (New York: W. W. Norton and Company, 1984), p. 55.

15. Ibid., p. 33.

16. Polsby, *Consequences of Party Reform,* p. 158.

17. Fred Siegel, " 'Republicanizing' the Democrats," *Dissent* 32, no. 2 (Spring 1985): 299–304.

18. See Thomas E. Mann and Norman Ornstein, *The New Congress* (Washington D.C.: American Enterprise Institute, 1981) and LeRoy N. Rieselbach, *Congressional Reform in the Seventies* (Morristown, N.J.: General Learning Press, 1977).

19. Edsall, *The New Politics of Inequality,* pp. 144–145.

20. Michael Barone and Grant Ujifusa, *The Almanac of American Politics: 1986* (Washington, D.C.: National Journal, 1985), p. 137. *Almanac of American Politics: 1990,* p. 124.

21. Edsall, *The New Politics of Inequality,* p. 43.

22. Allen Schick, "How the Budget was Won and Lost," in *President and Congress: Assessing Reagan's First Year,* ed. Norman Ornstein (Washington D.C.: American Enterprise Institute, 1982), pp. 14–43.

23. Barbara Sinclair, "Agenda Control and Policy Success: Ronald Reagan and the 97th Congress," *Legislative Studies Quarterly* 10 (August 1985): 291–314.

24. See Thomas Ferguson and Joel Rogers, *Right Turn: The Decline of the Democrats and the Future of American Politics* (New York: Hill & Wang, 1986).

25. Darrell M. West, *Congress and Economic Policymaking* (Pittsburgh: University of Pittsburgh Press, 1987).

26. Ibid., p. 55.

27. See John J. Harrigan, *Politics and the American Future,* 2nd ed. (New York: Random House, 1987), pp. 87–88.

28. West, *Congress and Economic Policymaking,* p. 49.

29. Phillips, *The Politics of Rich and Poor: Wealth and the American Electorate in the Reagan Aftermath.*

30. Ibid., pp. xviii.

31. See David W. Brady and Charles S. Bullock III, "Is There a Conservative Coalition in the House?" *Journal of Politics* 42, no. 2 (May 1980): 549–559.

32. See Mack C. Shelley, *The Permanent Majority: The Conservative Coalition in the United States Congress* (University, Ala.: University of Alabama Press, 1983).

33. *Congressional Quarterly Almanac: 1981* (Washington, D.C.: Congressional Quarterly, 1982), p. 36C.

34. The Senator was Rudy Boschwitz (R, MN) in 1986.

CHAPTER 8

Bias in the American Presidency

Introduction

We saw in Chapter 7 that it takes presidential leadership to achieve progressive economic legislation benefiting the lower-status population. But the prospects that any president will provide sustained leadership to improve the economic condition of the lower-status population are not very encouraging. The presidency is inherently conservative, and there is little to be gained for a president who commits his prestige and reputation to helping out the lower-status population.

On the face of it, this must seem an absurd statement, for the most successful presidents in the twentieth century (Woodrow Wilson, both Roosevelts, and Lyndon Johnson before Vietnam) were quite progressive. It was usually Congress, dominated by its conservative coalition, that threatened the great liberal causes such as the graduated income tax, regulation of the economy, assistance to the poor, Medicare, and civil rights. Enacting these measures usually required strong and skillful leadership from the White House. This liberal agenda, all accomplished since 1930, was achieved through what some view as a "plebiscitary presidency."[1] This is a presidency in which the incumbent president views his election as a mandate from the people and seeks to use that mandate to dominate Congress.*

Their electoral mandates for progressive government gave the progressive presidents (especially Woodrow Wilson, Franklin Roosevelt and Lyndon Johnson) a great weapon with which to dominate Congress. In this sense, not only were the greatest presidents of the twentieth century liberal presidents, but it was their liberal achievements that made them great. Theodore Lowi wrote that "the plebiscitary presidency has been built on a liberal base, just as much as it has been built on a democratic one."[2]

---

* A plebiscite is an expression of the will of the people through an election. The plebiscitary president thus views the election as a mandate from the people and tries to use that mandate to override the constitutional system of checks and balances.

The presidency is inherently conservative, and the president has little to gain in committing his prestige and reputation to helping the lower-status population.

In the light of this history, it may seem strange to argue that the presidency is inherently conservative, and that the conservative presidencies of Richard Nixon, Ronald Reagan, and George Bush were surely aberrations. And some day liberal Democrats will once again control the White House and reverse the conservative trends that Reagan and Bush rode into office.

Maybe.

But maybe not.

We need to consider the possibility that the great liberal advances of Wilson, the Roosevelts, and Johnson were the aberrations, while the conservative regimes of Nixon, Reagan, and Bush are the norm. That indeed is what this chapter will argue. We assert that: (1) there is a strong rationale and considerable evidence suggesting that the presidency is inherently conservative, (2) the Reagan–Bush years illustrate why the inherently conservative presidency prevails, (3) without significant restructuring of the political parties, neither the Democrats nor the Republicans are likely to produce a resurgent liberal presidential period, and (4) television imposes severe structural limitations on presidential progressivity.

The Logic of Presidential Conservatism _____

It is true that the most liberal periods in the twentieth century occurred under progressive presidents such as Wilson, the Roosevelts, and Johnson. But the liberal impulses of those presidents were quickly curbed by political forces beyond the presidents' control. Two of those forces in particular stand out.

Small and Infrequent Windows of Opportunity

Achieving significantly progressive legislation is a little like putting a Boeing 747 jet liner into flight. It takes an enormous boost of power to get the thing off the ground. In the case of progressive legislation, the power boost requires not only a president committed to change, but also an overwhelming majority in Congress to vote for the president's program, and the solid backing of public belief that action is required on a longstanding backlog of unmet needs. Since 1900, there have only been three small windows of opportunity in which all of these conditions were met:

Woodrow Wilson's New Freedom years (1913–1914)
Franklin Roosevelt's New Deal years (1933–1935)
Lyndon Johnson's Great Society years (1964–1966)

The Great Society as a Window of Opportunity. How these windows of opportunity work can be seen by examining the conditions that made possible the domestic achievements of President Lyndon Johnson's Great Society (1964–1966). First was a growing public support for government action to deal with a backlog of unmet public needs. The most severe of these was the oppressed and segregated condition of blacks, which had existed since slavery ended a century earlier. Unrelenting civil rights demonstrations for the previous 10 years, many under the masterful and eloquent leadership of Martin Luther King, Jr. helped persuade a growing body of public opinion that civil rights legislation was needed to guarantee blacks the right to vote and the full rights of citizenship. Other unmet needs were also gaining in public attention. Recently constructed poverty indexes showed that 25 percent of the population lived in poverty in 1960. Medical treatment was simply unavailable to large segments of the population, especially the elderly poor.

Not only did there need to be public support for doing something about these unmet needs, but there needed to be political support in Congress as well. As early as 1949, Senator Hubert Humphrey (D, MN) had introduced a civil rights bill and a bill for medical care for the elderly. But year after year those bills went down to defeat in Congress at the hands of the Conservative Coalition that we studied in Chapter 7. It was not until Lyndon Johnson's Great Society years that Congress passed the Civil Rights Act, the Voting Rights Act, and Medicare. What enabled these measures to succeed under President Johnson, whereas they had failed previously, were two events. First, Johnson was helped by a strong emotional wave of public support following the 1963 assassination of John F. Kennedy. Second, and more important, however, was the fact that he won the 1964 election in a manner that enabled him to claim a mandate to address the unmet needs.

There were three elements of the 1964 election that enabled Johnson to claim a mandate. First, he won it by a landslide, gaining 61 percent of the popular vote. Second, he won it by drawing a clear distinction between himself as the candidate pledged to addressing the country's unmet needs and his opponent as the candidate opposed to addressing those needs. His opponent, Barry Goldwater, had waged an ideologically conservative campaign opposed to the Civil Rights Act of 1964 and in favor of giving battlefield commanders the right to decide for themselves to use nuclear weapons. Third, 37 new Democrats won election to Congress in 1964 on the "coat tails" of Johnson's victory, and this coattail effect gave him the extra votes he needed to overcome

TABLE 8–1   The Origins of the Progressive State

Woodrow Wilson's Window of Opportunity,
1913–1916:
1913   Federal Reserve Board
1914   Clayton Anti-Trust Act
1914   Federal Trade Commission
1916   Child Labor Act

Franklin Roosevelt's Window of Opportunity,
1933–1935:
1933   Tennessee Valley Authority
1933   Agricultural Adjustment Act
1933   Securities Exchange Commission created
1933   Federal Deposit Insurance Corporation created
1933   Home Owners' Loan Corporation Board created
1934   Federal Housing Act
1934   Federal Communications Commission created
1935   Farm Security Act
1935   National Labor Relations Act

Lyndon Johnson's Window of Opportunity,
1964–1966:
1964   Equal Employment Opportunity Commission created
1964   Civil Rights Act
1965   Voting Rights Act
1965   Economic Opportunity Act
1965   Department of Housing and Urban Development created
1965   Elementary and Secondary Education Act
1965   Medicare established
1966   Medicaid established
1966   Food Stamp Program created

Progressive Legislation Passed Outside the
Windows of Opportunity:
1887   Interstate Commerce Commission established
1890   Sherman Anti-Trust Act
1906   Pure Food and Drug Act
1906   Hepburn Act
1910   Mann-Elkins Act
1937   Public Housing Act
1938   Federal Trade Act expanded
1938   Food and Drug Act expanded
1946   National Employment Act
1949   National Housing Act created urban renewal program
1956   Interstate Highway System funded
1970   Environmental Protection Agency established
1970   Clean Air Act passed
1970   Occupational Safety and Health Administration established
1971   Clean Water Act passed
1972   Consumer Product Safety Commission established

the conservative coalition. For the next two years, Congress passed an outpouring of economically and socially progressive legislation ranging from the Voting Rights Act (1965) to the Medicare program of health insurance for the elderly. Then in 1966, Johnson's party lost 48 House seats and 4 Senate seats, and the Great Society was over. The window of opportunity slammed shut.

The Prerequisites for Claiming Mandates. It takes all three of these elements to enable presidents to claim mandates: a landslide victory, a campaign promising identifiable direction in public policy, and a coat tail effect on Congress.[3] The importance of these three effects could be seen later in the elections of the 1980s. Republicans won all three elections by landslides, but only one of the campaigns was pledged to an identifiable policy direction and had a coattail effect on Congress. That was Ronald Reagan's 1980 landslide victory over Jimmy Carter in which Reagan pledged to cut taxes, reduce governmental regulation, and build up the military. The conservative theme of the campaign, the landslide victory, and the coattail effect that put Republicans in control of the Senate for the first time in 25 years gave Reagan a huge boost in selling his programs to Congress in 1981.[4] Despite substantial public opinion polls showing that the public at large did not want to decimate the welfare system,[5] many Democrats as well as Republicans in Congress perceived the president's 1980 election as a mandate. This notion was expressed succinctly by an aide to Democratic Speaker of the House Tip O'Neill:

> What the Democrats did, in extraordinary fashion, was to recognize the cataclysmic nature of the 1980 election results. The American public wanted this new president to be given a chance to try out his program. We aren't going to come across as being obstructionists.[6]

Four years later, Reagan waged an issueless campaign and failed to have the same impact on Congress. "A landslide without coattails [such as 1984] leaves the claim of a mandate . . . open to serious doubt," wrote political scientist Gary C. Jacobson. It permits members of the opposition to "refuse to recognize the mandate" and confronts them with "little psychological or political pressure to cooperate with the president on his own terms."[7]

Progressive Legislation Outside the Windows of Opportunity. To be sure, progressive legislation has occurred outside of the three windows of opportunity named here. Environmental legislation, for example, was largely a product of the 1970s, when the conservative Richard Nixon was in the White House. But, as Table 8–1 shows, a disproportionate share of America's social regulatory system was constructed during those three very short time periods. Most of what happened subsequently was fine tuning and tinkering with the basic progressive thrusts established then.

The Conservative Bias to Presidential Prestige

One reason why the windows of opportunity for progressive legislation are so small and open so infrequently is that there is a conservative bias to the actions that presidents must take to bolster their prestige in the eyes of the public. Presidential prestige has been tracked for more than 50 years by the Gallup Poll's simple question: "Do you approve or disapprove of the way that _____ is handling the job of president?" A 50-year summary of those ratings is shown in Figure 8–1.

Presidents pay close attention to these ratings. A high rating can help shield a president from attack. It can also give him a little more leverage in dealing with congressional members who are undecided about supporting the president's high-priority legislative proposals. In the early 1980s, for example, Ronald Reagan's immense popularity helped the Republican Party raise huge sums of money for campaign purposes, and the combination of a popular president with significant campaign funds to give away strengthened White House aides in seeking Republican votes in Congress. One aide secured the votes of two representatives for the president's 1981 budget cuts by promising to give them the maximum of campaign contributions permitted under law. When asked what he would have done had the Congressmen not voted for the budget cuts, the aide replied, "I would have nailed them to the wall."[8] Given the possibility of presidential retaliation of this sort, members of Congress are careful not to cross swords publicly with an extremely popular president. Richard Neustadt called this phenomenon the law of anticipated reactions.[9] Marginal members are afraid to challenge a highly popular president for fear that public opinion will burn against them.

The Dangers of Unpopularity. When presidential approval ratings drop, however, it becomes harder for White House aides to apply pressure tactics of this sort. When the president's approval ratings drop below the 40 percent mark, he falls prey to sniping from the press and members of Congress. Jimmy Carter's Gallup Poll ratings, for example (see Figure 8–1), were languishing in the low 30s in the fall of 1979 when Iranian students invaded the American embassy in Teheran and took 53 diplomats hostage. Prospering from the public's tendency to rally around the president during foreign crises, Carter's Gallup-Poll ratings shot up 30 percentage points, the highest single jump in the history of the Gallup Poll. Unfortunately for Carter, and

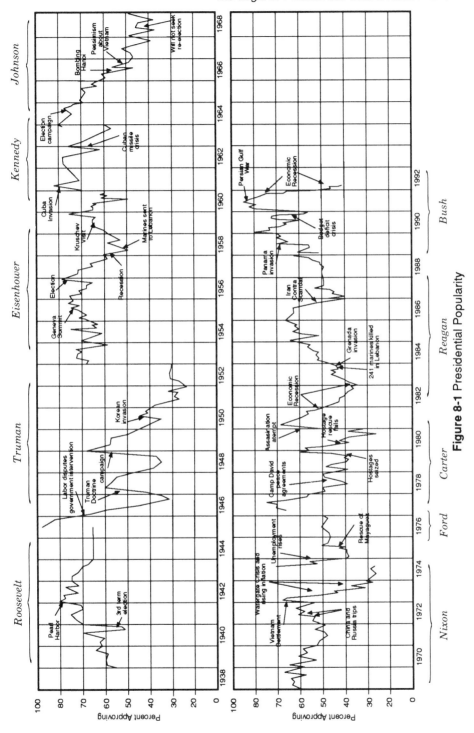

Figure 8-1 Presidential Popularity

the hostages, however, the president was unable to resolve that crisis, and his approval ratings began to fall again. As they fell, he became the target of increasingly sharp criticism from the press and from within his own party. His image was further damaged when Congress launched an investigation into the antics of his brother Billy Carter who had accepted money to lobby for Libya with the American government. The most drastic challenge to the president was a rebellion within the Democratic ranks that sought to replace Carter with Edward Kennedy as the Democrats' 1980 presidential candidate.

Reflecting the difficulty of exercising leadership while the president's ratings were dropping, one Carter aide said: "When the President is low in public opinion polls, the Members of Congress see little hazard in bucking him. . . . [They] read the polls and from that they feel secure in turning their backs on the President with political impunity. Unquestionably, the success of the president's policy bears a tremendous relationship to his popularity in the polls."[10] Another Carter aide commented: "When you go up to the Hill and the latest polls show Carter isn't doing well, there isn't much reason for a member to go along with him. There's little we can do if the member isn't persuaded on the issue."[11]

In sum, low public-opinion ratings endanger presidential success. The problem is, as Figure 8–1 shows, that most presidents see their approval ratings begin to drop after the first year. Only one president since 1945, Reagan, has left office more popular than he was when he came in. This deterioration of public approval gives presidents an enormous incentive to do whatever they can to stem the decline and boost their ratings whenever possible.

How Presidents Bolster Their Ratings. Unfortunately for the lower-status population, the things that presidents do to enhance their approval ratings do not lead to progressive domestic policies. If anything, domestic political developments bring drops in presidential approval. Figure 8–1 shows several instances in which drops in presidential approval coincided with economic recession (Eisenhower and Reagan), labor strife (Truman), civil rights struggles (Kennedy), or the federal budget, taxes, and economic recession (Bush). Even worse, Table 8–2 suggests that presidential attempts to address those domestic issues are more often than not followed by drops in presidential ratings. The president gets greater rewards in the Gallup Poll for defense and foreign initiatives than he does for domestic initiatives. Table 8–2 shows that this pattern has existed for five decades.

In the 1960s, for example, after President Kennedy presented a message to Congress in support of civil rights legislation, he saw his Gallup Poll ratings drop by 4 percent points. On the other hand, when he

TABLE 8–2   Public Opinion on Foreign and Domestic Initiatives of the President

Date	Domestic Events	Approval rating (%)	Date	Foreign Events	Approval Rating (%)
May–July 1947	Truman veto of the anti-union Taft–Hartley bill.		June–July 1950	Truman sends U.S. military forces to Korea.	
	Before veto	57		Before	37
	After veto	54		After	46
May–June 1963	Kennedy makes statement favoring civil rights legislation.		March–April 1961	Kennedy launches unsuccessful Bay of Pigs invasion of Cuba.	
	Before	65		Before	78
	After	61		After	83
November 1981 through January 1983	Economic recession, Nov. 1981, peak Reagan rating before recession		October–November 1983	Bombing of Marine barracks in Lebanon followed by Reagan's Grenada invasion.	
	January 1983,	54			
	lowest rating at			Before the bombing	45
	end of recession	35		After the invasion	53
June–July 1990	Bush accepts tax increase to resolve a federal budget crisis.		July 1990–February 1991	Bush sends troops to Persian Gulf to counter Iraq invasion of Kuwait.	
	Before	69		Before invasion	60
	In midst			At conclusion	
	of crisis	60		of Persian Gulf War	89

Sources: Data from the American Institute of Public Opinion (Gallup Poll). Used by permission. Adapted from Theodore Lowi, *Politics of Disorder* (New York: Basic Books, 1971), p. 94.

launched his disastrously unsuccessful Bay of Pigs invasion of Cuba in 1961, his public opinion ratings jumped up by 15 percentage points.

This same phenomenon is still at work today. In December 1989, President Bush invaded Panama to overthrow the government and bring its leader, Manuel Noriega, back to the United States to face drug charges. Even though this action was a direct violation of international law and treaties that the United States itself had signed, Bush's public-opinion ratings shot up by 10 percentage points after the invasion,[12] and Republican National Chairman Lee Atwater gleefully announced that Bush had won a political jackpot.[13] On the other hand, a few months later, the president's Gallup Poll ratings dropped when he hinted that he might accept some tax increases in order to deal with the long-standing budget-deficit problem (an action that seemingly violated his election campaign pledge "Read my lips: No new taxes").

By late summer of 1990, when Congress and the White House were deadlocked over the budget impasse and the nation began slipping into an economic recession, Bush's ratings began to fall precipitously. Then Iraq invaded Kuwait. Bush responded with military action, and his approval ratings rose once more. At the end of the successful Persian Gulf War Bush's ratings topped 89 percent, an all-time high for any president. Within a year, however, economic recovery sputtered, and Bush's approval ratings tumbled once again.

The message to presidents is clear. Domestic policy is a quagmire that can easily bog down a president and offer no quick path to broad public support. There also is no guarantee that foreign or defense initiatives will bolster presidential approval,[14] but at least there is a realistic hope that in those areas public opinion will reward decisive, short-term actions that give the appearance of strength.

Recognizing the short-term boost that foreign actions can give to their ratings, presidents are tempted to promote "rally events" to rally public opinion around them.[15] Few presidents were better at this than Ronald Reagan. In 1983 alone, three rally events helped boost Reagan's approval ratings as he geared up for his reelection campaign: the bombing of the U.S. embassy in Beirut in April, the Soviet downing of a Korean Air Line passenger plane in September, and the Grenada invasion in October. Rally events do not always boost presidential approval, of course, and the spurt is usually brief. But given the likelihood that almost any domestic policy initiative will depress approval ratings, foreign or defense initiatives at least offer a possible way to check a slide in public opinion.[16]

The Two-Presidency Phenomenon. Not only does public opinion reward the president more for foreign initiative than for domestic initiatives, so does Congress. Table 8–3 reflects what is sometimes called the two-presidency phenomenon.[17] As the table shows, Congress has been much more responsive to presidential initiatives in foreign and defense policy than in domestic policy. From 1948 to 1965, fewer than half of the president's domestic initiatives passed Congress, while more than half of their foreign initiatives and substantially more than half of their defense initiatives passed. These differences narrowed somewhat after 1965, probably because of the domestic legislative successes of Lyndon Johnson's Great Society programs as well as the growing criticism within Congress of foreign policy as the Vietnam War progressed. Nevertheless, there was still a greater tendency for Congress to pass presidents' foreign and defense bills than their domestic bills, as Table 8–3 shows.

The foreign and defense policy arena has a deep appeal for most presidents, and they give it from one-half to two-thirds of their time.[18]

"AND WHEN YOU'RE IN REAL TROUBLE YOU PRESS THIS BUTTON"

Cartoonist Herblock satirizes the tendency of presidents to use military decisions to bolster their public support.
(Source: Copyright © 1988 by Herblock in *The Washington Post.)*

TABLE 8–3 The Two Presidencies[a]

Policy Arena	1948–1964	1965–1975
Domestic Policy	40%	46%
Defense and Foreign Policy	70	55
Defense	73	61
Foreign	59	50

[a] Each score is the percentage of presidential proposals enacted by Congress.

Source: Adapted from Lance T. LeLoup and Steven A. Shull, "Congress Versus the Executive: The Two Presidencies' Reconsidered," *Social Science Quarterly* 59 (March 1979): 708. Used by permission of the University of Texas Press and the authors.

President Bush has been no exception to this, as he admitted when he was caught between two crises in 1990—a domestic crisis over the federal budget deficit and a foreign crisis over the Persian Gulf following Iraq's invasion of Kuwait. To counter that invasion, Bush sent 400,000 military personnel to the Persian Gulf area and built an international coalition to contain Iraq. Bush commented:

> When you get a problem with the complexities . . . that the Middle East has now and the gulf has now, I enjoy trying to . . . put the coalition together and keep it together and work toward what I think is a proper end. I can't say I just rejoice every time I go up and talk to [Ways and Means Committee chairman] Danny Rostenkowski . . . about what he's going to do on taxes.[19]

It is not hard to see why presidents prefer to deal with foreign crises rather than domestic ones. Domestic policy initiatives almost inevitably step on the toes of some entrenched domestic political interests in a way that is unlikely with foreign policy. When Bush invaded Panama, captured its president Manuel Noriega, and overthrew the Panamanian government, there was barely a murmur of dissent against those acts. And most of the murmur was restricted to the left-wing alternative press that is pretty much ignored in official Washington. By contrast, when Bush went on television eight months later and asked the public to support a budget and tax compromise he had worked out, a majority of Congress voted against him, including a substantial bloc of Republicans. Presidents face less competition from other political elites on foreign issues than they do on domestic ones, and this gives them a freer hand in shaping foreign policy. As the Panama example shows, in foreign relations presidents can take dramatic actions without Congressional interference that they cannot take in domestic affairs.

The Bias of the Two Presidencies. The reason the two-presidency phenomenon is biased against the lower-status population is that the lower-status population gains few benefits from foreign or defense-policy posturing. Addressing the economic problems facing the lower-status population calls for strong presidential leadership; but it is very risky for presidents to offer strong leadership in these areas, because there often is no consensus in the country about the proper action to take. While the country will rally around the president in confronting a short-term foreign crisis, virtually any initiative the president takes on urban problems, welfare programs, poverty, public transit, or tax policy will generate vocal and effective opposition.

To maintain popularity, presidents will be tempted to leave the complex domestic problems to others while the White House focuses on foreign affairs, on rhetoric, on the presidential image, and on symbolic gestures that improve that image.

War as a Short-Circuit to Lower-Status Interests. Not only does the two-presidency phenomenon work to the disadvantage of the lower-status population, but when presidents have focused on improving the economic conditions of the lower-status population, that focus often has been cut short by war. This tendency of war to short-circuit domestic liberal trends is not well-recognized. To the contrary, one of the key items in American mythology has been the belief that war is a democratizing and progressive experience. According to this mythology, rich and poor alike mingle in the Army barracks. Military build-ups spur the economy on to new heights and produce tens of thousands of new jobs.

Much of this myth derived from American experience in World War II, which stands as an exception to most American wartime experience. It is certainly true that World War II was more likely than any other American war to bring about a mingling of social classes. It is also true that gearing up for war production in the 1940s produced full employment for the first time in a generation. The manpower needs were so huge that blacks and women found work in the factories, and this experience with a steady income provided some of the underpinnings of the civil-rights and feminist movements that came later. More immediately progressive was the so-called GI Bill of Rights legislation that was passed near the war's end and provided a tremendous force for improving the lives of large numbers of people on the bottom half of the income ladder. The GI Bill's home mortgage program made it possible for average Americans to purchase houses. For the families of veterans, mortgages were now available on easy terms that had never before existed. The GI mortgage required no down payment, provided an interest rate slightly below prevailing commercial rates, and strung the mortgage payments out over an unheard of 30-year period so that the monthly payments were affordable to the average family. Furthermore, the mortgages were guaranteed, and this made them very attractive to mortgage-lending institutions. The net result was that home ownership increased from about 43 percent of all homes in 1940 to 65 percent two decades later in 1960.[20] As much as any other single piece of legislation, the GI Bill facilitated the vast suburbanization that took place in the 1950s.

Not only did World War II's GI Bill help veterans buy homes, it also facilitated their college education and vocational training. It provided them with a regular cash payment for 36 months as long as they passed accredited courses.

But the progressive results that flowed from World War II were the exception. Most wars have been bad news for the lower-status population. World War I (1917–1918), Vietnam (1965–1973), and even Korea (1950–1953) turned national attention away from domestic programs that might assist the lower-status population. The most dramatic instance of this occurred in 1965 when President Lyndon B. Johnson introduced American combat forces into Vietnam. Johnson refused to choose between budgeting to fight the war or to support his many liberal domestic programs. Faced with choosing between guns (fighting the war), or butter (funding his domestic programs), Johnson chose both. He also refused to make the tax increases that were necessary to fund the war. The net result was a boost in inflation rates that in the long run put pressure on federal budgeting. With a major war going on, defense expenditures continued to rise, and domestic programs absorbed most of the squeeze. Politically, the Vietnam War drew the nation's attention away from dealing with its domestic problems. It divided the nation sharply, contributed to the huge loss of Democratic seats in Congress in 1966, and slowly led to discrediting Lyndon Johnson himself. For all practical purposes, the Great Society was dead by the end of 1966. Except for passage of the Fair Housing Act in 1968, there were no more new initiatives from the Great Society after 1966.

A similar phenomenon occurred prior to World War I. In 1916, Woodrow Wilson won reelection on the success of his domestic program that he called the New Freedom and his campaign slogan, "He kept us out of war." But barely a month after his second inauguration, Wilson asked Congress to declare war on Germany. His New Freedom domestic initiatives were put on the back burner while the nation's attention focused on the war in Europe.

The Korean War which broke out in 1950 also turned President Truman's attention away from domestic problems. Prior to 1950 Truman showed great concern for the lower-status population. He called his administration the Fair Deal to distinguish it from Roosevelt's New Deal. He supported the Employment Act of 1946; he vetoed the anti-labor Taft–Hartley Act in 1947, only to have his veto overridden; and he supported the 1949 Housing Act that brought the federal government in a big way into urban housing and redevelopment. But this

War, in short, is bad news for the lower-status population.

marked the high tide of the Fair Deal. After the start of the Korean War in 1950, Truman got bogged down by bitter Washington politics that were filled with recriminations over the conduct of the war in Korea and alleged communist conspiracies.

War, in short, is bad news for the lower-status population. It draws national attention away from domestic problems. It absorbs huge portions of the budget. And it generally spreads its burden of battle deaths disproportionately among the racial minorities and the lower-status population.

Given the historically negative impact of war on progressive agendas, it is instructive to note that following the end of the Cold War in 1989, political leaders predicted a peace dividend. Without the Soviet Union as a mortal threat, American defense forces could be cut and the savings used for a variety of purposes ranging from budget-deficit reduction to increased funding for domestic social programs. Then, in August 1990, Iraq invaded Kuwait, and the United States sent 400,000 military personnel to Saudi Arabia and the Persian Gulf. Suddenly the peace dividend no longer seemed so certain. Now that the threat from Communist Russia was diminished, the Pentagon argued that it needed to retool itself to cope with third-world threats. If military procurement in the 1990s follows the pattern of the previous 40 years of Cold War, the United States will find an endless succession of military crises that will be used to justify a large defense budget; and domestic programs will continue to compete with military programs for budget supports.

The Negative Presidency and Its Conservative Tendencies

Generally it takes positive leadership for the president to advance lower-status concerns. Public opinion must be led to support lower-status causes, and Congress must be convinced to pass new programs or to expand budgets for old progressive programs. Since the budget is not infinite, any expansion or creation of programs in one area usually means no expansion in others, and this gives many congressional subcommittee chairs considerable inertia in supporting new initiatives outside their own domain. Overcoming this inertia requires strong positive presidential leadership.

The nay-saying president, the negative president, on the other hand, can stymie liberal causes merely by failing to exert progressive leadership and by administrative actions such as cutting the budget for progressive programs, reducing staff positions for such programs, and digging in one's heels in carrying out Congressional directives for such programs.

The Reagan Presidency as a Negative Presidency

How the negative presidency can have a conservative impact can be seen in the Reagan presidency in the 1980s. Having campaigned under the slogan that government is not the solution, it's the problem, Reagan proceeded to slash spending in critical domestic areas. Despite sharp criticism of the public school system, the federal share of public education funding dropped from 9.2 percent in 1980 to 6.2 percent by 1988.[21] Despite growing rates of teenage pregnancy and children living in poverty, federal spending for education, job training, and social services dropped by 13 percent during Reagan's first term.[22] And under the guise of New Federalism discussed in Chapter 3, Reagan reduced federal responsibilities for social services, environmental protection, and occupational health and safety, and turned a bigger share of these responsibilities over to the states. Despite growing numbers of the homeless, federal spending for commerce and housing dropped by 48 percent during Reagan's first term.[23]

Richard Nathan has documented that much of Reagan's assault on the welfare state in the early 1980s was administrative in nature rather than legislative. The Reagan White House took special pains to ensure that persons appointed to cabinet and subcabinet positions were stalwart supporters of Reaganomics and would attack rather than defend the status quo in the bureaucracies they were being sent to administer.[24] The administration consistently used the Office of Management and Budget to hold down domestic spending. Contracts and grants were deliberately awarded to recipients pledged to support Reagan politics and philosophies.[25] In the regulation of the environment and occupational safety, the administration deliberately appointed regulatory heads who distrusted federal regulations. They greatly reduced the number of rules issued by regulatory agencies. In the Labor Department, for example, the new assistant secretary, Albert Angrisani, a banker, made sharp cuts in the department employment and training programs and stopped all grants and contracts that had been awarded before his appointment but were not yet spent.[26] Under the Reagan administration, there was a dramatic reduction in the number of regulatory rules issued.[27]

Although these largely administrative attacks on the welfare state terminated very little of the welfare system and left the system's basic structure intact, they nevertheless scaled back the welfare system. Funding as a percent of the federal budget dropped sharply. To reverse this will take substantial new funding, new authority, and perhaps new agencies.

Finally, because of the huge budget deficits that Reagan left for his successors, there is no leeway for expanding social-welfare programs. Figure 8–2 shows the cumulative budget deficits of the presidents since 1953. By the end of the Reagan years, the cost of servicing this growing mountain of debt was having a negative impact on government finances and the American economy. But cutting the deficit meant a combination of raising taxes and cutting domestic expenditures. By 1992, the deficit reached $400 billion. To balance the budget left no room for increasing expenditures for domestic programs. Whether by accident or design, Ronald Reagan, without eliminating a single welfare agency or program, created a practical strategy for guaranteeing that no substantive expansion could occur in welfare programs until the U.S. government's fiscal house was put in order.

In sum, the negative president can do great damage to progressive programs purely through administrative actions. In the years succeeding Reagan, it is probably impossible for Congress to undo these administrative actions. And even if a new liberal president were to emerge in the 1990s, he would be so constrained by budget problems that it might also be impossible to make any substantive budget increases for progressive ideas.

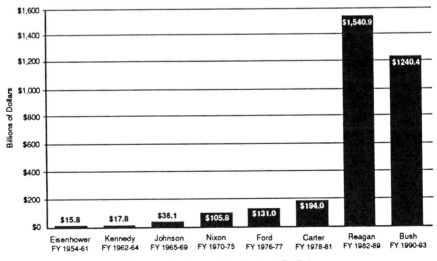

Figure 8-2 Cumulative Budget Deficits

The Prospects for a New Progressive Presidency _____

Even though the presidency may be inherently conservative and even though the Reagan years showed how presidential success can be built on the negative presidency, certainly, it will be argued, there will be moments of progressive presidencies in the future just as there were in the past. Indeed, these progressive periods seem to recur about once every generation. Franklin Roosevelt's New Deal started 20 years after Woodrow Wilson's New Freedom, and Lyndon Johnson's Great Society came 28 years after that. By this logic, another progressive presidency is due in the mid-1990s, possibly following the 1992 or the 1996 elections.

While there will no doubt be progressive presidential periods someday, and while such a period certainly is due by the mid-1990s, it is difficult to see how such a president can be produced by either political party as the parties are currently configured. First the Democrats.

Prospects for a Progressive Democratic President

Since all progressive presidents since 1913 have been Democrats, it is easy to assume that the Democrats are more likely to produce a progressive presidency. They draw their voter support from a lower-status constituency, and the rhetoric of recent Democratic presidential hopefuls in the 1980s (from Jesse Jackson as the most liberal to Richard Gephardt as the most conservative) is much more progressive than is the rhetoric of recent Republican hopefuls (George Bush, Robert Dole, Jack Kemp, and Pat Buchanan). However, there are several obstacles that will have to be overcome by any Democrat who hopes to become a progressive president pursuing the interests of the lower-status population.

Inherent Weakness of the Democratic Liberals. First, any liberal Democrat running on a progressive platform will face a broad uphill battle against not only a more conservative Republican but again a public that has been socialized for two decades into believing slogans such as "government is not the solution; government is the problem." Indeed, so strong is this bias in public opinion that most Democratic presidential nominees since 1970 (Carter in 1976 and 1980 and Dukakis in 1988) sought to distance themselves from their image as economically liberal. The other two (McGovern in 1972 and Mondale in 1984) lost their campaigns in no small measure because they failed to establish that distance. In 1972, Democrat George McGovern was ridiculed for his proposal to give $1,000 to every citizen each year. And in 1984, Mondale was pointed out as beholden to organized labor, social liberals, and feminists, and in favor of raising the income tax.

In sum, the would-be progressive Democratic president faces a serious dilemma. To advocate progressive measures as did McGovern and Mondale is to campaign in the face of strongly held conservative economic biases and a well-heeled business-interest lobby willing to spend millions of dollars attacking the liberal leanings of such candidates. On the other hand, to refrain from campaigning on a progressive platform is to risk failing to draw a sharp enough distinction between the Democrat and the Republican candidate to mobilize support from lower-status people.

Internal Contradictions in Democratic Constituencies. A second obstacle facing the progressive Democratic presidential candidate stems from internal contradictions within the Democratic constituencies. The main constituencies involved are blacks, lower-status whites, organized labor, Hispanics, and upper-status white feminists. Without huge majorities from all of these categories, it is hard to see how Democrats can regain the White House. But this potential majority is hindered by deep splits in their reactions to a variety of social issues ranging from abortion to affirmative action.

The Role of Affirmative Action in Splitting Democrats. A central issue splitting these various elements of the Democratic coalition is affirmative action. Affirmative action is a policy of positively seeking minorities and women when hiring for career positions or when admitting applicants to law schools, medical schools, and other professional schools. For many black leaders, affirmative action is a nonnegotiable demand. They perceive blacks, not inaccurately, as being victimized by racist hiring practices throughout the country. And they see affirmative action as the key way to redress that victimization. Upper-middle-class white feminists also see affirmative action as an important tool to give women preference over white males when competing for jobs or for admission to professional schools.

In contrast to the affirmative-action preferences of blacks and upper-middle-class white females, many lower-status white males see affirmative action as a policy of reverse discrimination targeted at them. Given that perception, it is not surprising that many of them deserted the Democratic party during the 1980s to vote for Reagan and Bush, who flatly opposed affirmative action.

The Need for Lower-Status Unity. What would work for the Democrats, of course, would be to find a presidential nominee who would unite lower-status white males, lower-status white females, lower-status blacks, and lower-status Hispanics around their common economic needs: jobs, health insurance, day care, decent schools, and safe neighborhoods. If such unity existed, a Democratic class-based campaign might win. In the absence of such unity, a class-based election is likely to lose.

The problem facing the progressive Democratic presidential candidate is that leadership does not come from lower-status white men, lower-status black man, lower-status Hispanics, and lower-status white women. It comes from blacks, Hispanics, and whites of upper-middle-class backgrounds. And it is not usually in the interests of these people to promote a lower-status coalition. In some instances, these leaders come to power and maintain their influence by promoting rather than alleviating racial and gender divisions.

None of this is to say that electing a progressive Democratic president is impossible. Only that there are important obstacles to be overcome before it is possible.

Prospects for a Progressive Republican Presidency

Although there has been a progressive Republican President in the twentieth century [Theodore Roosevelt (1900–1908)], it is difficult to see where one would spring from in the 1990s. All realistic Republican candidates for the White House in the 1980s came from the conservative side of the party. President Bush might, in some respects, be the least conservative of all the republicans who sought their party's nomination in 1988.

The Republican strategy for success since 1968 has been to split off a large proportion of lower-status whites from their Democratic allegiances. Ronald Reagan was very successful at this. He directed his appeal at lower-status Southern whites and lower-status Northern whites of European ethnic backgrounds. Substantial numbers of both of these groups were attracted by Reagan's focus on patriotism and conservative social causes such as being in favor of prayer in public schools, and against abortion and pornography. In the South, Reagan's financial backers provided "funds and organizational support" to evangelical churches "for voter registration activities."[28] In the North, his administration combined his appeal on social issues with a deliberate effort to weaken the institutional links between the urban European ethnic groups and the Democratic Party. In the view of Benjamin Ginsberg and Martin Shefter, the administration broke the union of the air traffic controllers in 1981 to encourage "employers to engage in anti-union practices," and followed deregulation policies as well as fiscal and monetary policies that decimated heavy industry and thus dealt a big blow to the bargaining power of organized labor. Finally, under Reagan the Justice Department selectively prosecuted abuses of big-city political machines in Democratic areas, "whose primary targets were large cities controlled by the Democrats." In their words:

The attack on labor unions, political machines, and municipal bureaucracies diminished these institutions' ability to provide benefits to members of urban ethnic groups, and thus undermined the institutional linkage between these voters and the Democratic party. As in the case of southern whites, the disruption of these institutional foundations gave the Republicans an opportunity to win the support of what formerly had been a staunch Democratic constituency.[29]

Finally, the administration used tax cuts to persuade many lower-status citizens that they had more in common with the upper-status population than they did with the poor. By emphasizing tax cuts throughout his presidency, Reagan demonstrated more sympathy with taxpayers who paid for social-welfare programs than he did for the poor and near-poor people who were the beneficiaries of those programs. He achieved a substantial cut in income-tax rates in 1981, and in his 1984 reelection campaign maneuvered his opponent Mondale into the position of trying to take away the tax cuts. The administration hoped in this way to erode public support for domestic expenditures in general.[30]

Kevin Phillips, as we saw, charged that Ronald Reagan converted lower-status Democrats to his cause and then betrayed them by redistributing income upward.[31] This is too harsh a judgment. Reagan did not betray them. He offered them symbolic benefits, and made no pretense of offering domestic programs for them. He opposed affirmative action, busing, and comparable worth, and he took conservative positions on other social issues popular with this group: for prayers in public schools, for patriotism, and for toughness on crime. Many of the lower-status citizens who voted for Reagan doubted that the welfare and anti-poverty programs were bringing them many tangible benefits. While believing that they would not get tangible benefits no matter which party won the White House, at least from Reagan they received symbolic benefits. This was the only way that Reagan could win and keep the presidency.

Is it possible that a Republican president could go beyond Reagan and not only attract lower-status voters but also then use the presidency to advance an agenda in the the economic interests of those lower-status voters? In other words, could a Republican president in the late twentieth century be a progressive president?

Probably not.

But there are some ways in which a Republican rather than a Democratic president might be better positioned to bridge the gap of mistrust between lower-status whites and lower-status minorities. A moderate Republican president who does not wish to alienate the lower-status population and is willing to make symbolic gestures to them might be able to capture some political support from blacks and Hispanics. He would not need a major portion of those voters to turn the

Republicans into the majority party—just enough to solidify his gains among the lower-status whites. How could this come about? Two ways.

First, many blacks and Hispanics are more conservative on some key social issues (abortion, crime) than are upper-middle-class whites. On some social issues unrelated to race or sex, blacks and Hispanics are not ideologically distant from lower-status white men. Since nobody expects a Republican president to be liberal on affirmative action, there might be significant black and Hispanic support for a moderate Republican president who appealed to conservative blacks and Hispanics on social issues other than affirmative action. This president would need to convince large numbers of minorities that he was not looking out solely for the interests of upper-status whites.

Second, a Republican President might be able to bridge the gap between lower-status people and the traditional Republican upper-status core of white voters by focusing on universalistic, as distinct from targeted, programs. Universalistic programs are those such as Social Security old age assistance, the GI Bill of post-World War II fame, Medicare, or government-subsidized loans for post-secondary education that distribute benefits to people in all income categories and are important to upper-status as well as lower-status citizens. Because the benefits of universalistic programs are spread broadly among the population, they draw much stronger support from upper-status voters than do redistributive programs. They also have some advantages for the lower-status population. They provide assistance without it being viewed as demeaning, as welfare assistance unfortunately often is viewed. And because lower-status people usually live on marginal incomes, distributive benefits as a percentage of their incomes are much more important to them than they would be to upper-status people. This would enable them to gain upward mobility without alienating the traditional conservative upper-status Republican interests.

In essence, because nobody expects any Republican president to push redistributive policies, a moderate Republican president has a unique opportunity unavailable to a Democratic president. As the experience of President Carter shows, a moderate Democratic president would risk alienating key elements of his political base if he temporized on certain social issues or focused on universalistic rather than targeted programs. A Republican president who did the same thing, however, might add to his base of political support.

Television and the Conservative Presidency _____

Television has become an important instrument for exercising presidential leadership,[32] especially in the era of the plebiscitary presidency. A president such as Ronald Reagan, who masters the use of television,[33] is able to prop up his public-approval ratings and, as we saw earlier, use that public support to help him negotiate with Congress. However, presidents such as Richard Nixon, Gerald Ford, and Jimmy Carter, who failed to make effective use of television, often found television being used against them.[34]

Television is not a neutral instrument of presidential politics. It has its own biases independent of presidential intentions. Television imposes a structure on presidential communications in ways that reinforce presidential conservatism. First, television is not a very friendly forum for the president to advocate redistributive taxing and spending policies that would assist the lower-status population. Second, television promotes a presidency of overblown expectations. And third, it puts a premium on staging media spectacles that center on symbolic gestures as distinct from substantive accomplishments.

Redistribution as a Nonstarter on Television

A key reason why television facilitates the conservative presidency is that it forces the president to address the entire nation, which necessarily means that presidential addresses cannot stray too far from a core of values shared by a broad cross section of the population. Before television, a president could make different appeals to the different ethnic, sectional, and political groups, but that is harder to do today. Since any presidential appearance is apt to be videotaped, presidents must address their rhetoric at core values that are shared by large pluralities across class lines. A nationwide address targeted to a specific constituency is very apt to turn off other constituencies. This was a clear lesson of Walter Mondale's 1984 presidential campaign when he followed a timeworn Democratic route of securing endorsements from different Democratic constituencies: organized labor, teachers, environmentalists, and the National Organization of Women. This tactic backfired, however, because he quickly was tabbed as the candidate of "special interests." Reagan, by contrast, directed his appeal to a set of core patriotic values shared by a broad cross-section of the American middle class.

Clearly outside the core values of the American middle class are redistributive policies that would increase taxes on upper-income people and spend the proceeds on programs for the poor and near-poor segments of the population. Because of this, even presidents who rely

---

Television imposes a structure on presidential communications in ways that reinforce presidential conservativism.

on the votes of lower-status constituents must be careful of how they use their television time to discuss domestic policy. This is a great change from the pre-television rhetoric of President Franklin D. Roosevelt. In his 1936 reelection campaign, Roosevelt deliberately invoked a redistributive theme and attacked the "economic royalists." In one speech late in the campaign, Roosevelt told a crowd of avid Democrats:

> I should like it said of my first Administration that in it the forces of selfishness and of lust for power met their match. I should like to have it said of my second Administration that in it those forces met their master.[35]

It would be difficult for a president to use such rhetoric successfully in a television address in the 1990s. Such rhetoric would alienate the upper-status audiences that would be watching him make this speech. Instead of pitching redistribution, liberal candidates today speak of fairness. But this fools very few upper-middle-income voters. Such speeches are regularly panned as "class warfare" by conservative and business publications, whose editors fully understand that tax fairness means raising their own taxes.[36]

The Presidency of Overblown Expectations

Second, television promotes a presidency of overblown expectations. To gain the presidency, candidates necessarily promise more than they can deliver. One study of Jimmy Carter's 1976 campaign counted 111 specific promises that Carter made to various constituencies.[37] Once in office, however, and hemmed in by the system of checks and balances, Carter found that he was able to deliver on only a few of those promises. By overblowing expectations, presidential candidates necessarily set the stage for disillusioning the public.[38] George Bush committed the same error in his 1988 campaign with his pledge not to raise taxes. ("Read my lips! No new taxes!") By the time his term was half over, however, he had agreed to significant tax increases, and this earned him the outrage of several conservative groups that accused him of reneging on his campaign pledge.

As presidential expectations get inflated in the face of severe constitutional and political checks and balances that restrict presidential power, serious scholars question whether any president can cope effectively with the nation's domestic challenges,[39] and other scholars charge that the presidency itself is in the process of failing[40] or that it has become a "no-win presidency" in which expectations about what presidents can accomplish have grown while their ability to make substantive accomplishments has declined.[41]

The more presidents inflate expectations, the more they contribute to public distrust of government. And the more distrust in government grows, the more difficult it becomes to use government as an instrument to improve the lives of the lower-status population. Distrust in government feeds into the hands of those who want to keep the government from helping the lower-status population.

The presidency of overblown expectations is in no small measure a consequence of television and the plebiscitary presidency. Given the declining influence of political parties and other political linkage institutions in recent decades, presidents find it more and more necessary to use television to appeal directly to the public. And the most likely way to get public support this way is to inflate public expectations about what presidential programs can achieve.

The Presidency as Spectacle

Finally, television also encourages the White House to stage what Bruce Miroff calls presidential spectacles.[42] White House aides feel a need to create a visual spectacle or media event each day that will get the president on the evening news in a favorable way. Reagan's public relations guru, Michael Deaver, told an interviewer:

> You get only 40 to 80 seconds on a given night on the network news, and unless you can find a visual that explains your message you can't make it stick.[43]

To get these precious seconds of news time, Deaver often created visual spectacles for the president. He "carefully scripted every second of the president's public appearances right down to placing tapes on the floor telling Reagan where to stand for the best camera angles."[44] In one instance Reagan appeared at the opening ceremonies for a senior citizens center in New York. In another instance he toured an apartment construction project in Texas. Despite the fact that Reagan's budget cuts had sharply reduced government funds for constructing such senior citizens centers and had brought public housing construction to a standstill, in both instances the visual "spectacle" of the president's appearances left the impression of a president who was committed to housing for the elderly and the poor.[45]

In presidential spectacles of this sort, writes Miroff, "Gestures overshadow results." In Reagan's case, the "presidency was a triumph of spectacle. . . . The image of masculine toughness was played up repeatedly" with the president shown riding horses, co-opting phrases from movie hero Clint Eastwood ("Go ahead. Make my day!") and repeatedly telling tales of symbolic American heroes.[46]

The most impressive Reagan spectacle, according to Miroff, was the invasion of Grenada in 1983. In explaining the invasion to the public, the president claimed that he was rescuing American medical students living on the island whose live were threatened by the "brutal group of leftist thugs" who ran Grenada and who were using their control to foment revolution throughout the Caribbean. None of these claims was later borne out to be true. But the students were happy to be evacuated from the island, and when some of them kissed the ground in thanks on arrival at the American airport, "the resulting pictures on television and in the newspapers were better than anything the administration could have orchestrated. . . . Here was a second hostage crisis—but where Carter had been helpless to release captive Americans, Reagan had swiftly come to the rescue."[47] Eventually, facts came out that disproved the president's claims about Grenada, but by that time, Grenada was old news, and the media had little interest. What was left in the public's mind was the first impression of Reagan making a decisive stand against communism.[48] The net impact of Grenada was an immediate jump in Reagan's public approval ratings. A White House aide told *Newsweek* magazine: "You can scream and shout and gnash your teeth all you want, but the folks out there like it. It was done right and done with dispatch."[49]

Conclusion _____

The biases against a progressive presidency are not impossible to overcome. Just as there have been windows of opportunity for presidents in the past to enact policies beneficial to the lower-status population, there will also be similar windows of opportunity in the future. But future presidents will have to operate under the constraints facing recent presidents. Namely, that the presidency itself has a conservative bias that is not generally receptive to promoting the interests of lower-status people.

As we have seen, there are several reasons for this. The emergency of the plebiscitary presidency since the 1930s has weakened the political parties and organized labor, two institutions which in the past have been major channels for articulating lower-status interests. Although Franklin D. Roosevelt and Lyndon Johnson were able to use the plebiscitary presidency to advance progressive legislation, in general the plebiscitary presidency is an appeal to the upper-status population that votes. Consequently, presidents who must appeal to that upper-status population for support are not well advised to do so by pleading with the upper-status population to support lower-status interests.

Notes _____

1. Theodore Lowi, *The Personal President: Power Invested, Promise Unfulfilled* (Ithaca, New York: Cornell University Press, 1985), p. 154.

2. Ibid.

3. George C. Edwards III and Stephen J. Wayne, *Presidential Leadership: Politics and Policy Making,* 2nd ed. (New York: St. Martin's Press, 1990), p. 300.

4. John H. Aldrich and Thomas Weko, "The Presidency and the Election Process: Campaign Strategy, Voting and Governance," in *The Presidency and the Political System,* 2nd ed., Michael Nelson, ed. (Washington, D.C.: CQ Press, 1988), pp. 251–252.

5. Thomas Ferguson and Joel Rogers, "The Myth of America's Turn to the Right," *Atlantic* 257, no. 5 (May 1986): 43–53.

6. Erwin C. Hargrove and Michael Nelson, *Presidents, Politics, and Policy* (Baltimore: Johns Hopkins University Press, 1984), p. 200.

7. Gary C. Jacobson, "Congress: Politics after a Landslide without Coattails," *Elections of 1984,* ed. Michael Nelson (Washington D.C.: CQ Press, 1985), pp. 228–229. Also see Aldrich and Weko in Nelson, p. 265.

8. See "Playing Hardball," *Wall Street Journal,* August 18, 1982, p. 1.

9. Richard E. Neustadt, *Presidential Power: The Politics of Power from FDR to Carter* (New York: John Wiley and Sons, 1980), p. 45.

10. Dom Bonafede, "The Strained Relationship," *National Journal,* May 19, 1979, p. 830.

11. Quoted in *Congressional Quarterly Weekly,* March 4, 1978, p. 585.

12. *The Gallup Poll Monthly,* no. 297 (June 1990): 6.

13. Tom Wicker, "Beyond the Jackpot," *New York Times,* January 22, 1990.

14. George C. Edwards studied the relationships between presidential approval ratings and significant international events. He concluded that there is no consistent relationship. The phenomenon "rarely appears and the events that generate it are highly idiosyncratic and do not seem to differ significantly from other events that were not followed by surges in presidential approval. Moreover, the events that cause sudden increases in public support are not restricted to international affairs." Edwards and Wayne, p. 111. Also see Edwards, *The Public Presidency: The Pursuit of Popular Support* (New York: St. Martin's, 1983), p. 247. For a disagreement with Edwards' thesis, see Lowi, *The Personal President,* p. 16.

15. The term "rally event" was coined by John Mueller. See his *Wars, Presidents, and Public Opinion* (New York: Wiley, 1970), pp. 208–213.

16. Lowi, *The Personal President,* argues, "Given the fact that almost all domestic events *depress* rather than rally approval ratings, any increase in approval ratings has to be taken as interesting, if not significant." p. 16.

17. Aaron Wildavsky, "The Two Presidencies," *Transaction* 4, no. 2 (December 1966): 7–14; Lance T. LeLoup and Steven A. Shull, "Congress versus the Executive: The 'Two Presidencies' Reconsidered," *Social Science Quarterly* 59, no. 4 (March 1979): 704–719.

18. Thomas E. Cronin, *The State of the Presidency,* 2nd ed. (Boston: Little, Brown and Co., 1980), pp. 146–147, cites an analysis of State of the Union addresses, which found that presidents devote increasing attention in them to foreign affairs until their reelection years, when domestic concerns rise once again. If the president wins reelection, the attention given to foreign affairs once again increases.

19. Quoted in *Washington Post National Weekly Edition,* October 22–28, 1990, p. 4.

20. Bureau of the Census, *Statistical Abstract of the United States: 1986* (Washington, D.C.: U.S. Government Printing Office, 1985, p. 731;

21. Calculated from the Bureau of the Census, *Statistical Abstract of the United States: 1982–83* (Washington, D.C.: U.S. Government Printing Office, 1982), p. 154; *Statistical Abstract of the United States: 1989* (Washington, D.C.: U. S. Government Printing Office, 1988), p. 140.

22. Office of Management and Budget, *Budget of the United States: Fiscal Year 1986* (Table 20) and *Fiscal Year 1987* (Table 18). Spending for education, job training, and social services dropped from $33.7 billion to $29.3 billion from 1981 to 1985.

23. Ibid. Spending on commerce and housing dropped from $8.2 billion in 1981 to $4.2 billion in 1985.

24. Nathan, *The Administrative Presidency,* p. 74.

25. Ibid., p. 76.

26. Ibid., pp. 77–79.

27. In its first year the Reagan Administration claimed to have made a 25 percent reduction in the size of the *Federal Register,* the document that publishes all regulations. Roger Thompson, "Regulatory Reform," *Editorial Research Reports* (May 11, 1984): 354.

28. Benjamin Ginsberg and Martin Shefter, "The Presidency and the Organization of Interests," in Nelson, *The Presidency and the Political System,* 2nd ed., pp. 314–316.

29. Ginsberg and Shefter, "The Presidency and the Organization of Interests," p. 315. As a specific example of the Justice Department singling out Democratic political machines for prosecution, Ginsberg and Shefter refer to Operation Graylord in Chicago, in which federal prosecutors convicted several Chicago judges of various illegal practices.

30. Ginsberg and Shefter, "The Presidency and the Organization of Interests," p. 317.

31. Kevin Phillips, *Politics of Rich and Poor.*

32. Samuel Kernell, *Going Public: New Strategies of Presidential Leadership* (Washington, D.C.: CQ Press, 1986).

33. See Mark Hertsgaard, *On Bended Knee* (New York: Farrar Straus Giroux, 1988). Hertsgaard details how the Reagan White House effectively used the media to its advantage. This point was also conceded by Reagan's deputy press secretary, Larry Speakes, who admitted that the media had given the administration a "fair shake" and "probably gave us a longer honeymoon than we deserved." Quoted in Edwards and Stevens, *Presidential Leadership,* 2nd ed. p. 152.

34. By one count, nearly 60 percent of the stories on the president during Nixon's last six months were hostile to the president. Michael Baruch Grossman and Martha Joynt Kumar, *Portraying the President: The White House and the News Media* (Baltimore: Johns Hopkins University Press, 1981), p. 262. Coverage of Carter's presidency was also highly negative. See Doris A. Graber, *Mass Media and American Politics,* 2nd ed. (Washington, D.C.: Congressional Quarterly, 1989), pp. 242–243. For a generally negative assessment of television's coverage of the president, see Austin Ranney, *Channels of Power: The Impact of Television on American Politics* (New York: Basic Books, 1983).

35. Franklin D. Roosevelt speech at Madison Square Garden, October 31, 1936.

36. For example, see Michael Novak, "Dead but Fair," *Forbes,* (March 16, 1992), p. 122.

37. Lowi, *The Personal President,* p. 115.

38. Ranney, *Channels of Power,* pp. 140–141.

39. See, for example, Richard Rose, *The Postmodern President: The White House Meets the World* (Chatham, New Jersey: Chatham House, 1988).

40. Donald L. Horowitz, "Is the Presidency Failing?" *The Public Interest* no. 88 (Summer 1987): 3–27.

41. Paul C. Light, *The President's Agenda* (Baltimore: Johns Hopkins University Press, 1982), p. 217.

42. Bruce Miroff, "The Presidency and the Public: Leadership as Spectacle," in *The Presidency and the Political System,* 2nd ed., pp. 271–292.

43. Quoted in Edwards and Wayne, *Presidential Leadership,* p. 125.

44. Ibid.

45. Taken from a Bill Moyers PBS Special.

46. Bruce Miroff, pp. 282–283, 287.

47. Ibid.

48. Anthony Lewis, "What Was He hiding?," *New York Times,* October 31, 1983.

49. *Newsweek,* November 14, 1982.

CHAPTER 9

Bias in the Executive Branch

Lower-status people have a great stake in the government bureaucracy. For several reasons, however, it is difficult for the average person to sort out what that stake is. The popular culture paints such a negative picture of federal, state, and local employees that it is hard for any American citizen to believe that the bureaucracy works for him or her. This negative image is reinforced by activists of the political left as well as the political right. Furthermore, the bureaucracy itself is so large and complicated that average lower-status people have difficulty sorting out the bureaucratic units that benefit them from other units. And finally, the bureaucrats themselves so visibly protect their own self-interest that the average citizen can be forgiven for doubting that the bureaucracy has his or her best interest at heart.

None of these perceptions changes the fact, however, that the federal bureaucracy does a great many things that are very important to the well-being of average Americans. And lower-status Americans in particular have a great stake in how well federal bureaucrats carry out their responsibilities. Consider, for example:

- Factory workers, restaurant workers, health-care workers, and all workers suffer fewer workplace injuries and acquire fewer work-related chronic illnesses if federal health and safety regulations are well-conceived and well-implemented.
- Average Americans suffer fewer accidents from lawnmowers, household appliances, and other consumer products if consumer product safety regulations are well-conceived and well-implemented.
- Lower-status persons who are laid off from their jobs, get divorced, or suffer disabling injuries will get their lives back in order faster if they can turn to help from an effective federal safety net involving sufficient welfare assistance, food stamps, unemployment compensation, workers' compensation, and Social Security.
- Lower-status families have a better chance of seeing their children enjoy upward social mobility if state and local education bureaucra-

cies function well and if federally guaranteed student loans exist for college education.

These four examples illustrate that the government bureaucracy is not neutral. But calculating the overall patterns of political bias in the bureaucracy is complicated by three factors. First, as the examples imply, there is no such thing as *the* bureaucracy; there are several hundred federal agencies, each with its own pattern of bias. Second, in each of the four examples, the bureaucracy does not operate in a political vacuum. The rules and regulations a bureaucracy can adopt are vitally affected by the president, by Congress, and by interest groups in the private sector. These outside forces interfere often enough in the affairs of the federal bureaucracy so that it is at times difficult to distinguish between biases brought about solely by the bureaucracy and those brought about by congressional or presidential direction. And third, different units of the federal bureaucracy implement different types of public policies, each with its own pattern of bias.

To draw a picture of how the federal bureaucracies affect the lower-status population, this chapter first will outline the structure of the federal bureaucracy and pinpoint those units that most concern the lower-status population. Second, we will focus our attention on a specific area of federal policy that is very important to the lower-status population—regulatory policy. We will outline the evolution of regulatory policy in the twentieth century. Third, we will examine the biases of the deregulation movement that predominated in the 1980s. Finally, we will explore the impact of these regulatory and deregulatory forces on one specific area of regulatory policy of special importance to the lower-status population—the policy area of occupational safety and health.

The Three Facets of Bureaucratic Bias _____

To understand the bias of the federal bureaucracy, we must first recognize three different aspects of bureaucratic bias. First, different units of the federal bureaucracy have different biases. Second, the federal bureaucracy is heavily influenced by the president and Con-

---

The federal bureaucracy does a great many things of great importance to the well-being of average Americans. And lower-status Americans in particular have a great stake in how well federal bureaucrats carry out their responsibilities.

gress and other political forces, each of which seeks to impose its own biases on the bureaucracy. Third, different parts of the federal bureaucracy are charged with implementing policies that have differing biases.

Different Units, Different Biases

Calculating the bias of the federal bureaucracy is difficult, because there is no such thing as *the* federal bureaucracy. There are many different units of the federal executive branch, which employs more than three million civilians and two million military personnel. These organizations can be grouped into five categories, as shown in Figure 9–1, and each grouping pursues its own distinct set of self-interests.

Cabinet Departments. First, and best-known, are the 14 cabinet departments, which employ slightly less than two-thirds of all federal civilian employees. Except for the Justice Department (which is headed by the Attorney General), each of these departments is headed by a person called a secretary who is also a member of the president's cabinet. The cabinet consists of the 14 department secretaries, the director of the budget, and any other officials to whom the president gives cabinet status. Although the cabinet is nominally the president's main advisory body, the fact is that few presidents make much use of it.[1] Instead, most presidents deal with cabinet members and agency heads on an issue-area basis. If they need to make a major economic decision, for example, rather than seeking the advice of the whole cabinet, they consult with the heads of the Treasury Department, the Council of Economic Advisers, the Office of Management and Budget, or other agencies whose duties impinge on the economy.

Because most cabinet departments are large organizations conducting some of the major business of government, these departments and their secretaries often share a bias favorable to the sector of society that the department services. The Agriculture Department, for example, is responsible for developing and implementing a workable policy for producing sufficient food for the nation each year under conditions that will keep farmers financially solvent. The Labor Department's mandate is less clear, but it is responsible for promoting effective management–labor relations under conditions that will benefit organized labor and the nation's work force. Given these responsibilities, it would be surprising if bureaucrats in the Agriculture Department failed to have a bias in favor of farmers or if those in the Labor Department failed to have a bias in favor of organized labor. Also, these departments have long histories of being attached to specific policies in their sectors of the private economy. The Agriculture Department, for example, has a long history of providing subsidies and price supports for various crops. These long-established arrangements often put the department's professional bureaucracy in conflict with a new president seeking to set new policies. We will see this phenomenon in practice later when we examine the attempts of the Reagan administration to influence the occupational safety and health policies of the Department of Labor.

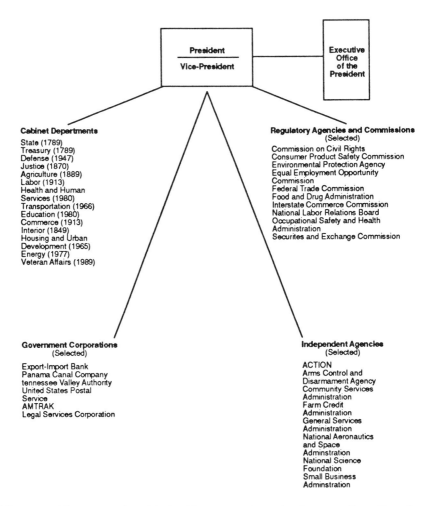

Figure 9-1 Five categories of federal bureaucracies exist: the executive office of the president, the cabinet departments, independent agencies, regulatory commissions and agencies, and government corporations.

The Executive Office of the President. A second set of governmental organizations are those comprising the Executive Office of the President. These are mainly the White House Office, the Office of Management and Budget, the Council of Economic Advisers, and the National Security Council. These agencies are directly accountable to the president, and their main reason for existence is to help the president manage the rest of the government. The Office of Management and Budget (OMB), for example, puts together the president's annual budget request to Congress, oversees the spending decisions of executive agencies, and issues management directives that other agencies are obliged to take seriously. Because the main purpose of the Executive Office of the President is to assist the president in managing the government, most of its agencies are more biased in favor of presidential policies than are the cabinet departments.

Independent Agencies. A third group of governmental organizations are the independent agencies, the most visible of which are indicated in Figure 9–1. Each of these was set up to perform a specific function that neither Congress nor the president wanted to assign to one of the cabinet departments. For example, when the National Aeronautics and Space Administration (NASA) was set up in 1959, it might logically have been housed in the Department of Defense, since that department already had considerable experience with space exploration. Instead, NASA was created as an independent agency to show that the nation's civilian space program would not have military objectives.

Independent Regulatory Commissions. A fourth bureaucratic organization is the independent regulatory commission set up to oversee a particular economic activity. The Federal Communications Commission (FCC), for example, regulates radio and television broadcasting. Most of the regulatory commissions were established during the early twentieth century when it was felt that effective economic regulation required the regulatory body to be independent of both the president and Congress. For this reason, the commissions were given quasi-legislative and quasi-judicial powers as well as administrative powers. The FCC, for instance, exercises quasi-legislative powers in that it establishes rules and regulations that broadcasters must obey, and it exercises quasi-judicial powers when it imposes penalties on broadcasters that it determines violate the rules. The regulatory commissions are made further independent of the president in that the commission members are appointed for overlapping terms of office. This was intended to reduce the chance that a single president could appoint a majority of the members of any commission.

Government Corporations. Finally, a fifth type of organization is the government corporation. Examples include the U.S. Postal Service, which delivers your mail, or the Federal Deposit Insurance Corporation (FDIC), which insures your bank accounts. Government corporations are usually created to provide essential services that either are too costly to be performed by any private sector corporation or cannot be operated profitably. Private corporations, such as Federal Express, can make a tidy profit specializing in overnight delivery of mail, but it is unlikely that any private corporation would make a profit delivering the volume and wide range of mail that is handled by the U.S. Postal Service.

The bias or political orientation of a federal agency is likely to differ, depending on what type of organization it is. Independent agencies or those belonging to the Executive Office of the President are most likely to be responsive to policy changes effected by a new president. At the other extreme, government corporations are likely to think of themselves as nonpolitical bodies performing public services in a business-like fashion, and they are least likely to respond to policy changes initiated by a new president. Somewhat in the middle are the cabinet departments and the independent regulatory commissions.

Different Actors, Different Biases

Not only do different bureaucratic units reflect different biases, but federal bureaucrats are also influenced by other political actors who each have their own biases that they try to impose on the executive branch. We conceptually distinguish between the president and Congress on the one hand as policymakers, and the bureaucracy on the other hand as policy implementers, but in practice this distinction is quite fuzzy. The bureaucrats not only implement policy, but they regularly interact with Congress and private-sector interest groups to influence what the policy should be. The best known example of this is the Department of Defense, which takes a keen interest in the passage of laws and budgets relating to the development and purchase of very expensive military hardware. For its part, Congress and the president also involve themselves deeply in the details of the Pentagon's bureaucratic affairs. It is a rare member of Congress who would fail to interfere with a Pentagon proposal to close a military installation in his or her district. Presidents, too, interfere with the bureaucracy. During the Vietnam War, the White House attempted to micro-manage the conduct of the war, down to the details of approving specific bombing targets.

We cite these examples of the Defense Department only because they are the most obvious examples of the confusion that exists between policy making and policy implementation. Our concern is not with foreign policy but with the implementation of domestic policy and whether there are persistent biases that permeate the executive branch.

Different Policies, Different Biases

In addition to political biases attributable to the type of agency, there are also different types of policies that have different biases. Political scientists traditionally distinguish between three types of policies—distributive, redistributive, and regulatory.[2] Distributive policies differ from redistributive ones in that redistributive policies seek to gather taxes from upper-income persons and use them for programs that target their benefits to the lower-status population, while distributive policies seek to divide their benefits evenly among the population. Thus, public education is essentially a distributive-policy area, because every citizen is eligible to attend the public schools. Welfare programs such as Food Stamps, Aid for Families with Dependent Children, or Unemployment Compensation, on the other hand, are redistributive programs. They are funded by income taxes drawn from the middle and upper-middle sectors of the population, and the benefits of the programs are redistributed down to the poor and near-poor sectors of the population. Policies targeted for the upper-status population (such as a lower income tax on capital gains) could also be called redistributive. But common convention uses the term "redistribution" primarily for benefits targeted to the lower-status population. Policies that take taxes from the lower-status population and target benefits to the upper-status population are generally called "regressive" policies.

There are some policies that are intended to be distributive, but in fact have a redistributive impact. Social Security is such a policy. During your working years the FICA deduction from your paycheck is placed into a Social Security Trust Fund that provides benefits for you when you retire. Since everybody's benefits are tied to the amount they contribute, this is intended to be a distributive policy. To date, however, almost everybody's benefits have far exceeded their contributions and have been subsidized by the public treasury.

A third category of policy is regulatory policy. This is a policy that reduces the discretion of a person, business, or organization to conduct its affairs as it wants to without taking into consideration the broader interests of society and other people.[3] Usually the goal of regulation is to induce businesses to promote some public good, such as preventing pollution or protecting occupational health and safety. Regulatory policies can be either distributive or redistributive. Environmental protection is a distributive regulatory policy. The poor person benefits from clean air as much as the rich person does. Regulation of occupational health and safety, on the other hand, is a redistributive policy area, because most of the hazardous and unhealthy workplace environments occur among the lower-status population. It is not the coal company executive, but the lower-status coal miner who risks death from mine cave-ins or black-lung disease from years of exposure to coal dust. Thus, attempts to regulate mine safety or to eliminate unhealthy conditions from the work environment are potentially among the most redistributive of all regulatory policies.

Bureaucracies for the Lower-Status Population

Table 9–1 outlines some of the major units of the federal bureaucracy that have specific importance to the lower-status population. It is not surprising that many of the units listed in this table are regulatory agencies. As we will see below, the political motivation that led to the creation of most regulatory agencies in the first place resulted from abuses being perpetrated either on the broad mass of the population or powerless sectors of the population.

The Background of Federal Regulation _____

Because of this heightened importance of occupational health and safety regulation to the lower-status work force, we want to focus on it as an example of bias in the federal bureaucracy. To see how occupational health and safety regulation fits into the history of regulatory policy, however, it is necessary first to examine the evolution of governmental regulation in the United States and the rise of the deregulation movement in the 1980s.

Historically, the federal government played a minimal role in regulating American business. The American economy was mostly governed by what economists call "market forces." That is, businesses decided for themselves what they would produce, what prices they would charge for their products or services, and whether they should be concerned about the impact their operations had on the environment, the occupational health and safety of workers, and the living conditions of their employees. If a factory wanted to hire 11-year-old children to work 12 hours a day, the factory owner was free to make that choice. If a business owner wanted to provide no pension or health insurance or sick leave for the company's permanent work force, the business owner was also free to make that choice. And if a railroad controlled the only transportation link for a farming community to ship its produce to markets, it was free to raise shipping rates without

TABLE 9–1   Bureaucratic Units of Special Concern to Lower-Status People

Redistributive Units that Provide Direct Assistance to Lower-Status People

Social Security Administration 1935 (Health and Human Services Dept)	Administers federal trust funds for Old Age Assistance, disability assistance, and Medicare. Administers the Supplemental Security Income program for the elderly, the blind, and the disabled.
Family Support Administration 1988 (Health and Human Services Dept)	Administers basic welfare programs such as Aid for Families with Dependent Children (AFDC), child-support enforcement, refugee resettlement, and a variety of community service programs.
Food and Nutrition Service 1969 (Agriculture Dept)	Runs Food Stamp program and other nutrition programs such as the school breakfast program and the special milk program for school children. Also provides supplemental food programs under the WIC program for pregnant women and for women and children.
Employment and Training Administration 1935 (Dept of Labor)	Administers federal programs for unemployment insurance compensation, employment services, and the Job Training Partnership program.
ACTION 1971 (Independent agency)	Administers several volunteer programs ranging from VISTA (Volunteers in Service to America) to the Foster Grandparent program.
Legal Services Corporation 1947 (Government Corporation)	Provides legal services in civil cases for persons too poor to hire an attorney.
Department of Housing and Urban Development 1965	Administers a wide variety of federal housing programs ranging from traditional public housing to rent-subsidy programs for low-income families, to the federal mortgage insurance program of the Federal Housing Administration. Also administers the federal Community Development Block Grant and the Urban Development Action Grant programs to assist states in community-development efforts.
Administration for Children Youth and Families (Health and Human Services Dept)	Administers several social service programs set up by the Social Security Act dealing with adoption, temporary child care, Head Start, child abuse and child neglect, child welfare.
Pension Benefit Guaranty Corporation 1974 (Government Corporation)	Provides pension-guarantee benefits for more than 40 million workers.
Farmers Home Administration 1949 (Agriculture Dept)	Provides credits, emergency loans, and loans for youth for low-income farm families.
Administration on Aging 1965 (Health and Human Services Dept)	The lead agency for the aged within the Department of Health and Human Services. Administers grant programs to states and communities.
Administration for Native Americans (Health and Human Services Dept)	Administers several grant programs relating to Native Americans and seeks to represent the interest of Native Americans within the Department of Health and Human Services.

Regulatory Agencies with Special Importance to the Lower-Status Population

Occupational Safety and Health Administration 1970 (Dept of Labor)	Regulates safety and health in the workplace.
Occupational Safety and Health Review Commission 1970 (Independent Commission)	Hears appeals on regulatory decisions made by OSHA.
Mine Safety and Health Administration 1969 (Dept of Labor)	Regulates safety and health in the nation's mines.
Federal Mine Safety and Health Review Commission 1977 (Independent Commission)	A review commission for cases involving health and safety in the nation's mines.
National Labor Relations Board 1935 (Independent Commission)	Regulates labor–management relations. Oversees collective bargaining elections. Goal is to prevent and remedy unfair labor practices by either management or labor.
Federal Mediation and Conciliation Service 1947	Promotes the resolution of labor management disputes through mediation and conciliation.
National Mediation Board 1934 (Independent Commission)	Provides mediation services for labor–management conflicts in the railroad and airline industries.
Pension and Welfare Benefits Administration 1974 (Dept of Labor)	Requires private pension plans to adhere to federal standards governing those plans.
Federal Deposit Insurance Corporation 1933 (Government Corporation)	Insures your savings accounts in federally insured banks up to $100,000. In 1989 the FDIC was also given authority over the administration of federal deposit insurance at the federally chartered savings and loans associations.
National Credit Union Administration 1970 (Independent Commission)	Regulates and insures federally chartered credit unions.
Office of Thrift Supervision 1989 (Dept of the Treasury)	The primary regulator of the nation's federally chartered savings and loans associations. Established in the wake of the savings and loan crisis of the late 1980s.
Employment Standards Administration (Dept of Labor)	Regulates employment standards such as minimum wage and discrimination.
Office of Workers' Compensation Programs (Dept of Labor)	Administers workers' compensation programs for federal employees and employees covered by certain programs such as the Black Lung benefit program.
Food and Drug Administration 1906 (Public Health Service)	Regulates and approves drugs for use in the American marketplace.
Consumer Product Safety Commission 1970 (Independent Commission)	Sets rules that seek to protect the public from unsafe consumer products. Enforces those rules.

Federal Trade Commission 1914 (Independent Commission)	Seeks to safeguard the public from unfair methods of competition and unfair or deceptive business practices.
Indian Health Service (Public Health Service)	Assists Indian tribes in providing health programs and improving the health of Native Americans.
Bureau of Indian Affairs 1824 (Interior Dept)	Administers federal educational and other programs targeted to Native Americans.
Women's Bureau (Dept of Labor)	Promotes the welfare of working women.

Distributive Units Whose Benefits Go to a Wide Range of Income Classes but Are Especially Helpful to Lower-Status People

Public Health Service 1944 (Health and Human Services Dept)	Promotes a wide range of health research; seeks to coordinate state health policies; sponsors programs to develop health resources; and provides health resources to the states. Is the parent agency for the Centers for Disease Control, the Alcohol, Drug Abuse, and Mental Health Administration, the National Institutes of Health, and other health-related agencies.
Department of Education 1979	Provides general educational assistance to states and local school districts. Also funds a number of redistributive educational programs directed toward minorities and toward compensatory education for the culturally deprived. Also provides funding for Gallaudet University (for the deaf), for Howard University (predominantly black) and the National Technical Institute for the Deaf.
Bureau of Labor Management Relations (Dept of Labor)	Offers educational and public affairs programs promoting better labor–management relations.
Rural Electrification Administration 1936 (Agricultural Dept)	Provides credits to rural electrification projects. Effect is to lower the cost of electricity for consumers.
Tennessee Valley Authority 1933 (Government Corporation)	Operates a system of dams that facilitate navigation on rivers in the Tennessee River Valley and provide cheap hydroelectric power for residents of that region.
Urban Mass Transportation Administration 1964 (Dept of Transportation)	Administers federal aid programs for urban transit, rapid-rail and light-rail construction.
National Railroad Passenger Corporation (AMTRAK) 1970 (Government Corporation)	Operates the nation's passenger rail service.
Economic Development Administration 1965 (Commerce Dept)	Provides grants and loans for job-development projects by local governments.
Minority Business Development Agency 1972 (Commerce Dept)	Provides assistance to minority entrepreneurs seeking to establish businesses.
Veterans' Employment and Training Service (Dept of Labor)	Administers employment and training programs directed at veterans.

Department of Veterans Affairs 1990	Runs veterans' hospitals and other programs targeted to the nation's veterans. These include pension programs, compensation programs for survivors of veterans, vocational rehabilitation and training programs, and guaranteed mortgages for veterans.
National Highway Traffic Safety Administration 1970 (Dept of Transportation)	A major regulatory body in the field of consumer protection. Regulates safety on the highways by setting rules on highway safety and enforcing those rules. Sets fuel standards for autos and regulations for safety devices such as seat belts.
Environmental Protection Agency 1970 (Independent Agency)	Sets rules seeking to implement the nation's environmental-protection laws. Enforces those rules.
Civil Rights Division of the Department of Justice 1957	Responsible for implementing various civil-rights laws and securing the enforcement of civil rights that prohibit discrimination based on race, national origin, sex, or religion.
Equal Employment Opportunity Commission 1964 (Independent Commission)	Responsible for enforcing the nation's laws dealing with equal employment opportunities and affirmative action. Goal is to prevent workplace discrimination based on race, sex, age, religion, country of national origin, or handicapped status.
Commission on Civil Rights 1957 (Independent Commission)	Sets rules implementing the nation's civil-rights laws and enforces those rules.
National Transportation Safety Board 1975 (Independent Commission)	Conducts independent investigations of transportation accidents, and formulates safety-improvement recommendations.

Source: United States Government Manual: 1990–1991.

interference from the state or federal government. Under a "market economy," the only restraints on these businesses were the restraints of competition and profitability. If the action was unprofitable, they probably would not do it; if profitable, there was nothing to stop them from doing it.

Up to the time of the Civil War when most economic activity consisted of individual tradesmen or shop owners operating in a local or regional market, this free-market economy worked well enough. But the period after the Civil War saw rapid industrial growth and the emergence of the large corporations that soon came to dominate the economy. The locally based shopkeeper economy was supplanted by a corporate-based economy. The corporations swallowed up small companies and created monopolies, such as Standard Oil, that dominated entire industries. Farmers were at the mercy of monopoly railroads that charged exorbitant rates to ship their produce to market. Workers, who in an earlier day might have been independent skilled tradesmen, now became anonymous employees in large factories that blatantly exploited the workers with low wages and unsafe working conditions.

Competitive Regulation: The First Wave

Widespread protest over these changing economic conditions led Congress to establish the first regulatory commission in 1887. This was the Interstate Commerce Commission (ICC), and it was charged with regulating railroad rates. Three decades later, in 1913, Congress created the Federal Reserve System to regulate national monetary policy and the banking system. And two decades after that, in the 1930s, came a wave of legislation setting up new regulatory agencies to deal with the securities industry, the communications industry, the fledgling airline industry, agricultural policy, and labor–management policy.

This wave of regulatory legislation in the 1930s has been called "competitive regulation."[4] Most of the regulatory agencies created during this period were industry-specific, and their regulatory efforts were directed at limiting the competition within any given industry. For example, the broadcast industry is regulated by the Federal Communications Commission (FCC), created in 1934. Limited competition is crucial in this industry because of the limited number of channels available on the television and radio spectrums. If more than one station were to broadcast or telecast on the same radio frequency, the results would be chaotic. Because it could limit competition, the FCC was looked on favorably by the broadcast industry. This was especially the case during the 1950s and 1960s when the FCC made it difficult for cable television to expand. Most companies in regulated industries support the idea of competitive regulation because of its effect of limiting competitors.

Capture Theory. When first established, regulatory commissions zealously protected the public interest. But some critics charge that in time the regulatory agencies began to defend the interests of the industries they were supposed to regulate. In this view, the regulatory agencies were "captured" by the industries they were supposed to be regulating. The creation of a regulatory commission was seen primarily as a symbolic act to calm down public concern over specific economic abuses without making any major assault on those abuses.[5] Once the commission was established, public outcry over the issue would dissipate, and the attention of Congress and the president would turn to

---

Under a "market economy," the only restraints on these businesses were the restraints of competition and profitability. If the action was unprofitable, they probably would not do it; if profitable, there was nothing to stop them from doing it.

other issues. As this began to happen, interest groups in the regulated industries came to have increasing influence on their regulatory agencies.[6] Thus, broadcasters were seen as having captured the FCC, drug companies the FDA, and major airlines the CAB. While still applicable in some instances, the capture theory is seen today as an overgeneralization.[7]

Revolving-Door Theory. The part of capture theory that seems to be most applicable today is that of the revolving-door theory. According to this theory, regulatory commissioners are drawn from the industries they are supposed to regulate, and they expect to go back and work in those industries after they leave the commission. Critics charge that commissioners such as these, who hope to move on to high paying jobs in their industries, are unable to regulate those industries with any zeal or independence. Not only do the commissioners have ties to industry, but it is tempting for the agencies' staff technicians to leave their agencies and seek jobs in their regulated industries, where they can command higher salaries. Recent studies have shown, however, that the revolving door is much more common among the commissioners than it is among the staff workers.[8] One study of employment patterns of high-ranking staff workers in eight regulatory agencies found relatively few cases where workers resigned to take positions in their regulated industries.[9] Among commissioners, however, the reverse was true. Twenty percent of recent commissioners on three regulatory commissions found jobs in their industries immediately after leaving their commissions.[10] When Congress passed legislation to close the revolving door, however, it closed it only for the staff workers. They can no longer move directly from a regulatory staff position into a company in their regulated areas. Commissioners, on the other hand, are free to move back and forth between agencies and their regulated industries.

The New Regulation: Protective

During the 1970s, important changes took place in the regulatory system. Following the turbulent decade of the 1960s which saw the birth of new political movements, especially the environmental movement, there was a dramatic expansion of regulatory activity. This new regulation of the 1970s differed from that of the 1930s in three key respects. First, not only were new regulatory agencies created, but they took on a different, more controversial focus. Whereas the older regulatory agencies of the 1930s aimed at limiting competition within specific industries, most of the new agencies created in the 1970s pushed for broad social goals across the entire spectrum of economic activity.

The Occupational Safety and Health Administration (OSHA), for example, was created to improve occupational health and safety throughout the country, not just within a specific industry. The Environmental Protection Agency was created to cut pollution and enforce environmental laws throughout the entire United States. The Equal Employment Opportunities Commission (EEOC) sought to eliminate racial and sexual biases in hiring practices. All three of these examples of new regulation differed from the old in their emphasis on protective regulation.[11]

A More Overtly Political Orientation. These new agencies were also less independent than the older regulatory commissions. Whereas the typical older regulatory commission was governed by a board of commissioners who served long, overlapping terms of office, were not removable by the president, and were required by law to be from different political parties, the EPA and OSHA were governed by an administrator appointed by and removable by the president. This lesser degree of independence makes the new regulatory agencies much more amenable to policy direction from the White House than was true for the older regulatory commissions.

A More Radical Ideological Tradition. Finally, the New Regulation of the 1970s stemmed from a more radical ideological tradition than did the Old Regulation of the 1930s and earlier. Proponents of regulation in both periods were critical of the American capitalist economy, but the Old Regulation of the Franklin Roosevelt administration essentially accepted capitalism while seeking to reform it. Roosevelt's Secretary of Labor, Frances Perkins, wrote that Roosevelt "took the status quo in our economic system as much for granted as his family."[12] And a prominent New Deal historian wrote that "Roosevelt's program rested on the assumption that a just society could be secured by imposing a welfare state on a capitalist foundation."[13] If only true competition could be imposed on the capitalist economy, especially on the sectors of the economy dominated by monopolies, the public interest would be served. It was for this reason that the Old Regulation was dubbed competitive regulation.

The public-affairs lobbyists pushing for the New Regulation in the 1970s, however, came out of the New Left intellectual tradition of the 1960s, which was much more critical of the capitalist system and professed a deep doubt that political institutions (such as the Democratic Party) could ever be counted on to permit effective regulation of capitalism. Instead, New Left advocates demanded that new institutions be created and widespread individual participation be relied on more than the traditional political institutions to promote the regulation of capitalism. For example, an important public lobbyist for New Regulation of equal employment opportunity and affirmative action has been John Lewis. During a 1960s speech Lewis expressed his mistrust of the political parties and other mainstream political institutions:

> The party of Kennedy [i.e., a Democrat] is also the party of Eastland. The party of Javits [i.e., a Republican] is also the party of Goldwater. Where is our party? . . . We all recognize that if any social, political and economic changes are to take place in our society, the people, the masses, must bring them about.[14]

As these words suggest, the public affairs lobbyists who advocated for the New Regulation of the 1970s simply mistrusted traditional political and governmental institutions. They especially denied that the Democratic Party or the president could be agents of the kind of social change that they wanted to bring to American society. They put great faith in citizen participation as a mechanism for achieving social regulation. In a sense, they held a political position that was self-contradictory. They mistrusted traditional governmental institutions, but needed to gain control of those institutions if they were to bring about social change. As one pair of scholars said, "Thus, public lobbyists had one foot in the establishment and one foot outside of it; they participated in the enhancement of the administrative state, then drew their political and spiritual sustenance from attacking it."[15]

Disenchantment with the New Regulation

Because the New Regulation is nationwide rather than tied to specific industries and because the new regulatory agencies were initially very zealous in carrying out their responsibilities, some of the new agencies came under sharp attack from the business community. This was especially true of the Environmental Protection Agency (EPA) and the Occupational Safety and Health Administration (OSHA). The EPA was created in 1970 to enforce environmental protection laws. It issues thousands of regulations that determine what companies must do to limit their pollution of the environment. This specific approach often put the EPA at odds with Congress, which often writes very vague environmental laws, and with business companies, who resented the way the EPA implemented the laws.[16] The environmental movement declined in the late 1970s and the 1980s, which left the EPA vulnerable to attacks by businesses that did not want to meet EPA standards and by conservatives who thought that the high cost of complying with the EPA's regulations put a drag on economic growth.

When Reagan became president in 1981, he moved to make the EPA more accommodating to business. His appointee as EPA director, Anne

Gorsuch Burford, held up new environmental regulations, cut staff, refused to prosecute some key violators, and generally took an anti-environment stance. These actions brought the agency into conflict with members of Congress who charged that EPA was illegally failing to enforce environmental legislation. This conflict brought about Burford's replacement by a more environment-oriented director.[17] Nevertheless, throughout the balance of the Reagan years, the EPA was plagued by persistent underbudgeting, the exodus of important staff workers, and an antiregulatory political environment. By 1990, the EPA had become a pale imitation of the agency it had been a decade earlier.

Unrecognized Benefits of Regulation

Despite the disenchantment with regulation that emerged in the late 1970s, it would be wrong to assume that regulation was an unmitigated cost to business. There were many instances in which regulation provided benefits for the business community. For example, one of the early actions of the EPA was banning the use of fluorocarbons as a propellant in aerosol spray cans. EPA took this action because of fear that the continued release of fluorocarbons in the atmosphere would deplete the ozone layer that protects the earth from dangerous ultraviolet rays. Instead of the ban imposing a cost on business, however, many businesses benefited from the ban. While it cost 71 cents to produce a can of antiperspirant spray if fluorocarbons were used, the cost dropped to 46 cents per can if a mechanical pump rather than a fluorocarbon-based aerosol was used. Individual companies were reluctant to abandon the more expensive fluorocarbon-based aerosol spray on their own, however, for fear that consumers would not buy the products in the pump container; but when the EPA banned the use of fluorocarbons for all antiperspirant sprays, it lowered the production costs of all the companies involved.[18]

Deregulation _____

Notwithstanding examples of the benefits of regulation, complaints against OSHA, the EPA, and other regulatory agencies began to grow. The business world stepped up its political agitation to cut back on economic regulation. A 1980 study by the prestigious business group, The Conference Board, asserted that businesses did not want to get rid of regulation *per se,* but they wanted major reforms in how regulation was practiced. Specifically, they complained about overlapping jurisdictions between regulatory agencies, with conflicting rules coming from each. The EPA, for example, often issued regulations that conflicted with ones issued by OSHA. Business leaders also complained that regulatory agencies went beyond their legal mandates by writing rules that exceeded their legal authority. They complained of the over-regulation in the sense that regulatory agencies would get deeply involved in the detailed operations of a specific company. They complained of delays by regulatory agencies in resolving disputes and of an adversarial attitude toward business that they felt typified many of the staff members of the new regulatory agencies.[19]

In response to complaints such as these, Congress and the White House in the late 1970s began to experiment with the idea of bringing regulatory relief to the business community.

Early Deregulation: The Carter Years, 1977–1980

The first steps toward deregulation took place in the old competitive area of the transportation sector. Starting in 1978 the airlines were deregulated. Under competitive regulation, airline fares and routes set by the Civil Aeronautics Board consistently protected the interests of the large carriers and effectively impeded new airline companies from starting up. Starting in 1978, authority to set air fares and air routes was taken from the CAB, and the CAB was gradually phased out of existence. The immediate results of this deregulation were to lower air fares between large cities; to stimulate the formation of new, smaller airlines that began to dominate services to smaller cities; and to stimulate intense price wars that drove several airlines into the red and some others into bankruptcy. By 1990, these forces were leading to the consolidation and merger of the major airlines into a small number of giant airlines.

After deregulating the airlines, Congress moved to undo regulatory controls over other industries as well. Railroad and freight trucking were made more competitive as authority was removed from the Interstate Commerce Commission to set rates and routes. Takeover wars also bid up the prices of television and radio stations as the FCC relaxed its ownership rules. Automobile manufacturers found it easier to delay installing passive-restraint systems such as air bags and to delay increasing the gasoline efficiency of their fleets.

While the Carter administration initiated regulatory reform, there was a key ideological difference between Carter's regulators and those who came into power under Ronald Reagan. Carter accepted the premise that regulatory reform might make the economy function more efficiently, but he did not accept the notion that regulation in itself was bad. Indeed, very little of Carter's regulatory reform touched the new protective regulations in areas such as environmental protection, civil rights, or consumer protection. Reagan, however, in his speeches, appeared to reject the basic idea of regulation, and he left the impression that deregulation under a Reagan presidency would aim not to make regulation more efficient, but to eliminate it. Reagan blamed regulation, for example, for setting up "barriers of investment, production, and employment," for being a "very significant factor" in inflation and the "retardation of economic growth." And he blamed regulation for imposing $100 billion per year in costs on the economy.[20]

These sentiments expressed by Reagan left Carter's regulators fearing that the thrust of a Reagan presidency would be not to make regulation more efficient, but to eliminate it. Accordingly they sought to get as many new regulations on the books as possible before the new president took over. The result was the issuance of more than 200 new, so-called "midnight rules" in the last few weeks of Carter's presidency.[21]

Deregulation: The Reagan Years, 1981–1988

Given his antiregulatory bias, Reagan followed a five-pronged attack on regulation. First, he used his appointive power to put antiregulatory people into office. He appointed Murray Wiedenbaum, an economist who had made a career of pointing out the economic inefficiencies of regulation, to be chair of the Council of Economic Advisers. We have already seen that Reagan's first appointee to head the EPA was the antiregulatory Anne Gorsuch Burford. And as we shall see below, his first OSHA director was a man who basically was opposed to a vigilant federal role in regulating occupational health and safety.

Second, the president imposed sharp budget restraints on the regulatory agencies.[22] These budget restraints meant that the EPA, for example, suffered a 19 percent drop in its number of employees during the first two years under Reagan.[23]

Third, Reagan issued an executive order requiring that any new regulations be submitted to a cost–benefit analysis conducted by the Office of Management and Budget. The intent was to ensure that the benefits of any such regulation would outweigh the costs imposed on the American economy or the companies concerned.

Fourth, the president appointed a Task Force on Regulatory Relief headed by Vice President George Bush. The task force combed through existing regulations to find ones that could be submitted to the cost–benefit rules and eliminated. At the conclusion of its work, the Task Force asserted that these cost–benefit measures had saved billions of dollars and reduced by 25 percent the size of the *Federal Register,* which is the document that must publish all federal rules before they can take effect.[24]

Finally, Reagan regulators reinterpreted existing regulations more narrowly than had been true in the past, in an effort to minimize their impact. For example, one area of federal benefits was for coal miners who had contracted black lung disease. The new regulators restricted those benefits to current sufferers and scrapped the existing preventive maintenance mechanisms that were designed to limit the number of new cases.[25]

The Consequences of Deregulation

Despite the glee in some sectors over the progress of deregulation during the early 1980s, there were limits to the benefits that could be achieved. Most of the progress toward deregulation had been achieved by executive order and budget cutting rather than by legislative change. This meant that a new president, who might be more regulatory-minded, could easily undo Reagan's deregulation simply by increasing budgets and reversing Reagan's executive orders.

Indeed, by the end of the 1980s, Congress was beginning to feel a backlash against the deregulation that had been put in place. Some industries, such as trucking, had been lukewarm in the first place to facing the greater competition that accompanies deregulation. Some groups began asking for reregulation of areas that had already been deregulated—railroad freight hauling, for example.[26] Along the way, some of deregulation's most prized goals were strongly opposed by most organized-labor groups and consumer groups. The administration received a sharp setback in 1981 when the Supreme Court blocked its attempt to apply cost–benefit analysis to an OSHA rule regulating the levels of cotton dust allowed in textile plants.[27] Prolonged exposure to cotton dust leads to a respiratory ailment called brown-lung disease, which OSHA regulations were seeking to prevent.

Deregulating the Airlines. The most worrisome consequences of deregulation occurred in the airline and financial services industries. Despite assertions by proponents that the public had benefited on balance from airline deregulation,[28] there was growing concern over safety, congestion, quality of service, and dominance of the industry by a few large carriers. Increased competitiveness reduced airline profitability, and with smaller profits, the companies had less money to spend on safety. Investigations showed that expenditures on aircraft maintenance declined after deregulation and that the average age of planes in service was increasing.[29] Safety records were the worst for the commuter airlines serving small communities. Deregulation was intended to increase competitiveness between the airlines, but by the end of the Reagan administration, several major airlines had gone bankrupt, the remaining giants enjoyed near-monopoly conditions in over a dozen major hubs, and 150 small airlines that had started up in the early days of deregulation were now out of business.[30] Most of the small airlines that managed to survive did so by linking up with one of the giants to provide its local commuter service.

Deregulating the Savings and Loan Industry. Financially, the most costly deregulation was that involving savings and loans associations (S&Ls).[31] These associations were created in the late nineteenth century to give workers a place to save small amounts of money and to get mortgage loans to buy homes. Until 1980 they were strictly regulated in the amounts of interest they could pay on deposits, and they were allowed to make loans only for mortgages. Because of these restrictions, they suffered in the inflation of the 1970s when they lost depositors to money-market mutual funds and to other institutions that could pay higher interest rates. To overcome these problems, Congress in 1980 and 1982 passed deregulation statutes that expanded the types of loans S&Ls could make and let them decide for themselves how much interest they would pay depositors. By the end of the decade hundreds of S&Ls had become insolvent and the federal government became responsible for the missing assets that will eventually cost taxpayers at least $500 billion.

In the absence of effective regulatory controls, many S&Ls offered above-market interest rates to attract depositors, but to raise revenue to cover those interest payments they had to make risky investments in poorly planned real-estate developments, shopping-center complexes, and junk bonds. When the commercial real-estate and junk-bond markets collapsed, these S&Ls were unable to pay off their depositors. Since each deposit was insured up to $100,00 by the Federal Savings and Loan Insurance Corporation (FSLIC), the federal government had to pick up much of the estimated $500-billion cost. To do so, Congress overhauled the savings and loan regulatory apparatus in 1989 and created the Resolution Trust Corporation to seize the insolvent S&Ls and sell their assets.

Not only were there bad management practices at the S&Ls, but outright fraud was discovered in more than half of those that failed.[32] Phony real estate appraisals were common, as were loans to family members, and kickbacks from loan recipients. But the owners of the S&Ls faced little risk, because the government deposit insurance would pay off depositors. Federal regulators should have pulled the plug on these activities, but they were hampered by antiregulatory attitudes in the Reagan administration and the staff cutbacks imposed by the Office of Management and Budget. When regulators did object to questionable practices, they sometimes got in trouble with Congress. In the case of one Arizona S&L, the company president got key senators, to whom he had made substantial campaign contributions, to put pressure on officials of the Federal Home Loan Bank Board who were trying to put limits on that S&L's risky investments.[33]

There were many reasons for the S&L debacle of the 1980s. Difficult economic conditions, fraud, and mismanagement were the main culprits. But the debacle would never have reached the level it did had it not been for the lax regulatory environment which made it impossible for federal regulators to exercise effective oversight of the industry.[34]

Occupational Safety as a Case Study of Regulation and Deregulation _____

Of all the areas of government regulation, it is hard to overestimate the importance of occupational health and safety to the lower-status population. Prior to the establishment of the Occupational Safety and Health Administration (OSHA) in 1970, there was little national concern over health and safety in the workplace. Consistent with the prevailing philosophy of dual federalism that we studied in Chapter 3, this was an issue left to the states. But the states had proved incapable of dealing with it. It was not until 1911 that the first state (New Jersey) passed a workers' compensation law. This is a law that sets up a trust fund into which employers pay a premium based in part on their histories of accidents in the workplace. When a worker loses an eye or an arm or suffers some other disability, he or she receives a dollar settlement from the trust fund. By mid-century, all states had workers' compensation laws, but they did little to deter occupational hazards. It was very difficult for injured workers to win a lawsuit charging a company with negligence when accidents occurred, and states that tried to set strict safety standards or generous workers' compensation benefits ran the risk of being labeled as anti-business. This label would deter new businesses from moving in and encourage existing businesses to expand elsewhere rather than in the home state.

It was clear that significant headway on occupational safety and health would require federal action, but federal legislation passed in the 1930s (the Walsh–Healy Act of 1936) went largely unenforced. By 1967 a report by the United States Surgeon General indicated that two-thirds of the labor force in industrial plants faced exposure to harmful chemicals, but only one-fourth of them were given adequate protection.[35] In 1970, the year of OSHA's passage, there were nearly 14,000 deaths in the workplace and 2.2 million disabling injuries.[36] When workplace-induced diseases such as cancer from working in toxic environments were taken into consideration, as many as 100,000 persons may have died each year from occupational diseases.[37]

Despite these gruesome statistics on hazards in the workplace and the inability of the states to deal effectively with them, Congress was slow to pass legislation. Organized labor, focusing historically on wage and benefit issues, was also slow to press for action on occupational safety.

But several factors coalesced in the late 1960s to place occupational safety on the nation's policy-making agenda. First, some widely publicized coal-mining disasters helped focus attention on the issue. In 1968, for example, 73 miners died in a West Virginia coal mine explosion. A second factor leading to federal action was grass-roots action by workers who were angry about safety and health issues. Staging walk-outs, rejecting collective-bargaining contracts that failed to address safety issues, and precipitating wildcat strikes, workers literally pushed union leaders to pay attention to safety issues. Finally, in 1969, a new Republican President, Richard Nixon, was seeking to show concern for blue-collar workers in the hope of attracting them away from the Democrats, and the White House introduced the bill which eventually led to the creation of OSHA the following year.[38]

The OSHA legislation in 1970 created the Occupational Safety and Health Administration within the Department of Labor to implement the act's provisions. It also created a National Institute of Occupational Safety and Health (NIOSH) to conduct the research necessary for OSHA to produce effective safety and health regulations.

OSHA's Early Days

From the beginning, OSHA ran into trouble. Its enabling act of 1970 gave OSHA two main jobs, both of which brought it criticism. First, OSHA was made responsible for establishing federal standards on occupational safety and health. OSHA did not have to reinvent the wheel to do this, since a wide variety of safety and so-called consensus standards had already been set by other federal agencies and private organizations such as the National Fire Protection Association. Without any scientific review, within its first month OSHA simply adopted these existing consensus standards as mandatory national standards. Not having conducted a scientific review of the standards before adopting them, OSHA standards necessarily ended up including many outdated and sometimes trivial regulations. One original standard, for example, prohibited the use of ice in drinking water.[39] This standard probably made sense in the nineteenth century when it was common to cut ice from polluted lakes and waterways, but it clearly made no sense in the waning decades of the twentieth century. If OSHA had conducted a scientific review of the standards before issuing them, no doubt it would have deleted this one and many others. In the absence of such a review, however, many nonsensical rules were issued along with sensible ones, and OSHA quickly established a reputation for causing endless grief to businesses over trivial matters.

OSHA's second main job was to develop a staff of safety and health inspectors who would visit workplaces around the nation and issue citations when firms violated one of the standards. If a citation was upheld, the firm would be forced to pay a fine. Problems arose, however, because OSHA's original staff of inspectors was given minimal training and they quickly fell into the habit of following a tight enforcement policy on all violations, the trivial as well as the serious. This naturally drew the wrath of business people, but it also drew criticism from organized labor, which felt that over-attention to minor violations was keeping OSHA from coming to grips with serious problems of health and safety in the workplace. Organized labor was especially critical of OSHA's bias toward safety issues rather than health issues in the workplace. Most OSHA citations were for safety violations, and most of the standards OSHA set were safety rather than health standards.

Early Reform

By 1977, when President Jimmy Carter took office, public-opinion polls showed OSHA to be the most disliked of all federal agencies.[40] The Carter administration sought to reform OSHA's tarnished image by focusing more on health issues as distinguished from safety issues and by getting away from the agency's practice of concentrating on trivial violations. Carter supported an attempt to eliminate 1,100 of what were now called "nuisance standards" that had been issued at OSHA's inception. As OSHA sought to put these reforms into place, however, it found itself caught in a political battle between organized labor and the business community. Union leaders objected to eliminating existing standards and criticized the agency for moving too slowly

OSHA, of course, never forced anybody to install a roll bar on a hammock. But that did not stop the cartoonists from reinforcing OSHA's image as a maker of ridiculous rules.
Source: MacNelly © 1978. Reprinted by permission of Tribune Media Services.

in protecting workers' health. Business lobbyists, on the other hand, resisted the agency's efforts to enforce standards and typically viewed the agency as antibusiness.[41]

The Cotton Dust Controversy. These conflicts came to a head in 1977 over OSHA's attempts to set standards for cotton dust in textile plants. As we noted before, prolonged exposure to cotton dust leads to the debilitating and irreversible condition called brown-lung disease, which destroys people's capacity to breathe and forces them to spend their lives on oxygen support. OSHA first issued a very rigid standard, but relaxed it after pressure from President Carter's economic advisers, who were concerned about reaction from the business community. They pressured OSHA to relax the standard even further on the grounds that implementing it would put a huge financial burden on the textile plants that would have to install expensive equipment. The president's Secretary of Labor, on the other hand, was receiving pressure from organized labor, and he resisted these efforts to make any further changes in OSHA's new cotton-dust standard. In the last analysis, Carter supported OSHA, but he ended up alienating both business and labor who each filed suits in the federal courts hoping to overturn the president's decision. Business people were adamant that the standard needed further relaxation, while labor leaders were equally adamant that the relaxations already made had endangered workers' health and violated the law. The Supreme Court upheld OSHA's ruling.

Attacking OSHA Through the Courts and Congress. Appealing the issue to the federal courts, however, set a precedent. As OSHA's focus shifted from safety to health issues, the business organizations involved repeatedly filed lawsuits. Finally, in 1980 the Supreme Court ruled that before OSHA could issue a health standard it had to prove not only that a significant risk to worker health existed, but also that the proposed standard would eliminate or lessen that risk.[42] This was a significant defeat for OSHA, leading to considerable demoralization within the agency and encouraging the business community to continue to attack the agency in court. Not only did business attack the agency in court, but business lobbyists also succeeded in getting Congress to pass legislation that exempted small firms from OSHA inspections. A further bill that would have exempted up to 90 percent of the nation's workplaces from OSHA regulation failed to pass, however.

OSHA and the Reagan Administration

As we have seen, President Reagan launched a five-pronged attack on regulation. Most of the five prongs were illustrated by the administration's attempt to rein in OSHA. First, following the appointment prong, Reagan appointed an OSHA director, Thorne Auchter, who shared the business community's antipathy toward OSHA. Auchter had been a vice president of a Florida construction firm that had received 48 safety violations from OSHA, six of which were deemed serious.[43] Auchter determined to reverse OSHA's adversarial relationship with business and seek a more cooperative, voluntary relationship. To do so, he put into effect most of the OSHA recommendations that had been made by the U.S. Chamber of Commerce and the pro-business Heritage Foundation. These actions included the use of cost–benefit analysis to assess proposed OSHA standards, and the transfer of important OSHA powers to the states.[44]

Following the budget prong of his deregulation approach, Reagan also made substantial cuts in OSHA's budget which brought about a reduction in the number of OSHA inspectors from 1,700 to 1,200. Staff reductions necessarily brought about a reduction in the number of inspections and citations for serious violations.

Following the deregulatory prong of narrowly interpreting the rules, Auchter ordered his staff to limit the number of safety citations in areas where the citation might lead to a court challenge by the cited company. Even where employers were cited for violations of standards, OSHA greatly decreased the number of fines and penalties levied on the violators. Auchter explained, "Our job is health and safety. We're not interested in crime and punishment."[45] Finally, Auchter issued more than two dozen new health standards, most of which weakened existing health standards. One casualty of these new standards was the cotton-dust standard that OSHA had originally issued in 1977. Under the new rules, more than 340,000 workers were exempted from the cotton-dust standards, and even in covered industries plant owners would be allowed to delay installing the required equipment to control cotton dust.

Another problem that the Reagan administration posed for OSHA was changeovers in top leadership. Auchter's reign over OSHA lasted only three years, and his successor's lasted less than a year. Because of OSHA's poor reputation, President Reagan had difficulty finding a new director. By the time a permanent director was found, the agency had suffered a severe loss of staff and morale due to the lack of sympathetic leadership under Auchter and the lack of permanent leadership in the two years following him.

Occupational Safety and Health Regulation in Retrospect

This short history of OSHA illustrates some of the key problems inherent in the attempt to regulate occupational health and safety.

Some of these problems were self-induced from OSHA's mismanagement, but some resulted from political conditions beyond OSHA's control. First, from the contrast between Carter and Reagan, it is obvious that it makes a great deal of difference to occupational safety and health regulation whether the president is sympathetic or hostile to the goals of regulation.

Second, it is also obvious that no attempt to regulate occupational health and safety can be divorced from the overall political process. Throughout the history of OSHA the interest groups of organized labor have held a view of health and safety regulation that is diametrically opposed to that of the major interest-groups of organized business.

Third, there can be no doubt that health and safety regulation increases the cost of doing business in America. These costs are significantly increased in industrial areas that make extensive use of chemicals and toxic materials.

Fourth, there also can be no doubt that failure to regulate occupational health and safety imposes financial costs on American society. Whether they be insurance companies, federal medical programs, Social Security disability resources, or private individuals, some group pays a bill every time a worker dies or suffers a disabling injury on the job. Without regulation, employers successfully push the cost onto other sectors of society. By being able to avoid that cost themselves, they necessarily have less incentive to reduce workplace hazards.

Fifth, there does not seem to be any reliable and accurate assessment of just how effective OSHA standards and inspections have been in making the workplace a safer and healthier environment. Deaths in the workplace dropped from about 13,800 per year when OSHA was created in 1970 to about 10,400 in 1989, and disabling injuries over the same time period dropped from 2.2 million to 1.7 million,[46] but there is no way to know whether these reductions are *because* of OSHA's actions, are independent of OSHA's actions, or even despite OSHA's actions. Some scholarly studies have found that OSHA inspections had only a marginal impact on reducing workplace injuries, but other studies have concluded that OSHA standards and inspections have reduced the number of accidents by tens of thousands each year.[47]

An Alternative Approach to Regulation _____

There can be no doubt that OSHA or something like OSHA is absolutely necessary to keep an eye on occupational health and safety. But is OSHA's method of setting standards, conducting inspections, and penalizing violators the best way to enforce this regulation?

OSHA Standards

I have conducted no detailed evaluation studies of OSHA to determine whether it has successfully improved safety in the workplace. But one anecdote from my own life leads me to suspect that it has. As a college student in the pre-OSHA days, I once earned my living operating a punch press in a small, low technology, non-unionized factory in a dingy Chicago neighborhood. My job was to sit on a wooden barrel, slide a long metal bar to a stopping point, and then step on a pedal which then sent a steel spike plunging through the metal bar as cleanly and easily as a spindle going through a sheet of paper. After a few hours of this repetitive task job on a sultry summer day, one became slightly drowsy, and I lived in fear that at some sleepy moment my hand was going to slip under that metal spike just before it punched through the steel.

Fortunately that never happened—to me. But it, or worse things, no doubt happened to others.

Today, OSHA standards would never permit such an unsafe punch press to be in use. Today the operator's hands must grasp handles on the machine before the punch press will work, thus preventing the hands from being injured.

Although experience has shown that government regulation is needed to protect the environment, public health, safety, and other public interests, the controversy over our present regulatory practices suggests that the system has some inherent problems that ought to be rectified. Charles Schultze, chair of the Council of Economic Advisers under President Carter, made some novel and valuable suggestions for solving these problems. Schultze describes our current regulatory system as one of command and control.[48] Under this command-and-control system, the EPA, OSHA, and other agencies issue regulations and then command industries to obey them. Implementation requires inspectors to investigate complaints. Neither the EPA nor OSHA has enough inspectors to investigate the implementation of all the rules. Consequently, inspection is spotty. This is a common business complaint. Knowing that implementation is spotty, a company that complies with the rules might make a big expenditure to implement them and then never be inspected. The company could easily have saved that expenditure by ignoring the rule.

In Schultze's view, the system of command and control has not worked well. Instead, he believes we should develop an incentive regulatory system. In the area of occupational safety and health, for example, instead of ordering companies to install specific pieces of safety equipment, OSHA should simply monitor accidents, injuries, and deaths at the plant and issue heavy fines when accidents, injuries, and deaths exceed certain limits. To keep down the level of its fines, a company would most likely take whatever safety measures were necessary voluntarily. Any fines collected could be used to conduct research on occupational safety and health. Advocates believe that a similar incentive system could be applied to many areas currently subject to command-and-control regulation, including affirmative action, environmental protection, and others.

An incentive-based regulatory system would preserve the positive features of the free-market economy while giving companies strong financial incentives to meet regulatory goals. It would also relieve the regulators of the impossible burden of getting all the necessary information to issue the very specific regulations needed to apply to thousands of unique situations. However, incentive-based regulation would not apply to all situations. For example, it is not clear how the threat of fines levied today will prevent health problems such as brown lung, which do not show up until many years after exposure to the dangerous substances. In situations such as this, there will still be a need for command-and-control regulations.

Summary: Bias in the Regulatory Process _____

This chapter has not sought to outline the complex pattern of biases underlying the entire federal executive branch. Instead it has focused on the federal government's regulatory role and the effects of the deregulation movement of the 1980s. From this review, four biases seem to predominate in the regulatory role of the federal government.

1. It makes a great deal of difference who inhabits the White House. The change from Carter to Reagan saw a change from a White House that was receptive to regulatory reform to a White House devoted to eliminating as much regulation as possible. The change from Reagan to Bush saw a White House that was more conciliatory toward regulation. Indeed, one of Bush's first acts as president was to signal his willingness to go along with a rewriting of the Clean Air Act that had been held up by White House intransigence for eight years.

2. Regulation does not cut evenly across all industries. Some companies benefit from regulation. We saw that the EPA's ban on the use of fluorocarbons in antiperspirant sprays reduced the production costs for antiperspirant manufacturers. Environmental protection laws also opened up opportunities for new business enterprises, such as waste-management firms, for example. Finally, the elimination of existing regulations would not benefit all industries. Those industries, for example, that had already gone to the expense of installing costly pollution-control equipment would see an edge given to new competitors if this equipment were no longer required.

3. In OSHA, the costs of deregulation fell heavily on the lower-status population.

4. The lower-status population suffered from deregulation of occupational safety and health in no small measure because of the political weakness of organized labor and the Democratic Party. As organized labor lost power in the 1980s, its ability to influence OSHA decreased.

Notes

1. For an historical review of presidents' use of their cabinets, see R. Gordon Hoxie, "The Cabinet in the American Presidency: 1789–1984," *Presidential Studies Quarterly* 14, no. 2 (Spring 1984): 209–230.

2. On this division of policy types, see Theodore J. Lowi, "American Business, Public Policy, Case Studies, and Political Theory," *World Politics* 16 (July 1964): 667–715.

3. Edward Paul Fuchs, *President, Management, and Regulation* (Englewood Cliffs, N.J.: Prentice-Hall, 1988), p. 13.

4. Randall B. Ripley and Grace A. Franklin, *Bureaucracy and Policy Implementation* (Homewood, Ill.: Dorsey, 1982), p. 34.

5. See Murray Edelman, *The Symbolic Uses of Politics* (Urbana: University of Illinois Press, 1964).

6. Marver Bernstein, *Regulating Business by Independent Regulatory Commissions* (Princeton, N.J.: Princeton University Press, 1955).

7. Michael D. Reagan, "The Politics of Regulatory Reform," *Western Political Quarterly* 36, no. 1 (March 1983): 164.

8. Kenneth J. Meier and John Plumlee studied employment patterns of high-ranking staff workers in eight regulatory agencies. But they found relatively few cases where workers resigned to take positions in their related industries. "Regulatory Administration and Organizational Rigidity," *Western Political Quarterly* 31, no. 1 (March 1978): 80–93.

9. Ibid.

10. Ross D. Eckert found that 20 percent of the commissioners on three regulatory commissions found jobs in their industries immediately after leaving their commissions. "The Life Cycle of Regulatory Commissions," *Journal of Law and Economics* 24 (1981): 113–130. A study of FCC records found that FCC commissioners were significantly more likely to vote for radio and television broadcasters during their last year in office than they were during their earlier years. It was as though they hoped to improve their job prospects with their broadcasters by becoming favorable to them. See Jeffrey E. Cohen, "The Dynamics of the Revolving Door on the FCC," (a paper presented at the 1984 Convention of the American Political Science Association, Washington, D.C., August 30–September 2, 1984).

11. See Ripley and Franklin, *Bureaucracy and Policy Implementation,* p. 34.

12. Richard A. Harris and Sidney M. Milkins, *The Politics of Regulatory Change: A Tale of Two Agencies* (New York: Oxford University Press, 1989), p. 63.

13. Ibid.

14. Ibid., p. 70.

15. Ibid., pp. 80–84.

16. Ibid.

17. See *New York Times,* March 10, 1982, p. 1; March 16, 1983, p. 1.

18. Robert A. Leone, *Who Profits: Winners, Losers, and Government Regulation* (New York: Basic books, 1986), pp. 34–36.

19. *Regulatory Problems and Regulatory Reform: The Perceptions of Business* (New York: The Conference Board, 1980), pp. 6–11.

20. Fuchs, *Presidents, Management, and Regulation,* p. 87.

21. Ibid., p. 85.

22. One estimate put the reduction at 8 percent of budget and 10 percent of regulatory personnel during Reagan's first term. See Ann Cooper, "Regulations: Taming the Base," *National Journal* 16, no. 48 (December 1, 1984): 2284.

23. United States Bureau of the Census, *Statistical Abstract of the United States: 1989* (Washington, D.C.: Bureau of the Census, 1989), p. 321.

24. Roger Thompson, "Regulatory Reform," *Editorial Research Reports* (May 11, 1984): 354.

25. Fuchs, *Presidents, Management, and Regulation,* p. 95.

26. *New York Times,* October 29, 1984, p. 14.

27. *Wall Street Journal,* June 10, 1981, p. 3.

28. See Larry N. Gerston, Cynthia Fraleigh, and Robert Schwab, *The Deregulated Society* (Pacific Grove, Calif.: Brooks/Cole, 1988). In a balanced account of airline deregulation, these authors conclude, "Airline deregulation can be considered to be a success for now." p. 111.

29. Ibid., pp. 100–108.

30. See Hobart Rowen, "Deregulation Revisited," *The Washington Post National Weekly Edition,* October 24–30, 1988, p. 5. In ten major cities, a single airline enjoyed two-thirds of the traffic, while in several others, three-fourths of the traffic was divided between only two airlines.

31. For background on the deregulation of S&Ls and other financial institutions, see Gerston, Fraleigh, and Schwab, *The Deregulated Society,* chap. 6.

32. *New York Times,* June 6, 1990, p. 1. Also see "Bonfire of the S&Ls," *Newsweek,* May 21, 1990, pp. 20–32.

33. For background, see Charles R. Babcock, "In the Matter of Lincoln Savings and Loan," *The Washington Post National Weekly Edition,* November 27–December 3, 1989, p. 10.

34. For an excellent background of deregulating the financial services industry, see Gerston, Fraleigh, and Schwab, *The Deregulated Society,* chap. 6.

35. Paul M. Bangser, "An Inherent Role for Cost–Benefit Analysis in Judicial Review of Agency Decisions: A New Perspective on OSHA Rulemaking," *Boston College Environmental Affairs Law Review,* 10 (1982): 370–371. See Gerston, Fraleigh, and Schwab, *The Deregulated Society,* p. 173.

36. *Statistical Abstract of the United States: 1990,* p. 416.

37. Bangser, "An Inherent Role for Cost–Benefit Analysis in Judicial Review of Agency Decisions: A New Perspective on OSHA Rulemaking," p. 46. See Gerston, Fraleigh, and Schwab, *The Deregulated Society,* p. 173.

38. It was Ralph Nader who speculated that the White House's bill on occupational safety was motivated by political hopes of attracting blue-collar votes from the Democrats. Gerston et al., p. 174.

39. Gerston, Fraleigh, and Schwab, *The Deregulated Society,* p. 177.

40. "OSHA Befriends Industry, but Draws Fire," *Washington Post,* July 5, 1983, p. A12.

41. "OSHA: Hardest to Live With," *Business Week,* April 4, 1977, p. 79.

42. *Industrial Union Department* v. *American Petroleum Institute* 448 U.S. 607 (1980).

43. Joan Claybrook, *Retreat From Safety* (New York: Pantheon, 1984), pp. 72–73.

44. Gerston, Fraleigh, and Schwab, *The Deregulated Society,* p. 184.

45. Quoted in Claybrook, *Retreat From Safety,* p. 99.

46. United States Bureau of the Census, *Statistical Abstract of the United States: 1991* (Washington, D.C.: Bureau of the Census, 1990), p. 422.

47. Gerston, Fraleigh, and Schwab, *The Deregulated Society,*

48. See Charles L. Schultze, *Public Use of the Private Interest* (Washington, D.C.: Brookings Institution, 1977).

CHAPTER 10

Money Justice: Lower-Strata People and the Courts

Introduction

Courts, as well as other political institutions, are important to the lives of lower-status people. One illustration of that importance took place in 1983 when the Reagan administration stiffened the eligibility rules for Social Security Disability Insurance and notified more than 490,000 people with incapacities of some sort that they could no longer receive their disability benefits.[1] When some of these affected people sued in the federal courts to have their benefits reinstated, the Social Security Administration declared a policy of "nonacquiescence" by which it meant that it would apply district court rulings only to the specific case of the specific individual and not to other individuals similarly afflicted. For example, pretend that your father and my father both were denied the disability payments they had received for many years because of a disabling disease caused by working in a toxic environment. If my father sued and successfully had his benefits reinstated, your father's benefits would not automatically be reinstated even though he shared the exact same situation. He would have to file a successful suit himself. The only rulings that the administration would consider as a precedent binding on all similar situations were those made by the Supreme Court, not a lower-level district court. However, the administration did not appeal any district decisions to the Supreme Court, and because of this, there was no way for the Supreme Court to rule on the issue.

This decision provoked hot protest. The administration was criticized not only for cutting the benefits of the low-income Social Security recipients but for attacking the integrity of the federal judiciary itself.[2] Congress reacted with the Social Security Disability Benefits Reform Act of 1984 that required the Social Security Administration either to apply adverse district court rulings to all similar cases or to appeal the court ruling to the Supreme Court. In response, the administration modified its policy somewhat but refused to drop the nonacquiesence policy entirely. Several interest groups converged on Congress to complain about the administration,[3] and in 1985 a federal judge in New York ordered the administration to drop its policy of nonacquiescence.[4]

The administration then discussed a plan to remove these cases from the federal district court system by seeking a law that would create a new Social Security Court. Once again, a collection of liberal-interest groups protested the administration's plans, and the idea was killed.[5] In the last analysis, the administration was forced to give in, and 200,000 of the people denied benefits eventually had their eligibility restored.

This anecdote raises some important questions about the role of the federal courts and the lower-status population. How did the judicial process get to be as politicized as this illustration shows? Is contemporary politicization of the judicial process a good idea? And do lower-status people usually fare as well in the judicial process as they did in this instance? To answer those questions we need to explore several facets of the judicial system and its interface with the lower-status population. We will do that in this chapter by examining: (1) the experience of lower-status people in criminal court, (2) the experience of the lower-strata in civil court, (3) the politicization of the federal courts in the 1970s and 1980s, and (4) implications for the lower strata of the growing conservatism of the federal courts in the 1990s.

Money in the Criminal Justice System _____

A criminal case is one in which a person is prosecuted on charges of having broken a criminal law. One usually enters the criminal justice system when picked up by law-enforcement officers on charges of having violated some law. Once brought into the system, one cannot leave until those charges are dropped or resolved through the judicial process. In some instances the charges are resolved immediately if the police decide that they picked up the wrong person and then release that person. In some instances, one leaves the system when the prosecuting attorney decides the case does not merit prosecution. In some instances, one is brought to trial and leaves the system when acquitted. And in some instances, one is brought to trial, is found guilty, and leaves the the criminal justice system to enter the corrections system that carries out the judge's sentence.

At each of these steps along the way through the criminal justice system, you need money to defend yourself. Either your own money, which is better, or the state's money in the form of a state-appointed attorney, which is worse. The less of your own money you have to devote to defending yourself, the less control you have over your fate. Money affects your fate in several ways, starting with law-enforcement patterns, then the setting of bail, the hiring of a lawyer, the composition of juries, and the patterns of sentences. In each of these areas, socioeconomic status makes a sharp difference.[6]

Law-Enforcement Patterns and the Lower Strata

A key hallmark of law enforcement which works against lower-strata people is the high level of discretion the police officer has.[7] When confronting situations such as a domestic dispute, for example, police officers have discretion to choose from a wide range of responses. They can calm down the couple and leave. They can take one side of the dispute. They can issue a warning to the couple and leave. They can arrest one or both members of the couple. If obliged to restrain a suspect physically, they can use the minimal amount of force needed, or they may lose control and beat the person badly, as occurred in a celebrated, videotaped Los Angeles incident in 1991. The lower one is on the social strata, the more likely one is to be treated harshly during a police investigation. A 1981 study concluded that police systematically arrested lower-status people more often than they did upper-status people in the same situations.[8] This is a long-standing finding. As far back as 1945 a study of juvenile justice in Philadelphia found that in similar kinds of situations, poor teenagers were much more likely than middle-class teenagers to be arrested and turned over to the juvenile justice system.[9] This was true even after adjusting for the severity of the offense and the prior records of the suspects.

Not only do police officers arrest lower-status people more frequently, they also are more suspicious of them than they are of upper-status people. James Q. Wilson observed that police surveillance patterns focus more intently on lower-income people, and especially on racial minorities. "Because the urban lower class is today disproportionately black (just as it was once disproportionately Irish), a dark skin is to the police a statistically significant cue to social status, and thus to potential criminality."[10]

At each of these steps along the way through the criminal justice system, you need money to defend yourself. . . . The less of your own money you have to devote to defending yourself the less control you have over your fate.

Bail and Pretrial Detention

Shortly after being arrested, the accused person is brought before a magistrate who determines whether the person can be released from detention before the trial. To ensure that the defendant shows up for the trial, the magistrate will often set a bail of several hundred or, in the case of serious crimes, several thousand dollars. Lower-strata people are less able to produce bail money than are upper-strata people, and poor people are least able to provide it. A study in Baltimore found that 38 percent of the felony defendants were not released from jail before their trial, and another 48 percent spent at least a week in jail before being released. Considering that 56 percent of the felony defendants ended up either being acquitted or having their cases dropped, this means that a substantial number of people ended up spending time incarcerated for a crime that they were not found guilty of committing.[11] They spent that time locked up for no reason other than that they lacked the bail money. This situation in Baltimore is probably common throughout the country. A 1986 study found that 53 percent of all the people in jail at the time of the study had not been convicted of any crime. In most cases, they simply could not afford to pay for bail.[12]

Being detained while awaiting trial is very costly in many ways.[13] You cannot go to work while you are sitting in jail, and your absence from work may well cost you your job. While in jail it is harder to find witnesses to aid in your defense or to make contact with your attorney and inform him or her about items that will aid in your defense. These are important matters, and studies indicate that failure to get out of jail on bail is strongly associated with higher conviction rates and more frequent prison sentences.[14] Perhaps the greatest cost is the psychological toll of sitting helplessly in jail awaiting the trial which may or may not convict you. During this time you are subject to all the degrading conditions of jail life in American cities—overcrowding, lack of privacy, verbal abuse, potential physical violence, possible strip searches, and body cavity searches. When you must make a court appearance while on pretrial detention, chances are you will be wearing scruffy jail clothing and may well be handcuffed. The person who made bail will, if he or she is well coached, make the court appearance wearing middle-class dress and looking neat.

So unfair are the consequences of the bail system to lower-status people that many efforts have been made to reform it. New York State had considerable success with a program for interviewing and keeping contact with defendants to ensure their court appearance.[15]

State-Provided Lawyers

The lower strata also have a distinct disadvantage in not being able to afford the best defense attorneys available. If you cannot afford to hire an attorney, states are required to provide one for you. About 37 percent of local courts use a public-defender system for doing this. Public-defender systems are government agencies that maintain a permanent staff of lawyers to defend indigent persons. About 52 percent of local courts use a system of assigned counsels for this purpose. Instead of having a permanent staff of attorneys to handle cases for the indigent, they assign the cases out to private lawyers on a case-by-case basis. Finally, about 11 percent of local courts use a system under which a law firm contracts with the court to handle its poor defendants for an entire year.[16]

Whichever method is used, the quality of state-provided representation seldom equals the representation that you would obtain if you could afford to hire your own criminal lawyer. If you hired a private lawyer you would have a better possibility of hiring one who specializes in your type of case. The private lawyer would probably make more money from the case than the public lawyer would, and presumably would be motivated to do a better job because of this. Moreover, lawyers working in the public-defender or contract lawyer system often are so overloaded with cases that they find it impossible to devote much time or effort to any specific case. So poorly regarded is the public-defender system, in fact, that one law journal article on the topic was entitled: "Did You Have a Lawyer When You Went to Court? No, I had a Public Defender."[17] Defendants assigned lawyers and contract lawyers may avoid some of the pitfalls of getting public defenders, but these two methods have pitfalls of their own. Fees for reimbursing these lawyers are sometimes set by judges, and this might motivate these lawyers not to pursue their defenses more vigorously than the judge wanted them to. Also, because assigned lawyers are paid on a per-case basis rather than an hourly basis, they have a great incentive to speed up the cases as much as possible. This may lead them to urge their clients to make guilty pleas or to accept plea-bargains that are not in the clients' interest.

Other Issues

The lower strata are also at a disadvantage in court because of some other factors. Juries drawn from voter lists represent a cross-section of the middle-class population, but they necessarily underrepresent racial minorities, transient people, and poor people. This may lead to juries that are less sympathetic to poor or near-poor defendants. In addition, lower-strata people are also much more likely than upper-strata people to receive harsh sentences.[18] This is especially true of the poor. Even where a judge is sympathetic to lower-status people, these people are still put at a disadvantage before that judge if they suffered pretrial detention and did not have good legal representation.

Money in the Civil Law System _____

In contrast to criminal cases, which involve violations of laws, civil cases involve disputes between people or organizations. If you and your landlord have a dispute about the terms of your rental agreement, the civil courts offer you a place where this dispute can be resolved peaceably. For the average lower-status person, however, the civil judicial system has some key drawbacks as a place to resolve personal disputes.

Cost of Civil Litigation

Perhaps the biggest drawback for lower-status people are the costs of litigation. These are high. Lawyers' fees are expensive and are charged on an hourly basis. Also, litigants must pay filing fees as well as other court fees such as those for obtaining copies of critical court documents. In a personal injury case, it could easily cost $1,000 to get a doctor to testify as an expert witness. Because of these costs, the wealthier party in a dispute can afford to delay and prolong the dispute and so force its less-affluent adversaries to settle at an early stage for a smaller settlement than they might otherwise receive. This is especially the case for a low-income litigant who needs money now and cannot afford to wait three or four years in the hope of receiving double or triple the amount.

Some of the costs of litigation are eased if the attorney takes the case on a contingency-fee basis. In such a case the lawyer bears all the costs of the case but typically receives 30 percent of the settlement. Add another 35 percent for state and federal income taxes (the settlement will boost the litigant into a higher income-tax bracket), and a $50,000 settlement is reduced to $17,500 by the time it reaches the individual's bank account.

An additional cost of litigation is the risk of not winning the suit. This chance is very high when the individual is sued by a business

For the average lower-status person, however, the civil judicial system has some key drawbacks as a place to resolve personal disputes.

corporation or a government agency. These institutions frequently go to court for one reason or another. And the frequent user of the courts has a much higher success rate than the individual one-shot user.

> [Frequent users have] a number of advantages in the litigation process. Briefly, these advantages include: ability to structure the transaction; expertise, economies of scale, low start-up costs; informal relations with institutional incumbents, bargaining credibility; ability to adopt optimal strategies; ability to play for rules in both political forums and in litigation itself by litigation strategy and settlement policy; and ability to invest to secure penetration of favorable rules.[19]

Alternatives to Litigation

Small Claims Courts. One alternative to a full blown law suit is the small claims court which hears cases that involve sums of up to a few thousand dollars. Litigants can present their own cases before the judge without the expense of hiring a lawyer to represent them, and the filing fees are minimal. Ideally created as a device for individuals to press claims against each other or businesses, the small claims court has largely resulted in the opposite. It is a cheap way for a business to collect debt claims from lower-status individuals. One critic wrote:

> Far from providing a forum for the poor (that is individual, blue- or perhaps white-collar) litigant to afford him his day in court simply and inexpensively, these tribunals have largely become collection agencies for the 'haves' of our society against the 'have nots.'[20]

Even when the individual does succeed in getting a small claims court judgment, the judgment is not automatically carried out. If you win a $500 judgment against your landlord but the landlord refuses to pay, you will have to go back to a regular court to enforce the judgment of the small claims court. Naturally, lower-status people are less likely to have the resources or inclination to pursue the case further.

Arbitration and Mediation. Many personal disputes can be resolved by hiring a neutral mediator who can discuss the dispute with both parties and facilitate a compromise resolution. Most divorce courts provide social workers who are available to mediate disputes over custody, visitation, and other divorce-related issues. Arbitration also involves a neutral third party to hear both sides of the dispute. But while the mediator's job is to facilitate a compromise between the two parties, the arbitrator is given authority to impose a binding settlement on them.

Pro Bono Work. Another avenue of mitigating the costs of litigation for the lower strata is for lawyers to accept more pro bono work; that is, handling cases for which they give up their fee. The American Bar Association has an ethical rule requiring lawyers to accept pro bono cases in the public interest. But research suggests that few lawyers comply with the rule to any great extent. One study found that nearly half of all lawyers spent *no* time at all on pro bono work. Forty percent spent more than 5 percent of their time on pro bono work, but further investigation showed that many of them counted as pro bono work cases in which they had charged the client but the client had simply refused to pay.[21]

Legal Services Corporation. The Legal Services Corporation is a government corporation that provides legal services in civil cases for people who are too poor to hire their own lawyers. Under this program, federally paid lawyers handle legal problems such as divorce filings, disputes with landlords, and consumer complaints of individuals against government bureaucracies. In 1974 Congress forbade its lawyers from engaging in political activities or giving legal advice on controversial political issues such as abortion, the draft, military desertion, school desegregation, and homosexual rights. The Reagan and Bush administrations sought to abolish the corporation and eliminate its funding, but considerable support for it in Congress has kept it alive. Nevertheless, it is funded at a minimal level and does not even come close to meeting the legal needs of poor people.

Politicizing the Courts

Politicization of the courts is not a new phenomenon in American history. As early as 1835 Alexis de Tocqueville wrote, "There is hardly a political question in the United States which does not sooner or later turn into a judicial one."[22] The most important way in which the political issues enter the judicial arena is through the Supreme Court's power of judicial review, the power to decide whether the acts of other government bodies are consistent with the Constitution or with existing law. The Supreme Court's exercise of this great power has generally been to support the prevailing political values of the times. One study of Supreme Court decisions and public opinion from 1937 through 1986 found that Supreme Court decisions were consistent with previously published public-opinion polls 62 percent of the time.[23] But it was when the Court challenged these prevailing opinions that some of the most explosive conflicts erupted between the federal courts and other bodies of government. And when the court strayed too far from the mainstream political values, as it did in the 1930s by trying to undermine President Roosevelt's New Deal program, political forces in Congress, the White House, and the nation at large eventually nudged the court back to a more mainstream position.

Finally, whether by election or appointment, it is through politics that people become judges in the first place.[24] Once judges are on the bench, their decisions are affected by their social and political values. In workers' compensation cases, for example, Catholic or Democratic judges were found to be much more likely than Protestant or Republican judges to make decisions favoring workers over employers.[25] In criminal cases, black judges were found to send defendants to prison much more frequently than white judges. They also sent black and white defendants to prison in equal proportions, in contrast to white judges who tended to imprison a higher proportion of black defendants than white defendants.[26] Judges in Pittsburgh (who disproportionately came from working-class backgrounds and lived in working-class neighborhoods) gave less harsh sentences than did judges in Minneapolis (who disproportionately came from affluent, elite backgrounds).[27]

These findings do not mean that judges are arbitrary or that courts are so politicized as to make justice impossible. But they do mean that when judges have to grapple with fundamental issues of their times, their treatment of those issues is influenced by the value system they have acquired over a lifetime, in part as a result of their religious, political, and racial backgrounds.

A Quantum Change in the 1970s

Notwithstanding this historical intertwining of courts and politics, two developments in the 1960s and 1970s led to a quantum leap in the politicization of the courts. First, the role of the Supreme Court in public-policy formation has been strengthened during periods of divided government and periods of divided public opinion accompanied by paralyzed government. Divided government occurred during most of the 1970s and 1980s when the Democrats controlled Congress and the Republicans the White House. Because of this division, the courts often provided avenues of influence for liberal groups that could sometimes get legislation through a Democratic Congress only to have its

---

As early as 1835 Alexis de Tocqueville wrote, "There is hardly a political question in the United States which does not sooner or later turn into a judicial one."

implementation bogged down by an unreceptive Republican White House. The Supreme Court also saw its hand strengthened during periods of governmental paralysis on critical issues over which public opinion was divided. This could be seen in the civil-rights struggle of the 1950s and early 1960s. During these years Congress and the president were essentially paralyzed on the task of ending racial segregation. The Court moved into this leadership vacuum by striking down state segregation laws for education, lunch rooms, buses, trains, libraries, and other public facilities.

The second development that hastened the politicization of federal courts was action by the Supreme Court in broadening "access" to the federal courts. This essentially was the issue in the Social Security Disability Insurance noted struggle earlier. Interest groups for disability insurance recipients wanted to have access to the federal courts to seek judicial decisions that would overturn policies of the Reagan administration. The administration in turn wanted to limit Court access so that the disabled would not be able to fight back effectively.

How did the Supreme Court broaden access in the 1960s and 1970s? First, in 1966 the Court made it much easier to file class-action lawsuits.[28] These are suits that affect an entire class of people. If you and 999 other people purchased a defective product, all one thousand of you normally would have to file individual lawsuits to recover your losses from the seller. A class-action lawsuit, however, would permit a group of you to file suit in the name of the entire class of people who purchased the defective product, and if you won your suit, the seller would be obliged to make recompense to everybody who bought the product.

The second thing the courts did in the 1960s and 1970s was to expand the judicial remedies available to groups filing civil lawsuits against corporations or government agencies.[29] Judges showed an increased willingness to issue injunctions that forced corporations or government agencies to stop doing something. Courts also issued judicial orders forcing corporations and government agencies to undertake some action. Another tool was the appointment of what are called "special masters" to investigate situations and report remedies back to the judges. Judges then sometimes used the results of these investigations to justify taking over the administration of certain public bodies. Federal courts made use of special masters, for example, in taking over the operations of the South Boston public high school in the 1970s to impose racial desegregation. Other federal courts issued orders forcing states to relieve the overcrowding of prisons and to improve facilities in state mental hospitals.

Even when judges were reluctant to intrude themselves into these sticky political affairs, they often felt they had no other choice. In the spring of 1981, for example, the Boston public schools were threatened with having to shorten the school year by two months because they had run out of money. In addition to the Boston School Committee, several different political actors were responsible for funding the city's schools. These included the governor, the state legislature, the Boston mayor and the city council. But when confronted with a possible early closing (that would violate a state law requiring a 180-day school year) none of these actors took any action to remedy the situation. The Boston City Council would not even meet with the mayor on the subject. So parents groups asked a Massachusetts court to force the schools to stay open as the law required. The court ordered the schools to stay open, appointed a special master to investigate the school finances, and personally forced the city council, the mayor, the school committee, and legislative leaders to negotiate with him and each other until they finally worked out a financial solution.[30]

Most judicial scholars have mixed feelings about judicial activity of this sort. Normally, most judges do not want to take on the headaches of trying to resolve issues in areas such as these where they have neither expertise nor an electoral mandate. But consider the dilemma of the judge in this case. If he intervened, he was bound to be criticized for unwarranted judicial activism. But if he failed to intervene, he would be joining other political leaders who were abdicating their responsibility to carry out the law's requirement that the schools remain open for 180 days. Regarding instances such as this one, Harvard law professor Lloyd L. Weinreb argued that judges did not seek deliberately to expand their power. Rather, the responsibility for intervention was thrust on them by the inaction of other political actors.

> Far from usurping authority, the courts have on the whole exercised their authority reluctantly. Our political leaders have often been only too glad to leave to the courts responsibility for unpopular measures favoring the weak, powerless, and disfavored of our society. Sometimes, legislatures have made the shift of responsibility explicit, by enacting very general measures that the courts must interpret and, in effect, administer.[31]

Judicial Politicization and the Lower Strata

In the early stages of this new politicization, the primary beneficiaries of the opened access to the courts were liberal groups with public-policy agendas dealing with civil rights, the environment, consumer protection, and feminist causes. When it became impossible to get favorable action from Congress, a state legislature, or a local government or school board on an issue such as desegregation, sexual equality in sports, stopping a proposed freeway, ceasing the dumping of carcinogous agents into a major water body, requiring the inclusion of public housing in a city's housing plan, or increasing state spending for mental hospitals, the broadened access to the courts sometimes made it possible to get a federal or state judge to issue an injunction, appoint a special master, or make a judicial order achieving the same goal. The Boston school-year case was an instance of this.

As they saw that a broadened judicial access increased their own influence on public policy, liberal political groups in the 1970s increasingly became judicial activists.[32] What broadened judicial access meant for the lower strata generally, however, is not clear. In one respect, the lower strata were significant beneficiaries. Since it is primarily lower-strata people who attend the Boston public schools, it is primarily the lower strata that benefited from the judicial intervention to keep those schools open. Since Social Security disability recipients are primarily lower-status people, again it is primarily the lower strata that benefited from access to the courts to appeal their cases.

But there is a respect in which the lower strata generally have not benefited from the politicization of the courts in the 1970s and 1980s. Courts intervene at the behest of some interest groups or citizens groups that take the initiative to file suit. These usually are groups with specific functional purposes. For example, the American Foundation for the Blind and the National Senior Citizens Law Center were groups opposing the Reagan administration disability insurance cuts. These organizations are run by upper-middle-class professionals, and, on other issues affecting the lower strata but not affecting the blind or senior citizens, these two organizations would have no reason to seek judicial intervention. Greater court access benefits only those segments of the lower strata that have interest groups capable of pursuing judicial remedies. But the fundamental problem facing the lower strata is that it lacks interest groups capable of doing for it as a class of people what the American Foundation for the Blind does for the blind or what the National Senior Citizens Law Center can do for senior citizens.

This problem is especially acute for the poorest levels of the lower strata. One critic wrote

> This link between judicial decisions and political mobilization has produced few benefits for the poor . . . there have been few judicial decisions basing symbolic declarations upon recognition that poor people constitute an identifiable, unfairly disadvantaged group. By contrast, there have been many decisions concerning racial and gender discrimination which have helped to mobilize political action and social change. Even if the courts issued rulings supporting rights for the poor, poor people would have less ability to capitalize upon these symbolic declarations in order to achieve political gains.[33]

In sum, politicization of the courts in the 1970s and 1980s was a mixed blessing for the lower-status population. Certain members of the lower strata benefited when feminist groups, civil-rights groups, environmental groups, and others used the courts to further their own public-policy agendas. But the lack of interest groups that could represent the lower strata directly meant that the general concerns of many members of the lower strata still went unrepresented before the courts. Furthermore, as we will see at the end of this chapter, although contemporary court politicization was pioneered by liberal groups sympathetic to the lower strata, the same tactics would eventually be taken up by conservative groups who were less sympathetic.

Reemergent Judicial Conservatism 1987–? _____

Whatever gains the judicial politicization brought to the lower strata in the 1970s, most of those gains were put in doubt by the 1990s. Part of this doubt was due to increasing success that conservative interest-groups were having in using the legal process for conservative purposes much as liberal groups were using it for liberal purposes.[34] Many of these conservative efforts were not as dangerous to lower-status economic interests as might be assumed, however, because most of the conservative effort addressed social issues rather than economic issues. There were, for example, several lawsuits over the direction of public school curricula.

More important than the increased litigation of conservative groups was the success that the Reagan and Bush administrations had in reshaping the face of the federal judiciary. By the end of 1990, there were 825 judges on the federal courts. Fifty-four percent of them had been appointed by Reagan and Bush, and those two presidents consistently appointed conservative jurists to the bench,[35] including five of the nine Supreme Court justices.

The symbolic event marking the judiciary's reemergent conservatism was the promotion of William Rehnquist from Associate Justice to Chief Justice of the United States Supreme Court in 1987. An avowed advocate of judicial conservatism, Rehnquist was a forceful spokesman for the death penalty, for letting the states decide on the legality of abortion, and for closing much of the access to federal courts that had been opened up during the 1970s.

Whatever gains the judicial politicization brought to the lower strata in the 1970s, most of those gains were put in doubt by the 1990s.

It is the issue of access to federal courts that is most important to the economic concerns of lower-status people. Without access to the courts, the disabled people described at the beginning of this chapter would have been unable to wage a successful fight against the Reagan administration's cutbacks on Social Security Disability Insurance benefits.

Court Access and Affirmative Action

Probably the most pronounced area of Rehnquist-Court conservatism has come in the field of affirmative action. Prior to the Rehnquist Court, the Supreme Court was inconsistent on issues of affirmative action. At times it supported efforts to increase minority presence in the workplace and in professional schools, while at other times it rejected those efforts.

Court Inconsistency on Affirmative Action. This pre-Rehnquist-Court inconsistency could be seen in a number of cases from the late 1970s through the 1980s. The most famous was the University of California–Davis Medical School case in 1978. Alan Bakke charged the university with reverse discrimination because it had denied him admission to the medical school in order to make room for minorities and women who had lower entrance qualifications. The Court came up with a compromise solution that solved Bakke's problem but did not give much satisfaction to either the opponents or proponents of affirmative action. It ordered the university to admit Bakke but also permitted the use of separate entrance requirements for minority and female applicants as long as those requirements did not impose a rigid quota system.[36]

This pattern of compromise solutions was also seen in the Boston fire fighters case in 1983. Faced with budget cutbacks, the City of Boston, in a deliberate commitment to its affirmative action policy, laid off a number of white fire fighters who had more job seniority than blacks who were kept on. This contradicted the city's collective bargaining contract with the fire fighter's union which provided that seniority would be followed when layoffs were imposed. The laid off white workers sued, claiming that this affirmative-action policy violated their seniority rights under both their collective bargaining agreement and the city's civil service ordinance. The legality of the issues was muddled by the time the case reached the Supreme Court, however, because in the meantime Massachusetts passed a law rehiring the laid-off workers and imposing the seniority rule on all future layoffs. Nevertheless, there was a sharp legal conflict between the NAACP, which wanted the Supreme Court to give an unambiguous endorsement of the affirmative-action principle, and the union (supported by the Reagan administration), which wanted the Court to uphold the seniority principle. The Court satisfied neither side, however, when it dismissed the case as moot, since the fired workers had been re-hired.[37]

Although these cases fell short of a ringing endorsement of affirmative action, there were other cases in which the Court did come out squarely for affirmative-action principles. In 1986 it upheld a Cleveland plan that gave black and Hispanic fire fighters promotion preference over whites. And this was followed up in 1987 by a decision approving an affirmative-action plan that allowed the Santa Clara County (California) Transportation Agency to promote women to supervisory positions over better-qualified male applicants.[38]

Court Opposition to Affirmative Action. With the conservative faction of the Court solidifying since 1987, however, the Court has become less receptive to affirmative action or other plans that would oblige employers to hire minorities in the absence of convincing evidence that those specific employers had discriminated in the past. The most influential case along these lines was *Wards Cove,* decided in 1989. It was important because it presented one of the key dilemmas facing U.S. social policy in the 1990s.

Two salmon-canning establishments in Alaska had practiced a dual employment pattern. Low-paid cannery workers were hired primarily from the local pool of Filipino and Native Alaskan laborers; high-paid non-cannery workers were recruited principally from a predominantly white pool of applicants in Oregon and Washington where the company was headquartered. There were also separate dining and dormitory facilities for the two groups of workers, and the company did not follow a practice of promotion from within. The net result was what the courts termed a *"disparate impact"* in employment. The minorities were disproportionately concentrated in the cannery jobs, while the whites were disproportionately concentrated in the higher-paid non-cannery jobs.

Had the Supreme Court adhered to a precedent it had followed since 1971, the existence of such a "disparate impact" would have put the burden of proof on the company to show that it had not intentionally discriminated and that its recruitment practices constituted a business necessity. But in *Wards Cove* in 1989, the Supreme Court ruled:

1. A company may use objective tests and standards such as aptitudes tests and strength tests and other measures of hiring if these tests are related to the business and constitute a business necessity.

2. The burden of proof is on the worker to show that a racially "disparate impact" resulting from these standards is due to active discrimination by the company.

In opinion of the Court, Justice Byron White wrote,

> If the absence of minorities holding such skilled positions is due to a dearth of qualified non-white applicants (for reasons that are not the petitioners' fault), petitioner's selection methods or employment practices cannot be said to have had a "disparate impact on non-whites."[39]

If this ruling prevailed, it would have a definite effect of reducing the access to the federal courts of minorities who feel discriminated against. Formally, they would still have access, because they could still sue. But in practice the access would be reduced, because requiring them to prove that the employer discriminated would greatly reduce the number of suits initiated.

The Court's new antipathy to forcing employers to hire minorities was reinforced by another 1989 case that threw into question the viability of the entire concept of voluntary affirmative-action agreements. In this case, the Supreme Court made a complete reversal from affirmative action by allowing white fire fighters in Birmingham, Alabama, to challenge an eight-year-old affirmative-action plan designed to increase the hiring and promotion of minorities.[40] This decision was a blow to affirmative action because it opened the door for future white employees to be exempt from affirmative-action plans drawn up before they were hired.

Federal Court Access and Set-Aside Programs

Related to affirmative action has been the practice of set-aside programs for minority-owned businesses. Cities normally award contracts for equipment purchases, maintenance, road construction, insurance, or other work through competitive bidding. The lowest bidders who meet the contract specifications are then awarded the contracts. In order to stimulate minority or female-owned businesses, cities often set aside a certain percentage of their contracts exclusively for minority contractors. While we do not normally think of lower-status people as business people, the ownership of small businesses has historically been an important avenue of upward mobility among many immigrant groups, and for this reason set-aside programs have the potential to facilitate upward-mobility among minorities.

However, this practice, too, was thrown into question by the Rehnquist Court in 1989 when it struck down a Richmond, Virginia, plan that had set aside 30 percent of city construction projects for minority-owned businesses.[41] To be acceptable, ruled the Court, such plans needed to serve a "compelling state interest" of redressing "identified discrimination." Considering that 36 states and 190 cities around the country had similar plans, the impact of this decision on minority businesses could be considerable.

Reaction to the Court's Reemergent Conservatism

In summary, the Rehnquist Court since 1987 has sent out several signals that it does not intend to make any further advances in the groundwork laid by earlier Courts for maintaining open access to the federal courts for groups representing lower-status people. Highly controversial here are the access issues surrounding affirmative action and the attempts to give minorities and women preferential consideration for admission to professional schools and for lucrative employment opportunities.

It is these issues that we will address here, because few issues divide the lower-status population more than those surrounding affirmative action. They have also provoked an extremely bitter debate within the alliance of liberals who historically provided the political clout for many of the civil-rights movement's successes. There are blacks on both sides of this bitter divide, and there are whites on both sides. To sort out these divisions and the biases of the reemergent conservatism of the Rehnquist Court, we need to distinguish between differing assessments made by the civil-rights establishment and a growing group of moderating liberals.

Reaction of the Civil Rights Establishment. Because the lower-status population is split racially, ethnically, and geographically, the immediate impact of the Court's renewed conservatism does not necessarily have a consistent anti-lower-status bias. Instead, it puts into question the advantages that some people derived from affirmative action. The biggest beneficiaries of affirmative action probably have not been lower-status people at all. They probably have been upper-middle-class white women, who have seen a dramatic explosion of employment opportunities as governments and companies scramble to demonstrate their commitment to employing and promoting women.

... the Rehnquist Court since 1987 has sent out several signals that it does not intend to make any further advances in the groundwork laid by earlier courts for maintaining open access to the federal courts for groups representing lower-status people.

Racial minorities have certainly benefited to the extent that affirmative action has forced open jobs that previously were closed. But here as well, the primary beneficiaries probably have been the upper-middle-class minorities more than the lower-status minorities. It has been predominantly upper-middle-class minorities and upper-middle-class white female liberals who have formed the most potent political force for enacting racial and sexual preferences into the law in recent years.

If upper-middle-class minorities and white females have been the prime beneficiaries of racial and sexual preference policies, it is not surprising that they also have been among the most vocal critics of the Rehnquist Court's rightward turn. Probably no institution is more symbolic of the civil rights establishment than the National Association for the Advancement of Colored People (NAACP), which, since its founding nearly a century ago, has labored steadfastly for racial equality. Benjamin L. Hooks, executive director of the NAACP until 1992, called the Rehnquist Court an even greater threat to black people than the active segregationists who had opposed the civil rights movement a generation earlier.[42] Many within the civil rights establishment also hold a very bitter view of white Americans whom they see not only as turning their backs today on civil rights, but as wanting to prop up a system of widespread discrimination against blacks. Roger Wilkins, journalist and commentator on race relations, said, "We still have [preference programs] and the preferred are white men. But somehow in the debate all the victims are white men worried that black people are going to take their jobs. The only place in America where blacks have taken jobs in a major way from whites is the National Basketball Association."[43]

These attitudes of the civil-rights leadership have also filtered down to the black population at large. A survey conducted by the Leadership Conference on Civil Rights showed a consensus among blacks that whites who resist the current goals of the black civil-rights leadership are essentially racists who have turned their backs on the civil rights movement itself.[44]

New Civil-Rights Legislation. Perceiving the Rehnquist Court's affirmative-action rulings of the late 1980s as negative for black people and women, the civil-rights establishment pressed Congress to pass new civil-rights legislation that would overturn the Rehnquist Court decisions by bolstering affirmative-action programs in hiring and promoting minorities. Congress responded with a civil-rights act in 1992 that will allow women and minorities to sue employers whose own payrolls do not contain a number of women and minorities proportionate to their number in the local work force. The act also puts the burden of proof on employers in such suits to demonstrate that any hiring criteria they used were both work-related and essential to job performance.

Reaction of the Moderating Liberals

In contrast to the civil rights establishment are a growing number of moderating liberals who resist the imposition of racial quotas for hiring and professional-school admissions. These moderating liberals include whites, blacks, and other minorities. They have spent much of their lives supporting integration and racial equality but argue that the goals of the civil-rights establishment changed during the 1980s. Prior to the 1980s, they argue, the goals of the civil-rights establishment were essentially those expressed by Martin Luther King in his famous "I have a dream" speech when he called for a society in which people are judged not by the color of their skin but by the content of their character.[45] With this emphasis on a color-blind society King staked out the high moral ground for the civil-rights movement.

This high moral ground, say the moderating liberals, has been abandoned by the current civil-rights establishment. Black columnist William Raspberry expressed the heart of the moderating liberal argument when he wrote:

> My own view is not that white people have changed but that our own goals have been transformed. We still say we want to be judged by the 'content of our character,' but our agenda is based on the color of our skin.
>
> [Whites] . . . do not see themselves as opponents of equal opportunity and fairness. What they oppose are efforts to provide preferential benefits for minorities. They aren't buying. How could civil rights leaders expect them to buy a product we have spent 400 years trying to have recalled: race-based advantage enshrined in the law?[46]

From this viewpoint, the civil-rights establishment is making a serious error in focusing its attention on the civil-rights bill that Bush vetoed on the grounds that it was a quota bill. This focus is an error because it dilutes the necessary support for the civil-rights movement from liberal whites and saps the movement of its moral authority. Princeton University Professor Cornell West argued, "The power of the civil rights movement under Martin Luther King was its universalism. Now, instead of the civil rights movement being viewed as a moral crusade for freedom, it's become an expression of a particular group. Once you have lost that moral high ground, all you have is a power struggle, and that has never been a persuasive means for the weaker to deal with the stronger."[47]

Note that these arguments from the moderating liberals do not seek to end government aid to underclass blacks or to cut programs that would assist upwardly mobile minorities get into college or professional schools. And this is what distinguishes the moderating liberals from the conservatives who dominated the Reagan administration. Those conservatives went to enormous lengths to undermine the enforcement of civil-rights laws and to cut budgets for programs that helped the underclass and upwardly mobile minorities.

But the moderating liberals reject what they feel is hyperbole and overstatement associated with many in the contemporary civil-rights establishment. Black scholar Shelby Steele wrote that black–white dialogue since the 1960s has been characterized by a "harangue–flagellation ritual" in which black militants claim victimhood and blame it on their white oppressors and in which white liberals get off the hook through symbolic flagellation, by joining in the harangue, and throwing support behind black entitlements. The trouble with the "harangue–flagellation ritual," says Steele, is that it draws the attention of society away from coming to grips with the horrendous economic and social problems of the growing black-urban underclass.[48]

Reactions of Lower-Status Whites

To a great extent, the dialogue over the Supreme Court's retreat from affirmative action has been primarily a dialogue of the upper-middle class, both whites and minorities. Another important group of people is the lower-status white population. Its voice is virtually absent from this dialogue, but its actions have had enormous significance.

The people most likely to see themselves as losers in the battle for affirmative action were young, lower-status whites—especially white males—for whom contemporary social change has meant fewer opportunities for job advancement and upward social mobility. To the extent that they perceive racial and sexual preference policies as limiting their own career prospects, it is not surprising that they resist such policies.

White Opinion on Racial Issues. What *is* surprising is that large percentages of whites generally support special programs to help minorities. A CBS News/*New York Times* survey in 1977 found that 68 percent of whites interviewed agreed that the government should give a better break to people who had been discriminated against in the past. Fifty-nine percent agreed that universities should give special consideration to the admissions applications of the best minority applicants for admission. Sixty-three percent agreed that large companies should set up special training programs for minorities. And a 1979 Gallup Poll found that 56 percent of whites interviewed wanted the federal government to set up special courses to help minorities do better on admissions tests for universities and professional schools.[49]

Where most whites draw the line, however, is at quotas and racial or sexual preferences. A 1983 ABC News/*Washington Post* poll asked whether blacks should get special help that is denied to white people in similar circumstances. Only 28 percent of whites agreed with that statement; interestingly, barely a majority of blacks (51 percent) agreed with it.[50] Furthermore, there seems to be evidence that whites are less supportive of preferences for minorities today than previously. A CBS/*New York Times* poll found that 42 percent of whites in 1985 agreed to preferential treatment of minorities; by 1990 that number dropped to 32 percent.[51]

Because people's responses to surveys on race vary widely depending on how the questions are worded, one has to be careful interpreting these data. But the data do seem to support three conclusions about the opinion of whites on racial issues. First, most whites generally support special government assistance to help minorities prepare themselves to meet testing standards for professional schools and lucrative jobs. Second, most whites resist the idea of lowering standards for admission to such schools or giving preference to minorities who are less qualified than whites on the admissions criteria. They tend to view this as reverse discrimination. Third, very few whites support the use of quotas as a tool for improving the status of minorities.

The White Lower-Strata Vote. Because there are no national interest groups representing lower-status whites as such, there is no voice to their concerns in the media. There is, however, one place where lower-status whites can express their opinion with some efficacy, and that is the voting booth. People vote for a wide variety of reasons, but it is difficult to avoid the conclusion that one key reason for the defection of many young, white lower-status males to the Republicans throughout the 1980s was the association of the Democratic Party with the idea of quotas and racial preferences.[52]

In sum, the reaction of many whites has been a quiet migration away from Democratic Party candidates toward the Republican Party candidates. Survey data do not suggest that most of these whites are any less committed to equality for women and racial minorities than their parents were a generation earlier; but they resist using the power of government to give other groups of people an advantage over them.

Bias Overcome

Although the Supreme Court justices were not the prime cause of the growing political divisions between lower-status whites and lower-status minorities, Supreme Court decisions since the mid-1970s have nevertheless contributed to that division. It makes a great deal of difference to the lower strata who the judges are. We live under a constitution, Oliver Wendell Holmes is reputed to have quipped, but the Constitution is what the judges say it is. In the 1970s, a predominantly liberal federal judiciary made great strides in opening access to the federal courts, and this gave many different groups representing disadvantaged people a further mechanism for influencing national public policy.

In the 1990s, the most relevant judicial fact of life for the lower-status population has been the success of the Reagan and Bush administrations in staffing the federal courts with conservative judges. While these judges are not likely to undo the civil rights advances that were made over the previous four decades, they have clearly signaled their reluctance to be on the leading edge of new civil rights advances. And they have clearly signaled their intention to reduce the access of disadvantaged people to the federal courts.

Conclusion

It is no easy matter to sort out the implications of judicial action for the lower-status population. As of this writing, the Rehnquist Court has struck a sharp symbolic blow to the civil rights and feminist establishments. How extensively that blow will impede social mobility for lower-status minorities is not known, but it certainly seems unlikely to assist that social mobility. On the face of it, lower-status whites would seem to be the beneficiaries of the Court's reemergent conservatism. But since an essential part of reemergent judicial conservatism aims to reduce access to the federal courts, lower-status whites too will find it more difficult to press some of the kinds of claims we have discussed in this chapter (appealing negative decisions by the Social Security Administration, for example, or forcing the schools to stay open for the entire year).

Summary

1. The criminal court system has many costly features that put the lower-status defendant at an extreme disadvantage compared to the upper-status defendant. The most dramatic of these are law enforcement practices that focus on the lower strata, the setting of bail, pretrial detention, and representation of accused persons by lawyers.

2. The system of civil law also has many costly features which put lower-status litigants at an extreme disadvantage compared to upper-status litigants and institutions such as businesses and government agencies.

3. The 1960s and 1970s saw an opening of access to the federal courts which directly benefited public-policy interest groups and indirectly benefited many lower-status persons. Because of the lack of interest-group representation, however, a great many lower-status people drew very few benefits from this increased access to the courts.

4. The 1980s saw a concerted effort to close access to the federal courts. Symbolically, this effort reached its most successful peak with the appointment of William Rehnquist as chief justice in 1987. In the next few years, the Rehnquist Court made several key decisions that reduced the access of the lower strata to the federal court system. These decisions have contributed to bitter political divisions among many liberal interests.

5. The key to overcoming bias in the court system is electing judges who are committed to retaining access to the federal courts for the lower-status population.

Notes

1. *Congressional Quarterly Weekly Report,* September 22, 1984, pp. 2332–2334.

2. See Anthony Lewis, "A Profound Contempt," *New York Times,* May 21, 1984.

3. These included the National Senior Citizens Law Center, the Save Our Security Association, the Commission on Legal Problems of the Elderly, the National Mental Health Association, the American Foundation of the Blind, and the National Governors' Association. See Mark Silverstein and Benjamin Ginsberg, "The Supreme Court and the New Politics of Judicial Power," *Political Science Quarterly* 102, no. 3 (Fall 1987): 371–385.

4. Ibid., p. 386.

5. Robert Pear, "New Court Sought for Benefit Cases," *New York Times,* March 9, 1986.

6. The treatment here of criminal and civil justice relies heavily on Christopher E. Smith, *Courts and the Poor* (Chicago: Nelson–Hall Publishers, 1991).

7. On the importance of discretion on the job among police officers and other urban professionals, see Michael Lipsky, *Street-Level Bureaucracy* (New York: Russell Sage Foundation, 1980).

8. Douglas A. Smith and Christy A. Visher, "Street-Level Justice: Situational Determinants of Police Arrest Decisions," *Social Problems,* 29 (1981): 174.

9. Smith, *Courts and the Poor,* p. 21.

10. James Q. Wilson, *Thinking About Crime,* rev. ed. (New York: Basic Books, 1983), p. 83.

11. Cited in Smith, *Courts and the Poor,* p. 24

12. Ibid.

13. Malcolm Feeley, *The Process Is the Punishment* (New York: Russell Sage Foundation, 1979), pp. 199–243.

14. Smith, *Courts and the Poor,* p. 25.

15. Ibid.

16. Ibid., p. 29.

17. Jonathan D. Caster, "Did You Have a Lawyer When You Went to Court? No, I Had a Public Defender" *Yale Review of Law and Social Action* 1971, i, 4–9.

18. Smith, *Courts and the Poor,* p. 35.

19. Marc Galanter, "Afterward: Explaining Litigation," *Law and Society Review* 9 (1975): 347. Quoted in Smith, *Courts and the Poor,* p. 48.

20. Harry P. Stumpf, *American Judicial Politics* (New York: Harcourt Brace Jovanovich, 1988), p. 234. Quoted in Smith, *Courts and the Poor,* p. 49.

21. Smith, *Courts and the Poor,* p. 55.

22. Alexis de Tocqueville, *Democracy in America,* tr. by J. P. Mayer. (New York: Anchor Books, 1969), p. 270.

23. Thomas R. Marshall, "Public Opinion, Representation, and the Modern Supreme Court," *American Politics Quarterly* 16, no. 3 (July 1988): 296–316.

24. There is a substantial body of research on the politics of judicial selection. See, for example, Craig F. Emmert and Henry R. Glick, "The Selection of State Supreme Court Justices," *American Politics Quarterly* 16, no. 4 (October 1988): 445–465. Also see Richard A. Watson and Rondal G. Downing, *The Politics of Bench and Bar: Judicial Selection Under the Missouri Non-Partisan Plan* (New York: Wiley, 1969).

25. Stuart Nagel, "Political Party Affiliation and Judges' Decisions," *American Political Science Review* 55 (December 1961): 851–943; Nagel, "Ethnic Affiliation and Judicial Propensities," *Journal of Politics* 24 (1962): 92–110; Sidney Ulmer, "The Political Variable in the Michigan Supreme Court," *Journal of Political Law* 11 (1963): 552–562.

26. Susan Welch, Michael Combs, and John Gruhl, "Do Black Judges Make a Difference?" *American Journal of Political Science* 32, no. 1 (February 1988): 126–136.

27. Smith, *Courts and the Poor,* p. 36.

28. Silverstein and Ginsburg, "The Supreme Court and the New Politics of Judicial Power," 371–385.

29. Ibid.

30. Anthony Lewis, "When Politicians Fail," *New York Times,* May 7, 1981, p. 27.

31. Lloyd L. Weinreb, "Judicial Activism," *New York Times,* May 7, 1981, p. 71.

32. Silverstein and Ginsberg, "The Supreme Court and the New Politics of Judicial Power," p. 38.

33. Smith, *Courts and the Poor,* p. 98.

34. See Lee Epstein, *Conservatives in Court.*

35. *Congressional Quarterly Weekly Report,* January 19, 1991, pp. 174–175.

36. *Bakke* v. *Regents of the University of California–Davis* 438 U.S. 265 (1978).

37. *Boston Firefighters Union* v. *Boston Chapter NAACP* 103 S. Ct. 2076 (1983).

38. *Johnson* v. *Transportation Agency, Santa Clara County* 480 U.S. 616 (1987).

39. *Wards Cove Packing Company, Inc.* v. *Atonio* 109 S. Ct. 2115 (1989).

40. *Martin* v. *Wilk* 109 S. Ct. 2180 (1989).

41. *City of Richmond, Virginia* v. *Croson* 488 U.S. 469.

42. Hooks made those remarks at the 1989 annual convention of the NAACP. See *New York Times,* July 10, 1989, p. 7.

43. For Wilkins' quote, see *New York Times,* April 3, 1991, p. 1.

44. See William Raspberry, "'91 Model Civil Rights Might Sell," *Minneapolis Star Tribune,* March 19, 1991, p. 12A.

45. Martin Luther King, Jr., speech to the March on Washington Rally, 1963.

46. Raspberry, "'91 Model Civil Rights Might Sell," p. 12A

47. Cornell West, quoted in the *New York Times,* April 13, 1991, p. 1.

48. Shelby Steele, *The Content of Our Character: A New Vision of Race in America* (New York: St. Martin's Press, 1990).

49. For a review of this survey data, see John H. Bunzel, "Affirmative Re-Actions," *Public Opinion* (February/March 1986): 45–49.

50. Ibid.

51. Ibid.

52. John B. Judis, "Democrats Go Wrong on Civil-Rights Revisions," *In These Times,* July 4–17, 1990, p. 8.

Epilogue: Overcoming Bias in American Politics

We have drawn a portrait of American politics as seen from the underside—the effect of political institutions and processes on the bottom 60 percent of the income earners. And a dismal portrait it is. There are many admirable features of American society. But the political treatment of our lower-status population is not one of them.

If politics is the struggle for who gets what, when, and how, as Harold Lasswell[1] defined it, the lower strata of American society get less of what there is to be gotten through politics than do the upper strata. From early socialization experiences, they learn a very passive role in the political system. For a variety of reasons, some having to do with these same socialization experiences, many lower-status people are literally absent from the electoral arena. And this absence gives elected officials very little practical reason to be responsive to them. Members of Congress want electoral support from the people they champion, and not many members of Congress are inclined to stick their necks out for people who do not give that support.

We saw that there are a multitude of interest groups to represent virtually every functional, ethnic, religious, and regional agglomeration of Americans but one—lower-strata people as such. There is in this country no interest group that represents lower-strata people as a class. The closest approximation is organized labor, which represents workers. But unions have fallen on hard times; the most successful ones these days are those representing the upper end of the lower strata (such as teachers, nurses, police officers), and the prospects for a renaissance of the union movement seem slim.

There are many admirable and positive features of American society. But the political treatment of our lower-status population is not one of them.

The failure of representation through interest groups has been compounded by the weakening of political parties, especially the Democratic Party. Neither major party today really draws its central strength from the vote of lower-status constituents as the New Deal Democrats did from the 1930s through the 1960s. Having a large constituency of minorities, the Democrats are certainly closer to the New Deal model than are the Republicans. But partisan reforms in the 1970s helped weaken the Democratic party and the influence of blue-collar unions in that party. As the influence of blue-collar people declined in the Democratic Party, there was a growth in influence of upper-middle-class professionals who (at least in Thomas Edsall's analysis)[2] appeared to be less concerned with improving the economic situation of the average American than they were with using political-reform strategies to bolster their own influence within the party and within the government.

With such weakness in the political institutions that purport to represent them, it is not surprising that lower-status people also began to lose influence on the institutions of government itself. Congress, as we saw in Chapter 7, despite being controlled by the Democrats for most of the 1970s and 1980s, made a series of tax-law changes in those years that gave one of the largest tax breaks in history to the top four or five percent of income earners. The presidency, as we saw in Chapter 8, has an inherently conservative bent that can be mitigated by a liberal president but never totally overcome. In Chapter 9 we observed that the federal bureaucracy, once seen as a central set of institutions for promoting the social welfare of average Americans, was itself brought under attack in the 1980s. Some of the most important regulatory agencies for environmental protection, for occupational safety and health, and for consumer protection were gutted during the Reagan years. And the federal court system, which carries the motto "Equal Justice Under the Law" above the entrance to the Supreme Court building, is itself a very inhospitable place for those who lack the money to walk through its costly, Byzantine, legal labyrinth.

Overcoming Bias _____

Along with this dismal picture of the underside of American politics, however, we have also seen important examples of bias overcome, or at least bias mitigated. The lower-status Anti-Federalists did not succeed in blocking passage of the new Constitution in 1788, but they did succeed in adding the Bill of Rights to it. And we are all better off because of that. Black civil-rights leaders did not succeed in eradicating racial discrimination or racial inequalities from American society, but they enjoyed great success in stripping away segregation's worst manifestations of racial injustice. Presidents may be inherently conservative, but at least once each generation some president is given a window of opportunity for making progressive advances.

Unless Americans someday become ready for a true social revolution, and I do not think they will, this is what we must aim for—windows of opportunity to mitigate bias and overcome bias. The great journalist Walter Lippman, we noted in Chapter 1, defined politics as the art of the possible.[3] One thing we must do is to distinguish between what is possible and what is not. It is not possible, in my judgment, to overturn the class structure of American society or the capitalist nature of the American economy. What is possible is to take concrete steps that help overcome bias, help mitigate bias, help improve the political representation of those in the lower strata, and help ease the economic uncertainties of their lives.

How can we overcome the biases against the lower strata? And what can you do about it? The first step is simply to learn how to recognize biases when they appear and to adopt a mental framework that rejects them. Accordingly, I offer the following nine precepts. These nine precepts are so simple and so obvious that I would be embarrassed to stress them in a serious book, except for one thing. And that one thing is that these nine precepts are violated more often than they are adhered to in today's politics. I argue that lower-status people will enjoy better political influence to the degree that they understand these nine precepts and recognize when they are being violated. When you vote, or contribute to a cause, or join a movement, or march in a protest, or simply discuss politics with peers, I urge you to remember these precepts. Support the candidates, the tactics and the groups that are consistent with them. Oppose those that are inconsistent with them.

1. *Improve Civic Education among the Lower Strata.* Civic education of the lower strata is much too important to be left to the public schools. Lower-strata people must be taught to overcome their early socialization experiences that promote nonparticipation, authoritarianism, and intolerance. Harry Boyte conducted successful experiments with teenagers in Minnesota that taught them not only to participate effectively but to take a more positive view

---

What is possible is to take concrete steps that help overcome bias, help mitigate bias, help improve the political representation of those in the lower strata, and help ease the economic uncertainties of their lives.

of politics as something that can improve their lives.[4] John L. Sullivan, also in Minnesota, conducted successful experiments with teenagers that show promise for making them more tolerant and receptive of others from different racial backgrounds and different social values.[5] Building on these academic experiments, there is a great deal that could be done by neighborhood associations, labor unions, and other locally oriented interest groups to build up the participatory skills of lower-status people.

2. *Strengthen the Political Parties.* One key thing missing in today's politics is a strong political party whose leaders depend on lower-strata support to hold their positions. Political parties are, as the great political scientist V. O. Key expressed it, "the basic institutions for the translation of mass preferences into public policy.[6] Because of this, "democracy is unthinkable save in terms of parties."[7] Throughout the twentieth century, it has been the Democratic Party that most successfully translated lower-status references into public policy. Today, however, neither party has the strong ties to the lower-status population that the Democrats held from the 1930s through the 1960s. The Republicans won the presidency in the 1980s on the votes of a great many working-class voters, but then pursued economic policies unabashedly favoring the wealthy over those working-class voters. The Democrats rhetorically stand for the lower strata, but they have lost their appeal to a great many lower-status whites and increasingly are viewed by them as the party of racial minorities and upper-middle-class, white, left-wing ideologues. The longer the Democrats remain with a diminished ability to draw votes from throughout the lower strata and to compete for the presidency, the more it becomes an open question as to which party might better address the needs of the lower strata today.

Whether minority or white, whether Democrat or Republican, lower-status people should commit this precept to memory: A system of strong political parties works to their advantage; a system of weak parties works to their disadvantage.

3. *Create Interest Groups for the Lower Strata.* In addition to lacking a strong political party to champion their interests, most lower-status people lack powerful interest groups. There is no group doing for lower-status people today what organized labor did for blue-collar workers in the 1930s, what the civil rights movement did for blacks in the 1960s, or what feminists did for women in the 1970s. In part this problem stems from upward social mobility and from the natural inclination of the interest-group system to coopt lower-status leaders.[8] Women who move from a blue-collar background to upper-middle-class professions can still play a role

in the women's movement, but most find a huge cultural gap between their professional lives and the lives of lower-status women. Racial minorities who move from blue-collar backgrounds to upper-middle-class professions can still play meaningful roles in the civil-rights movement and in the advancement of fellow blacks, but they too find that their professional status often creates a huge gap between them and low-income blacks. By definition, when these people become upper-middle-class professionals, they necessarily leave the lower-strata behind. The success of our society in promoting upward social mobility is laudatory. But that very success robs the lower-strata of effective leadership.

What can be done? The most successful examples of mobilizing lower-strata groups to action occurred when their leadership emerged from those groups themselves. The labor-union movement stands out as the most striking instance of indigenous leadership of lower-status groups. A production worker, a social worker, or a teacher does not lose contact with his or her social roots when he or she becomes a union steward or a business agent. The model of neighborhood organization is another response. The most successfully organized lower-strata neighborhoods also have some upper-middle-income residents who are forced by circumstances to interact with their less-affluent neighbors.[9] This interaction leads to a fertile social dynamic that gives the lower-strata residents of these neighborhoods more clout with city hall than they would otherwise possess. Another widely copied model is that of the civil rights movement of the 1950s and 1960s in which middle-class blacks trained future leaders and mobilized lower-status blacks to political action. In all these instances, the leaders of movements were indigenous to the groups of people being mobilized.

There are no doubt other models equally successful in organizing lower-strata Americans. What is critical is to experiment with these models and to give them support. The more successful activity that occurs, the greater will be the number of lower-strata people who begin to learn how to use politics to improve their economic and political position.

What is critical for lower-status people to understand is that they need to join groups, work with groups, and contribute to groups that benefit them. Historically, the single most effective organization at this task has been the labor union.

4. *Reject Right-Wing Demagoguery*. Lower-strata people often have been kept at odds with one another by demagogic rhetoric that prevented them from perceiving their common economic self-interest. We saw in Chapter 6 that upper-status white Southern-

ers effectively used the tactic of race-baiting to keep lower-status whites from uniting politically with poor blacks. If these black and white lower-status voters had been united during the populist movement of the 1890s, they most certainly would have had a bigger impact on Southern welfare policies throughout the next century. Disunited, lower-status Southern whites went along with movements to disenfranchise blacks. But the same literacy tests and poll taxes that disenfranchised the blacks eventually brought disenfranchisement to large numbers of lower-status whites as well. In the 1950s, right-wing demagoguery took the form of the famous McCarthy anti-communist crusades. In the 1970s and 1980s, it took the form of law-and-order campaigns, reaching its peak, perhaps, in the famous Willie Horton commercials in the 1988 presidential campaign. In the 1990s, as this is being written, great battles are taking place over political correctness. These battles have the potential to pit lower-status whites against lower-status minorities, with the same disastrous consequences as the earlier demagogic movements had. There are black demagogues as well as white demagogues who have more to gain from disunity than unity.

For the great mass of black and white lower-status people, however, it is essential to recognize the difference between a healthy ethnic pride and demagogic appeals to racial hatreds. The first does not hinder cross-ethnic cooperation, but the second makes such cooperation virtually impossible.

5. *Reject Media Attempts to Discredit Lower-Status Groups.* In Chapter 4, we took a fairly detailed look at the media's treatment of coal-mine strikers in the 1970s and 1980s. One result of that treatment was to discredit the strikers, to make it seem that they were extremists with unreasonable demands. We also saw that there is a great disenchantment with the way in which specific lower-strata people are treated in the entertainment media. Studies by organized labor complain that ordinary workers are treated negatively by the entertainment media. I suggest you simply watch a few episodes of the "Roseanne" show, or a few back episodes of the once popular "All in the Family" and decide for yourself how sympathetically the entertainment media treat lower-status Americans.

There are many other categories of people who also complain about their portrayal in the media. Blacks, Native Americans, and women especially have been stereotyped in damaging ways. Politicians are almost universally treated with contempt in the entertainment media. Even conservative business people complain that the entertainment media creates negative stereotypes of them. Our concern, however, is with the lower strata in general. What is important to recognize is that lower-status people will find it difficult to gain respect in society if they are regularly portrayed by the media as buffoons, incompetents, slackards, and troublemakers. One net result of the negative stereotypes is that lower-strata people deny their own membership in the lower strata. Instead they look upon themselves as part of the elusive American middle class. And who can blame them? If Roseanne and her husband are typical lower-status people, who in their right minds would want to be thought of as belonging to such a category? Another net result is that it reinforces people's reluctance to join lower-status movements. If the media in general treat strikers as negatively as they did the coal-mine strikers in the 1970s and 1980s, what reasonable person would want to join a strike and be pictured in such negative terms?

For average Americans, it is important to recognize these negative portrayals when they occur and understand how they can undermine the political effectiveness of lower-status people.

6. *Demand Open Access to the Courts.* Although the courts, as we saw in Chapter 10, are not especially hospitable to lower-status people as individuals, it is important that the courts be open to hear the grievances of groups of lower-status people. The attempts of Boston parents to keep their schools open for the entire school year in 1981 might well have foundered if they had been denied the right to sue in the courts. Civil-rights advances for minorities would most certainly be more limited today if minority groups had been denied access to courts to press their grievances.

For lower-status people, it is important to reject the currently popular argument that it is necessary to reduce access to the courts in order to reduce the amount of litigation that goes on in American society. Reduction of access to the courts would make it even harder than it is now for lower-status people to have an influence on the political system.

7. *Think of Politics as a Non-Zero-Sum Game.* There is a tendency today to view politics as a zero-sum game. This is a game, like boxing, in which there is a loser for every winner. Politics as a zero-sum game pits the elements of the lower strata against each other in the quest for scarce resources, instead of joining together to expand the resources. In my region of the country, for example, there has been a substantial immigration of Southeast Asians, and they have come to predominate in the public housing projects where blacks once predominated. This competition over a limited supply of housing has given rise to a fair amount of tension between blacks and Southeast Asians. On a wider scale, similar

tensions exist between whites and blacks over a limited supply of good jobs. If growing numbers of blacks and whites compete for a more slowly growing number of jobs, racial tensions are bound to escalate.

The lower strata needs a growing national economy. If the number of jobs grows and the housing supply grows, housing and employment can be transformed into a non-zero-sum game, and there is a greater possibility of gaining interracial cooperation among the lower strata.

One policy area in which some commentators argue it is necessary to transform politics to a non-zero-sum game is that of welfare policy. Most welfare programs today are means-tested; that is, an applicant's income must fall below a certain level for the person to qualify. Because of this, many working people in the financially precarious and the near-poor categories fail to qualify for much public assistance. And it is not surprising that many of them resent the people who do qualify. The most successful social welfare program, Social Security, is not means-tested, however. And this gives Social Security much greater political support than any other social welfare program. Because of this, some commentators argue that we should pursue fewer means-tested welfare policies and more *universal* welfare policies.[10] This would put more assistance into the pockets of people who need it without generating political opposition from the upper strata and the higher levels of the lower strata. It would also help to turn a difficult political issue from a zero-sum game to a non-zero-sum game in which most of the players turn out to be winners.

For lower-strata people, the lesson to be learned is that the more that politics can take place in a non-zero-sum-game environment, the better off they will be. There will be more cooperation between minorities and whites, and less opposition from the upper strata.

8. *Demand Progressivity in the Tax System.* The one area where lower-strata people should reject the non-zero-sum approach, however, is in tax policy. They should demand a taxation system based on the ability to pay. The more income one has, the greater the percentage of income should be paid in taxes. There have to be upper limits, of course, but with an upper limit of only 28 percent for the highest earners, America's tax structure is a long way from treating the rich unfairly.

Our analysis of tax changes in Chapter 8 showed a significant shift of the tax burden from the shoulders of the well-off onto middle sectors of the income earners. Except for the poor, who were given substantial relief, the average citizen would have been better off if no tax changes had occurred between 1978 and 1990. Ironically, these changes, which benefited the rich, had broad support from lower-strata people who wanted an income-tax cut as much as anybody.

Lower-status people in general have nothing to lose from a progressive tax structure. They should understand that when business executives call for cutting taxes they usually want to cut the taxes on the rich, which will have the inevitable effect of boosting the tax burden on everybody else. For lower-strata people to be taken in by these arguments is to agree to a strategy that is against their own self-interest.

9. *Reject the Idea of a Minimal State.* One of the most popular phrases in American political culture is "The government that governs best is the one that governs least." But lower-status people would be well advised to reject that phrase and replace it with a saying of the great Republican president, Theodore Roosevelt, "The object of government is the welfare of the people."[11]

The average lower-status person needs a great many things that can be achieved only by a strong and dynamic government—clean water, clear air, effective regulation of occupational safety and health, adequate health insurance, good schools, and effective public transit, among other social goods. How these social goals can be achieved is open to debate. Sometimes conservative policies may make more sense than liberal ones, and vice versa. What should not be open to debate among lower-strata people, however, is the principle that the federal government has a strong and vital role to play in achieving these goals.

For lower-strata people, the point to remember is that the surest role to dominance by the upper strata is to have a government that governs least.

Conclusion _____

Political developments since about 1970 have reduced the political influence of the bottom 60 percent of the American income earners. It has been a great mistake to allow this to occur. Bankers have made a shambles of America's credit industry. Mergers and acquisitions specialists have placed a huge burden of debt on American corporations. Manufacturers, for whatever reason, have failed to stay competitive with the rest of the world and have exported lucrative American jobs by setting up off-shore factories. Republicans and Democrats went along with a Reagan economic program that pushed such a huge budget deficit on the federal government that we approach the end of the century with the federal government in no fiscal condition to address important domestic needs. If American citizens had simply been chosen at random to fill the top positions of government and industry over the past two decades, I am not certain that they would have left the nation any worse off than it has been left under governance by its best and brightest and most privileged.

For those in the lower strata, declining political influence has been accompanied by a worsened economic situation. Regaining political influence will not reverse the economic trends at work in the world today. But it will give members of Congress a practical reason to use the power of government to mitigate the impact of economic change on the lower strata.

Whether you are in the lower strata or not, as you close this book, I urge you to keep in mind the nine precepts outlined above and to impress on your friends and acquaintances the words of Theodore Roosevelt that "The object of government is the welfare of the people," all of the people—those at the bottom half of the population as well as those at the top.

Notes

1. Harold Lasswell, *Politics: Who Gets What, When, How* (New York: McGraw-Hill, 1936).
2. Thomas B. Edsall, *The New Politics of Inequality* (New York: W. W. Norton, 1984).
3. Walter Lippman, *Essays in the Public Philosophy* (Boston: Little, Brown, 1955).
4. Harry Boyte, "Beyond Community Service: Turning On Youth to Politics." *The Nation* 252, no. 18 (May 13, 1991): 626–628.
5. John L. Sullivan, et al., "Political Tolerance Among Adolescents: The Potential Role of Curricular Socialization," a paper presented to the Midwest Political Science Association, April 1991. Chicago, Illinois.
6. V. O. Key, *Public Opinion and American Democracy* (New York: Knopf, 1961), p. 432.
7. E. E. Schattschneider, *Party Government* (New York: Rinehart, 1942), p. 7.
8. Herbert Marcuse, *One Dimensional Man: Studies in the Ideology of Advanced Industrial Society* (Boston: Beacon Press, 1964).
9. Matthew Crenson, *Neighborhood Politics:* (Cambridge, Mass.: Harvard University Press, 1983).
10. Theda Skocpol, "Sustainable Social Policy: Fighting Poverty without Poverty Programs," *The American Prospect* no. 2 (Summer, 1990): 58–70.
11. Cited in *Bartlett's Familiar Quotations* (Boston: Little, Brown, 1980), p. 687.

Index